# First Globalization

**WORLD SOCIAL CHANGE**
Series Editor: Mark Selden

# First Globalization

## The Eurasian Exchange, 1500–1800

Geoffrey C. Gunn

ROWMAN & LITTLEFIELD PUBLISHERS, INC.
*Lanham • Boulder • New York • Toronto • Oxford*

ROWMAN & LITTLEFIELD PUBLISHERS, INC.

Published in the United States of America
by Rowman & Littlefield Publishers, Inc.
A Member of the Rowman & Littlefield Publishing Group
4501 Forbes Boulevard, Suite 200, Lanham, Maryland 20706
www.rowmanlittlefield.com

P.O. Box 317
Oxford
OX2 9RU, UK

British Library Cataloguing in Publication Information Available

**Library of Congress Cataloging-in-Publication Data**

Gunn, Geoffrey C.
    First globalization : the Eurasian exchange, 1500–1800 / Geoffrey C. Gunn.
      p. cm. — (World social change)
Includes bibliographical references and index.
    ISBN 0-7425-2661-5 (cloth : alk. paper) — ISBN 0-7425-2662-3 (pbk. :
alk. paper)
    1. Europe—Relations—Asia. 2. Asia—Relations—Europe. 3. East and
West. 4. Europe—Civilization—Oriental influences. 5. Asia—Foreign
public opinion, Western.  I. Title. II. Series.
    CB251 .G87 2003
    303.48'2504—dc21

                                                    2002153801

Printed in the United States of America

♾ ™ The paper used in this publication meets the minimum requirements of
American National Standard for Information Sciences—Permanence of Paper
for Printed Library Materials, ANSI/NISO Z39.48-1992.

# Contents

# Preface

*First Globalization* offers a reappraisal of binary East-West history, including both the Orientalist critique and the work of the "Asian values" school. Where incorporation has come to define the making of a European-centered world system, we are concerned here with the cultural exchanges and symmetries across the Eurasian landmass in the course of centuries before the rise to dominance of the West. The "Eurasian exchange," in our definition, involves complex crossovers of ideas, languages, and philosophies that engaged and transformed Europe and Asia in the sixteenth to eighteenth centuries, the era of the discoveries. But just as Europe impacted on new worlds, so, reflexively, did the revelation of Asia change Europe irrevocably.

European knowledge of eastern lands reached back to Ptolemy and the Greeks, but the new discoveries pioneered by the Iberians awakened both wonderment and prejudice. Such was reflected in the Jesuit school, in the front line of East-West ideological contest a century before the arrival of the Dutch and English chartered companies. Nevertheless, European Enlightenment, as borne by the English, Dutch, French, and other navigators and traders, passed beyond mere self-interested curiosity to laying the scientific basis of European empire. Ineluctably, as the examples of modern Macau, the Philippines, East Timor, and many other sites reveal, the first wave of globalization introduced new exchanges, hybrid forms, and especially creolized cultures.

As a thematic or nonlinear history, this work offers an alternative frame of reference to a vast geocultural zone outside the established categories of modern nation-state and region. Drawing on cultural, linguistic, geographical, and social studies, utilizing an array of world historical texts, we seek to break down the inherent bias and boundaries of both national and imperial history. Rather than taking the asymmetric development of East and West for granted, rather than accepting European exceptionalism as a given, we demonstrate that ultimate European hegemony was in many ways contingent on three centuries of intellectual negotiation and ideological contestation with the East.

# Acknowledgments

Having commenced work on this text in 1998, little did I know that I would be caught up in the sometimes violent events leading to the birth of a new nation, East Timor. My intermittent work in East Timor with the United Nations Transitional Administration in 2000–2001 slowed the pace of writing but in the process undoubtedly enriched it.

Looking further back, the book builds on three of my recently published "regional world histories," namely, *Encountering Macau* (1997), *Timor Lorosae: 500 Years* (1999), and *Nagasaki in the Asian Bullion Trade Networks* (1999).

Further back, I simply highlight a youthful life traveling the Afroeurasia world, not only crisscrossing the Persian and Afghanistan deserts and plateaus and other "terrestrial" silk roads but more than once plying the "Sinbad route" through the China seas, the archipelago, along the two coasts of India and Sri Lanka, westward across the Indian Ocean to Dar es Salaam, and through the Red Sea from Massawa to the Gulf of Aquaba, feats almost unimaginable in present times. All the more luck to have held teaching positions in, respectively, the Arab (North Africa), Chinese (Singapore), Malay (Brunei), Indochinese (Laos), and Japanese worlds. My deepest appreciation to my wife Chieko and son Kenji for sharing this adventure and experience.

Needless to say, teaching Asia-oriented courses to students in Asia in general has also offered a new dimension on the Eurasia exchange. I particularly appreciate my Nagasaki University seminar class of 2000–2002 on whose ears the basic concepts of this book were first tested, otherwise known as the class who insisted on accompanying me "on mission" to East Timor in the spring of 2001.

Research for this book was achieved almost exclusively in libraries in Nagasaki, Macau, and Dili (East Timor), and I extend my thanks to librarians and archivists in those places.

Especially, I am indebted to commissioning editor Mark Selden for extreme patience, skillful editing, and a rare mastery of the metageography and historical-cultural issues encompassed in this book. More than that, Mark came close across many pages to collaborating on certain issues and themes. Driving even harder after an appropriate first meeting in the cultural crossroads of the lovely Okinawan islands, to my mild consternation he suggested yet another chapter. Similarly, I thank Susan McEachern and Alden Perkins of Rowman & Littlefield, who supervised final editing and questions of style, along with Bruce R. Owens, who critically copyedited the entire manuscript.

In dedicating this book to the East Timorese people and their nation's victory, I am mindful of their unconscionable suffering at the hands of outsiders and the debt owed to them by most of the rest of the world.

# Glossary

A = Arabic; C = Chinese; D = Dutch; F = French; I = Indonesian; J = Japanese; K = Korean; L = Latin; M = Malay; P = Portuguese; S = Spanish; Sa = Sanskrit; Ta = Tagalog; Te = Tetum; Th = Thai; V = Vietnamese

amok (M)—murderous frenzy attributed to Malays
anito (Ta)—spirit, soul of dead
Asia Extrema (L)—Far East
Aurea Chersoesus (L)—Golden Peninsula
azulejos (P)—hand-painted ceramic tiles

Baba (M)—Malayanized Chinese
bairro (P)—district
bandores (P)—Renaissance musical instrument resembling a guitar
bastinado (P)—split bamboo baton used to punish criminals in China
baybayin (Ta)—Tagalog writing system
bolo (P)—Portuguese cake
bombacha (P, S)—baggy pantaloon trousers
bongiois (J)—personal servant of the governor
byobu (J)—screen

cangue (F)—from (P) canga; wooden frame placed around neck of criminals in China
carroza (S)—float
carta (P)—card, map, or letter
castella (P)—*see* kasutera

Cathay—China
chaomuang (Th)—lord of the realm
chef de suco (P)—head of district
ching (C)—canonical books
cho nom (V)—Sino-Vietnamese ideograms
Cipangu—Japan
cofraida (S)—Catholic religious procession
confreira (P)—Catholic religious procession
conquista (S, P)—the conquest
conquistadores (S)—(Iberian) conquerors
crioloes (S)—local (Latin America)-born Spanish
crioulo (P)—creole language

daimyo (J)—Japanese feudal lord
Darul Islam (A)—world of Islam
deva raja (Sa)—god king
dobashi (J)—two languages, interpreter
dunia Melayu (M)—Malay world

Edo—former name for Tokyo
emaki-mono (J)—picture scroll portraits
Estado da India (P)—lit. state of India; Portuguese political-economic
   trading empire in the Asia region

fado (P)—Portuguese musical form
feng shui (C)—lit. wind and water, geomancy
festa (P)—festival
fidalgo (P)—aristocrat
filhos de terra (P)—sons of the soil

gamba (P)—violin
gentio (P)—nonbeliever
gyogi-zu (J)—Japanese maps formed from oval shapes representing
   provinces

haj (A)—Muslim pilgrimage to Mecca
hanafuda (J)—flower cards
han'gul (K)—Korean alphabet
hiragana (J)—Japanese syllabary
hojas volantes (S)—lit. flying pages, news bulletins

illustrados (P)—educated
India Meridional (L)—southern India

India Orientalis (L)—east of India
Indios (S)—natives of the Philippines
inimigo (P)—enemy
intramura (S)—within the walls of the fortress
iroha karuta (J)—ABC cards

jefumi (J)—figure treading
jurubassa (M)—lit. language specialist, translator

kakure (J)—lit. hidden, underground Christians
kana (J)—*see* hiragana; katakana
kanji (J)—Chinese character
Kannon (Kuan Yin)—goddess of mercy
karuta (J)—playing card
kasutera (P)—castella, cake from Castelo
katakana (J)—Japanese syllabary used for loanwords
katana (J), (P), (Te)—knife
keroncong (I)—genre of Indonesian music influenced by Portuguese
    melodies
kling (M)—people of Indian descent
kraak (D)—lit. carrack (tableware)
kudit (Ta)—diacritical mark
kurofune (J)—lit. black ships, Portuguese ships

ladinos (S)—bilingual Filipinos
Larantuqueiros (P)—mixed-race people from Larantuca on Flores island
    in the Indonesian archipelago
lingua (L, P)—language; interpreter
lingua Macaista (P)—language of the Macanese
livres de cartes (F)—lit. book of maps

Macaense (Macanese) (P)—mixed Portuguese-Asian residing in Macau
Makista (P)—Portuguese creole of Macau
mappa mundi (L)—world map
mappe monde (F)—world map
mestiço (P)—mixed race
mestizen (D)—mixed race
mestizo (S)—mixed race
miso (J)—soybean food derivative

Nanban (J)—southern barbarian
negara (M)—state

Nihon-machi (J)—Japan towns
nuoc nam (V)—fermented fish sauce

orang kaya (M)—lit. rich man or noble
orbis terrarum (L)—terrestrial globe

Panca Sila (Sa, I)—five principles
patung (M)—statue
payson (S)—passion
pedras (P)—stones or rock mountains
pesta (I)—festival derived from festa (P)
portolan—from Italian *portolano*; charts derived from empirical observa-
    tion of mariners

quoc ngu (V)—lit. national language, Vietnamese Latin script

raja (M)—king
Rangaku (J)—Dutch learning
Reduction (S)—Jesuit-controlled Indian reservations in Paraguay and
    Uruguay
reina (P)—queen
relation (P)—letter missive
retabulos (P)—altar piece, decorated panel
roja (J)—jail
romaji (J)—Romanized Japanese script
roteiro (P)—travel directions

sakoku (J)—closed country
santos (S)—saint
Serani (M)—Christian
syair (M)—epic poem

Tatary—region in Asia (and Europe)
Terra Australis Incognita (L)—lit. unknown land of Australia
tofu (J)—soybean food derivative
topasse—term describing mixed Portuguese-Asian descendants
tranquiera (P)—palisade, stockade

Ukio-e (J)—woodblock print
ummat (A, M)—community of believers in Islam
uta karuta (J)—poem cards

VOC (D)—Dutch East India Company

waiguo (C)—foreign countries

# Illustrations

# Introduction

Global studies of the "Rise of the West" now acknowledge the importance of developments in key zones of Asia, especially East Asia. In this new argument, Asia, not Europe, held center stage in the world economy for most of early modern history. The leading proponents of this view are Andre Gunder Frank, *Re-Orient* (1998); R. Bin Wong, *China Transformed* (1997); and Kenneth Pomeranz, *The Great Divergence* (2000), who contend that Europe and East Asia attained comparable levels of development between 1500 and 1800. The debate continues, especially as to the question of European exceptionalism in the making of the modern world system. Eurocentricity, postcolonial critical theory, and accidental or optional European domination are all raised in this discussion. Taking the spatial bounds of this inquiry as the broad sweep of what is best evoked in the term "Eurasia," *First Globalization* seeks to explore the interplay of cultures commensurate with the European discoveries and expansion. This we term the "Eurasian exchange."

While globalization[1] today is generally associated with processes of economic incorporation and an emerging worldwide consumer culture, in this book we shift the terrain to the world of ideas and culture in order to address a range of questions. How, since the age of Columbus and Vasco da Gama, did ideas travel, both eastward and westward, and who were the prime agents of dissemination? In other words, how were mutually alien or variant ideas and philosophies received, transacted, translated, and even canonized in text and image? Why, in the first wave of globalization, were some peoples and civilizations more receptive to new ideas and exchanges, some selective, and some downright hostile? Alongside

1

the plunder associated with the Columbian exchange and the obvious benefits accruing to Europe from the early trade in Asian exotics, including the lucrative Asian bullion trade (Flynn 1996; Frank 1998; Gunn 1999a), can we also explain the great divergence between West and East on the route to modernity as a result of an unequal intellectual exchange during the crucial centuries of the first globalization? Having acquired knowledge of mathematics, astronomy, and crucial navigational information from the Arabs, did early modern Europe already have an edge over the Orient in the production and reproduction of knowledge? But if, as shown in the following pages, the first Europeans in the East were awestruck by the civilizations they encountered, why in these centuries did not a réverse revolution in the acceptance of new ideas and scientific paradigms occur throughout Asia?

## FIRST GLOBALIZATION

This book traces the epoch of first globalization as it touched the maritime vector of the Eurasian landmass. Just as late Renaissance Europe expanded its mercantile and military sway over literally a New World, so its ideas and values entered a contested terrain, both at home and abroad. At home, the new discoveries challenged the tenets of medievalism, albeit not Euro-Christian-centrism. In Asian lands, the messages—both religious and secular—plied by missionaries and traders received a mixed reception, at times even outright rejection. In its late medieval heyday, European cosmography upheld a holistic view of the world and the universe, its physical description, and order. While cosmography—defined in Webster's dictionary as "the science that deals with the constitution of the whole order of nature"—came to be challenged and subordinated by the new philosophy of Enlightenment skepticism and rejection of the irrational, we may well ask, How did a resurgent Europe seek to intellectually accommodate civilizations outside the familiar?

In tracing the rise of a European canon on Asia, we are not merely recording the image of Asia in Europe or even Asia in the "making of Europe" (cf. Lach 1969). To the contrary, we defend the thesis that the accumulation of knowledge of Asia in Europe not only offered the ideological empowerment and legitimation for future military and commercial hegemony in Africa and the Americas but also developed—reflexively—out of that grand project of control and conquest. European precocity led to European primacy. But while our method is also generalizable to Africa and the Americas, we recall that in the first European interactions with the tribute-trading systems of India and China, systems that extended across the Indian Ocean world and embraced East and Southeast Asia, European interlopers on the Asian mainland met their peers in civilization, military prowess, and science. Early European interactions with Asian empires, we shall argue, went beyond mere physical conquest (although there was plenty of that) and often took the form of didactic exchanges, philosophical conversation, and argument. *First Globalization* seeks to herald three centuries of mental struggle to accommodate the new discoveries within the ambit of the various, albeit evolving, European religious and philosophical establishments.

The contrast between Europe's rapacious Columbian exchange and the Eurasian exchange, we argue, offers certain oblique differences in approach as much as outcomes. The broad-scale decimation of populations and cultures in Central and South America that occurred within generations of the arrival of the first conquistadores was not repeated in Asia. Where the Iberians looted and enslaved at the sources of silver and gold in the Americas, in Asia the Europeans entered elaborate and mannered trading networks on their best behavior, meaning that they could not summarily destroy or subjugate at will. Neither was Asia demographically transformed as was the New World of the Americas by the Atlantic trade in African slaves and the creation of settler colonies. Whereas the Europeans laid waste by disease much of the Americas, with important exceptions, Asia was spared this scourge.

To be sure, the Asian peripheries were transformed by miscegenation, creolization, genocide, or some combination thereof. At least that was the fate of the indigenous populations of the Molucca or Spice Islands of Ambon and Banda in the Indonesian archipelago. It was also the fate of the Chamorro people of the remote Pacific islands of the Marianas astride the famous Mexico–Manila galleon route. Lacking a centralized state system, the Philippine islands also fell into the pattern, with the important caveat that the demographic outcome was markedly different. Other zones, such as the sandalwood-trading circuits of Flores and Timor island, also within the Indonesian archipelago, were tested by centuries of indigenous resistance against European interlopers, only succumbing with the advent of steam-powered gunboats.

Piratical acts and local skirmishes aside, the epoch of the first globalization in Asia preceded "pacification" and colonial settlement with contact restricted to a relatively small, albeit influential, group of officials, soldiers, missionaries, merchants, adventurers, and others dispersed through a string of isolated ports and maritime strong points. True, the Iberians sought to outflank or destroy Arab or Arabized trading networks from the Indian Ocean to the China Sea, yet the conquest of the three great centers of Asian civilization—respectively, India, China, and Japan—was not seriously entertained, short-lived Spanish designs on China (and Japan) excepted. In placing the Eurasian exchange at the fore of our study, at the same time we cannot be seen as standing apart from contemporaneous developments in Africa and the Americas, especially as the Europeans themselves rode at the crest of the wave of a truly global commerce and cultural exchange.

## ORIENTAL TEXTS AND THE
## RISE OF THE EUROPEAN CANON

But in privileging European texts and accounts of Asia, have we not "Orientalized" the colonial (actually precolonial) "other," as Edward Said (1978) has cautioned? In any case, should not such an obvious Eurocentricity be interpolated with reference to indigenous Asian texts?[2] As Chakraborti (1994, viii), an Indian economic historian of Anglo-Mughal relations has written, while Muslim scholars, mainly Arab, Persian, and Turkish, recorded events, they failed to produce historical epics, and, with few exceptions, their attention was not drawn to economic historiography. "They were more interested in politico-religious aspects." Rather, "it was the European historiographers especially the English traveler and merchant-adventurers [who] have meticulously recorded the contemporary conditions and events of trade and commerce in India." It might also be objected that states sharing Chinese bureaucratic traditions, including Korea, Japan, and Vietnam, also assiduously collected data on population, trade, taxes, households, and so on. This is certainly true, but little entered the public domain, much less the intelligence of contemporary European reporters. Writing in *The Cambridge History of Southeast Asia*, John Legge (2000, 2) observes that Vietnamese dynastic historians aside, indigenous chronicles from Southeast Asia performed largely "moral functions." Historian Anthony Reid clarifies that the sixteenth and seventeenth centuries is the earliest epoch for which a substantial body of indigenous writing survives in Southeast Asia. But while such texts are essential for an understanding of ideology, law, religion, and the ceremonial, he contends, for the life of ordinary people we must turn to the first generation of European visitors, even in preference to accounts of Chinese, Arabs, and other Asians who lacked "the same astonished interest in the life-style of the people they encountered" (Reid 1988, xv–xvi).

To strike a position, we must allow that the European tradition of recording, archiving, and publishing not only made public to an expanding literate audience the observations of wide-eyed travelers but also, as analyzed in chapter 1, produced a veritable canon of travel literature. Cultural studies helps us understand how representations of knowledge, print, and graphics, as in the case of maps, are much less coherent and ordered and much more contestatory than presupposed by the traditional archiving of facts and the application of systematics (cf. Edney 1997, 16–17). In this light, we must acknowledge that, whatever their intrinsic interest, the European reports are not exact copies of reality. We could say the same of the Asian traveler accounts with the rider that, as cultural products of different civilizations, they answered different needs. But a tradition of collection and study of Asian documents also developed in Europe. Entering translation into European languages by the late eighteenth century, Chinese, Japanese, Sanskrit, Arabic, Persian, Malay, and other Asian-language texts all came to be creatively interpreted by Enlightenment philosophers importantly entering the debate at home as to the nature of clericalism and the ideal form of government. From the Asian side, late Tokugawa Japan was an outstanding example of a bureaucracy that also sought to archive, document, translate, and apply knowledge gained from Europe.

The truth is, however, that translations of major works of Asian literature, philosophy, and holy books lagged by centuries. Very few non-European accounts entered the late medieval European canon. But where they do, we should be conscious of them. From St. Francis Xavier on, missionary accounts, whatever their biases and blind spots, not only prove to be reliable witnesses; they also bequeath rare late Renaissance to early Enlightenment views of Mughal India, Ming China, and early Tokugawa Japan. Outstanding was Jesuit Luis Fróis (1994), writing on Japan in 1585, who easily meets Reid's test of "astonished interest," one matched also with literary style. As the example of Fróis offers, antiquity may be as much merit as demerit, especially as earlier-arriving Europeans sometimes lacked the prejudice of subsequent generations of European visitors, especially where (as in Japan) they had overstayed their visit. Again, we would have to answer on a case-by-case basis, but it is also true, as elaborated here, that innovations in printing and publishing evolved rapidly in this age.

With time (indeed, short time), histories of the Portuguese in Asia began to appear in Europe, inevitably followed by Dutch, French, and English counterparts. As historiographies, we may well ask, What value can be ascribed to these works of national and religious prejudice? To some extent there is no substitute for these histories, especially where the original documentary sources relating to the early discovery voyages entered the realm of state secrecy, therefore defying reproduction, at least in their time, or are simply missing. But, on the other hand, where the great European travel collections are available, lending themselves to deconstruction, then we agree that they are useful, even indispensable, to the modern researcher.

A final caution awaits, what Ana Paula Laborinho (1993, 141) has termed the rise or rather the trap of exoticism: "not so much a description of a reality as the formulation of an ideal which gains increasing light and color the more distant [and] inaccessible it is." Such an alternative geographical or imagined place thus becomes the stuff of European travel writing. The rise of exoticism and its critique returns us full circle to Said's objection and a postmodernist critique of an Orientalizing mind-set. While the transition from report, to narrative, to exoticizing the "other" might not always have been watertight, we nevertheless seek in these texts to maximize Laborinho's sense of their "surprise of civilization." For all these reasons, we draw the line in our inquiry at the late eighteenth century not as watertight but in order to establish the temporal boundaries of late Renaissance to early Enlightenment precocity.

## EUROCENTRICITY VERSUS
## THE EURASIAN EXCHANGE

The Eurocentricity debate has also engaged practitioners of history from a global viewpoint. As James Blaut (2000, 391) posits, race and environment, as well as culture, have all been advanced over the centuries to validate Eurocentric world history. But with racial determinism long since dead, or at least no longer respectable, Eurocentric history today rests on but two legs: environment and culture. But today, just as the critique of the supposed superior cultural qualities of Europeans deepens (such as unique Western rationality), so the need for environmentalist arguments to counter this critique seems to be growing. Over a long time and to the present, he argues, the "marriage" between environmentalism and Eurocentrism has become self-serving, especially in the hands of practitioners of "popular" environmentally reductionist texts. Historically, Europeans always took it for granted that they (and Europe) were favored racially, culturally, and environmentally by a Christian God, especially alongside "nasty" tropical zones. As explained in chapter 6, one who promoted a view of climatic determinism was French Enlightenment philosopher Montesquieu, finding all kinds of moral fallibility in hotter climes. The nineteenth-century German geographer Carl Ritter, as mentioned in chapter 1, was another who fitted the environmental determinist mode.

A variation on the theme is Jack Goody's *The East in the West* (1996). No less a polemic against European exceptionalism, Goody, whose reputation has been established as an Africanist, offers homage to an integrated planet. Goody challenges the assumptions of Europe's unique institutions by mapping a world where East and West are broadly portrayed as equals, with their common roots reaching back to Mesopotamia. Offering particularly notable examples from India, Goody seeks to blur the division between the West and the "rest" by binding the historical trajectories of Europe and Asia. In offering a materialist conception of the entire Eurasian landmass, albeit at the expense of Africa, Goody also offers a powerful critique of constructions of the Other.

Another text entering the world history canon is Robert B. Marks's *The Origins of the Modern World* (2002). As suggested by the subtitle, *A Global and Ecological Narrative,* Marks is concerned to correlate broad demographic and ecological shifts in explaining East-West parallels and divergence. Of particular interest in Marks's analysis is the varying ability of China, India, and Europe to harness New World crop imports to escape the ecological constraints of "the biological old regime." Our bias, then, is to subordinate or, at least, to situate environmental/ecological considerations within a broad social science matrix that would equally privilege culture, including material culture, allowing for a broad parity in civilizational achievements between East and West, at least within our time frame.

The new world history scholarship,[3] written in response to the recent rise of East Asia, has debated the contention that the real divergence between the West and the "rest" dates only from the eighteenth or even the early nineteenth century. Central in this debate, as mentioned, have been the texts of Andre Gunder Frank (1998), Kenneth Pomeranz (2000), and R. Bin Wong (1997). Needless to say, this argument addresses seminal questions concerning the rise of the industrial revolution in Europe, the preeminence in the global economy of Great Britain from the 1800s, and so on. But in confirming the counterpart role of, especially, China in the making of the early modern world system, the divergence literature has also provided a powerful antidote and, in the writings of Wong, an alternative to Eurocentrism. Specifically, Wong is convinced of the importance of viewing Europe from a Chinese perspective as well as the other way around. Rather than offering up a reexamination of global economic history as a reflex to the Asian economic "miracle," or, in other words, reading back from recent trends, the recent world history literature finds its lodestone in a complex set of correlated global interactions that have their origins in millennium-old world empires.[4]

*First Globalization* thus seeks to enter the literature on the early modern world system with a difference. While we are conscious of the globalizing forces unleashed by seaborne trade and commerce of unprecedented proportions (the stuff of economic historians), we are here concerned with the ideological and cultural contestation that accompanied the trader-missionaries and conquistadores. The other side of the coin of economic supremacy, such as was achieved in the high tide of European imperialism, this book argues, was the scientific and humanistic revolution that incubated in the medieval European courts, churches, and centers of learning. To be sure, casting aside medievalism and embracing the new Enlightenment was not an even trajectory, especially in the face of such powerful mediating institutions as the Church and the courts. At the end of the day, we seek to demonstrate, the "divergence" was as much intellectual as it was material. Eventually, European science and technology triumphed. Indisputably, the West still maintains its edge in research and development, even if the Asia Pacific region, the world's most dynamic zone since recovery from World War II, has rapidly bridged the gap. Still, in the first age of globalization, as this book demonstrates, Eurasia was the premium global arena of intellectual contestation and exchange, especially in contrast to the lands of the New World *conquista,* suffering, variously, deracination along with cultural imperialism. The longevity of Confucianism, Hinduism, Buddhism, Islam, and other Asian civilizational values suggests a major disconnect between economic exchanges and culture transfers. Nevertheless, a major theme this book addresses is the appearance of hybrid forms and cultures across the Eurasian landscape during the first wave of globalization just as cultural transfers East and West reached a new peak.

## EURASIA AS REGION

Rather than offering a focused or single state-centered narrative, albeit within a regional world history perspective, such as I sought to achieve in my studies of Macau (Gunn 1997), Nagasaki (Gunn 1999a), and Timor (Gunn 1999b), *First Globalization* offers a multicentered study of the vast Eurasian world, as a second tier of analysis that would incorporate all functionally interacting regions of the globe. Highlighting the Eurasia world also draws attention to, as we reflect here, the postwar construction of region. Even today, such terms as "Near East," "Middle East," and "Far East" betray an imperial approach to European expansion that had its beginnings in the first wave of Oriental studies emerging in such European centers of learning as Leiden and Paris. Stripped of Eurocentric bias, the reconceptualization of Asia divided into West, South, and East has gained a new politically correct flavor (cf. Emmerson 1994).

Asia, both the term and the construct, we agree, has a long pedigree and, from Ptolemy down, might be considered that part of the Eurasian landmass that is not Europe. The "Southeast Asia" region was known to classical Greece and Rome as *Aurea Chersonesus,* or the "golden peninsula." For Ptolemy and Renaissance Europe, it was known as "India beyond the Ganges" or further "India" or, echoing Marco Polo, the "gold and silver islands." Ancient mariners knew this monsoon zone simply as the "land below the winds." For China, the region was glossed "Nanyang," emphasizing its southern location relative to the "Middle Kingdom." For ancient India, this was "Suvarnaduipa." Above all, as the historical and cultural patterning of this tropical zone of archipelagos and river deltas reveals, it was a pivotal zone through which traders and ideas passed, a buffer zone between the great civilizations of India and China. As Janet L. Abu-Lughod (1989, 185–211) has explained of the "Sindbad way," long before Europeans entered the Persian Gulf and Indian Ocean, Muslim traders had already reached the China Sea area, just as Islam established beachheads across this vast maritime zone.

There is also an important sense that East–Southeast Asia fell into a tribute-trading zone with China, the Middle Kingdom at the center. As elaborated by Hamashita Takeshi, a Japanese historian of China, the Ming and Qing codes ranked and modified, according to circumstances, the various geographical groupings of tributaries. Such ranged from Korea, Japan, Vietnam, Cambodia, Ryukyu, Mongolia, Java, Mongolia, and Tibet and even came to incorporate "barbarian" traders from Europe. Hamashita describes the Chinese-based world economy as "a unified system characterized by internal tribute/tribute-trade relations with China at the center . . . an organic entity with center-periphery relations of southeast, northeast, central and northwest Asia . . . connected with the adjacent India trade area" (Hamashita 1994, cited in Frank 1998, 114). It is also true that, from Japan to Vietnam, erstwhile tributary states established their own versions of tributary or, rather, subtributary power and diplomatic relations more or less along the Chinese model. By highlighting an East–Southeast Asia regional world system, Hamashita is also countering the Wallersteinean conception of a bifurcated world where, historically, local economies are simply incorporated into a European-centered world economy (Hamashita 1994; Ikeda 1996, 52).

Even so, the Portuguese, Dutch, and English imposed their own divisioning of the region on the southern or maritime tier of Asia, usually with reference to seat of empire, whether centered locally on, respectively, Goa, Batavia, or Calcutta. For example, historian Manuel de Faria Sousa, writing at the end of the seventeenth century, divided Portuguese Asia (the so-called *Estado da India*) into seven regions in a crescent reaching from Mombassa to Liampo, the lost Portuguese outpost on the coast of China near modern Ningpo.[5]

With the establishment of Macau in 1557 and Spanish Manila in 1571, and the entry of the Dutch and English into the China Sea zone, all in pursuit of the lucrative and indispensable China trade, a new sense of bounded region emerged. This became all the more obvious with the decline of the ancient spice trade focused on the Moluccas (not even mentioned in Sousa's divisioning) and with the shift in center of gravity of trade to the Macau–Guangzhou (Canton)–Taiwan–Nagasaki–Manila axis. By the early seventeenth century, the Dutch blockade of Goa, the Dutch capture of the Moluccas and Malacca, English inroads into Indian commerce, and the eventual opening of China to European maritime trade confirmed this shift, just as it signaled the hegemonic sequence of the northern European powers over the Iberian.

The revelation of Eurasia also awaited the production of post-Ptolemaic atlases and cartographic reproductions with increasingly accurate renditions of China, Korea, Japan, and the archipelago. *India Orientalis* thus took Cartesian form, to adopt the term used by a Dutch cartographer to denote the vast lands east of India. It is of interest that in early eighteenth-century collections, such as that of John Harris (1745), East Asia was already used to refer to the China, Japan, and the Korea area alongside the generic term "Tartary." Such enterprise in publishing and map production in the European core, we should understand, was part and parcel of what Anderson (1998) has termed the rise of "print capitalism."

## THE SOUTHEAST ASIA REGION?

Observing the wartime origins of "Southeast Asia" and the "imagined reality" that it became only with the advent and prosecution of the Cold War, Anderson (1998, 3–8) also reflects on the sense of region in an earlier age. As an artifice, he reminds us, outsiders named this region. Victorian naturalist Alfred Russel Wallace (1869) had simply termed the region the "Malay Archipelago" in his book of the same name. John Crawfurd (1820, 1), British Resident to the Court of Yogyakarta (1811–1814, 1816) termed the European discovery of the "Indian Archipelago" "a transaction of history as recent as that of the Americas . . . [comparable] . . . even with the New World itself to which, in fact, its moral and physical state have a closer resemblance than any other portion of the globe." Even today, China contests with Vietnam ownership of large parts of the South "China" Sea on the basis of prior historical contact and interest reaching back to antiquity (Gunn 1991). In any case, Anderson observes, it was imperialism that supplied the boundaries, drawing the line through the island of New Guinea, hiving off Vietnam from the cultural orbit of the Middle Kingdom, and rupturing the millennium-long link between Ceylon/Sri Lanka and its Theravada Buddhist emulators in Thailand, Cambodia, and Laos (Anderson 1998, 3–8).

Nevertheless, the intellectual construction of Southeast Asia continues. As Denys Lombard suggested in a number of publications, with rich allusion to French Annales historian Fernand Braudel, even if Southeast Asia lacked the equivalent of the Roman Empire's ability to politically unify both shores of the Mediterranean during four or five centuries, there were sufficient shared linguistic, cultural, and even political features in the region to suggest an oriental Mediterranean. Such a picture would not ignore southern China (Hainan and Taiwan included) and even Japan, especially in connecting up the agrarian and harbor cities of Southeast Asia through western (Philippines) and eastern (Cham) maritime trade routes. Lombard (1990), in his classic study of Java, *Le Carrefour Javanais* (Javanese Crossroads), develops the theory of cultural hybridization to explain the grafting of Indian, Islamic, Sinic, and European influences on animist Java. But as with Braudel's Mediterranean, so the archipelago is defined by its connections across diverse regions. For Lombard, it is only by making use of a supranational framework, and by adopting an "integrated approach," that we can apprehend this reality (Lombard 1997, 126). Others, such as Lieberman (1990, 1995), caution that, in bounding Southeast Asia, fundamental differences exist between island and mainland Southeast Asia, underlying differential cultural and mercantile penetration.

Following the work of K. N. Chaudhuri (1985) in attempting to construct an image of the Indian Ocean in the way that Braudel (1976) achieved for the Mediterranean, Anthony Reid has likewise drawn from the method of the Annales school in his two-volume (1988, 1993) study of commerce and historical change in the "Land below the Winds." The debt to Braudel is clearly acknowledged in the first volume, where the master is praised for his ability to call on a range of disciplines, especially geography, to demonstrate the "collective destinies" of the people of a region. Reid (2000, 4–6) emphasizes the coherence of Southeast Asia as a geographical and human region, even compared with the Mediterranean.

Yet, as Wong (2001) has pointed out in a seminal essay exploring "Braudelian regions" of Asia writ large, the "Chinese Mediterranean" imposes its attention. He writes that not only was the Chinese empire more economically developed than Southeast Asia, but its political power also enjoyed an edge. In making this assertion, Wong is influenced by the writings of Hamashita (for example, 1995) on the modus operandi of the tributary trade system. He also observes that while Lombard allows a Chinese dynamic in his construction of maritime Southeast Asia, Reid presents a more autonomous region. Wong further comments that a Braudelian concept of region is less defined by a particular configuration of space than a multiplicity of bonds between peoples such as implied by a "total human experience." But whereas in Braudel's Mediterranean, Latin Christians and Turkish Muslims each retained their respective centers of gravity, Southeast Asia, as Lombard emphasized, was above all defined by its diversity and hybridity.

## DEFINING THE EURASIAN
## MARITIME WORLD SYSTEM

Disputes over definitions of boundaries of world systems as well as the parts that constitute systems have also entered the debate among practitioners of world history. Appropriately, as a work of metageography, we should also clarify our sense of a Eurasian maritime world system. It is now recognized that very small world systems can be brought into the analysis, as in the study of seminomadic desert tribes. The emergence of the largest tributary system ever known, that of Afroeurasia circa 500 B.C. to A.D. 1400 out of trade connections between Rome and China along the famous silk roads, raises theoretical issues related to the rise of world systems. Chase-Dunn and Hall (1997, 148–86) denote a major difference between the Afroeurasian system and the Europe-centered global system that eventually emerged. Both systems were politically multicentered in the sense that no state controlled the whole system. The trade network was larger than any one state. But, in contrast to the truly global Europe-centered modern world system, the ancient Afroeurasian system comprised three noncontiguous cores linked only by the exchange of prestige goods. Afroeurasian sea links were important in this two-millennium exchange, as acknowledged by Abu-Lughod (1989, 172–73, 202, 252), but the terrestrial silk roads were the center stage of both long-distance trade and political-military conflict, especially with the Mongol ascendance.

The interruption of the terrestrial Silk Road trade by the Ottoman Turks and the quest by the Portuguese to outflank and, with the defeat of the Mamluk fleet at Diu in 1509, to ultimately choke the Arab trade in the Indian Ocean was epochal. But equally, the substitution of Portuguese for Ottoman control over shipping routes in the northern part of the Arabian Sea has profound implications for theorizing a newly bounded maritime world system. Just as the central Asian empires imploded, so the Iberian traders reenergized a vast maritime crescent reaching from Japan, the China coastal littoral, the East Indies, the two coasts of India and beyond, the African-Atlantic zone, and the European terminus. Indeed, it is tempting to say that the shift from terrestrial silk roads to the maritime zones is still playing its way out as testified by the surging economies of maritime East Asia, particularly those in the China coast region. Such historians as J. C. van Leur acknowledge the importance of early eastern trade prior to the advent of the European trading companies. Writing in Dutch but entering translation in English in the early 1960s, van Leur also went far in challenging Eurocentric approaches to the study of Asian history.[6] By redefining the boundaries of Eurasia to invoke its maritime dimension and interconnectedness within a world history perspective, we are also in line with recent research of Frank (1998) and Hamashita (1994).[7]

As Chase-Dunn and Hall (1997, 16–17) have summarized, basically two camps have emerged in world system studies: the "culturalists," who stress the homogeneity of central values in defining civilizations, and the "structuralists," who use criteria of interconnectedness rather than homogeneity. The positions among an array of world system practitioners are varied and complex, but *First Globalization* seeks to define the Eurasian maritime world system as one bounded by intersocietal networks that go beyond trade and warfare to include information, technology, and especially hybridization of cultures inside and outside the European and Chinese (Indian and Japanese) cores. Silk is a perfect example of the ambiguous status of a prestige commodity and the value it accrues across differential marketplaces, civilizations, and cultures, suggesting, in turn, important ways in which the culturalist and structuralist approaches may well be complementary. But tea, spices, and other Asian rarities entering European marketplaces support this sense of cultural complementarity. Especially, as we shall highlight here, more so than continental Asia, where powerful centralized states prevailed, the archipelagic zone of Southeast Asia, including zones of contact on the littorals of India and China, was the locus of intense European cultural and racial creolization.

No matter where we live in today's globalized world, it is worth reflecting on the origins of many of our traditions. *First Globalization* helps remind us of where we have been, mentally and materially, and just how so many of our treasured cultural icons have been, variously, imported, transacted, translated, invented, contrived or confabulated. Whether we (in Europe or Asia) are reflecting on tea culture; the habit of smoking tobacco; the act of consuming coffee, spicy food, fusion food, the "English" potato, the sweet potato, or "herbal" remedies; or on more imaginative tropes, such as sea monsters, mermaids, humanoids, science fiction, Catholic passion plays, fado music, Latin rhythms, European fashions, Chinoiserie, and Japanware, we should look back not only to Vasco da Gama and Magellan and their entourage of traders and missionaries but also to the great Arab, Chinese, and other Asian seafarers, traders, and emissaries, bearers of what we have described as the Eurasian Exchange. The East-West exchange between 1500 and 1800 was not simply a transfer of material goods and exotics such as implied in the "Columbian exchange" but in its heyday also involved intense cultural crossovers and exchanges between civilizations that changed forever the way we (in Europe and Asia) situated ourselves versus fellow humankind, the physical earth, and, indeed, the universe.

## THE BOOK

Chapter 1 seeks to identify a European discovery canon, inter alia, the key texts and genres guiding the construction of European discourses on Asia in the premodern era. Chapter 2 explains how the empirical discoveries were often fantasized as literature. Chapter 3 seeks to identify how the natural world fitted the cosmology of the age. Chapter 4 expands on the theme of the mapping and geographical framing of Asia. Chapter 5 examines the role of the Catholic mission in Asia as frontline crusaders in a grand cosmological contest. Chapter 6 looks at Enlightenment views of Asian governance. In chapter 7, we investigate the various receptions of Europe by Asian civilizations. Chapter 8 looks at European perceptions of livelihoods in Asia. Chapter 9 turns to a discussion of language in the rise of European Oriental studies, and chapter 10 links the discussion with new emergent identities and the creolization of cultures. A conclusion offers a final reflection on the "Eurasian exchange."

## NOTES

1. Our version of globalization should not be confused with the current popularized sense of globalized finance and production processes associated with advanced capitalism and globalized consumerism, tracing its origins back some twenty years in some versions or to the 1870s in others. Simply stated, in this book "first globalization" refers to the deepening interactions within the Afroeurasian region attendant on the expansion of Europe following the voyages of Columbus and Vasco da Gama. We are neither propounding nor testing a theory of modernity or globalization but hold to a sense of globalization as the extension of economic, social, and cultural relations over time and space. This also includes the sets of processes affecting individuals in a truly phenomenological sense. As such, we acknowledge Anthony Giddens (1991), among his other writings.

2. For an accessible text on Arab source material, see Tibbetts (1979).
For a pioneering European work on Chinese source materials relating to Southeast Asia, see Groeneveldt (1880).

3. For a discussion, see Goldstone (1987), who also allows that his own interest is in cultural blocks on non-European progress. See also Goldstone (2002).

4. The sense of an integrated world economy from the thirteenth century is most forcefully presented in Abu-Lughod (1989), which describes a world system spanning Afroeurasia persisting through to the eighteenth century.

5. In this divisioning, according to Sousa (1695), Malacca represented the sixth and "the last place we possess in the Eastern Continent" in a subregion that comprised Bengal, Pegu, Tanassarim, and Cape Singapore. A seventh division extended from Singapore to Siam, Ligor, Cambodia, Champa, Cochin China (already so named), Macau, and the coast of China as far north as Liampo (Ningpo?). Ceylon and a fort on the island of Timor constituted extras.

In its time, British India embraced not only the vast Indian subcontinent but also Burma, Penang, Singapore, and, in a general sense, Malaya and Java when that island came under British domination during the Napoleonic Wars. All Dutch outposts in the sprawling and ethnically heterogeneous Dutch East Indies, as with Dutch outposts in Taiwan and Japan, answered first to Batavia, just as Goa served as seat of the *Estado da India* for the Portuguese in all its eastern settlements, including Macau and Timor, albeit answerable to European courts and company directors. The Spanish in Manila, in turn, answering to New Spain (Mexico), were, via the galleon trade, much more focused on a China-centered Asia.

6. Van Leur's critique of Eurocentrism is summarized in Legge (1965, 21–23).

7. In fact, such purpose was achieved by the work of Lombard and Aubin (2000), first published in Paris in 1988 as *Marchands et Hommes d'Affaires Asiatiques*. Besides exploring the links across vast space from the coast of Africa to Japan, Lombard sought in this publication to promote the view that, notwithstanding the European presence after 1500, Asian history continued according to its own rhythms.

# 1

# The Discovery Canon

Inasmuch as we have sought to limit our inquiry to European print works on Asia from the late sixteenth to the eighteenth century, it would be relevant to arrive at some understanding of how this knowledge entered vernacular languages and how it was shared and disseminated across European audiences with what end.[1] While media studies today form part of an invigorated social sciences repertoire, relatively little critical apparatus has been applied to bodies of pre-Enlightenment and early modern literatures or even to the creation and early dissemination of print material as a genre. Following the method of Derrida and others, we seek to select canonical texts that stood before European audiences as cultural icons of their age. We reserve for a separate chapter the corpus of church, especially Jesuit, writing on Asia, much of it actually published in Asia. But we are also concerned to track the rise in the emerging European core of "print capitalism," to borrow the terminology of Benedict Anderson (1983), as the Gutenberg revolution was also part and parcel of the Eurasian exchange between the East and the West.

## MEDIEVAL TRAVELERS

Famously, travels and voyages and the general theme of discovery became familiar in Europe from accounts of the thirteenth-century Venetian traveler Marco Polo (1254–1323?), even if not given much credence in his lifetime. After a reported seventeen years in China, Polo returned to Venice and, in 1298, dictated *La Meraviglie del Monde* (The Marvels of the

World), also known as *Il Milion*, to his cell mate Rustichello (Bencardino 1998, 14). In any case, Polo's adventures entered various manuscript versions in Paris and Germany long before its first publication. This went by the title *Divisament Dou Monde* (Description of the World), first printed in woodblock in Nuremberg in 1477. As the seminal source for European images of Asia, its priority was confirmed with at least seventy reprintings by the early 1500s—in Latin at Gouda in 1483, in English at London in 1579, in French at Paris in 1586, and at Venice in 1533 and 1620. Setting aside interpretations of Poloean history[2] (a theme returned to in subsequent chapters), Marco Polo's travels constituted the original Oriental travelogue, believed to have been read by Christopher Columbus prior to his first landmark journey (1492–1493) in search of the Indies. It is also important, as Mackerras (1989, 19) has pointed out, that Polo's *Description* is "immensely laudatory" of China and its civilization, especially of commerce, regional trade, and the splendor of cities.

Cathay, or at least the Mongol court, was well known to medieval Europe.[3] The Mongol invasion of Europe forced Pope Innocent IV (elected 1243–1254) to step up diplomatic relations with the "barbarians." In 1245, the Council of Lyons led to the dispatch of two diplomatic missions east. In 1245, the Italian Franciscan Giovannida Pian del Carpine (1182–1251) traveled as far as Karakorum in Mongolia. Deemed a diplomatic and religious failure, it nevertheless led to the circulation of his manuscript *Historia Mongolorum* (History of Mongolia), the first European description of Mongolian civilization. Two additional missions to Asia, initiated by Louis IX (r. 1214–1226) of France and Innocent IV, included William of Rubruck, Lourenco de P., and other merchant travelers. In turn, Marco Polo's account of the Mongol court inspired such new religious missions as Giovanni de Montecorvino (1278), leading to the foundation of the (largely symbolic) archbishopric of Cambaluc (Beijing) (Bencardino 1998, 14).

In medieval Europe, where oral accounts of semimythologized voyages had great currency, a veritable canon of travelogues to the East found publication in the rising age of print. Notable was the journey of Nicoli de Conti (1395–1469), who departed Damascus in 1414, crossed Mesopotamia, and reached India, Burma, Java, Borneo, and Indochina. A manuscript version of his travels was included in Gian Francesco Poggio Bracciolini's (1380–1459) *Historia de Varietate Fortunae* (1431–1448) (Bencardino 1998, 14). The merchant handbook of Francesco de Balducci Pegolotti, *Practica della Mercatura* (ca. 1340), was another source of European knowledge on Cathay, although not published until the eighteenth century from a 1471 manuscript. Another important early sixteenth-century account was the itinerary of Ludovico Varthema, whose *Itinerario*, or account of his travels from Europe to Asia between 1502 and 1508, first published in Italian in Rome in 1508, was reprinted at Bologne in 1510, Milan in 1511, Augsburg in 1515, Seville in 1520, and Venice in 1550. The first non-Muslim to offer a firsthand account of a pilgrimage to Mecca, Varthema plausibly journeyed as far east as Banda in the Moluccas in 1505. Lach explains that it was from Varthema that Europe received its first knowledge of the places where nutmegs and cloves were grown (Lach 1969, 593–94). We recall that, within a mere five years of the publication of Varthema's account, the Portuguese under António de Abreu pushed beyond Malacca to the Moluccas.

It is important that the medieval voyages fed into revisions of geographical texts passed down from antiquity, characteristically a three-continent description (Europe, Africa, Asia) of the world. One of the closest students and revisionists of the classical view was Pope Pius II (1458–1464), better known as Aeneas Sylviis Piccolomini, author of *Cosmographia Pii Papae i Asiae et Europae Eleganti Descriptione* (The Pope Pius Cosmography of Asia and Europe Elegantly Described), first published in 1461. The importance of the text, according to Lach, is that while assimilating the classic Ptolemaic picture, it adds information about China and western Asia derived from Polo and Odoric de Pordenone. He also borrowed from Conti's description of India in rejecting the theory of an enclosed Indian Ocean. As such, Pius II lent his support and prestige to the idea that India could be reached by rounding Africa. His ideas apparently influenced Columbus (Lach 1965, 70–71) and the trailblazing cosmographic vision of mapmaker Sebastien Munster.

But the announcement in 1493 by Columbus of his successful voyage to the "Indies" or, in some versions, "India beyond the Ganges," namely, his Barcelona Letter of May 1493, quickly gained major attention in Europe. At least eleven editions of his letter were published in 1493 with six more in 1494–1497. Generally, print and manuscript versions of Columbus's *Book of Prophecies* and *Book of Privileges* "canonized" the Italian New World prophet in European circles. As Boxer (1951, 14) has pointed out, a republication of Columbus with mention of Xipangu (Japan) as a source of gold was also inspirational. We recall also that when Columbus set out from Spain, he carried a letter from the Spanish throne to the "Great Khan of Cathay." It is also believed that Columbus perused *Itineranium* or *The Travels of Sir John Mandeville*, a medieval travel account of the Orient first printed in Milan in 1480 and in Augsburg in 1481. Originally written in French, by 1540 *Travels* was available in every major European language. Mandeville, in turn, is believed to have embellished his account with sources such as those of the Franciscan monk Odoric de Pordenone (1266–1331), author of *Descriptio Orientalium Patrium* (Description of Oriental Countries), an account of his travels to and from Beijing via Persia, India, Sumatra, Borneo, and Guangzhou. While we defer discussion of Mandeville as literature to the following chapter, it is important that Columbus held Mandeville's romantic tales to be truthful account of various islands off the eastern coast of India or China. Until he died, Columbus believed he had revisited the Indies, or Mandeville's "Isle of Cathay." But Columbus was not alone in his credence of the Mandeville legend. According to W. R. D. Moseley (1993), Mandeville's *Travels* were source material for, inter alia, Richard Wills's *History of Travayle* (1557), early editions of Hakluyt, and, as discussed in chapter 5, the 1492 globe by Martin Behaim and mapmaker Gerhard Mercator.

Obviously, as Ana Paula Laborinho (1993, 141–42) has written, great travel narratives have a long pedigree, from *Odysseus* to the Chinese classic *Tao Te Ching* to *Journey to the East*. Nevertheless, the need to describe reality became paramount with the age of discovery. One such document was Pero Vaz de Carminho's letter on the discovery of Brazil to King Manuel in 1500. More influential, albeit controversial as to authenticity, was Amerigo Vespucci's (1451–1512) letter *Mundus Novo* (New World) to the king of Spain in 1503. Variously published in Lisbon (1504), Paris (1504), Augsburg (1504), and Florence (1505–1506), along with the letter of his claimed first four voyages, versions of *Mundus Novo* became early best-sellers going through Italian-, French-, and German-language editions besides the original Latin. A unique copy of Vespucci's third voyage to America, addressed to Laurentio de Medici, was printed at Antwerp in 1506–1510.

But while modifications to the Ptolemaic view of the world came to be assimilated within the Catholic cosmology, the revelations by Copernicus, Kepler, and Galileo of a sun-centered solar system famously met with firm papal resistance. Notably, in 1543, Nicholas Copernicus (1473–1543) published his treatise *De Revolutionibus Orbium Coslestium* (Revolution of the Celestial Sphere), advancing the theory that the earth and all the other planets revolved around the sun while rotating on its axis. By removing man from the center of the universe, Copernicus not only threw down a challenge to the Catholic orthodoxy (his book was accordingly prohibited by the Catholic Church in 1616) but also paved the way for innovations in science that would sweep Protestant ahead of Catholic Europe. Galileo Gallilei (1564–1642), who in 1635 published his *Systema Cosmicum* (Cosmic System) as a snub to the establishment, was dragged to Rome to stand trial in 1633. Galileo's work remained on the *Index Librorum Prohibitorum*, or the List of Prohibited Books, issued by the Roman Office of the Inquisition until 1823.

## THE IBERIAN DISCOVERY LITERATURE

With the rise of northern European cities such as Mainz, Strasbourg, and Lyon as early centers of printing, followed by Paris in 1470 and the Low Countries in 1473, by the 1470s the art had migrated south of the Alps to Venice, Florence, and Milan. With time, Seville, Lisbon, and other Iberian centers had also established their presses (Chatterton 1927; Lucas 1960, 373), announcing, in Derrida's language, "the civilization of the book."

Pioneers of print in Portugal were Jewish immigrants from Spires in Germany, and the first book published in Portugal was *Pentateuch*, a Hebrew work printed by Samuel Gacon at Faro in 1487. The second book, also in Hebrew, appeared in Lisbon in 1489. It was not until 1494 that the first Latin book appeared in Lisbon. Certain Jewish immigrants found favor at the court. Notable was Abraham Zacuto (1450–1510), author of *Almanach Perpetuum* (Perpetual Almanac), printed in Leiria in 1496 and translated from Hebrew to Latin in 1496. Appointed court astronomer and historiographer to John II (r. 1481–1495) and holding office under Manuel I (r. 1495–1521) until the expulsion of Jews from Portugal, Zacuto's scientific material, it is held, "had a decisive influence on the maritime voyages and discoveries." Notably, he presented an astrolabe, an instrument used for measuring altitude of heavenly bodies, to Vasco da Gama, who famously led the Portuguese advance to Asia with his epic journey to India in 1498. Long known to the Arabs, the astrolabe was then considered a breakthrough in Europe as a navigational aid. Columbus also possessed a copy of the *Almanach* but may not have put it to good use. It is noteworthy as well that a Portuguese edition of the *Livro do Marco Polo* appeared in Lisbon in 1502 after da Gama's return to Lisbon, printed expressly "for the service of God and for the information of those who are now going to the said Indies" (Anonymous 1935).

Even so, the Spanish discoveries of the New World were bound to ramify in print. The first collection on the Spanish expeditions was that of Pietro Martyr (Peter Martire), first published in Venice in 1504. As with Columbus, an Italian in the service of the Spanish court, Martyr brought out a series of publications triumphing the Spanish achievements. Martyr's work *Mondo Nuovo* was translated by Richard Eden and published in 1555 as the *Decades of the Newe Worlde or West India*, with the view to encouraging English enterprise to emulate the Spanish.

In the years before Magellan's voyage, it is clear that whatever fascination awaited a European audience of discoveries in the East, it was the conquest of the New World that held Europe in awe. It was with this knowledge that in 1521 Cortes published his self-serving letter on the collapse of the Aztec capital in the future Mexico City. The following year, his first letter to Charles V, Holy Roman emperor (r. 1519–1556), was printed at Seville by the German publisher Cromberger, a figure associated with the establishment of the Spanish press in Latin America.

The westward circumnavigation of the globe by the Magellan voyage and the return to Europe in 1521 of the *Victoria*, captained by Juan Sebastian del Cano, was deservedly epochal. It produced three near-contemporary accounts: those of Maxmillian of Transylvania and Antonio Pigafetta, an Italian scribe aboard the *Victoria*, and one in Portuguese by Antonio de Brito, Portuguese captain at Ternate who offered an account of the Spanish arrival but apparently not published until much later. Maxmillian's Latin account *De Moluccis Insulis* (Molucca Islands), published at both Cologne and Rome in 1523 and based on an interview with del Cano, provides, according to one biographer, "useful information on the life of the people of the Moluccas and the spice trade there." Pigafetta's eyewitness account, completed in 1524 (his original diaries having been lost), was first published in summary in Paris in 1525 as *Le Voyage et Navigation fait pas les Espaignoiz es Isles Molucques* (The Voyage and Navigations of the Spanish to the Molucca Islands), followed by an Italian translation from the French in Venice in 1536. However, the complete Pigafetta manuscript was not published until 1780 (Silva 1987, 86). Collectively, the survivor accounts offer the first contextualized European accounts of the Philippines, Brunei, the Moluccas, and Timor. The Moluccas conquest theme also entered Bartolomeu Argensola's (1562–1635) triumphalist *Conquista de las Islas Moluucas al Rey Pilipe* (1609), an enduring text in Europe entering English translation as *The Discovery and Conquest of the Moluccas and the*

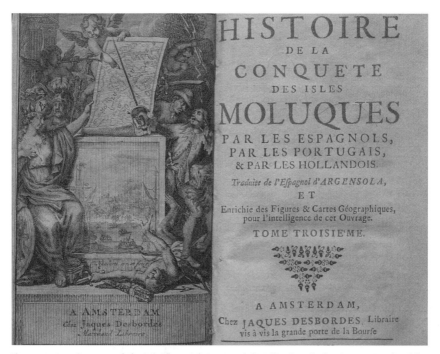

**Figure 1.1.    Cover and frontispiece of Argensola's *Histoire de la Conquete des isles Moluques par les Espagnols, par les Portugais & par les Hollandais* (1707). A triumphalist text, evoking the age of discovery and conquest of the Asian peripheries. (Author's collection)

*Philippine Islands* (1708). Commissioned by the Spanish crown, Argensola drew on royal archives in Seville, including numerous sources of Portuguese origin.

Nevertheless, as Lach underlines, the Portuguese state deliberately controlled information on its overseas discoveries from Africa to Asia in the sixteenth century. As evidence, he offers that the *Suma Oriental* of Tomé Pires, the celebrated manuscript description of Asian trade compiled by the author in Malacca, and the *Book* of Duarte Barbosa, both written before 1520, were not published even in part until, as mentioned later in this chapter, the Italian Ramusio obtained some sections. Lach observes that the rigid control broke down by only midcentury, especially as Jesuit letters reached a wide audience and Portugal's monopoly on the spice trade was broken (Lach 1969, 154, 338).[4]

## THE PORTUGUESE HISTORIES

The great tradition of Portuguese histories of discoveries undoubtedly began with the publication of Fernão Lopes de Castanheda's (1500–1559) *História do Livro Secundo do Descobrimentos & Conquista da India pelos Portugueses* (History of the Second Book of Discoveries and Conquest of India by the Portuguese), published in Coimbra in 1552. This historicizing genre of writing, as explained here, had many emulators. Typically, the Portuguese histories offered slavish paeans to king and country, tending to be organized around the triannual governorships of the *Estado da India*, or the seat of the Portuguese government in Asia at Goa in India. The genre also reflected Portuguese concerns for documentation, not only the practice of copying and archiving in Europe (the Tombe de Correa archives in Lisbon goes back to the fourteenth century) but also the creation of local archives, notably in Goa. Arriving in India in 1528, Castanheda spent ten years in Asia before returning to Coimbra, devoting another twenty years to compiling his *História*. The first of ten intended books, the first volume was nevertheless suppressed although reprinted as a second book with two additional chapters in 1554, offering praise to King Manuel I (r. 1495–1521) for "predicting" the discoveries. The third book appeared in 1552; the fourth, fifth, sixth, and seventh appeared in 1554; and the eighth was printed by his sons. Such was the impact of the book in Europe that a French edition appeared in Paris in 1553, a Spanish edition in Antwerp in 1554, an Italian edition in 1578, and an English edition in London in 1582. As such, Castanheda preceded the better-known João de Barros by a decade.

Still read today is João de Barros's (1496–1570) *Asia: Dos Factos que os Portugueses Fizeram no Descobrimento e Conquista dos Mares e Terras do Oriente* (Asia: Facts Relating to the Portuguese Discovery and Conquest of

Oriental Seas and Lands), published in Lisbon in 1552–1553. The first three volumes of *Decadas*, as this work is commonly known, remain a valuable source for modern historians of the Portuguese encounter with Asia. The first Italian edition of Barros's two first *Decadas*, published in Venice in 1562, signaled his rising fame. Much later (1707), a translation into Dutch was printed in Leiden. Although lacking firsthand experience of Asia, Barros gathered information from a wide range of Asian, including Chinese, informants in his employ besides having access to rare documents and even Asian chronicle sources. More so than Castanheda, Barros stood out as "apologist as well as narrator of Portuguese achievements" (Anonymous 1935, 289). According to Boxer (1948, 9–19), the value of Barros's work is uneven as to region. China aroused his deepest interest, but he also drew on early Portuguese travelers to Siam and Jesuit letters from Japan. While strong on Sumatra, he was not the best informed on Malacca.

This historicizing genre of writing by quasi-official chroniclers was also emulated by Diogo do Couto, keeper of the archives in Goa and literary heir to Barros. Do Couto's *Decada IV*, sent to Europe in 1597, was printed in 1602 with his *Decada Quinta da Asia*, printed in 1612 although dogged by censorship, theft, and neglect. This volume, covering the period 1536–1544, included comment on Indochina, Japan, Goa, Ceylon, Mozambique, and Hormuz.

But what was the influence of Barros's and Couto's published works during their lifetimes? Boxer answers that aside from the Italian translation, the work made little stir in Renaissance Europe. Moreover, the first edition of the *Decadas* may have had a print run of less than 500. In any case, the *Decadas* were admired rather than read. Couto fared even worse, being able to sell only thirty copies of his *Decadas*, giving away forty, with original stock still on sale a century later (Boxer 1948, 9–19). Nevertheless, both Barros's *Decadas I–IV* and Couto's *Decadas IV–XII* were republished in Lisbon in 1777–1778.

Several other Portuguese histories dating from the early expansion phase merit attention. One is *Commontarios de Alfonso De Albuquerque*, published at Lisbon in 1557 and reprinted in Dutch at Leiden in 1706. Albuquerque (1453–1515) first arrived in India via the Cape of Good Hope in 1503 in the employ of Manuel II, but *Commentaries* was compiled and reworked by his son as homage to his father and to the Portuguese discoveries. As narrative, it weaves the victories and defeats of the Portuguese in various battles along with the difficulties of administrating a string of fortresses connecting the Portuguese conquests in the Indian Ocean. Another is by Gaspar Corrêa (1496–1563), who arrived in Goa in 1512, serving as secretary to Albuquerque. He was thus well positioned to write his *Lendas da India* (Legends of India), a history of Portuguese activities in Asia. However, the original manuscript of *Lendas*, plausibly suppressed, was not published until recovered in the nineteenth century.[5]

One of the most influential of the seventeenth-century Portuguese histories was Faria e Sousa's *Da Asia Portuguesa*, first published in Portuguese in 1666. This was translated by John Stevens from the Spanish edition as *Portuguese Asia, or The History of the Discovery & Conquest of India by the Portuguese from the Coast of Africa to the Furthest Parts of China and Japan* (1695). In essence, Sousa's history or, rather, historiography ranges over the entire canvas of the maritime route from the coasts of Africa to Japan. While expanding on some topics such as China, on which Sousa wrote a separate book, chapters follow closely the chronology imposed by the usual triannual governorship of Goa. Sousa is, however, explicit as to his print and manuscript sources, including Castanheda, Barros, Couto, and Ferdinand Mendez Pinto, among others. As McIntyre (1987, 5) explains, this work popularized the Portuguese discoveries to an English readership.

## THE GREAT EUROPEAN COLLECTIONS

Pietro Martyr, we noted, launched the first collection on the Spanish voyages, albeit in the service of Spain. More inclusive was Giovanni Battista Ramusio (1485–1557), who in 1550–1559 published in Venice his *Delle Navigationi et Viaggi* (Some Voyages and Travels) in three volumes, a remarkable achievement for the times, preceding even the great English and Dutch collections by over half a century. Ramusio not only reproduced such texts as Marco Polo's *Travels* and the writings of Ludivico Varthema but also incorporated woodcut and, in some versions, copperplate engravings. In his 1550 volume, he also included, as intimated, a summary derived from Tomé Pires's version of the 1514 account of the first *roteiro* (sailing direction) from Malacca to China, in turn derived from a version owing to Alfonso Albuquerque. His collection was also the first to include an account of the Magellan circumnavigation. The first Portuguese collection, albeit originally published in Latin, was Geronomo Osorio's *Historie de Portugal* (History of Portugal), published in Paris in 1581. Osorio (1506–1580), the bishop of Silves, also incorporated the Magellan account along with other Portuguese discoverers, including Cabral, Cortereal, Vasco da Gama, and Gaspar de Lemos.

While Spanish historians labored under similar constraints as those of their Portuguese counterparts, the early seventeenth century saw the emergence in Madrid of the collection genre, albeit under royal patronage. Needless to say, the great Catholic voyages of Columbus, Vespucci, Ponce de Leon, and Pizarro were highlighted. Exemplary was Antonio de

Herrera's *Historia General del Mundo* (General History of the World), which appeared between 1601 and 1615. As official historian to, successively, Philip II, III, and IV, Herrera had rare access to official documentary sources. Translations of his book appeared in Latin in Amsterdam in 1622 and in reprint in Leiden in 1706. Broadly, English knowledge of the New World, including the Magellan circumnavigation as bequeathed by Pigafetta, entered learned circles with publication in London in 1555 of Richard Eden's *The Decades of the Newe Worlde*. Significantly, the Cambridge-educated Eden had translated from the Latin and published in 1552 Sebastian Munster's *Universal Cosmography: A Treatise of the Newe India* and, as mentioned, a 1555 translation of Pietro Martyr's *Decades*. In 1577, Richard Wills produced an expanded version of Eden's own *Decades* titled *The History of Travayle in the West and East Indies*. Inter alia, this work provided the earliest account of Japan in the English language by excerpting letters of Jesuit Luis Fróis. By this year, a tradition of translating Spanish and, to a lesser extent, Portuguese books was established in London, entering mass production at the turn of the century by Richard Hakluyt, and then expanded with the Purchas collection.

Setting aside the Poloean legend, arguably the most important single work in influencing the course of European expansion and imperialism in Asia was Dutchman J. H. van Linschoten's *Intinerario* (1595–1596). This was translated into English by John Wolfe as *John Huighen Van Linschoten: His Discovers of Voyages into Ye Easte and West Indies* (1598). French and German editions followed. Linschoten (1563–1611), secretary to the archbishop of Goa in 1583–1589, was well placed to collect a mass of trade data, including secret Portuguese *roteiro*, even though he did not travel further east than Goa. Originally published in Amsterdam by Cornelis Claesz in 1596 and copiously illustrated with maps and prints, the *Itinerario* was not only a narration of Linschoten's travels in the Azores and the East but is generally acknowledged as contributing to Portugal's loss of key commercial intelligence to the advantage of the Dutch, English, and French in their own commercial advances. Notably, the pioneering 1595–1597 expedition by the Dutch to the East Indies led by Cornelis de Houtman, named the *Eertse Scheepvaart*, or First Ship Sailing, was guided by travel information supplied by Linschoten.

Richard Hakluyt (1553–1616), the Westminster/Oxford-educated Englishman, published his first collection of *Voyages Touching the Discovery of America* in 1582. But during a five-year sojourn in Paris, he worked on his great collection *The Principall Navigations*, published in 1589. A second edition of *Voyages* also appeared in three volumes between 1598 and 1600. Among other texts reproduced by Hakluyt was a translation of Antonio Galvano's *Discoveries of the World* (1601). By openly plying his political influence to encourage exploration, colonization, and trade, the geographer

Hakluyt emerged in his time as a prime expositor of travel literature for political purposes.

Travel literature with a patriotic purpose was also the lifework of the English clergyman Samuel Purchas (1577–1626). By reworking the immense mass of manuscripts remaining in Hakluyt's possession on his death, Purchas published in 1625 four huge quartos: *Hakluytus Posthumus or, Purchas His Pilgrimes: Contayning a History of the World in Sea Voyages and Lande Travells by Englishmen and Others.* Even though Purchas was an inferior editor to Hakluyt, he nevertheless added many more Portuguese, Spanish, Dutch, and English voyages. He also incorporated many maps from the *Atlas Major* by Mercator-Hondius and the *Atlas Minor* map showing China and Korea. Importantly, for English knowledge of Japan, Purchas carried accounts of Japan by Will Adams, the first Englishman in Japan, having arrived in 1600, and John Saris, of the English East India Company, who visited in 1613. But also important for European cartographic perceptions of China, he included "Map of China, taken out of a China Map printed with China characters, etc. gotten at Bantam by Capt. John Saris," albeit derivative of Jesuit Matteo Ricci's famous world map produced for a Chinese audience in 1602 (cf. Needham 1959, 586).

Nevertheless, London was by no means the only northern European center of publishing, nor was it the only marketplace for the new literature, which, in itself, was becoming pan-European in the context of the rising bourgeoisie. In the early seventeenth century, the Protestant city of Frankfurt was a major print and distribution center in its own right. It was to this city that Johann Theodore de Bry (1528–1598), a convert to the Reformation, moved in 1570 from his former base in Strasbourg. Already known as an engraver, de Bry came into contact with Hakluyt, and his circle and was inspired to produce his own collection of voyages to the New World generically titled *Grand Voyages* (1590–1620). Almost simultaneously, de Bry, with Johann Israel de Bry, published *Petit Voyages* (1598–1634), devoted mainly but not entirely to the East Indies, including the voyages of Linschoten (1583–1592), the voyages of de Houtman (1595–1597) and Jacob von Neck and Wybrandt van Warwijck (1598–1599) to the East Indies, as well as Joris von Spilbergen's voyage to Ceylon in 1601–1604, Gaspero Balbi's voyage to Pegu via Syria in 1579–1588, Dutch voyages to the Spice Islands and China (1600–1606) revealing the rising power of the Dutch, Admiral Pieter Willemsz's voyage to the Spice Islands to seize them from the Portuguese (1612), along with a wealth of visual and cartographic material.

There is a sense that in emphasizing the great voyages of Protestant discovery with appropriate engravings, de Bry was waging a war of words against Spanish and Portuguese conquests around the world. The great collections and series brought down in Paris, London, Amsterdam, and elsewhere during the seventeenth and eighteenth centuries are also important in the way of both incorporating newer discoveries and foreshadowing the trajectory of European historical world incorporation. We are necessarily selective in the following enumerations, but it should be recalled that outside of state censorship, all the major voyages quickly entered translation in all the major European languages.

One of the first collections of the eighteenth century was Awnsham and John Churchill's *Collection of Voyages and Travels.* This first edition in four volumes appeared in London in 1704. A 1732 edition added two volumes, followed by a reprint in 1732 and a new third edition of 1744–1747, adding, besides an index, two more volumes drawn from the "Oxford Collection of Voyages," never before published in English. The third edition also included a preface by English philosopher John Locke (1632–1704) titled "The Whole History of Navigation from Its Original to This Time." The entire work is illustrated with 305 copperplate engravings and maps, including a new map of China.

Another in the collection genre was John Harris's *Navigantium Atque Itinerantium Bibliotecha . . . ,* first published in London in 1705 with only thirty-five plates and maps. A 1744 version of this monumental work of over 1,000 pages offers, besides original works in English, accounts translated from Latin, French, Italian, Spanish, Portuguese, and High and Low Dutch. The enlarged 1745 version of *Navigantium* in two volumes offers sixty-one engraved plates, including twenty-three copper-engraved maps. The second and third versions reprint Tasman's original map of the east coast of Australia. It also includes the voyages of Queiros, Dampier, Magellan, Drake, Cavendish, von Noort, Schouten, Funnell, Woods Rogers, and Roggewain, among others. In other words, Harris's work was a history of all known voyages, not just a selection of random accounts, as was Churchill's. Harris was a clergyman and amateur naturalist. Rare in this age of compilation, *Navigantium* also includes a text written by a Chinese scholar deemed "a very worthy, honest and pious man." This was Dionysius Kao, "being a native Chinese, and bred up on letters." Penned around 1674 and offering descriptive asides on the Chinese provinces in which he traveled, Kao's account was praised by Harris as "impartial" and not overly dependent on the Jesuits. Even so, as we shall discuss in chapter 7, such an ecumenical view of China did not survive the Enlightenment and would severely test many West-based China scholars today.

Also important among the English collections is Alexander Dalrymple's (1737–1808) *An Historical Collection of the Several Voyages and Discoveries in the South Pacific Ocean* (1770–1771). Published prior to Cook's discoveries of 1772–1775, the text comprises partial translations of such South Sea voyages as Magellan, Queiros, Roggewein, Schouten and Le Maire, and Tasman. Following an active career in Borneo and the Philippines and later as an admiralty hydrographer, Dalrymple sought in this compilation to encourage English discovery of the southern continent. The earliest and most valuable of the French collections was Melchisedech Thevenot's *Relations de Divers Voyages Curieux* (Account of Various Strange Voyages), published in Paris in 1663–1673. Thevenot (1620–1692), a founder of the French Academy of Sciences, was well placed as librarian of the Royal Library to assemble an array of printed and manuscript texts, including the Hakluyt and Purchas collections. Those of Asian interest included the voyages of Anthony Jenkins (or Jenkinson) to "Cathay"; John Hawkins, Thomas Roe, and Edward Trry to the Mughal court; Willem Schouten to Siam; and François Caron to Japan, as well as Martino Marini's description of China.[6]

More than a collection and more in the way of a global analysis was the work of literary freelancer and controversialist Abbé Guillaume-Thomas Raynal (1713–1796), author of the multivolume *Histoire Philosophique et Politique des Establissements et du Commerce des Européens dans les Deux Indes* (Philosophical and Political History of the Establishment and of the Commerce of the Europeans in the Two Indies). Rather than recycling the epochal voyages, and true to the title, Abbé Raynal offers a philosophical and political synthesis of the history of European expansion with numerous volumes devoted to Asia. Written with the participation of French Enlightenment leader Denis Diderot (1713–1784), the work was first published secretly in 1770. For his efforts, the book was condemned by the French parliament and Church dignitaries and, in 1774, placed on the Index by the Catholic Church. Raynal was forced to leave France, returning only during the Revolution. In any case, indicative of its success, *Histoire* ran to some forty versions across Europe by 1774. With Diderot's undoubted assistance, the work also offered declarations against despotism, religion, colonialism, and the Inquisition.

Almost contemporaneous was François Valentijn's monumental and copiously illustrated *Oud en Nieuw Oost-Indien* (Old and New East Indies), published in Amsterdam in 1724 although never appearing in translation. Valentijn (1666–1727), who served in the East Indies in the early eighteenth century as a pastor in the Dutch East India Company, in the words of two modern historians, "collected, pilfered, plagiarized, paraphrased and supplemented every relevant document upon which he could lay his hands, whether published or unpublished, official or private, in Portuguese, Spanish, Dutch and Arabic, script Malay, overlooking only those in English" (Hanna and Alwi 1990, 277–78). The contents of this multivolume opus include entries on Java and Bali, Ternate and Tidor, Ambon (including its marine life and flora), the Cape of Good Hope, Malabar, Ceylon, Persia, the Mughal court, Japan, Taiwan, and Timor, among many other locations wherever the Dutch Company traded. Besides plans and views, his work carries numerous maps and charts, including early maps of Australia drawn from manuscripts now lost. Still a source for modern historians of Asia, the legacy of Valentijn as a framer of European knowledge on Asia is taken up in separate chapters.

## ARAB-IBERIAN CROSSOVERS

Fettered by Christian cosmography, European geography, with its classical antecedents in Strabo, Ptolemy, and others, lagged during the Middle Ages behind the great Arab geographers and travelers from the eighth century. Ceuta-born and Cordoba-educated Al-Idrisi (1099–1166) is a foremost example of a Hispano-Arabic crossover figure. Considered by many as the finest medieval cartographer and mapmaker, Idrisi also presented the Norman king Roger II (r. 1130–1154) of Sicily a spherical silver globe. Sicily, alongside other European centers of learning under Muslim rule, such as Toledo in Spain, had been one point of entry to Europe of Arabic learning. Generally, translations from Greek done in Baghdad in the ninth century began arriving in the Islamic kingdom of al-Andulus on the Iberian Peninsula in the tenth century, in turn entering Latin translations. Certain of Idrisi's works on the geography of Asia and Africa had been translated into Latin, one published in Rome in 1619. It is plausible also that Columbus used a map derived from Al-Idrisi.

In fact, the Medici Oriental Press, based in Rome between 1588 and 1614, produced some of the earliest books ever printed in Arabic. George Saliba (2001) argues that, contrary to the received view that the press was concerned mainly with expanding the mission among Christians in Islamic lands, it was equally directed at the European market and, importantly, served as a major media for transmission of Arabic knowledge on astronomy and mathematics. He explains that numerous contemporaries of Copernicus, mostly Italian, were reading Arabic and involved in producing scientific commentaries of Arabic manuscripts, possibly even enabling the transmission to Copernicus of two Arabic mathematical theorems. Microhistorical studies of the key Renaissance European "Arabists," he argues, enables us to question the master narrative of "Western" science with its roots in ancient Greece and to challenge the assignation of specific linguistic, civilizational, and cultural adjectives to the term "science."

Arab knowledge of Afroeurasia expanded generally with the spread of Islam and the institution of the pilgrimage to Mecca but also with the journeys of individuals. Such was Tangiers-born Ibn Battuta (1304–1368?), author of *Tihlah* (Travels), an account of his journey to Mecca, Africa, India, China, Ceylon, and Sumatra. His contemporary, the Tunis-born Ibn Khaldun (1332–1395), was less traveled but produced a masterpiece of literature and philosophy of history and sociology in his *Muqaddinah* (Prologue). Influential in its times, this work offered a critical approach to historical facts, including the rise and fall of civilizations, a method then unknown in Christian Europe.

It can be said that while the concept of sphericity was well understood by the Greeks, the cosmopolitan Arabs advanced astronomy, geography, mapmaking, and navigation. Arab medicine did not reject experimentation. The leading centers of Arab learning, Damascus and Baghdad, also hosted celestial observatories. Arab scholars established longitude and latitude and, long before Galileo, even investigated the possibility of the earth's rotation around its own axis. Arab knowledge of algebra, trigonometry, and analytical geometry from the twelfth century anticipated the geometry of René Descartes and the notion that every point on a plane surface can be represented in relation to a point of origin. The Islamic faith demanded greater precision in the preparation of calendars, just as the pilgrimage required sophisticated knowledge of terrestrial and maritime route maps and direction. We should also note that Arab seafaring in the Indian Ocean long devoted great attention to geography, meteorology, and navigation. From the eighth century, as mentioned in chapter 5, Arab seafarers reaching China introduced geographical awareness of the Indian Ocean and knowledge of Africa. Long before Europe, Arab seafarers also adopted the magnetic compass.

The reconquest of the Iberian Peninsula from the Islamic kingdoms of al-Andalus opened up to Europe a wealth of scientific knowledge preserved in the great libraries of Toledo and Cordoba by Islamic scholars through the Dark Ages. Translated from Arabic to Latin by Jewish scholars and circulated in the new print media, Europe gained, besides algebra and trigonometry, advanced astronomy and advanced navigation and mapping. Just as astronomy depends on mathematics, so it requires instruments to match. The Arabs pioneered such instruments as the quadrant and, as mentioned, the astrolabe.[7] But the most determined effort on the part of Europe to harness the practicalities of Arab navigational lore was, famously, the project launched by the Portuguese prince dubbed Henry the Navigator (1394–1460).

Having established his nautical academy in 1419 on the Atlantic coast of his homeland, the prince consulted sailors and savants with a view to launching the tiny kingdom on the trailblazing path of expansion, conquest, and conversion. Even so, the adaptation of theoretical knowledge to the practicalities of navigation entailed much experimentation and innovation. In some accounts, the major achievement of Henry, besides developments in navigation, instruments, and cartography, was to produce the oceangoing caravel, the most revolutionary feature being the lateen sail, clearly adopted from Arab dhows (McIntyre 1987, 8–26).

Beginning with the Portuguese conquest of Islamic Ceuta in 1415, Portuguese mariners reached the Atlantic Ocean island of Madeira in 1420, before pushing south along the African coast, reaching Cape Bojador in 1434, Cape Branco in 1445, Cape Verde in 1445, Gambia in 1446, the mouth of the Zaire River in 1485, and around the Cape of Good Hope in 1487 (voyage of Barthelemeu Diaz). Vasco da Gama, who reached Calicut on the Malabar coast in 1498, not only opened up a new vein of commerce with maritime Asia but simultaneously led the Christian push to outflank the Islamic world already active in the Indian Ocean trade. To achieve these twin goals, exploration turned to conquest, especially of Islamic trading centers, and the creation of an arc of fortified islands and ports, beginning with the conquest of Ormuz in 1507, followed by Goa in 1510 and the sultanate of Malacca in 1511. Within two years of the conquest of the strategic Southeast Asia harbor port, the Portuguese sea captain Jorge Alvares reached the China coast. When, in 1557, Portugal gained permission from mandarinal authorities in China to establish an exclusive European trading presence in China on the peninsula of Macau, Portuguese seafarers had already infiltrated trading networks with Japan. Pushing west, Spanish expeditions in the wake of the Magellan circumnavigation had already come into conflict with the Portuguese in the Moluccan islands. But in finding colonies of "Moros" in Manila and the islands, the Iberian traders and Christian missionaries also came into collision with the easternmost expansion of Islam.

It is also important, as Said emphasizes, that from the Crusades on, the European medievalists upheld a vigilant militancy vis-à-vis Islam. Spain had scarcely evicted Muslims from Grenada when Columbus set sail. While Ceuta was a Portuguese beachhead, by 1453 Constantinople had fallen to the Turks. Cursed by his religious adversaries, Albuquerque and his successors blustered their way across the Indian Ocean. Future battles against the Moors awaited the Spanish as they emerged from across the Pacific Ocean. Fear and awe was the response to Islam in Europe, an attitude reinforced by the Ottoman "peril." Out of this mind-set, Said elaborates, "comes a restricted number of encapsulations: the journey, the fable, the stereotype, the polemical confrontation" (Said 1978, 58).

## THE VARENIUS REVOLUTION IN GEOGRAPHY

The European advance in geographical understanding obviously benefited from Arab precedent, but it also caught up. With its antecedents in Pliny and the ancient Greeks, the modern science of geography traces its origins back to the period between 1750 and 1850, more or less coincident with the rise of philological and other studies of the Orient conducted "scientifically" in the European centers of power and knowledge, a theme to which we shall return in separate chapters. German-born Bernard Varen (Latinized as Varenius) (1622–1651) is today credited with producing the first introductory textbook in general geography, although his was undoubtedly a derivative work. This was *Geographia Generalis* (General Geography), first published by Elsevier in Amsterdam in 1650. Anointed and improved by Sir Isaac Newton as a required text at Cambridge University, the work entered the debate between Cartesian and Newtonian scientific systems and was influential for 150 years. Varenius is also accredited with rejuvenating geography as an academic discipline and making current what today is termed physical geography, or the study of forms and dimensions of the earth, including climatic change, along with cultural geography, or the detailed study of regions of the earth using comparative cultural studies. Unlike earlier works, Varenius included ideas based on direct observation and original measurements, in other words, seeking out general laws through the application of applied mathematics to the study of the earth. Varenius, who died at the age of twenty-eight, also authored a pamphlet *Descriptio Regni Iaponae* (Description of the Kingdom of Japan; 1649).

Anticipating the rise of modern geography in the hands of Humboldt and Ritter, as discussed later in this chapter, the method of Varenius is suggested in the title of an English translation of 1733: *A Compleat System of General Geography; Explaining the Nature and Properties of the Earth; viz Its Figure, Magnitude, Motions, Situation, Contents, and Division into Land and Water, Mountains, Woods, Desarts, Lakes, Rivers &. With particular Accounts of the different Appearances of the Heavens in different Countries; the Seasons of the Year all over the Globe; the Tides of the Sea; Bays, Capes, Islands, Rocks, Sand-Banks, and Shelves. The State of the Atmosphere; the Nature of Exhalations; Winds, Storms, Tornados, &. The Origins of Springs, Mineral Waters, Burning Mountains, Mines &. The Uses and Making of Maps, Globes, and Sea Charts. The Foundations of Dialling; the Art of Measuring Heights and Distances; the Art of Ship-Building, Navigation, and the Ways of Finding the Longitude at Sea. Originally written in Latin by Bernhard Varenius, MD. Since improved and illustrated by Sir Isaac Newton and Dr. Jurin . . .*

Still, the Varenius revolution did not entirely displace the historical descriptive method as favored by the compilers of the great European travel collections. For example, English historian and Anglican clergyman Peter Heylyn (1559–1662) published his *Cosmographie in Four Books . . .* in 1652, in turn an expansion of his *Mikro'Kosmos*, first published in Oxford in 1621. *Cosmographie*, subtitled *Containing the Chorographie and Historie of the Whole World and All the Principal Kingdoms, Provinces, Seas and Isles Thereof*, was still being reprinted in the early eighteenth century. Written during the English civil wars, *Cosmographie* was in its time the most comprehensive description of the known world in the English language. In Heylyn's words, "Geography without History hath life and motion, but very unstable and at random, but History without geography, like a dead carkasse, has neither life nor motion at all."

But in the following century, the German philosopher Immanuel Kant (1724–1804) postulated that knowledge could be organized, alternatively, according to classifications of facts relating to objects studied, such as in botany and zoology; on a temporal basis, as in the field of history; or relative to spatial relationships, such as in the study of geography. Kant's lectures on physical geography, delivered from 1756 to 1796 at the University of Konigsberg, entered print only in 1802 as *Physical Geography*. But by 1820, the figures of Humboldt and Ritter, associated with the rise of scientific geography, were dominant. Alexander von Humboldt (1769–1859), German explorer of Central and South America and Siberia, was author of *Kosmos* (The Cosmos; 1845–1862). Carl Ritter (1779–1859), who took up the world's first chair of geography at the University of Berlin, authored the massive multivolume *Die Erdkunde* (Earth Science; 1817). With their concern for interactions between human cultures and environment, Humboldt and Ritter laid the ground for the rise of environmental determinism, a simplistic but self-serving view that human society is molded or determined by the particular environment in which it develops. Thriving in the high age of colonialism, climatic determinism serviced the generalized Western conceit of the "lazy native" in tropical climes.[8] Writing in the 1930s, the eminent geographer Richard Hartshorne (1939) allowed that the concept of natural boundaries, first developed as a framework for physical geography, was carried over "both into political geography and political practice." To interpret Hartshorne, it can be said that geography would emerge in the mid-nineteenth century all too often as a handmaiden of imperialist expansion and rivalry.

## CONCLUSION

Consonant with Derrida's sense of the "civilization of the book," the discovery canon that first emerged in late Renaissance Europe stamped itself with authority in a way that subverted the veracity of the old medieval and classical texts. Primarily, the discovery canon was a secular literature. Increasingly, the master narrative of the epochal voyages was commerce and material gain. Glory for God may have figured, but it did not necessarily sell books. As we shall see in a following chapter, a literature of the fantastic further drove a wedge between alchemic-religious literatures of the Middle Ages and the New World literature of a worldly as opposed to heavenly "Other." Based on empirical observation, the authorial quality of the discovery texts was further reified and canonized by their appearance in the great collections of the day. Beginning with the precocious Ramusio working in Venice, travel collections in European vernaculars introduced to a restricted, albeit expanding bourgeois readership outside the traditional centers of knowledge (that is, the church-universities and the courts) the deepest possible knowledge of the world outside Europe, an increasingly secularized genre soon emulated in London, Paris, Amsterdam, and elsewhere. While the centers of gravity of publishing and print capitalism in general shifted rapidly to northern Europe just as new commercial hegemonies replaced the Iberians, it was the Portuguese (and Spanish) who offered the first synthesis of knowledge about Asian lands at least since the age of Polo. But where northern European accounts would gain an unimpeachable literary priority, as explained in subsequent chapters, it was the semisecret but much plagiarized portalans, route maps, and chart manuscripts of the Iberians that offered the first half-believable accounts of new lands. The rise of a European discovery canon cannot be entirely disassociated with contemporary debates in the history and philosophy of science, a theme to which we shall return. Neither can we disassociate entirely the rise of new knowledge centers in Europe with the crossover of ideas, not only with the Islamic world but, as developed in subsequent chapters, engaging all major Asian civilizational centers as fleet after fleet of seaborne traders, soldiers, and missionaries launched themselves across the Indian and Pacific Oceans.

## NOTES

1. While excluding unpublished manuscript sources from this discussion, we are not oblivious to the contention of Lach (1969), that oral sources of information were "probably every bit as influential in shaping Europe's view of Asia." But setting aside the impossibility of reconstructing oral accounts, the impact of print, text, and picture nevertheless became determinant as the audience for visually consumed material expanded.

2. One who has challenged the veracity of the Poloean legend is Francis Wood, author of *Did Marco Polo Go to China?* (1995). Elsewhere, Wood (2000, 65–75) argues that for patrons of fourteenth-century manuscripts, it was regarded as "an exotic romance, a fantastic, probably invented, account of the unlikely realms of the distant East." We would certainly agree with Wood's contention that Polo manuscripts grew throughout the centuries as copyists came across new material on China that they freely added. But notwithstanding the annotation tradition on Polo already mastered by Giovanni Ramusio in his 1599 text and the problem of "manuscript complexity," Polo fed into a powerful imaginative current in late medieval Europe that undoubtedly contributed to the othering of the Orient, one that was grasped by Columbus and the early navigators.

3. The "medieval geography" of Asia or the reception by medieval Europe of the accounts of Polo, Odoric, Mandeville, Ibn Batuta, and others was the subject of elaborate investigation by the British Orientalist Henry Yule in his *Cathay and the Way Thither* (1866).

4. The Portuguese humanist Damião de Goes chose to publish his *De bello cambairo ultimo commontan tres* (1549) in Louvain, doubtless confirming the difficulty of satisfying the Portuguese censors. A work that defends Portugal's spice monopoly, it also relates Portuguese exploits in Asia.

A counterexample is that of Diego de Teiva's *Commentaries de Rebus in India apud Dium Gestirannosalatus Nostrae* (1548), published in Coimbra. As an exposition on the heroic deeds of the Portuguese in Diu in India, this work undoubtedly met the test of patriotism without challenge.

5. Our list of Portuguese authors on Asia is selective, but one that merits attention is António de Gouvea, author of *Relacam que se Tractam as Gueras e Grandes Victorias que Alançar o Grande Rey da Persia* (1611). Evidently defeating censorship, this work relates matters of diplomacy and commerce with Persia. Another early Portuguese work is *Historia da Provincia de St. Cruz* (History of the Province of St. Cruz; 1576). Santa Cruz was an early name for Goa.

6. Another of the great French collections was that of A. F. Prevost, *Histoire Générale des Voyages* (1746–1770), initiated as a translation of John Green's *New General Collection of Voyages and Travels* (1745). To this, Prevost added an additional eight volumes, eventually expanding to a massive sixty-five volumes between 1746 and 1789, incorporating newer voyages of discovery, such as those of Bougainville. Copiously illustrated with maps supplied by Jacques Nicole Bellin, the premier French mapmaker of the age, Prevost's *Histoire* was a major source lode for the French philosophers, Jean-Jacques Rousseau included.

7. It is of no small interest that English poet Geoffrey Chaucer based his literary reflection "Treatise on the Astrolabe" (1391) on *Compositio et Operatio Astrolabie* (Composition and Operation of the Astrolabe), the Latin translation of the eighth-century Arab astronomer Macha-allah, composed around 815. The Arabs also knew celestial globe-making.

8. For a lucid discussion on the evolution of environmental determinism in European geography, see Morris (2002).

# 2

# Historical Confabulators
# and Literary Geographers

Empirical knowledge of the European New World developed apace with the discoveries, so in the early to mid-seventeenth century, Copernican and Galileon theories came to challenge core assumptions of European cosmology. Nevertheless, a gray world of skepticism and doubt as to the new revelations took the form of a literature of the fantastic. In part a parody of the serious discovery canon, it also tapped into a medievalist alchemical literature, albeit transformed as utopian literature fed by fears and fantasies of the unknown but often informed by the new discovery literature. The allegorical literature also had its counterpart in allegorical maps, such as in depictions or paintings of hell or utopia. As literature, the allegories often come in the form of a journey in which the reader identifies with the traveler. While not all these European allegories concerned Asian themes, a surprising number fell into that mold. The practitioners of this genre might well be termed historical confabulators and literary geographers. But in the way of constructing a New World and, indeed, an Orient, in what way was Europe also discovering itself, at least in the way of marking its own identity and unity?

It is important that Europeans responded variously to the civilizations they confronted. To be cynical, the conquistadores took their measure by the yardstick of the military prowess of their adversary, far more powerful in Asian political systems than in both Africa and the Americas. As Laborinho (1993, 143) observes, Europe's great "Other" divided geographically into two broad groups, albeit offering "complementary reflections." On the one hand, the Americas (and remote islands) allowed a mythical return to European origins, while, on the other, Asia, particularly India, represented the fount of primitive wisdom. But just as postcolonial discourse alerts us to the master colonial narrative in modern world history, so in our discussion of the first wave of globalization we should be aware that the earliest attempts to construct a "European" identity were contestatory at best.

## CONSTRUCTIONS OF EUROPE AND THE LITERARY CLASSICS

Leshock (2000) has drawn attention to the *orbis terrarum,* or terrestrial globes, and other "cultural productions" of medieval Europe, especially in the way that they projected space that is "not Europe." Order and spatiality on medieval globes, he argues, typically fell into accepted boundaries of religious hierarchy and emplacement. Setting aside Jerusalem (often centered in such spheres), African and Asian space shades off into darkness and the unknown. Even so, an East is deliberately created and demarcated with respect to a West. As such, the *orbis terrarum* and *mappa mundi,* or world maps, are allegorical and symbolic rather than accurate depictions of the globe. Neither was medieval travel writing value free. As Leshock suggests, both Marco Polo and Sir John Mandeville also engaged in "mapping" the East. Mandeville was, in fact, specific as to his "west syde of the world" and saw his book as the basis for future *mappa mundi* after its approval by the pope. Polo also refers to "our countries of Christendom." Both narratives assume a shared or collective identity on the part of the reader, at once European and Christian. The ideology of European identity, he suggests, was further established by the deployment of geographical markers.

A "fantastical imaginative work," as the Italian scholar Bencardino describes Mandeville's *Travels,* it was "more consonant with the culture and traditionalism of medieval science . . . dominated by Ptolemaic conceptions and those of the Church." As this author declares, the scriptures remained the main source concerning cosmology and geography in the context of the decadence of medieval and especially late medieval geographical culture (Bencardino 1998, 3–14). Mandeville, whose journeys between 1322 and 1356 ranged imaginatively beyond Jerusalem to "India the Lesser and the Greater," specifically locates China, where he served the great khan, along with Arabia, Ethiopia, and various topoi that might be identified with Armenia, Sumatra, and Cambodia.

Of course, not all knowledge of the Orient was consumed visually or at least in print, just as not all travelogues recorded actual travel; moreover, not all print accounts of voyages were received as truth, confirmed (as discussed later in this chapter) by the reception given to Portuguese "novelist-narrator" Fernão Mendes Pinto. This is not the place to expand on the Orient in Elizabethan literatures, but, as Louis Wann (1915) has written in his article "The Oriental in Elizabethan Drama," the major British playwrights produced no fewer than forty-seven plays dealing with Oriental themes between 1558 and 1642. Shakespeare, for example, undoubtedly learned of the New World discoveries through reading Hakluyt's new collection, among other sources. In any case, the awakened fantasies of the Elizabethan public were well catered for by the playwrights whose audience may have been larger than that of the book literate.

Luis Vaz de Camões's classic *Lusiadas* (1572) provides a reference to the Portuguese or Lusitanians. First published in Lisbon in 1572, *Lusiadas* was singular not only as a European literature rooted in the "brooding epic tradition" of the *Odysseus* but also as world travelogue. As a herald of European imperialism, it stood, in the words of one analyst, "in the service of the state, fulfilling a national mission" (Santos 1999, 133). It is clear that Camões (1524–1588) stood astride the discovery tradition and, in producing a work redolent of the richness and aroma of the East, symbolized across the ages the "expansion" theme in Portuguese historiography. Although the details are controversial, Camões traveled as far east as Macau, where he held an official post until recalled to Goa in 1558 on charges of extortion. Surviving shipwreck in Cambodia and financial problems in Goa and Mozambique, he returned to Lisbon in 1570. Not only did Camões inscribe for a new European audience the now familiar toponyms of Asian ports and courts, but also, as some scholars who have researched the poet's itinerary observe, his lyric descriptions of Pegu, Tavoy, Malacca, and many other places he actually visited are accurate if matched with the historical record (Oliveira 1975). But more than travelogue, *Lusiadas* rejoices in Portugal's manifest destiny as revealed by Vasco da Gama's historic voyage to India. In Camões's telling, the gods are pleased with da Gama's exploits and arrange landfall on an island of amorous nymphs. But the poet ends on a somber note, bemoaning a nation "given/to avarice and philistinism,/heartlessness and degrading pessimism." The year of Camões's death (1580) was also the year that Philip II of Spain annexed Portugal, but by the time Portugal had regained its freedom, the old empire was under severe challenge from the Dutch and English. Nevertheless, even in its time, *Lusiadas* fed into an expansionist mentality or imagination, setting up a powerful master narrative that has endured. We recall that the *"poeta Portuguese"* is officially celebrated in Portugal on June 10, the anniversary of his death, and was celebrated in Macau until 1999.[1]

Special place must be reserved for Pinto's epic historical fiction of Asia, *Peregrinação . . .* (Peregrination, or Pilgrimage), first published in 1614. Like Marco Polo, Pinto (1510?–1583) was a merchant-adventurer, spending twenty-one years in Asia from 1537 until 1558. Based variously in Malacca,

Pegu (Burma), and Siam as an ambassador of the Portuguese viceroy of India, he also made four voyages to the China seas and Japan, falling in with missionary Francis Xavier. After a swashbuckling career in the East, he returned to domestic life in Lisbon and wrote his manuscript of over 600 pages. While in its time, indeed through the centuries, Jesuit and Portuguese detractors treated the work with some ridicule for its many obfuscations and imaginative tropes and the author was dubbed a liar, recent scholarship has assigned more credibility to Pinto's classic. For example, in her modern translation, Catz (1989) treats the work as if it were an elaborate satire on Portuguese expansion, albeit not the age of high colonialism.

Not published until long after his death, *Peregrination* is rare in its candid exposé of corruption and hypocrisy behind the ideology of glory for God and country. Catz also allows that the narration switches voices from, for example, the man of virtue to the rogue. She also points to the criticism of Europe that "comes in the voices of the Asians who give their views" (Catz 1989, xiv, xliv). Such is instanced by the persona of the Tatar king who had captured Pinto and his companions. Asking why they have traveled so far and hearing their answers, the king remarked to a courtier, "The fact that these people journey so far from home to conquer territory indicates clearly that there must be very little justice and a great deal of greed among them." The courtier answered that given their industry and ingenuity to "fly over waters in order to acquire possessions that God did not give them," it means that they were either driven by poverty, vanity, or such blindness so as to even deny God (Catz 1989, 254).

A second Portuguese version did not appear until 1688, but in the meantime Spanish translations were published in 1620, 1627, 1628, 1645, 1664, and 1666. Separate Dutch editions were published in 1652 and 1671 and English editions in 1653 and 1692 as *Voyages & Adventures of Ferdinand Mendez Pinto*. All told, ten editions of *Peregrination* were published in the seventeenth century, including three in French, two in Dutch, and three in English. Plausibly, *Peregrination* reached a wide European audience for its time, including, it is believed, Cervantes (see Santos 1999, 131). As a popularizer, albeit confabulator, it is significant that Pinto also introduced to a European audience a new geography of Asia, memorializing such states, polities, ports, and cities as Japan, China, Malaya, Siam, Laos, Champa, Cambodia, Cochinchina, Borneo (Brunei), Ryukyu, Malacca, Aceh, Kedah, Patani, Lugor, Pegu, Aracan, Martaban, Goto, Tanegashima, Nanjing, Beijing, Guangzhou, and Ningpo.

## TRADITION OF THE FANTASTIC

Lach has drawn attention to a tradition of the fantastic in European writing that continued through the Renaissance. One example was Balthazar

Springer's *Indienfahrt* (Journey to India; 1505–1506), progenitor, inter alia, of images of dog-headed men in Africa (Lach 1991, 5). Antonio Galvano, writing of Antonio de Breu's pioneering voyage to the Moluccas, related the existence of, besides Ternate's volcanic eruptions, "a kind of man that have spurs on their ankles like unto Cocks." He also heard it told by the king of Tidor (in the Moluccas) that in neighboring islands there were people who had tails and "a thing like unto a dug between their cods, out of which came milk" (Galvano, in Purchas 1905, 31).

It is possible, as Savage (1984, 42–47) allows, that the European imagination of Asia as a region populated by people that looked and lived like animals was fed by Ptolemy's evocation of *Anthropophagi*. But setting aside the medieval travelers' evocations of cannibalism and dog-headed humans in the remoter island regions of Asia, Savage contends that one of the most enduring myths was that of races of people who had tails. Precisely, Marco Polo related that in Lambri (northwestern Sumatra), where he passed on his return journey to Europe, "there are men with tails." Polo also offered a variation on the humanoid creature with his contention that pygmies were actually manufactured in "Java the Less" (Sumatra).

Even in serious books, such as one edited by pioneer Dutch natural historian of Brazil Willem Piso (1611–1678), *De Indiae Utrius re Naturali et Medica* (1658), Jakob de Bondt (Bontius), physician to the Dutch settlement at Batavia, claims to have seen a female satyr who "hid her face with great shyness for the strange man." In an otherwise scholarly book on nature, first printed in Leiden in 1642, Bontius offers a word picture of an "Ourang Outang": A "curious monster with its human face does exist as it has the human habit of sighing as well as that of shedding tears" (Lach 1991, 6). A version of this account was passed down by the Italian world traveler, Careri (1704, 280). The Englishman Beekman, author of *A Voyage to and from the Island of Borneo, in the East Indies* (1718, 13), as illustrated in an accompanying engraving, linked the orangutan (lit. "jungle man" in Malay) to ape-men, comparing them favorably to the Hottentots of southern Africa. As French naturalist Pierre Sonnerat (1782) confidently declared, even if the inhabitants of the island of Mindoro in the Philippines did not actually have tails, as "attested" by numerous travelers, then it was because their coccyx was "a little elongated." Such assertions would not have dispelled the monkey-man myth in European audiences, indeed a subject that would be given a scientific framework only with the advent of Darwin's theory of evolution (cf. Savage 1984, 46).

A variation on the theme, as mentioned elsewhere, was sightings of mermaids. Such was the "sighting" of a pig-faced *poisson-femme* by Mocquet (1996, 78) in his voyage of 1607–1610 on board a Portuguese carrack off Mozambique island in the Indian ocean. An artful creature by any standards, the *poisson-femme* (lit. fish-women) were said to be the object of amorous affairs, whether dead or alive, by local natives. Although

Mocquet's account was first published in Paris in 1617, an engraving of the reclining *pesce dona* also appeared in the edition of 1830. Clergyman-historian François Valentjin (1724) also gave detailed descriptions of *"zee-menschen"* and *"zee-wyven,"* mermen and mermaids, respectively, even relating instances of their capture in the waters of the East Indies.

But generally, the monster genre was given a fillip by the first map engravers, who characteristically embroidered distant realms with both land and sea creatures of fantastic or grotesque proportions. For example, the dangers of navigating the *baixos de India,* or the Sofala Strait, is well illustrated in an engraving of a shipwrecked carrack executed by Dutch mapmaker Abraham Ortelius in 1590. Adding to the image of general misery, giant lobsters are depicted clawing at the hapless crew.

## FANTASTIC SCIENCE

Needless to say, the European literary canon was also influenced by the swirl of philosophical debates and scientific advances, especially where they challenged the religious orthodoxy of the day. While Catholic Europe under the Counter-Reformation long continued to uphold the received Christian cosmologies derived from Aristotle, Ptolemy, and Aquinas, by the late seventeenth century, Protestant England in particular began to forge a new elite consensus largely in affirmation of the principle of discontinuity between heavenly and earthly spheres (Goldstone 2000). Such was the thrust of the writings of John Wilkins, master of Trinity College at Cambridge and bishop of Chester, notably his *Discovery of the New World,* first published in 1638. In this work, Wilkins defends the cosmology of Copernicus, Kepler, and Galileo by explaining that the moon is subject to the same physical laws as the earth. Wilkins also speculated that the moon may be inhabited and that travel or communication with the moon was feasible. Although proscribed by the pope on April 25, 1701, Wilkins's *Discovery* has been hailed as the earliest significant work of popular science and literally inspired a genre of voyages-to-the-moon literature.

Observations of the natural world, as developed in chapter 3, certainly had their roots in antiquity, but the revelation of the New World, along with the first circumnavigations, provided new empirical evidence, in turn feeding into the rising "scientific" productions of Europe. As we shall see, early European travelers to Asia were often scornful of alternative cosmographies where they did not conform to Christian verities, yet it is also true that their message was often garbled with fantastic elaborations. For example, Scotsman John Johnson published his *Theatrum Universale* (Universal Theater; 1650), a compendium of known animals graphically illustrated by master engraver Mathaus Merian.

First published in Frankfurt but going through many editions because of its great popularity, *Theatrum* included not only a standard repertoire of recognizable quadrupeds but also harpies, griffins, phoenixes, unicorns, mermaids, mermen, and great sea serpents. In 1663, after Dutch traders in Japan presented a Dutch translation of this work to Shogun Yoshimune, it became a major influence on the study of natural history in that country. Even so, in 1717 and 1718, the Dutch were questioned about names and habitats of each animal listed in Johnson's book (Goodman 1986, 36, 60).

The boundary between scientific investigation and confabulation was drawn very thin by Louis Renard (ca. 1678–1746), an agent of King George I who resided in Amsterdam, where he used his position to access purported authentic drawings of exotic fish of the Molucca islands. Although Renard never traveled east, the result of his "research" was a baroque production titled *Poissons, Ecrevisses et Crabes, de Diverses Couleurs et Figures Extraordinaires, que l'on Trouve Autour des Isles Moluques, et sur les Côtes des Terres Australes* (Fish, Crayfish and Crabs, in Various Colors and Extraordinary Shapes, as Found in the Moluccas and on the Coasts of Australia), first published in Amsterdam in 1719. Reprinted in limited editions in 1754 and 1782, each contains one hundred plates, in turn offering 460 richly colored engravings, mostly of fish and crustaceans, along with descriptions. With minor exceptions, according to Theodore Pietsch (1995, 2000), who has examined the plates with some objectivity, all the illustrations represent Indo-Pacific tropical fish. Of the 416 fish represented, Pietsch allows that about 60 percent can be identified according to species, an additional 60 percent to genus, and another 37 percent to family. Similarly, the crustaceans can mostly be identified along parallel lines. No doubt such estimation led to the book's ready reception by the scientific community when it appeared. One hundred years later, in his *Histoire Naturelle des Poissons* (Natural History of Fish; 1828), even eminent French anatomist George Cuvier described the book as "indispensable."

However, as should have been obvious to Enlightenment scientists, there were certain disturbing or fantastical features written into this book. One is a reproduction of a mermaid "captured" near the island of Ambon and "positively asserted." Realistically humanoid above the waist, the body is palpably that of a dugong. But what would scientific scrutiny have made of such additions to the fish as images of human faces, suns, moons, stars, and pots containing flowering plants? Moreover, what to make of an egg-laying, fruit-eating spiny lobster that lives in the mountains, a walking fish that follows like a dog, or a loudly whistling pipefish? If these fantastical elements, comprising some 9 percent of the total, were not sufficient to give the lie to the scientific veracity of

Figure 2.1. "Fantastic fish/mermaid," from Valentijn's *Oud en Nieuw Oost-Indien* (1724). While contemporary scholarship traces these images to Samuel Fallours of the Dutch East India Company, it is all the more surprising to find the fabrications reproduced in Valentjin's monumental scholarly study. (Reproduced with permission of Nagasaki University Library)

Renard's book, then what of the rich coloring, the signature attraction of the book? Here, too, the coloring is found to be completely arbitrary and has no reference to the purported originals.

The answer to this conundrum, Pietsch (1995, 2000) demonstrates, lies in the provenance of the illustrations attributed to Samuel Fallours, an Ambon-based Dutch East India Company soldier turned cleric who was recognized by respective governors of Ambon for his artistic talents. Beginning in 1703, Governor Balthasar Coyett commissioned drawings from Fallours, who in turn produced multiple copies. Fallours, who also supplied material to François Valentjin, produced at

**Figure 2.1.** (*continued*)

least four albums, each one different in contents and presentation. Valentjin, in turn, reproduced in his *Old and New East Indies* (1724) certain of these fantastic images in monochrome, including a likeness of a mermaid. Pietsch believes that, in the copying, the colors were added indiscriminately. Fallours might also have seen commercial advantage in pure invention of fantastical forms. Whether Renard was actively complicit in this embellishment, exaggeration, and deception is not altogether clear, but the inevitable result was that, once exposed as fraudulent, this surreal production soon dropped off the literature on marine fauna. But it is also true that the mentality of the age, fed by the literature of the fantastic, created a metropolitan demand for the bizarre and off key.

## THE PRESTER JOHN MYTH?

As has been well documented, the legend of Prester John, a medieval story of a powerful Christian king to the east of the Muslim world, played an important role in influencing the Portuguese expansionist imagination. During the Crusades, rumors of an Oriental priest-king reclaiming lands for Christendom reached popes and Christian monarchs. The term "Prester," like "priest," is a contraction of "prebster," meaning "elder." Identification shifted from the Mongols to "India." The Christian kingdom of Armenia was also a candidate. Such false imagining on the part of European courts and savants, at least until the identification with Abyssinia was made, led to a belief that this "utopian" topos was located in Asia. For example, a surviving medieval French letter-document deals with an Indian, as opposed to African, Christian ruler. Mandeville also embroidered the legend, making a faux dynastic linkage between the emperor Prester John and the great khan but also drawing an image of an exotic Christian king of fabulous wealth and power. Located "many dreadful journeys" distant, the land of Prester John was described as a veritable knight's paradise for those who entered this imaginative pilgrimage across vast Asian space. Notably, the world map of German mapmaker Henricus Martellus of 1489 marked the realm of Prester John as lying in China with the Latin inscription "Here rules Prester John, emperor of all the Indies" (Wyld 2000, 10).

Throughout the fifteenth century, the Portuguese sent voyages in search of this apparently beleaguered kingdom. As such, the search for Prester John in Africa slowed Portuguese expansion southward (Lach 1969, 25–27, 54). On his pioneering voyage of 1497 around the Cape of Good Hope, Vasco da Gama sought to verify the Prester John legend and sought out Christian communities on the east coast of Africa. From their new establishment in Goa, in 1520 the Portuguese sent a fleet under Diogo Lopes de Sequira to Massawa in the Red Sea with a view to making direct contact with Abyssinia. Having found its way to the British Museum, a record of the voyage, *Carta das Novas* . . . (New Charts . . .), subtitled *The Discovery of Abyssinia by the Portuguese in 1520,* was published by Cortesão and Thomas in 1938. A narration of the expedition was also published in Portugal by Luis Rodrigues, namely, *Verdadeira informação das terras do Preste João* (True Information on the Lands of Prester John; 1540), a work that very quickly appeared in Italian, French, Spanish, German, and English (1625). This was accomplished by Padre Francisco Alvares, who accompanied Lopes to the Abyssinian court and returned to Lisbon in 1527 bearing letters and a gold cross from King David of Ethiopia (Prester John) for presentation to the pope. The Portuguese "corpus" also appeared in Hakluyt (1589) as "The Portuguese expedition to Abyssinia in 1541–1543 as narrated by Castanhoso, with some contemporary letters, short account of Bermudez, and certain extracts from Correa" (namely, from Gaspar Correa's *Lendas da India*).

The eyewitness and therefore "factual" account was in fact by the Portuguese Jesuit Jeronimo Lobo (1596–1678), who, arriving from Goa, spent nine years in the African kingdom before returning to Portugal. The first full publication of his original manuscript was published by Abbé Joachim Legrand as *Voyage Historique d'Abissine du R. P. Herome Lobo de la Compagnie de Jesus* (Historic Voyage to Abyssinia by Herome Lobo of the Company of Jesus; 1728). An English version was prepared from this copy by English dramatist Samuel Johnson (1709–1784) in 1759.[2] The portrayal of the kingdom as an eastern Christian bastion against Islam was also apparent in John Wiles's *A True Relation of Their Great Victory . . .* (1684).

Despite the legend of Prester John, there is opinion that the kings of Portugal had received envoys from Abyssinia by 1446 or had established contacts in Venice or elsewhere by that date, information otherwise suppressed from general circulation. There is no doubt as well that King Manuel I, who dispatched presents of books to the Abyssinian court, albeit lost in India, was moved by the entreaties of Alfonso de Albuquerque, who linked the defense of religion with defense of the Red Sea in the heartland of Islam along with the development of Portuguese commerce (*Livros Antigos* II 1935, 13–43).[3]

With time, the realm of Prester John began to appear on European maps of Africa. Once the identification with Abyssinia had been confirmed, it was marked accordingly. Such was the case with Jodocus Hondius's *Abissinorum sive pretiori* (1609), a map of central Africa, the Ethiopia area, and the Horn. Even so, as Carvalo and Ramos (1999, 20) remark, the longstanding association of an imperial-like Ethiopia with the source of the Nile was a "cartographic cliché" not abandoned even in the eighteenth century. Portuguese navigators reaching the west coast of Africa even believed that they were in touch with the far-flung provinces of the Ethiopian kingdom. The utopian-earthly paradise image of Ethiopia in Europe only surrendered in the light of modern traveler accounts.

What is particularly surprising about the myth is that it has spawned a steady stream of scholarship to the present, undoubtedly encouraged by reprints of the Hakluyt Society (1902) of the sixteenth-century accounts of João Bermudes, Miguel de Castanhosa, and Gaspar Correa.[4] Nevertheless, as one recent researcher on a central Asian locus of the legend has written, "It is important to remember that despite the existence of genuine historical characters and events that molded his legend, Prester John was a purely European invention" (Wyld 2000, 12).

## LITERARY UTOPIAS

Literary utopias of imaginary new worlds entered European, especially French, imagination with some éclat in the mid-seventeenth century. Such we might define as narrative descriptions of imaginary communities or societies inviting the reader's vicarious participation.[5] From our own experience, we need look no farther than the writings of Jules Verne, Karl Marx, Aldous Huxley, George Orwell, or even Walt Disney.

Needless to say, the genre built on strong antecedents, as in Sir Thomas More's *Utopia* (1516). More's earthly utopia was made all the more credible through the persona of a philosopher/sailor from Portugal who had traveled to the New World and saw a society that worked well compared to Europe. Discovery and New World myths also fed Spanish and Portuguese utopias, although proscription by the Inquisition at the end of the sixteenth century doubtless explains the absence of a systematic literary utopia in these countries. One example from Enlightenment Spain dating from the eighteenth century, albeit remaining in manuscript form, was the anonymous *Description de la Sinapia, Peninsula en la Tierra Austral* (Cro 1975).

As David Fausset (1993) explains in his study of seventeenth-century imaginary voyages to the great southern continent, loosely identified as Australia, such evocations of a utopian southland, at least before the voyages of Englishman James Cook in 1772–1775, were validated because they were "u-topian," literally "without topos or place." But even with Dutch discoveries, the mythology of a southern continent was perpetuated. But the corpus of such literature, which includes *Robinson Crusoe* and *Gulliver's Travels*, had been set in the period from 1668 to 1708. Often couched in allegorical tones, such works were presented as philosophical works. Fausset further argues that such works—voyage-utopias or utopian novels—also embodied the "closed society's opening onto a wider world—its confrontation with history."

*New Atlantis* (1627) by Francis Bacon (1561–1626) is both a utopia and an elaborate allegory. Also known as the father of deductive reasoning, Bacon was a Renaissance man of parts. The voyage to New Atlantis in an "utterly unknown" part of the South Seas was described thus: "We have sailed from Peru, where we had continued by the space of one whole year, for China and Japan" only to blunder upon an island of Christians, between the binaries of the sea and land, life and death, beyond even the Old World and the New World, and "whether we shall see Europe, God only knoweth." But in setting up this duality between Europe and the "Other," Bacon revealed a precocious sense of Western exceptionalism. Scornful of China for closing its borders to foreigners and trade, Bacon's new commonwealth ruled by science and industry was undoubtedly America, not Asia.

Another utopia, but with an identifiable Asian locale, was *Civitas Solis* (City of the Sun; 1602) by Tommaso Campanella (1568–1639), an Italian-born Dominican philosopher and controversialist. Published in Italian in 1602 just before he was condemned to life imprisonment for sedition and heresy, the work was later revised and reprinted in Latin in 1611–1614 and again at Frankfurt in 1623. Believed to have influenced Bacon's own utopian novel, Campanella's city of the sun is identified as Taprobane, the Ptolemaic evocation of, variously, the island of Ceylon and, in some versions, Sumatra. While the description of Taprobane as "under the equator" better fits Sumatra than Ceylon, the references to India, Brahmans, and Arabic language suggest Ceylon. In a single geographical aside, Campanella writes, "There are treaties between them and the Chinese and many other nations, both insular and continental, such as Siam and Calicut, which they are only just able to explore." But, as a composite city of men from India in thrall to Greek and Roman heroes and the Chinese inventions of cannon and typography, *Civitas Solis* was like no place on earth and had no known coordinates.

Somewhat like *New Atlantis*, Campanella's Taprobane had been visited by all nations. In the following half century, Savinien Cyrano de Bergerac (1620–1655) wrote *Histoire Comique des États et Empires du Soleil* (1657), or, in the English version, *The Comick History of the States and Empires of the Worlds of the Moon and Sun* (1687). Arguably an alchemical text, it also fits into the mold of early science fiction. As a mix of science and romance, Cyrano de Bergerac's "Other Worlds" has been viewed as a model for Jonathan Swift and Edgar Allan Poe.[6]

As explained in a separate chapter, while we do not usually associate Jesuit scholarship with humor, a rare exception might be Padre João Sardinha Mimoso's *Relacion de la Real Tragicomedia . . .* (Account of a Royal Tragicomedy . . .; 1620), published in Lisbon. Originally a play by Antonio de Sousa, it describes the deeds of such Portuguese discoverers as Vasco da Gama and Alfonso de Albuquerque. Characters include Manuel I and his councilors, the Ocean, the Earth, Brazil, and Malabar in India. As an allegorical work, it relates a tragicomical tale of monkeys singing in Tupi, an indigenous language spoken in Brazil, in a play on the discoveries. One chorus has the king of Portugal and the Tapuias Indians singing in Portuguese and then in Tupi. In the course of five acts, some 350 animals, birds, and marine monsters are represented. In 1619, it was performed before Philip III of Spain (II of Portugal) and his queen, Isabel, at the Jesuit College in Lisbon.

As allegory, these works offered a new "moral world" for poets and intellectuals to create their own mental maps or space to be used, in the words of Franz Reitinger, "as a kind of projecting screen for social states and processes."[7] Madelaine de Scudéry, author of *Carte de tendre* (Map of the Heart; 1654), was long assumed to have been the progenitor of this genre of allegorical map. Such literary priority owed to the writings of Charles Sorel (1671), who identified "*livres de cartes*" as a special genre referring to books that contain allegorical maps as text or image. Yet, as Reitinger has analyzed, the production of allegorical maps reached back to the second half of the sixteenth to the mid-seventeenth centuries, albeit invented independently in different places under different circumstances. A single connecting theme, however, was Christian visionary thought or an ideological framework in which to pass moral judgment on fast unraveling religious orthodoxies and other ambiguities as unmasked by the new discoveries. Reitinger offers, as example, *Mappe-monde Nouvelle Papistique* (New Papist World Map; 1566), by an Italian refugee, Giovanni Battista Trento, in short, a Calvinist spoof on the papist world map. Finally, as Reitinger summarizes, while a growing concern across Europe emerged in the early seventeenth century for the didactic use of maps and moral geography, only in France after 1650 did a literary coterie emerge that would step back from the Christian world to which these images have been applied, to forge a new type of map allegory for mapping relationships of any kind, from friendship to sexuality (Reitinger 2000). Next we offer another example of the genre in relation to the imaginative discovery of a new southern continent.

## TERRA AUSTRALIS INCOGNITA

As explained in chapter 5, overcoming the Ptolemaic bias in European mapmaking also came to be associated with an enduring mythologizing over golden lands and sources of riches. But as the Pacific Ocean came to be incorporated into the bounds of the known realm, the search for *Terra Australis* entered, especially, Spanish political intelligence. The Dutch and English were not far behind. Yet it was surprising that the Portuguese, who traded regularly at the island of Timor, were not aware of the southern continent. In fact, in the opening years of the seventeenth century, the Luso-Malayan cartographer Manuel Godhinho Eridia entered the search for what he called *India Meridional* with his semi-imaginative maps and writings only to be actually eclipsed by Dutch discoveries (McIntyre 1987, 201–5). In 1601, from his base in Malacca, the self-proclaimed "cosmographer-general of the Esdado da India" actually announced the discovery of "Nuça Antara" (lit. "land between the islands" in Malay) or, in this sense, Australia.

In any case, the real world quest for *Terra Australis* quickened with the voyages of Pedro Fernando de Queiros (1560–1614), the Portuguese navigator in the employ of the expedition led by Alvaros Mendana de Neira to the Solomon Islands, as then so named, followed by the voyages of Abel Tasman, among others, at least until the discoveries by Cook confirmed a southern continent. In due time, a literary genre on this quest developed, in part as satire, in part as a special niche within the literary utopias.

One early believer in the great south land was Hakluyt, but once *Terra Australis Incognita* came to be marked on later sixteenth-century European charts as a vast undifferentiated south land, the continent became tangible. But much like Columbus's India, falsely attributed to the West Indies, so even the Spanish discovery of Australia by Queiros was misleading in the sense that he probably only visited Espiritu Santo in the New Hebrides and not the mainland. Nevertheless, with the printing in 1617 for John Hodgetts of Queiros's letter-petition to the Spanish king, the legend was tangible. As translated, this was *Terra Australis Incognita, or a New Southerne Discoverie, Containing a Fifth Part of the World, Lately Found Out by Ferndinand de Quir[o], a Spanish Captaine, Never Before Published.*

Important in this sense is Bishop Joseph Hall's (1574–1656) *Mundus Alter et Idem Sive Terra Australia Ante Hac Semper Incognita . . .* (Another World and the Same . . .; 1605), published in London and Frankfurt.[8] According to Reitinger, Hall offers a spoof on geography, and the myth, as embedded in the new *mappe monde*, or world maps (Ortelius), of the southern continent. While allegorical maps that introduce individual chapters impart some features of an atlas, continents are literally removed, blurring the division between the real world of discoveries and the legendary. But, as a satirical dystopia or "just censure of travel," Hall is also offering a dire moral judgment on the false expectations of explorers chasing terrestrial utopias (Reitinger 2000).

As satire, Fausset elaborates, *Mundus,* which carried an exaggerated map of a southern continent, had a basis in political realities, namely, commercial rivalries between Dutch and English and Iberians not only in the East but matched by religious rivalries at home, exactly issues of cultural interaction thrown up by the new discoveries. Fausset also highlights *History of the Severites or Severambi* by Denis Vairasse, or Veiras (ca. 1637–ca. 1683), first published in English in 1675 and subsequently in France in 1677. Claiming to be a true story, *Severites* invokes a country resembling explorer Abel Tasman's descriptions of New Zealand and Tasmania. Vairasse incorporated the story of the real-life wreck of the *Batavia* off the coast of Western Australia in 1629, with its scandalous and bizarre history of mutiny and savagery. Fausset speculates as to the success of this work, offering its importance as a blueprint for the Enlightenment, at least in the way of presenting various societal models (Fausset 1993, 113–29). Even so, this antipodean utopia rested on the pillar of slavery.

One of the more enduring of the new "*livres de cartes*" must be Gabriel de Foigny's *La Terre Australe Connue* (The Land of Australia Known; 1676). Originally published anonymously, this late seventeenth-century view of Australia was later published under Foigny's name as *Les Avantures de Jacques Sadeur dans la Decouverte et le Voiage de la Terre Australe. Contenant les Coûtumes & les Moeurs des Australiens* (The Adventures of Jacques

Sadeur in the Discovery and Voyage to Australia. Containing the Customs and Mores of the Australians; 1692). Conjuring up a classless island of hermaphrodites, Foigny's utopia is otherwise a "journey" of high fantasy. As an imaginary journey to a utopia, the work became known as one of the best known of the French "utopias" and a precursor to, as discussed later in this chapter, Jonathan Swift's *Gulliver's Travels* (1726).

## PSALMANAZAR'S FORMOSA: SCIENCE AS FICTION

The virtually unknown Formosa came to be linked irremediably in eighteenth-century Europe with one of the greatest literary frauds of the age. This was associated with the figure of one George Psalmanazar (ca. 1679–1763), a French-born poseur who successfully passed himself off to a gullible European public as a Latin-speaking Japanese and, when that was unmasked, took on the persona of an even more obscure identity, that of a Formosan. Psalmanazar was a take on Shalmaneser, a king of Assyria, although his real identity has never been uncovered. A celebrity in London and Rotterdam for his alleged ability to babble in Formosan language and to entertain those who would listen to his faux tales of a strange land on which he had never cast eyes, he was convinced to write an account of his "native" country. This appeared in 1704 in London as *An Historical and Geographical Description of Formosa, an Island Subject to the Emperor of Japan,* replete with lurid first-person descriptions of polygamy, human sacrifice, infanticide, and cannibalism, which he avowedly experienced. The "Chief Sacrificator," he wrote, "alone is to cut the throats of infants and pluck out their hearts. . . . Since our God requires the Hearts of so many young boys to be offered up to Sacrifice, therefore lest the whole Race of Mankind should by degrees be extirpated, he has permitted the Men, at least of the Laity, to keep more Wives than one" (Penzer 1926, 178). The work was also fancifully illustrated, including a map of Formosa bearing little resemblance to reality, along with an image of an animal-shaped idol that demanded to be fed the hearts of young boys. It is believed that what was not due to his lurid imagination was derived from Bernard Varenius's *Descriptio Regni Japoniae et Siam* (1649) or from the Dutch Protestant missionary Georgius Candidius's *A Short Account of the Island of Formosa,* first published in Germany in 1627 and recycled in the Churchill and Churchill collection. Originally printed in Latin, a French translation also appeared in Amsterdam in 1705 and a German version in Frankfurt in 1716, making it a best-seller for its time. Although Psalmanazar's deception was slowly unmasked by this date, he kept up an active career in writing and entered the select literary circle of Samuel Johnson, among others, and even spent a spell at Oxford. Jonathan Swift (1667–1745) had not only read Psalmanazar's bizarre accounts of traffic in bodies in Formosa but, heavy with irony, also suggested the same of several plump girls of Ireland in his *A Modest Proposal for Preventing the Children of Poor People in Ireland from Being a Burthen to Their Parents or Country . . .* (1729). In the last decades of his life, Psalmanazar composed a confession of his fraudulent past, published in 1764, the year after his death. This was *Memoirs of \*\*\*\* Commonly Known by the Name of George Psalmanazar, a Reputed Native of Formosa, Written by Himself, in Order to Be Published after His Death.*[9]

Jack Lynch (1999) links the Psalmanazar phenomenon with the advent of English philosopher John Locke's *Essay Concerning Human Understanding*, especially an essay titled "Identity and Diversity" in the second edition of 1694. This influential essay was published just prior to Psalmanazar's arrival in England. Personal identity to Locke is placed in the consciousness. For Lynch, Psalmanazar "located his identity outside the horizon of European perception." His imagined Formosa became "a sort of intellectual playground." Asian identity, then, emerges as "an 'Antipodes' to European identity." Remarkably, Psalmanazar's grotesque parody of Formosa was largely devoid of empirical data and therefore stands outside Said's sense of a European stake in a real Orient. Yet the compulsion to write about the Orient was there. Ultimately, Lynch confirms, Western preconception took over from Oriental perception. Part of Psalmanazer's glib reception in Protestant Europe might also be linked with his diatribes against his Jesuit detractors (Penzer 1926, xiii).[10]

## REMOTE ISLAND FANTASIES

A separate but related genre was that of remote island fantasies, the best known of which is Daniel Defoe's *The Life and Strange Surprising Adventures of Robinson Crusoe, etc.* (1719). The persona of Robinson Crusoe has long been identified with the story of Scottish sailor Alexander Selkirk, voluntarily marooned on and later rescued from Juan Fernandez Island off the coast of Chile by English buccaneer turned navigator William Dampier (1651–1715). In turn, the Selkirk story was first given currency by Edward Cooke in *A Voyage to the South Sea, and Round the World . . . in the Years 1708, 1709, 1710, and 1711 . . . Wherein an Account Is Given of Mr. Alexander Selhkirk . . . upon the Uninhabited Island of Juan Fernandes* (1712). Cooke was the commander of one of the ships of the buccaneering expedition of Captain Woodes Rogers (1679?–1732), who discovered the castaway. The two English buccaneers, Dampier and Rogers, along with mapmaker Herman Moll (1654–1732), closely interacted in the coffeehouses of

London with Defoe and Swift. Reinhartz (2000) states that Moll maps appeared in early editions of *Robinson Crusoe* and, as discussed later in this chapter, *Gulliver's Travels*. Plausibly, Gulliver was also modeled after the Dampier and Rogers exploits. The island was mapped by Frenchman J. N. Bellin and published in 1760.

A revisionist understanding of the remote island fantasy genre is offered by Ferreira (2000) in his text declaiming the Portuguese origins of *Robinson Crusoe*. He reasons that the Selkirk and Robinson Crusoe experience have little in common except where two men were marooned on an uninhabited island. In fact, the practice of abandoning mutineers and others on remote islands was not uncommon in that age. To wit, he cites the case of one Fernão Lopes and a black slave marooned in circumstances closer to that of Defoe's reconstruction and explicitly described in João de Barros's *Decadas da Asia* (1553, 2nd decade, sec. VII, 376), in Gaspar Corrêa's *Lendas da India*, and in Fernão Lopes de Castanheda's *Historia do Descobrimentos & Conquesta da India*, all three entering into English translations. More than that, Ferreira exactingly identifies Defoe's composite source material as drawing from, even plagiarizing, *Lusiadas*, *Peregrinação*, *Lendas da India*, and *Ethiopia Oriental*, among other classic fifteenth- and sixteenth-century Portuguese texts entering English translation.[11]

The remote island grand discovery genre also found its counterpart in satire. Such was François Gabriel Coyer's *A Supplement to Lord Anson's Voyage Round the World: Containing a Discovery and Description of the Island of Frivola . . . to Which Is Prefixed an Introductory Preface by the Translator*, published in London in 1752. In this work, Frivola is an imaginary island somewhere off the west coast of South America, described by Coyer as a land of obsequious inhabitants, provided that they are well paid. As such, this work was a satire on the follies of the present age and, seemingly, the grand discoveries genre at large. Anson's negative view of China as presented in his *A Voyage round the World in the Years MDCCXL* (1748) came to influence otherwise benign images of the Qing Empire held up to that time in England.

Entering European legend in 1668, with publication in Dutch, and in English translation in the Churchill and Churchill collection in 1704, the picaresque account of the fourteen-year sojourn, beginning in 1653, and escape from the erstwhile unknown hermit kingdom of Korea by the shipwrecked Dutch mariner Hendrik Hamel no doubt fed into this imaginary island narrative. No less, the story of Will Adams (1554–1620), the first Englishman in Japan and favorite at the shogunal court following his arrival in Japan in 1600 on a Dutch ship, entered this lore. Even so, this story in composite was resurrected only in the last century. As retold by Jack London in his last published novel, *The Jacket* (*Star Rover*) (1915), Adam Strong, an Englishman living between 1550 and 1650, fell in with Hendrik

Hamel and a shipwrecked Dutch party led half guest, half prisoner to the Cho-son court. As a work of travel and reincarnation, London drew on a powerful imaginative genre reaching back in European literary tradition.

## SWIFT'S JAPAN

No other author gained as much critical attention as Jonathan Swift (1667–1745), especially his *Gulliver's Travels* or *Travels into Several Remote Nations of the World Including the Voyages to Lilliput, Brobdingnag, Laputa, Balnibarbi, Luggnagg, Glubbdubdrib, and Japan*, published in 1726. Controversy over his work and the ultimate meaning of his writing has continued over 250 years. But rather than entering the vast critical literature on the Swiftian allegory, it will be sufficient to recall that, of all the remote regions of the globe visited by Gulliver, Japan is the only real place as such. At least, as described by Swift, it was both a flourishing island nation and a mysterious place. Perhaps because Swift read into the thin literature on Japan then at hand a land where so many verities were at odds with European norms, he had no better than describe that reality. In any case, such has been the research of Johnson, Kitagawa, and Williams (1977). These authors postulate that Swift gleaned his material on Japan from a reading of the account in Will Adams's *Purchas His Pilgrimes* (1625–1626). Additionally, these authors believe it highly plausible that Swift read a manuscript version of Dutchman Englebert Kaempfer's *The History of Japan*, appearing in English in 1727. The evidence becomes stronger with investigation of Part III of *Travels*, especially with reference to his "Alphabeta Japonum" and his language machine palpably adapted, albeit imaginatively, from Kaempfer. Overall, they find a series of paradoxes in Swift's narration of a real Japan, especially as *Travels* is a work of imagination and that the heathen Japanese are portrayed in a better light than the Protestant Dutch. It is also noteworthy that the historical materials that Swift consulted on Japan actually helped develop the characterization of Gulliver.

To embellish this narrative further, we are reminded that Swift, in the words of one analyst, was "notoriously anti-empire" and satirized grandiose imperialist visions in the light of what remained to be done closer to home or at least in his beloved Ireland (Reinhartz 2000). Japan also obliquely entered this trope with *An Account of the Court and Empire of Japan*, an unfinished essay penned by Swift in 1728, although only published in 1765 by his second cousin Deane Swift. Unlike *Gulliver's Travels*, where a richly imagined Japan becomes an arena for satirical play, Japan as thinly described in *An Account of the Court and Empire of Japan* merely serves as a device to satirize corruption in English politics under George I and, with his accession to the throne in 1727, George II (Johnson et al. 1977).

## BOUGAINVILLE, DIDEROT,
## ROUSSEAU, AND PARADISE LOST

First contacted by English circumnavigator Samuel Wallis in 1767, the South Pacific island of Tahiti was visited by French circumnavigator Louis Antonine de Bougainville (1729–1811) in 1768. The Frenchman dubbed it "La Nouvelle Cythère" after the island in Greece where mythology held that Venus first emerged from the sea. Bougainville's *Description d'un Voyage Autour du Monde* . . . (Description of a Voyage around the World . . .; 1771–1772) offered up a picture of Tahiti as an island of plenty where nature supplied all wants, the islanders held no private property, and the sexual taboos of Christian Europe were notably absent.

The importance of Bougainville's writings helped popularize Jean-Jacques Rousseau's (1712–1778) thesis on morality of man in a primitive or natural state such as published in *Discours sur l'Origine et les Fondements de l'Inégalité Parmi les Hommes* (Discourse on the Origins of Inequality among Men; 1755). It also inspired French philosophe and encyclopedist Denis Diderot's (1713–1784) *Supplément au Voyage de Bougainville* (Supplement to Bougainville's Voyage), written in 1772 but published posthumously in 1796. Diderot's mental voyage to Tahiti led him to compare the island's "natural" or precivilized society favorably to even European Enlightenment Christian society. An indictment of European slavery and colonialism, Diderot has an old Tahitian man tell the protagonist, "We are a free people; and now you have planted in our country the title deeds of our future slavery." He continued, "If a Tahitian landed one day on your shores, and scratched on one of your rocks or the bark of your trees: 'This country belongs to the people of Tahiti'—what would you think?" As Laborinho (1993, 144) interprets Diderot, "If these societies are different, then they do not share the same values and therefore one cannot pronounce moral judgment." Bougainville's text also offers Diderot a scientific understanding of human nature, just as travel texts offer new understandings and new points of departure in which to know the inhabitants. Rousseau is no less wary of ethnocentrism but places himself outside universalist currents, which saw men as equal without observing difference. As "ethnologist," Rousseau defends observation over metaphysical speculation. But in Rousseau's theory of "natural good" stressing innate principles of justice found in the depth of the soul (primitivism), we also find a philosophical beacon for the new nineteenth-century exoticism (Laborinho 1993, 144–45). But it is also true that the "noble savage" theme was earlier treated satirically by, respectively, Swift and Defoe.

As Kitson (1998, 19) remarks of Tahiti (or Otaheite, as it was known to Europe) in his study of European romanticism and colonialism, the Pacific island was made an "indicator for European attitudes to the peoples with whose culture Europeans were unfamiliar." But when Cook arrived in Tahiti in 1769 with return journeys in 1773, 1774, and 1777, he regarded the mythmaking of Diderot and Bougainville with some skepticism. In any case, by the time that William Bligh arrived in 1788 on a mission to secure the breadfruit plant for transplanting in the West Indies as a food source for slaves, Tahiti society had already been corrupted by European contact, awaiting only "salvation" with the arrival of the London Missionary Society in 1797.

## CONCLUSION

Not surprisingly, as the market for discovery or travel literature grew, a wide niche developed for historical confabulators and, alongside them, pure literary fabulists. Our analysis has borne out Fausset's understanding that utopian literature grew out of the juncture of global commerce and travel and the thirst for "knowledge." But this was also a transitional literature in the sense that reality caught up as the last tracts on earth became known and mapped and, indeed, the Newtonian revolution arrived. But such indulgence in imaginative literature, drawn from half-baked travel diaries and traveler's exploits, obscures the impact of the travelers themselves on the creation of an Oriental "Other." As discussed in chapter 4, the old Christian cosmography died hard, especially as it was the religious, especially Jesuits, who exceeded the ship captains and merchants in interpreting and even changing the East in the era before the great age of European imperialism and full-blown Orientalism.

## NOTES

1. In part, I have been guided in this paragraph by the feature article on the Macau "handover" by Morris Dye (1999), a piece of writing that also takes a wry look at the 500-year Lusitanian legacy.

2. Additionally, Johnson penned a didactic romance titled *The History of Rasselas, Prince of Abyssinia* (1739) about a prince who left the confines of the palace to explore the world. The exoticizing of the realm also led to a precocious literature on the source of the Nile. Such was Sir Peter Wyche (1689).

3. See Gumilev (1987).

4. Indeed, Ethiopia even began to appear on the linguistic map in Europe with the publication of the first grammar and dictionary in the Amharic language, that of Job Ludolph (1698).

5. In general, the genre is well researched. See Gove (1941).

6. See Cyrano de Bergerac (1976).

7. Arguably, falling into this mold was François Choisy's *Le Prince Kouchimen, Histoire Tartare, et Dom Alvar de Sol, Histoire Napolitaine* (1710). Choisy (1644–1724), eccentric son of a courtier to Louis XIV, and author of a journal of his 1685 voyage to Siam, produced in this imaginary biography a device to ridicule his contemporaries and mock the decadence of the court.

8. For major discussion of this work, see Wands (1981).

9. The bibliography on George Psalmanazar is long, befitting his notoriety, but the major modern study is Swiderski (1991). See also Adams (1962).

10. Another example of historical confabulation is a popularized work on Confucius by Frenchman Nicolas-Gabriel Clerc (1726–1798) titled *Yu le Grand et Confucius, Historie Chinois* (Yu the Great and Confucius; 1769), dedicated to the grand duke of Russia (later Czar Paul I). As Mungello (1999, 86–87) has elaborated, Clerc fictionalized Chinese history for didactic purposes, namely, for the instruction of the young Russian prince. While Clerc shared Enlightenment views on the improvement of men, he badly confused Confucian virtue with a Christian sense of egalitarianism.

11. A partial translation of *Robinson Crusoe* appeared in Japanese before the advent of the Meiji Restoration. This was *The Account of a Castaway*, translated from Dutch by Kuroda Kogen. According to Hisakawa (1989, 478–79), the translator, as much as his readership, was apparently unaware that "Robinson Crusoe" was a fictional product of Daniel Defoe.

# 3

# Observations on Nature

From Columbus on, the European explorers evinced as much appre-hension of the natural world as they did fascination, albeit almost always concerned with the search for either gold or silver or exotic trade products and even "elixirs of life." While naked plunder of the gold and silver mines of the Americas preceded the Promethean exploitation that accompanied the rise of industrial society in Europe, there were also those who looked to exotic plants and herbs as an adjunct to medieval medicine. Here we mention the pioneering studies of the Portuguese Garcia d'Orta in India. Apothecaries such as Tomé Pires joined the first Portuguese voyage to China. Soon it was Jesuits and others reporting on nature, in any case a tradition that went back to the Greeks. Certain of this literature takes the bizarre as its lodestone, and much of it hardly fits the tests of the Renaissance world, much less the Enlightenment-era fashion for great missions of botanical exploration. But what has been called the "Columbian exchange" with reference to the biological and cultural consequences of the first Iberian contacts with the New World has its echo in the Eurasian exchange.[1] Renaissance botany started as an "herbal" science, claiming to account for all plants used in medicine. By 1500, the number of known plants approximated 500, but as New World exotics came to be included, the number swelled dramatically. Gener-ally, efforts to produce local or regional lists of plants developed along-side encyclopedic compilation.[2]

## GREAT ASIAN HERBALS AND FLORAS

Still, we may well ask, Was the exchange on "nature" during the first globalization a reflex of European superiority, or were the shipboard doctors also in a learning mode when confronting age-old Asian, especially Indian- and Chinese-derived, systems of medical and botanical knowledge? As Roger French (1991, 40–41) has written in a reflection on European and Oriental health systems at the outset of the great maritime discoveries, "There is not a great deal of evidence that European medicine in the fifteenth century was more effective in strictly practical terms than that of other cultures." He offers the case of rational Chinese practice of acupuncture versus dubious European practices of bloodletting. "Profits and economics," French declares, led to the entrée of European medical practices into China and other eastern cultures. The export of European medicine simply "rode on the back" of the political success of an expanding Europe. Moreover, the discoveries of distant lands were perceived and realized through the frame of European medical knowledge, hence the shipboard presence of books, apothecaries, and later physicians. To be sure, as discussed in chapter 7, European knowledge of anatomy would revolutionize Asian concepts of medicine, but not before the Europeans themselves became enthralled with New World herbals, drugs, remedies, and other indigenous medical systems.

One of the first descriptions of the flora of Asia, or at least a region of Asia, was that by the French explorer-naturalist Pierre Belon (1517?–1564). This was *Les Observations de Plusieurs Singularitez et Choses Memorables, Trouvée en Grece, Asiae, Judée, Egypte, Arabie, & Autres Pays Estranges* (Observations on Several Singular and Memorable Things, Found in Greece, Judea, Egypt, Arabia and Other Foreign Countries; 1553). Not only was *Observations* the first description of the flora of this vast zone, but it was accomplished by fieldwork. Rare for its time, Belon's work was accompanied by woodcut illustrations showing certain Asian plants for the first time. Belon also advocated the acclimatization of Asian plants in France.

Undoubtedly the most acclaimed among the physicians and pharmacists traveling east on Portuguese ships was Garcia d'Orta (ca. 1500–1568), who resided over thirty years, between 1534 and 1564, in India, where he established a botanical garden in Bombay. Orta widely interviewed native physicians, his servants, and other sources to better understand local botanica and even psychopharmacology. He also drew from Jesuit sources as well as unpublished manuscripts of Couto and Bocarro. But by privileging indigenous medical and biological knowledge, including the Ayurvedic tradition, it is significant that Orta broke with Brahmanical as well as Arabic and European tradition.[3] His *Colóquios dos Simples, e Drogas he Cousas Mediçinais da India . . .* (Colloquium of the Simple and Medical Things of India . . .; 1563), published in Goa, was one of the very first European-language texts published in Asia. It took the form of a dialogue between Orta, representing local knowledge, and a European standing for the orthodoxy. Although concerned primarily with medicinal plants, including opium, datura, areca (betel nut), and concoctions made from hashish, Orta also introduced to Europe a range of then-unknown edible plants from southern India, such as mango, mangosteen, and durian, along with such spices as cardamom, pepper, cinnamon, and turmeric. Well received in Europe, although not in his native Portugal, where his Jewish background led to its banning, this work on tropical drugs and medicinal plants became a new standard, republished in Antwerp (1567, 1574, 1593), Venice (1589, 1616), Madrid (1572), Burgos (1578), Amsterdam (1658), and London (1612) under the title *History of Aromatic Plants.* In 1567, a Latin version appeared in Europe illustrated with woodcuts of Asian vegetables.

Orta also collaborated with Cristobal de Acosta (ca. 1525–ca. 1594), physician to the Portuguese viceroy of Goa and author of the first Spanish herbal on the Asian world. This was *Tractado de las Drogas y Medicinas de la India Orientales* (Treatise on the Drugs and Medicines of East India; 1578), published in Burgos, a work that came to rival Orta's authority and influence. Another standard was established by C. de L'Ecluse (Carolus Clusius) (1528–1609) in *Aliquot Notae in Garciae Aromatum Historium* (1592), a paraphrase of Orta's *Colóquios,* along with observations on New World plants and seeds collected by Drake's circumnavigation (1577–1580), including the first descriptions of cocoa and jasmine. Together, these works offered descriptions of specimens along with notes on locations and included woodcut illustrations. While we have mentioned the talents and energy of Johan Theodor de Bry as engraver and as pioneer chronicler of Eastern travel, he also illustrated his *Florilegium Novum* (New Anthology of Flowers; 1612–1614) with many non-European plants, including *Ananas fructus Indicus Orientalis,* or pineapple.

The medical theme may have become subordinated to botanical interest, but it was obviously awakened with the development of Enlightenment science in Europe as much by the problems of survival on long-distance shipping routes in hostile and unknown tropical regimes.[4] Jakob de Bondt (Jacobus Bertius/Bontius), author of *De Medicina Indorum* (Medicine of India; 1642), was undoubtedly one of the first to scientifically research tropical medicine. Certainly, his is the first Dutch work on tropical medicine, including the first modern descriptions of beriberi and cholera researched during his four years in the East Indies. But in the midst of a discussion on "quadrupeds, birds, and fishes," as alluded in chapter 2, he was not beyond offering a highly fanciful drawing of an orangutan. Nevertheless, his reputation has survived to the extent that he is hailed by some in modern Indonesia as that country's original scientist.

In the event, a new global standard in scientific botany was set by Carl Linnaeus (1707–1778), who published his *Fundamenta Botanica* in 1735 and *Classes Plantarum* in 1738. With the publication of *Species Plantarum* (1753), Linnaeus had achieved a systematic survey of all known plants and animals, achieving a scientific priority in botany, albeit short of the great nineteenth-century leap in scientific deduction made by the Spensorians and Darwinians. But, as described by Edney (1997, 50), Linnaeus's systematics, in which the observer distinguished degrees of identity and differences between objectified phenomenon, was part of an Enlightenment trend to carry this classificatory project from the vegetable to the animal and mineral worlds and even to the study of linguistics and human society. Even cartography fell into this mold. Linnaeus referred to his taxonomic system as the *mappa naturae*.

Possibly the greatest botanical feat of this era was *Hortus Indicus Malabaricus* (1683–1703) of Hendrik Reede totDrakestein (1637?–1691) on the flora of Malabar in India. As a collaborative effort, it involved the labors of one hundred European and Indian participants. All specimens are described in Latin, Arabic, Sanskrit, Malayalam, and Tamil. In this production, totDrakestein is known to have bypassed Brahmanical opinions and sources in favor of low-caste informants. According to Lach (1991, 9), this work was a prime source for Linnaeus's *Species Plantarum*. Another Indian flora, although removed in time, was that of A. W. Roth, *Novae Plantarum Species Praesertim Indiae Orientalis* (New Plant Species Especially of East India; 1821), in turn a catalog of plants collected by Benjamin Heyne, a German missionary based in Tranquebar in 1792 and superintendent of the Bangalore Garden from 1802 to 1808.

Yet another flora, drawing on the talents of Indian artists formerly employed by the Mughal Empire, was J. F. Royle's *Illustrations of the Botany and Other Branches of the Natural History of the Himalayan Mountains and the Flora of Cashmere* (1833–1839). As curator of the Saharunpore botanical gardens, Royle, in part, was instrumental in introducing quinine into India, though his special interest in "drug plants" connects him with the imperial "plant-hunters," as discussed later in this chapter.

From a natural history perspective, the works of Georgius Everhardus Rumphius are singular, gaining the author the reputation of an "Indian Pliny," a reference to the Roman natural historian and geographer. A German-born employee of the Dutch East India Company, Rumphius spent most of his life on the island of Ambon in the Moluccas, where he took up residence in 1653. His *Amboinishe Raritaten* (Ambonese Rarities), published posthumously in 1705, is a classic work on molluscan ecology. A meticulous field-worker, drawing strongly on Malay and indigenous Ambonese systems of classifications, Rumphius also authored *Herbarium Amboinense* (Ambonese Herbal; 1750–1755). This was a six-volume survey of the flora of the East Indies, the first to date. Even so, copies of his manuscript did not arrive until 1697 in Holland, where it languished thirty-two years before publication. The first to describe the *Nepenthes,* or pitcher plant, in its archipelagic setting, Rumphius was not beyond perpetuating, or at least exaggerating, certain myths as to the carnivorous features of this plant along with associated taboos.[5] Valentjin, in turn, used an unpublished manuscript by Rumphius titled "Amboinsch dierboek," in his *Old and New East Indies* (1724–1725), for descriptions of the natural history of Ambon.

The Dutch East India Company's presence on the artificial island of Deshima at Nagasaki in Japan also afforded a valuable perch from which to engage both social and natural observation. As taken up in chapter 7, Deshima would also serve as a bridgehead for the introduction of Western learning into Japan. Engelbert Kaempfer (1651–1716), the German-born employee of the Company, arrived in Deshima in 1689. Already a graduate of German and Swedish universities, he set about his practice of medicine while also imparting his knowledge of anatomy and physiology to his Japanese pupils. Returning to Holland in 1694, he submitted to Leiden University his thesis on botany, tropical medicine, and acupuncture (Plutschow 1991, 101). Drawing on accumulated knowledge acquired in Asia, his thesis was titled *Amoenitatum Exoticarum* (Exotic Pleasures; 1712).

The first flora on Japan published in Europe was by the Swedish-born botanist in the employ of the Dutch East India Company, Charles Peter Thunberg (1743–1828). This was *Flora Japonica . . .* (Plants of Japan . . .), published in 1784 and including thirty-nine folded engravings, the fruits of his sojourn in Deshima between 1775 and 1776. Altogether, Thunberg returned to Europe with some 800 Japanese plants, all of which he assigned scientific names. Known as the Linnaeus of Japan, his *Flora* was also printed in Japanese. Thunberg also authored *Florula Javanica* (Plants of Java), researched in Java between 1775 and 1777 and published in Uppsala in 1825. Thunberg was a pupil of Linnaeus and succeeded Linnaeus's son as professor of botany at the medical school at Uppsala. This tradition was carried on by the Bavarian-born Philip Franz von Siebold (1796–1866), a physician in the employ of the Company at Nagasaki from 1823 who commissioned drawings of local flora from Japanese artists. As revealed by the Siebold collection of Japanese botanical art, today preserved in Komarov Botanical Library of St. Petersburg, the Japanese aesthetic approach to the job did not meet European scientific standards. Accordingly, only copies of the Japanese originals executed by European artists saw publication.[6]

In turn, the first flora on Ceylon was Paul Hermann, *Musaeum Zeylanicum* (1717), although the first illustrated flora of the island was J. Burmann's *Thesaurus Zeylanicus . . .* (1737). Hermann, employed as a Dutch Company official in Colombo (1672–1677), subsequently took up the chair in botany at Leiden University. Hermann was another source for Linnaeus. Thunberg, who sojourned in Ceylon in 1777–1778, also published his dissertation *Florula Ceilanica* in Uppsala in 1825.

Of minor importance compared to the previously cited works, especially because it was not published until the modern period, is the undated folio of the Dominican father Alberto de São Tomas (1969) titled "Virtudes de algumas plantas, folhas, cascas e raizes de differente avores da Ilha de Timor" (The Virtues of Some Plants, Leaves, Barks and Roots of Various Trees and Bushes of the Island of Timor). From a Timor historical perspective, this is a rare collection of watercolor drawings with descriptions of various local trees and plants along with medicinal properties. Believed to have been executed in the late eighteenth century, it remained in manuscript form until published in 1969. Portuguese ethnographer Ruy Cinatti has also drawn attention to the botanical importance of the so-called Planta do Cailaco, a partly colored sketch map of a region of Timor executed in 1727 (Cinatti 1959).

The Spanish-born Augustinian Manuel Blanco (1779–1845) conducted a more grandiose and better-financed Iberian endeavor. Originally commissioned in 1786, Blanco's *Flora de Filipinas* (Plants of the Philippines) was not published until 1837, entering a second, posthumous edition in 1845, and a third in 1877. This monumental work carries 479 plates, listing 1,200 species reproduced from watercolor paintings, half of them color. A separate study of Philippines flora accomplished by Blanco's Filipino collaborator, Ignacio Mercado, was included in the third edition. The illustrations to *Flora*, which included orchids, was a collaborative work between a team of Filipino artists led by Felix Resurreccion Hidalgo and five Spanish painters led by Agustin Saez (Lizares 2000).

Jesuit interest in Asian botany was obviously not lacking, and there is every reason to believe that observations of the natural world entered their correspondence. Long before the age of commercial plant hunting, a Polish Jesuit, Michael Boym, authored what is believed to be the first European flora on China. This was *Flora Sinensis*, published in Venice in 1656. This work carried depictions of Chinese fruits and vegetables illustrated by hand-colored woodblocks. Boym also authored a work on Chinese medicine (1682). An obscure Franciscan text relating to China, Cambodia, and Goa was by Macau-born Jacinto de Deus (1612–1681), author of *Vergel de Plantes, e Flores . . .* (Orchard of Plants and Flowers . . .; 1690). Despite the title, the author was better known for his philosophy than his botany.

The first missionaries in Indochina also turned their attention to the natural world, but it was not scientifically explored until the late eighteenth century. Singular was the Jesuit Juan de Loureiro's *Flora Cochinchinesis . . .*, published in Lisbon in 1790. This work was written in Latin, and

Loureiro also offers counterpart "nominum Cochinchinensium," or *quoc-ngu*, transliterations, a system of writing Vietnamese in Latin as discussed in chapter 9. Based on the Linnaean system, Loureiro's (1715–1796) investigation included over 1,000 species. A native of Portugal, Loureiro had sojourned thirty-six years in Cochin China, entering the service of the Nguyen court as mathematician and naturalist.

To be sure, as R. K. Kochhar (1991) has argued in discussion on the pioneering botanical research conducted in India by the Portuguese and Dutch, not much was of "contemporary significance" for local knowledge, at least alongside the role of British East India Company doctors at the Mughal court. Only much later was botanical knowledge incorporated into the main body of local science. In any case, with the advent of British India, "science" had become a colonial tool. Kochhar offers the trigonometrical survey of the country beginning in Bengal in 1767 as a case in point. We would further argue that botanical and other research conducted by the Dutch in the archipelago failed to engage or stimulate a local tradition in classification and collection, even if it fed into the fast incubating scientific tradition back home. Still, as demonstrated in another chapter, the matter was otherwise in Japan, where Western medicine, alongside other branches of learning, was given an eager reception.

## THE LURE OF SPICES AND OTHER RICHES

As mentioned, some sixteenth- and seventeenth-century observations of the natural world also ran to the anthropomorphic. Certain renditions even entered the world of "fantastic science." But with the possible exception of "carnivorous" plants, the vegetable world was better apprehended, especially when and where it concerned spices. Tropical spices and the super profits they returned in European markets were the initial lure behind the entry of the Iberians and, in turn, the northern Europeans into the maritime trade with Asia.

One such observer of nature, from seasons to tides to tropical products, was van Linschoten, whose *Itinerario . . .* (1596), excerpted in Purchas (1905), made common in Europe such exotics as pepper, the aromatic resin benjoin, cinnamon, lack, snakewood, aloes (calambac/palo daguilla), and cardamom, among other products that would become familiar trade commodities through the next two or more centuries. Undoubtedly, Linschoten was the progenitor of the description of the durian, "a fruit that only groweth in Malacca and is so much commend by those who have proved the same that there is no fruit in the world to be compared with it." While observing that, on opening, it smelled like rotten onions, he continued that "the fruit is for color and taste like an excellent meate, much used in Spain, called Mangiar Blanco, which is made of henne's flesh, distilled with sugar."

Such dilettante interest in taste, however, masked a cool commercial appraisal of richer fruits, almost worth their weight in gold, namely, the fabled spices and aromatic woods of the archipelago. At its easternmost extremity lies the island of Timor, literally meaning "east" in Malay. Timor's famed sandalwood was well known to Yuan and Ming China and directly entered Chinese trading circuits. As Pigafetta (1969a, 141), scribe aboard the *Victoria*, the sole surviving ship of Magellan's circumnavigation, learned firsthand during his sojourn on Timor in January 1522, "All the sandalwood and wax which is traded by the people of Java and Malacca comes from this place, where we found a [Chinese] junk of Luzon." The aromatic wood and its location soon entered Portuguese commercial intelligence along with the riches of the miniature archipelago to the north of Timor known as the Moluccas. As Tomé Pires wrote in the *Suma Oriental . . .* (1944, 204), a manuscript text based on his travels to China via Malacca in 1512–1515, "The Malay merchants say that God made Timor for sandalwood and Banda for mace and the Moluccas for cloves and that this merchandise is not known anywhere else in the world." While Timor's sandalwood, destined for the production of incense sticks and luxury items in China, was basically only a product of intra-Asian trade, the spices entered both Asian and European markets.

Not for nothing did the Europeans—Portuguese, Spanish, Dutch, and English—wage war over these precious items, not only against native populations but also against each other, in part a reference to the massacre in Ambon of English prisoners by the Dutch in 1623. To achieve a monopoly over the nutmeg trade in the little archipelago and to complete the conquest, in 1621 the Dutch governor-general of the Indies, Jan Pieterzoon Coen, launched an expedition to crush all indigenous opposition, "an act of cruelty," in the words of Dutch historian Vlekke (1965, 141–42), "which shocked even contemporaries." Through the course of the seventeenth century, Hanna (1991, 80–81) explains that in order to preserve the monopoly, the Dutch dispatched an endless succession of expeditions to destroy nutmeg trees, especially on outlying islands, although the policy of "extirpation" never met with real success.

The Englishman Christopher Fryke also described the "noblefruit," of which Banda island was famous, namely, nutmeg (and mace). The nutmeg tree, he related, "is almost like the Pear-tree, but doth not spread so much, and its Leaf is somewhat rounder" and the fruit "like a Peach in bigness and looks, of an extraordinary fine taste and delicate smell, when it is ripe." The flower, he described as "fine Red, and very agreeable to look on, especially when the tree is pretty full of Fruit," while the whole fruit is an "excellent Confite." Cinnamon, he described, was the bark of a tree, "much of the bigness of an olive-tree. . . . The tree hath two barks, the cinnamon is the inner one of them, which is peeled off the tree, and cut into square pieces; then laid in the sun to dry, which makes it rowl up together, as we see it in Europe." The cinnamon of Malabar, he described, is "a bastard kind, and nothing near so well" (Fryke and Schweitzer 1997, 87–88, 91).

Observing that Ambon in the Moluccas produced such products as ginger, pepper, canes, and nutmeg, the Englishman William Funnel wrote of the island's famous clove tree that it was "rather slender," from twelve to thirty or forty feet in height, with small branches and leaves about five inches long and two inches wide with the end tapering. He explained that, if rubbed between the fingers, the leaf would smell very strong of cloves. "The cloves grow out at the tip of the branches, in clusters of ten, twelve or fourteen, first white, then green, then a dark copper color, signaling their ripeness." He went on to explain that while all trees—cloves, nutmeg, mace, and cinnamon—belong to "Freemen," they still had to deliver the goods to the Company on pain of losing their status (Funnell 1745, 131–50).

Monopoly control over the cinnamon trade eventually led to a treaty between Raja Singha II, the last great warrior king of Ceylon, and the Dutch at the expense of the Portuguese. Christopher Schweitzer (Fryke and Schweitzer 1997, 240–41), who served a five-year term with the Dutch East India Company on the island commencing in 1676, offers a vivid description of traditional pearl diving on an offshore bank some twenty miles long and two miles wide, seven to ten fathoms deep. Diving, he relates, was the specialization of "Malabar" fisherman, each of whom "hangs a stone upon his foot to sink him the sooner; when he is at the bottom, he fills his net with oysters, and then loosens himself from the stone." Formerly a royal monopoly, Schweitzer observed that the Hollanders were in complete control. For the first three days of the pearling season, the entire harvest went to the Company; thereafter, each boat was taxed a rixdollar, or Dutch silver coin, a day. A Dutch soldier attended each boat to ensure that the divers did not spirit away the coveted pearls.

## GLOBAL PLANT EXCHANGES

European herbal and physic gardens, often attached to medical schools of universities such as at Padua and Bologna, date back to the mid-sixteenth century, but in short time royal botanical gardens came to be established throughout Europe and in the colonies to "acclimatize" the New World botanical imports. To name a few, the Royal Botanical Gardens in Lisbon dates from the mid-sixteenth century. The Hortus Botanicus of Leiden, founded in 1590 by Carolus Clusius, is regarded as the earliest scientific garden in Europe. By 1635, a Jardin des Plantes was founded in Paris out of the original Jardin des Plantes Medicinal. New World plants soon found their place in this garden as French explorers in Quebec returned with specimens. In turn, the Amsterdam Botanical Gardens were founded in 1682, with the Royal Botanical Gardens founded in Edinburgh in 1673 and at Kew in London in 1772 under the "directorship" of the botanist aboard the Cook navigation, Sir Joseph Banks. Likewise, Charles III founded a Jardin Botanico (botanical garden) in Madrid for New World plants in 1781. The list of strategic gardens gets even longer if we include those at Utrecht, Leipzig, and Chelsea, among others. But probably because of the mixed success in domesticating the lucrative spices in Europe, the Europeans also established gardens closer to the source.

Dating from the Dutch settlement at the Cape of Good Hope in 1652, Company gardens were used to acclimatize edible and decorative plants from Africa, Java, China, and elsewhere. The English East India Company saw to the creation of a Royal Botanical Gardens in Calcutta, which, founded in 1787 to grow spices for trade, botanist William Roxburgh transformed into an herbarium in 1793. From that year, Indian artists were commissioned to prepare sketches of specimens matching descriptions made by Scottish botanists in Edinburgh. The famed Peradeniya Royal Botanical Gardens, established in 1821 by the British in Kandy in Ceylon, became the site of major experiments in the cultivation of coffee, cinchona, and tea, among other "drugs." In 1811, the Dutch formally opened a Plantentuin at Buitenzorg or Bogor on Java, used for introducing tropical plants from other parts of the world. In another hemisphere, the Jardin Botanico of Rio de Janeiro, established by royal orders in 1808, sought to acclimatize plants imported from the East Indies. The French chose their Indian Ocean colony of Ile de France, or Mauritius, as a botanical base in which to acclimatize certain Asian species, while other strategically sited botanical gardens appeared in other colonies and territories.

Although genetic typing of plant specimens is a recent science, the New World–Old World exchange of food crops and exotics has entered historical lore. The global distribution and naturalization of such exotics as the potato, tomato, corn, capsicum pepper, and tobacco is common knowledge, but the rapidity of their globalization along lines of globe-girding commerce is less well documented and, as indicated later in this chapter, staggering. Moreover, the introduction of certain foods not only changed lifestyles but affected demographies as well.

In some accounts, beginning from the sixteenth century, Portuguese traders arriving in Macau were responsible for initiating major changes in the Chinese diet at least in the Pearl River delta region, especially by introducing maize, peanuts, sweet potato, yam, tomato, lettuce, watercress (still called "Portuguese greens"), okra, manioc, papaya, custard apple, guava, pineapple, varieties of onions, and pumpkin, among other introductions (Pires 1998, 77). The "revolutionary" demographic consequences of the introduction of American food plants into China have been widely analyzed by Ho Ping-ti (1955) and from a more global perspective by Marks (1998, 2002).

In his study of ecological change in southern China, Marks specifies the middle of the eighteenth century as the period when the New World imports became an important part of the Chinese peasant-farmer's basket of food crops. It also coincided with a peak in both population levels and cultivated land area in the region. Peanuts had entered the crop rotation of peasants in Jiangnan in the Yangtze River delta by the early sixteenth century. By the late sixteenth century, maize was being planted in inland Yunnan and Henan and sweet potato in coastal Fujian and Guangdong. A county gazetteer for Dongguan (adjacent Macau) registers the first planting of sweet potato in 1580, but by the late seventeenth century, the New World import had become a major cash crop and dietary supplement of the poor. For reasons not entirely clear, maize was better received and indeed linked with migratory patterns in the hills south of the Yangtze River (Marks 1998, 309–11).

To offer some examples of the new food crop introductions in Japan, the *Jacatra-imo* (Jakarta, or "English," potato), as known to Japanese, made a recorded entry in the early 1600s, while the *Satsuma-imo,* or sweet potato, of Central American origin found its way to Kyushu in western Japan in 1612. In 1772, the sweet potato crop saved local people in southern Kyushu from famine, the rice crop having failed because of a grasshopper plague. The authorities in Edo conducted experiments in the Koishikawa botanical gardens and encouraged further plantings. Also known as *kara-imo,* or Chinese potato, it was probably introduced via Ryukyu or China, having earlier been imported into the Philippines by the Spanish. Even so, the wide distribution of sweet potatoes across the Pacific Ocean has suggested to some that varieties of these tubers reached Polynesia several centuries before the advent of Columbus (Short 2001). Better adapted to Kyushu's warm moist climate than the English potato, the sweet potato is the third most important "indigenous" food crop in Japan today.

The case of the island of Timor, visited and settled by the Portuguese from the sixteenth century, is also illustrative. As observed by Englishman Dampier at the end of the seventeenth century, maize (*Zea mays,* L. Gramineae) of Brazilian provenance was already established as the staple of the population of Lifau in the north coast enclave territory of Oecusse. In fact, the first reference to the presence of maize in the archipelago was made by the Portuguese Gabriel Rebello in his *Historias das Molucas* (History of the Moluccas; 1561), based on his sojourn on the island of Ternate from 1543 to 1570. More or less in the same time frame, other New World imports to Timor, such as beans (*Phaseolus vulgaris,* L. Leguminosae), came to supplant indigenous varieties. Added to this list are groundnuts, papaya, manioc of various varieties, cashew nuts, guava, capsicum, sugar apples (of Mexican provenance), and so on. But the Portuguese also facilitated the import into Timor of other plants sourced from India, including mango, jackfruit, pimento, and cinnamon. Even so, certain introductions, such as ginger and citrus fruits, entered Timor in an even earlier period via Malay and Chinese trade networks (Almeida 1976; Thomaz 2001). Among the fruits arriving via India was undoubtedly *Ananassa sativa,* or the pineapple, native to Central America. Attested by the Florentine world traveler Francesco Carletti at Malacca in 1509, Jesuit Athanasius Kircher described the pineapple as in great abundance by the mid-seventeenth century in Guangdong, Jiangsu, and Fujian Provinces of China (Yule and Burnell 1903, 25–26).

Writing of plant introductions into the Indonesian archipelago at large, Crawfurd (1820, 352–54) also observed the wide distribution and adaptability of maize. Next to maize, he identified sweet potato (*Convolvulus batatas*) of American origin as the most extensively cultivated root crop. Known to Malays as *batata* to distinguish this import from indigenous yams, it is referred to by the people of the Moluccas as *Castilian,* or Spanish, yam. Another introduction, the "poisonous" manioc, is locally known by the name *Ubi Balanda,* suggesting its introduction by the Dutch. Similarly, a more recent introduction by the Dutch, the American potato, goes by the local name of *Ubi Europa* or *Kantang Holanda.* Crawfurd contested the assertion of Rumphius that the capsicum, or chili, was an American import, citing a wide variety of local nomenclature. In any case, the piquant capsicum in its many varieties had gained near universal acceptance in the archipelago by his time, especially useful as a spice and preservative in a tropical climate.

Among other indigenized New World imports into Asia borne by European merchants in the early wave of global transfer was tobacco.[7] First observed by the Columbus expedition, tobacco was cultivated for European consumption by the Portuguese in Brazil in 1548. In 1556, Andre Thevet brought seeds from Brazil to France, and two years later, seeds were planted in the Royal Gardens in Lisbon. In 1560, Jean Nicot de Villmain, who had been French ambassador in Lisbon, helped establish a European market in snuff and also lent his name to the plant variety *Nicotiana rustica.* In 1564, John Hawkins introduced tobacco to English nobility. Although touted by some Europeans as a medicinal, famously in 1601, King James I inveighed against the weed. But just as Sir Walter Raleigh popularized pipe smoking in England, by 1612 he had founded the slave-owning, tobacco-producing, and tax revenue–paying British colony of Virginia on Chesapeake Bay.

But how did tobacco arrive in Asia? Berthold Laufer (1924) theorized three routes. The first was via the galleon trade from Mexico to the Philippines, where tobacco in the form of cigars made an appearance at the end of the sixteenth century. Meanwhile, the Asian tendrils of the Manila trade took the drug to Taiwan and parts of China, Korea, Burma, and southern India, just as the eastward sailing Portuguese achieved the same by a second route. As a result, tobacco had arrived in Java by 1601 (Crawfurd 1820, 104; Reid 1988, 44) and was known in India in 1605. The reception of tobacco in India and Southeast Asia was undoubtedly eased by the established practice of chewing betel, to which tobacco was mixed (Laufer 1924; Rudgely 1998). Writing of Java in the opening decades of the nineteenth century, Crawfurd (1820, 105) explained that, unlike the case of opium, tobacco was no longer smoked but chewed. Even so, as John Nieuhoff observed in Patani in 1663, the population consumed so much tobacco that "the very children practice it to 4 or 5 years of age, and there are very few men and women among them who do not smoke" (Nieuhoff 1745, 220). Crawfurd (1820, 105) further explains that while the Arabs may have first introduced opium into Java and its usage stimulated by the "debauching influence of Chinese manners and example," its commerce is ascribed to the Europeans.

Tobacco was first accounted for in Japan around 1605, but, as documented in the August 7, 1615, diary entry of the English factor at Hirado, Richard Cocks, the authorities sought unsuccessfully to have tobacco fields already established in Nagasaki and elsewhere destroyed (Laufer 1924; Rudgely 1998). As Henry Hamel observed in mid-seventeenth-century Korea, fifty or sixty years prior to his arrival, the Japanese had introduced tobacco, and it was the Japanese who taught the Koreans "to grow tobacco, top dress and make use of it." According to Hamel, the Koreans even referred to tobacco after the Portuguese, as *Nanpankouk*, a play on *Nanban*, or southern barbarian (Hamel 1745, 631). The third route for the diffusion of tobacco was across Siberia to northern China.

Tobacco made a relatively late entry into the Pearl River delta region, becoming a significant commercial crop only in the eighteenth century. In the early eighteenth century, demand for tobacco in China was made up for by direct trade from Brazil to Macau, although not sanctioned by the Portuguese crown. Writing of southern China, Marks (1998, 311) explains that, unlike sweet potatoes or peanuts, tobacco exhausted the soil, but where there was profit, the tobacco plant could be accommodated on marginal land. Following the Portuguese introduction of snuff into China via Brazil, tobacco not only lent itself to a new social style for the elite but also gave birth to a new art form, the exquisitely decorated Chinese snuff bottle.

## REVERSE FLOW

But what of the reverse flow of exotics from Asia to Europe? Setting aside the exotic species that for ecological or other reasons could not be adapted to European climates, in fact Asian plants had been entering such European marketplaces as Venice since the age of Marco Polo. The list is long (and we are necessarily selective) but includes rice, sugar, tea, coffee, rhubarb, ornamental plants, and opium.

A native of China, the soybean (*Glicene max*) also entered Southeast Asia via trade routes at an early period. A major source of nutrition in East Asia, it is all the more surprising that Marco Polo did not mention the bean or its major food products: miso, soy sauce, and tofu. Nevertheless, the use of miso made from a bean as a flavor for fish and a gravy (soy sauce) was attested to by Francesco Carletti, who visited Nagasaki in 1597. In 1665, the Franciscan Domingo Navarrete observed in China the production of tofu from the milk of kidney beans. Englishman John Saris, visiting Hirado in 1613, was deceived in mistaking tofu for cheese. But within fifty years, soy sauce from the East Indies would be entering England as a trade product. With the publication in 1712 of Engelbert Kaempfer's *Exotic Pleasures*, including a drawing and description of the production of soy sauce, Europe gained a comprehensive knowledge of the soybean and its uses. Nevertheless, as Hymowitz (1990, 159–63) observes in his study of soybeans, the plant reached Europe only relatively late. Seeds sent by missionaries from China were planted in the Jardim des Plantes in Paris in 1739 and at Kew in 1790. With the exception of the Dubrovnik region of the former Yugoslavia, where seeds were planted in 1804 and gardens developed, soybeans were grown in Europe only for scientific purposes.

Sugar is a special case, especially as an example of an Asian plant that found its way to Europe, only to be re-created as an item of mass consumption produced under plantation conditions. Believed to be indigenous to India and the Pacific, sugarcane was probably imported to Europe from India by Muslim traders at an early date and flourished in parts of Italy and Spain and later the Canary Islands. By late Ming times (1368–1644), next to rice, sugarcane was the most important crop grown in the Pearl River delta counties of China. Southern China supplied all the sugar requirements of the Chinese Empire at that time (Marks 1998, 116). Recognizing the value of sugar as a trade item, the Portuguese introduced sugar cane in the early sixteenth century into the West African island of São Tomé, from where the traffic in slaves to the Americas was launched after the first plantations were opened in Brazil in 1530. By the seventeenth century, the Europeans had perfected the method of refining sugar, lending further stimulus to the creation of plantations in the Americas. But when the British and French established sugar colonies in the West Indies, they imported hybrids from Malabar, Batavia, and Tahiti believed to be superior to "indigenous" versions. The Chinese, who had already perfected the manufacture of sugar candy, made sugar a major export item to

Japan by the seventeenth century. Such at least is the gist of Benjamin Mosely's *Treatise on Sugar* (1800), a work that draws on a range of anti-quarian works to establish the medicinal properties of sugar. The Dutch went further in expanding the consumption of sugar in Japan by redirect-ing their exports of sugar on Java from newly founded Chinese-run plan-tations, an experiment repeated on Taiwan after the Dutch conquest.[8]

Undoubtedly introduced to Europe via the Eurasian silk roads, the first detailed description of tea and tea culture appeared in Gaspar da Cruz's *Treatise on Things Chinese* (1569). Other missionaries, such as the Por-tuguese Jesuit Alvaro Semedo, author of *Imperio de la China* (Empire of China; 1642), also described the uses and preparation of tea. The ceremo-nial uses of tea in Japan were first described by João Rodrigues in his *His-toria de Igreja da Japão* (History of the Church in Japan; 1620). His *Vocabu-lario de Japon Declarado* (ca. 1605) also offers numerous Japanese terms associated with tea culture. From an early date, tea was being exported from Macau and Manila to Europe.

In 1674–1678, Jacob Breyne and William Ten Rhijne published in Danzig their *Exoticarum . . . Plantarum Centuria Prima* (First Century of Exotic Plants). Offering a finely illustrated record of exotic plants from the Amer-icas, the East Indies, and South Africa, this work established Breyne as a leading European botanist. An appendix carried a description of the tea plant and the Japanese camphor tree by Ten Rhijne derived from his stay in 1674–1676 at Deshima in Nagasaki, where he studied tea culture, the tea plant, its manufacture, and the effect of the stimulant on the body. Tea (as well as coffee) and chocolate also attracted some literary attention in Europe, as specimens and knowledge of, especially the former, were gleaned from Dutch East India Company contacts at Deshima. Just as the Company researched the trade aspects of tea, so the botanists moved to analyze the plant. Such was P. S. Dufour's *Tractatus Novi de Potv Caphe, de Chinensium Thé et de Chocolata* (New and Curious Treatise on Coffee, Chi-nese Tea and Chocolate; 1685).

In Europe, tea remains an import from Asia, although it was planted in the Azores by the early 1800s. Around 1816, tea was also introduced into Brazil via the Jardin Botanico of Rio de Janeiro and subsequently to the Je-suit mission of Santa Cruz, where Chinese immigrants worked elaborate tea plantations (Pires 1998, 81).

Coffee had long entered Ottoman trade routes to Europe before the Dutch adopted, around 1690, mocha varieties for commercial cultivation in Ceylon and Java. The first major description of mocha, however, was established by the Marseilles merchant Jean de la Roque in his *Voyage de l'Arabie . . . Un Memoire Concernant l'Arbre et le Fruit de Café* (Voyage to Ara-bia . . . A Notice on the Coffee Tree and Fruit; 1715). Roque was associated with the first French scientific voyage to Arabia and the court of Yemen in

1708–1711. In short time, coffee cultivation was established in French Martinique by 1713, and with the establishment of coffee cultivation in Brazil by 1727, the social and commercial fortunes of that country were transformed. Similarly, the Portuguese introduced coffee in their African colonies, such as in São Tomé, in 1795. We may surmise that the Spanish introduced coffee into the Philippines from Java, but in introducing arabica coffee into Portuguese Timor also from Java in the first decades of the nineteenth century, later systematized by Portuguese Governor Affonso de Castro in the 1850s, the Portuguese pioneered an industry that remains the backbone of the agricultural economy of modern East Timor, a reference to the highly esteemed *hybrido de Timor*, the country's unique forest coffee, as in Madagascar, grown under towering *albizzia* mother trees.[9]

In his scholarly study of rhubarb, Foust (1992) reveals that the very best Chinese rhubarb, that found in the mountainous regions of Gansu Province, entered Europe from an early age through Russian caravans traveling overland in the north or through to Arabia or by coastal trade routes. Known to Polo, rhubarb, or *theum*, a plant of broad Asian distribution, was received by European and Chinese pharmacists alike as a medicinal. Known to Jesuit visitors, rhubarb was also attested to in the 1606 English edition of Ortelius's *Theatrum*. While plantings of rhubarb were recorded in Italy from 1608 and while various plantings were attempted in Europe, notably Russia, where the plant became a state monopoly, and America, from 1790, the European penchant for the plant as a medicinal and as a foodstuff was voracious and, as such, entered the English East India Company's trade in a big way.

## THE PLANT HUNTERS

While, to be sure, Eastern exotics had long entered European marts such as Venice via the overland silk roads, there was no precedent for the scale, reach, and depth of the globalizing impact of the Iberian exchanges. But European advances in classification—the penchant for collection and transplanting in metropolitan and strategically sited local gardens—merely presaged the imperial age of plant hunting. Following the first wave of globalized exchange with the New World, the plant hunters turned to Asia, where colonial rivalry, especially in the Moluccas, sometimes proved deadly for locals as well as rivals.

Anecdotal evidence also suggests that woody plants from Asia were imported into Europe dating back to Marco Polo, but the evidence from the eighteenth century is stronger. One of the first recorded imports of ornamental and landscape plants, also prized for its fruit, is that of the *Ginkgo biloba* L., the maidenhair tree, or gingko, in fact a plant now considered extinct in nature. In the mid-1730s, this plant was brought back from Nagasaki aboard a Dutch East India Company ship and planted in the Utrecht botanical gardens. The scope for smuggling plants out of Japan was limited, however, until Siebold successfully solicited seeds and specimens, planting some in a nursery at Deshima and secretly exporting others on Europe-bound ships, destined to enter the garden floras of Europe and America and beyond as commonplace ornamentals (Spongberg 1993).

Jesuit endeavor in China, we have observed, entered many domains. French missionary Pierre Nicholas le Chéron d'Incarville (1706–1757), who collected seeds of trees in the environs of Beijing, entrusted some to a member of a Russian caravan. Among them were seeds of the *Koelreureria paniculata Laxmann*, or golden rain tree, and *Sophora japonica* L., the pagoda, or scholar's, tree. Having safely arrived in Europe and eventually germinated in the Jardin des Plantes in Paris, these trees were later cultivated in other European and, eventually, American gardens. Another seed transmitted by d'Incarville to Europe and eventually America was that of the *Ailanthus altissama* (Miller), the tree of heaven, entering the Chelsea Physic Garden in 1751 and in later years invading American woodlands and suburbs alike (Spongberg 1993). Although mistaken into believing the seed was that of the lacquer tree, d'Incarville was already an authority on oriental lacquer techniques, then the rage in Europe. In 1760, he authored "Memoire sur le Vernis de la Chine" (Study on Chinese Varnishing), appearing as an appendix in Jean-Felix Watin's *L'Art de Peintre, Doreur, Vernisseur* (Art of Painting, Gilding, and Varnishing; 1772).

Doubtless such evocations of a wealth of spices grown and sold under tight Dutch monopoly through the seventeenth and early eighteenth centuries whetted the commercial appetite of other nations and actors. One seduced by the dream was French missionary turned entrepreneur turned colonial administrator Pierre Poivre (1719–1786). Having visited India, Java, and China on one mission and Indochina on another, Poivre came to be involved in a number of commercial adventures. Overcoming the difficulty of deceptive Dutch maps, Poivre made his way to the Moluccas and, passing through Timor, managed to smuggle out some 3,000 nutmeg plants, cloves, and other spices. Arriving in December 1753 at Mauritius, he planted the seeds in the Pamplemousses (Royal) Botanical Gardens before returning to France to solicit commercial interest. Returning in 1765 to the Mascarenes, as Mauritius and Réunion were also known, he was appointed administrator (cf. Hanna 1991, 195–206; Maverick 1941). The *Oeuvre Complêtes*, or complete works, of Pierre Poivre, containing his philosophical views and observations on Africa and Asia, was published in Paris in 1797. In turn, Poivre invested his grandson, Pierre Sonnerat (1749–1814), author of *Voyages aux Indes Orientales et a la Chine* (Voyage to the East Indies and China; 1782), to undertake an expedition to the Moluccas to follow up the

**Figure 3.1.** **"Plant hunters in Spice islands," from Valentijn's** *Oud en Nieuw Oost-Indien* **(1724). A rare if unabashed image of European plant hunters at work in the "spice islands." (Reproduced with permission of Nagasaki University Library)**

search for "spice plants" with a view to their acclimatization in the Mascarenes.

A more celebrated attempt at a New World–New World transfer of food crops was, as mentioned in chapter 2, that by English Captain William Bligh, who, in 1776, was expressly commissioned by London to sail to Tahiti to collect and transplant breadfruit plants to the West Indies, where they were to be used as a food source for black slaves on English sugar plantations. Breadfruit, or *Artocarpus altilis,* are believed to originate from the Malay archipelago, although they have a wide distribution in the Pacific. Ending in failure with the mutiny of the HMS *Bounty* and heroic open-boat navigation to the Dutch colony on Timor, Bligh's first mission is the stuff of legend. Bligh was successful a second time around with the arrival in the West Indies of 347 breadfruit plants aboard the HMS *Providence* on February 5, 1793. Breadfruit remains a culinary item and export fruit in the Caribbean today. The Pamplemousses Gardens in Mauritius became the center for French efforts to introduce breadfruit to their West Indian colonies, having obtained a single cultivar from Tonga in 1796.

Because of remoteness and historical conditions, the last great zone for the imperial plant hunters in Asia was China. Illustrations of Chinese flora appeared in Sir John Hill's *Exotic Botany Illustrated in Thirty-Five Figures* (1759) but were rendered from dried plants brought back from China on English merchant ships. The first plant hunter to successfully penetrate China after the Opium Wars (1839–1842) was Robert Fortune, author of *Three Years Wandering in the Northern Provinces of China . . . with an Account of the Agriculture and Horticulture of the Chinese, New Plants, etc.* (1847). Fortune, first employed as botanical collector for the Horticultural Society of London and subsequently by the English East India Company and the government of the United States, visited the eastern seaboard of China and other Asian countries four times between 1843 and 1859. Today, Fortune's name is associated with many now widely grown cultivars that he introduced into European and American gardens, such as the tree peony, varieties of camellia, and the golden larch, among many others (Spongberg 1993).

Not all Asian exotics commanded a European market, however. The most "famous" of the unwanted exotics, still exotic by today's European tastes, must be the ginseng root. To take an example from China (actually Korea), the account of the French Jesuit missionary Pierre Jartoux, writing from Beijing on April 12, 1711, of the European "discovery" of ginseng, is illustrative. Explaining that while in the employ of the emperor of China and engaged in producing a map of Tatary, he had the opportunity of "observing the famous plant called Gin-seng, so highly regarded in China and little known in Europe." This took place in July 1709 when he entered a village near the border with Korea, albeit an area inhabited by "Tatars." The ginseng plant, he relates, was collected from a neighboring mountain. Contrary to contemporary thinking, Jartoux was able to confirm that the plant was not endemic to China but localized. Not only did the Jesuit produce a skilled sketch of the plant, but he personally attested to its medicinal qualities, preferring it even to tea (Anonymous 1714).

## THE BOUNDS OF THE NATURAL WORLD

The age of the first globalization set no bounds on the natural world other than the fear of God invoked by storms, shipwrecks, war, and disease. The Varenius revolution in geographical awareness did not yet translate into environmental consciousness. If anything, the trepidation of medieval seafarers as to the natural world was assuaged by the advent of Enlightenment science that not only stimulated discovery in the natural world but also objectified and appropriated it. Even so, disease and pandemics remained largely unchecked in this age. Though environmental awareness belongs to the late twentieth century, the signs of ecological degradation, species loss, and even pollution must be read back to an earlier age alongside the better-observed omens of exploding volcanoes, flying comets, and devastating plagues.

Global species loss, as symbolized by the extinction of the proverbial dodo bird of the Indian Ocean island of Mauritius in 1680, had parallels in forest depletion. Again taking Mauritius as paradigmatic, the first seaborne visitors also plundered its ebony forests, source of prime timbers for naval construction, a practice emulated by the Europeans on the Malabar coast of India and by the Spanish in the Americas and at Cavite, the terminal port of the galleon trade in the Philippines. To be sure, the tropical forests of Asia fared better than converted forestlands pioneered by the Portuguese and Spanish in the Americas along with the forests of China, basically cleaned out ahead of the era of European expansion. Even so, the relative longevity of the forest zone of tropical Asia merely postponed the date of biological and species extinction.

But the navigators and other European observers were also quick to report on quirks of nature, such as the earthquakes of Japan, volcanic eruptions as in the Moluccas, typhoons of the China Sea, and other navigational dangers written into the first *roteiros*. Plague and pestilence were hardly everyday topics, but as the Dutch embassy to the Qing court witnessed on a river canal near the seacoast east of Beijing in 1656 or 1657, people were being organized into various groups "to defend their country against the grasshoppers (which occasion often times a very great dearth and scarcity)." As explained, the pests came once a year "with an easterly wind in mighty swarms or squadrons, that devour all they meet with and that in a few hours, leaving the fields utterly dismantled." In order to minimize the damage to their harvest, the inhabitants were seen marching through the fields "with their colors and ensigns flying, shouting and hollowing all the way they go" (Anonymous 1665, 111).

The bounds of the natural world were all the more tangible to the Dutch on the fortified spice island of Banda Neira, dominated by its antipodean Vesuvius, the 600-meter-high Gunung Api. Threatening major eruption at the time of the first Dutch arrival in 1599, Gunung Api (lit. "fire mountain" in Malay) erupted violently in 1615, 1629, 1638, and 1693. Hanna (1991, 85), from his reading of Valentjin and other Dutch sources, explains that the 1615 eruption was so severe that giant boulders rained down on Fort Nassau, pulverizing the garrison. In 1629, a tidal wave swept Neira anchorage, washing houses and cannon out to sea. Severe earthquakes struck the establishment from April to June 1636. Stinking sulfur vapors and showers of hot ash persisted from 1691 to 1696. The plantations were also vulnerable to lava flows and periodic hurricanes. Epidemics, which generally followed eruptions, such as in 1638 and 1693, along with two subsequent epidemics of 1702 and 1715, decimated the slave population. In the face of these human tragedies, Batavia considered curtailing its Banda operation, revised only after careful study of the balance sheets.

In an age when plague and pestilence were generalized, descriptions of poverty, illness, and social conditions of Eastern countries tended to be subordinated or sublimated in European accounts, at least alongside economic potential. We make exception here for the missionary doctors who, in the late sixteenth century, established Misericordia, or hospices, in such missionary enclaves as Goa, Macau, and Nagasaki. While, as seen, tropical medicine had its origins with the first European contacts, concern over, for example, demographic shifts, public health, and famines were concerns of future colonial administrators, not to mention the business of local empires and rulers.

But records of famine and natural disaster also entered the records of Asian dynasties with long writing traditions. Li Tana's (1998, 26–27) reading of the Vietnamese Le-Trinh dynasty annals offers illuminating data helping to explain large-scale migrations southward of Vietnamese from the troubled Thanh-Nghe region of central Vietnam from the late sixteenth century. Notably, drought and pestilence struck in Nghe-Anh in 1572 and 1594, altogether the most disastrous period recorded in Vietnamese annals, especially as fighting raged across the Red River delta in the north, leading to the losses of several hundred thousands in civil war.

Henrik Hamel's account of drought conditions and its consequences in Korea in 1680 is not only rare on the part of a European observer but also realistic in the light of reported famine and starvation in North Korea in the late 1990s. As Hamel witnessed, food was scarce in 1680, but the following year "was more miserable, abundance of people were famished to death, and the roads were full of robbers" although pursued by the authorities. Dead bodies found in the fields were ordered to be buried. People were obliged to collect acorns, pineapples, and other wild fruits, but even so, villages were plundered, and even some royal storehouses were broken open. The calamity continued through 1662, and the impact was felt in 1663 although mitigated by more plentiful harvests in better-watered places (Hamel 1745, 584).

Hitherto unknown in the New World until introduced by the Portuguese and Spanish, smallpox was identified in Santo Domingos from 1493, rapidly spreading to Puerto Rico, Antilles and Mexico, and elsewhere in Latin America, leading to catastrophic demographic consequences. With its Eurasian origins, smallpox was long part of the medical history of Asia and, indeed, entered Chinese medical texts as evidenced by their importation into Nagasaki in Japan during the Edo period (Mayanagi 2002). Nevertheless, the new global maritime routes were also

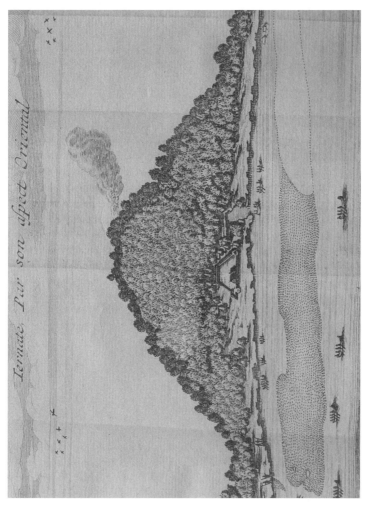

*Ternate, Par son aspect Oriental*

Figure 3.2. Eastern aspect of Ternate, from Argensola's *Histoire de la Conquete des isles Moluques par les Espagnols, par les Portugais & par les Hollandais* (1707). Exploding volcanoes like those of Ternate and Banda Neira in the Spice Islands symbolized the limits imposed by nature on foreign adventures, albeit not greed. (Author's collection)

conduits for the imports of new diseases and pandemics. This is acknowledged by Crawfurd (1820, 37), writing of the demographic toll taken by this disease in central Java, adding that smallpox was "probably" an Arab introduction alongside other "loathsome" disorders imported by the Europeans. Spanish and Portuguese sources record smallpox epidemics in Ternate in 1558, Ambon in 1564, and Balayan in the Philippines in 1592. Reid (1988, 59) reasons that smallpox was already endemic in major population centers of Southeast Asia by the sixteenth century,[10] while Campbell (2002) demonstrates that the disease was spread to the aboriginal peoples of northern Australia by visiting Macassan fishermen before and after the arrival in the continent of the first Europeans.

One Old World–New World import into Asia was syphilis, usually attributed to crews of Portuguese vessels. First identified in Europe in 1493, it reached India in 1498 and Guangzhou by 1505. Actually, it was Pigafetta (1969a, 141) who first mused on the presence of the Old World–New World malady of syphilis on Timor during his sojourn in 1519, taking it as a sign that other Iberians had preceded him to the island. While he might have mistaken "St. Job's" disease for yaws, his observation was prophetic of the globalization of disease and epidemics.

With its origins in India, indeed, attested to by Orta in 1563, cholera broke out in Calcutta in 1817 with dire results, soon cutting a demographic swath through Moscow in 1830 before arriving in western Europe and the United States in 1832. Cholera, usually not regarded as reaching Southeast Asia before 1820–1822 (Reid 1988, 61), added to Timor's reputation as a graveyard from the mid- to late nineteenth century (Gunn 1999b).[11]

There is no question that the first globalization introduced other "plagues" of an environmental nature. For example, the first Portuguese mariners arriving on Mauritius Island introduced pigs, goats, and such predators as rats, a practice continued over the centuries by various seafarers in different islands and oceans. But the Mariana Islands offer another example. By the time that the Jesuit Charles Le Gobien (1671–1708) published his *Histoire des Isles Mariannes . . .* (History of the Mariana Islands . . .) in Paris in 1700, not only was the indigenous Chamorro culture he recorded virtually extinct, but the Chamorro people were decimated by war and disease. Besides bringing epidemics, the annual galleon from Mexico also brought some unwanted visitors. In the words of a Chamorro chief recorded by Le Gobien, "Before they [the Spanish] arrived on the island, we did not know insects. Did we know rats, flies, mosquitoes, and all the other little animals that torment us? These are the beautiful presents they have made us . . . they have brought us their diseases and do not teach us the remedies."[12]

## CONCLUSION

Our focus on the Columbian exchange, especially in its Eurasian counter-part, is not to deny the historically significant exchanges across the terres-trial silk roads linking the Mediterranean with China dating back to Roman times. Nor is it to deny the role of especially Asian traders in the Eurasian exchange, whether astride the land or along maritime trading routes. But it is, however, to signal the new role played by the Europeans in the maritime trade hitherto monopolized by the Arabs, Gujaratis, Malays, Javanese, Chi-nese, Ryukyuans, and other Asian traders. Uniquely, as we have seen, the biological and cultural consequences of global exchanges opened up by the Columbus and Vasco da Gama revolutions were far reaching in both Eu-rope and Asia alongside the ancient terrestrial trade.

In the early age of globalization, the traffic in exotics was always two way. Just as the spices of Asia, from nutmeg to rhubarb to tea, would trans-form social habits and diets in Europe, so the New World introductions borne by the Europeans into Asia were quickly indigenized, leaving origins obscure. This, we have suggested, was the case of maize, sweet potato, and manioc. While cloves and nutmeg and, later, tobacco, tea, and coffee were developed by the European traders as plantation or export crops, it is im-portant to observe that the early plant and food crop introductions had a spontaneous character as to their dissemination and reception across a range of cultures. While it is beyond the scope of this work (cf. Marks 2002), the demographic consequences of the introduction of certain food crops, from southern China to Japan to the archipelago, may have been enormous, especially in checking famine, even in the early centuries of contact.

It is a cliché to suggest that a fascination for exotic plants and herbs was merely intellectual, as, then and now, the therapeutic quality of this or that product was widely noted. But it was always the commercial possibilities raised by the traffic in preciosities that drove the interest. Whether cloves, nutmeg, pepper, tea and coffee, or especially opium, the lure of profits over-whelmed mere scientific curiosity. Famously, the Dutch were prepared to destroy nutmeg to preserve their monopoly. The French, in the guise of sev-enteenth-century scientist-traveler Pierre Poivre, were not beyond botanical espionage for national gain. Plant hunting became a second vocation for the European adventurers, leading even to voyages and expeditions. In short time, the Dutch, English, and French, along with the Spanish and Por-tuguese, established strategic plant nurseries in their colonies as well as in metropoles, the precursors of colonial commercial agricultural estates.

## NOTES

1. For a study on the biological and cultural consequences of the Columbian ex-change, see Crosby (1973).

2. The first attempt to draw up a modern system of classification, however, owes to Caspar Bauhinus's *Pinex Theatri Botanici Caspari Bauhini* of 1623. All told, the *Pinex* included 6,000 entries, differentiated by genera and species, some of them of New World provenance. New World herbals include the little-known *Libellus de Medicinalibus Idorum Herbis* (Booklet of Indian Medicinal Herbs; 1552) dictated in Natuatl by Martin de la Cruz and translated into Latin by Juan Badiano, two Aztec acolytes of the College of Santa Cruz. Known as the de la Cruz/Badiano Codex, the value of the manuscript is its description of herbal remedies. The Spanish state also ventured into this field with the appointment to Mexico in 1550 by Philip II of Francisco Hernandez as royal physician. Returning to Spain, Hernandez published his *Historia Natural de la Nueva Espana* (Natural History of New Spain; 1570), including a description of 3,000 species of plants. As Paz (1999) points out in his geohistorical study of the Amazon, Hernandez had a keen eye to the medicinal uses of the plants and herbs he collected. By 1571, the Spanish crown had assigned a cosmographer to the "Indies" with a brief to draw up an inventory of plants for commercial uses. In a short time, Nicholas Monardes (1493–1588) had established a botanical garden in Seville to study the effects of New World drugs. His *Dos Libros el Uno Trata de Todas las Cosas q Trae de Nras Indias Occidentales* (Two Books about the Drugs from the West Indies Used in Medicine; 1565) offered the first major description of the tobacco plant along with Peruvian bark (cinchona), coca, sunflower, guava, and so on. An English rendering titled *Joyful News Out of the New Found Worlde* appeared in 1580. Descriptions of such New World "drugs" as tobacco, chocolate, and coca also entered João de Costa's *De Natura Novi Orbis* (New World Nature; 1588).

3. On the interplay between European botany and indigenous knowledge, see Grove (1996, 121–43).

4. The history of Western medicine should not detain us here, but it is noteworthy that the first Western monograph on Arabic medicine was Prosper Alpinius, *Medicine Aegyptiorum* (1745), describing medical practices in Cairo, where the author had lived in 1580–1584.

5. For a modern reprint and interpretation, see Beekman (1995).

6. Japanese botanical illustrations from Siebold's collection held in the Library of the Russian Academy of Science (Komarov Botanical Library, St. Petersburg) were exhibited at the Iwate Museum of Art, Iwate, Japan, June 15 to July 28, 2002. The author has inspected the catalog.

7. We should not confuse the East-West transfer of food crops and plants with intraregional exchanges, including the millennium-long transfer and naturalization of many Asian species of fruits and food crops, for example, rice, the mango of India, and the Chinese mandarin. For example, see the discussion on Malay world fruits in Burbidge (1989, 312). Writing in 1880, the naturalist Burbidge contended that Rumphius was mistaken in his belief that it was the Dutch who introduced the mango from the Moluccas to Java in 1655, as the mango grows in India and has long been naturalized in Malaya.

8. Dutchman André van Braam (1798, 44), who accompanied the embassy of the Dutch East India Company to the Chinese court in 1794 and 1795, was able to inspect a sugar mill in southern China in 1798, observing that the method and apparatus was identical to that in use in Java, leading him to conclude that it was Chinese who actually introduced the milling method in Java.

9. Lyrics to the exotic riches of the East took various forms. Even coffee fell into this category. The origin, preparation, and medical benefits of coffee were sung, actually as poem in Latin hexameters, by Thomas Bernard Fellows (1895), a humanist Jesuit from Avignon. Apollo, anxious to curb the drunken excesses of Bacchus, the author mused, introduced coffee into the world.

10. The writer and traveler Lady Mary Worsley Montague (1763) observed the practice of smallpox vaccinations in Turkey during her sojourn in 1717 and is responsible for introducing the practice to Europe. Dr. Edward Jenner began his first experiments with a smallpox vaccine in 1796. In short time (1803), the English East India Company introduced the vaccine into China experimentally. Success was achieved only in 1809 with the arrival in Macau of a fresh shipment via Manila. Over the subsequent thirty years, more than one million residents of Guangzhou had been vaccinated, confirming Macau's role as a conduit for the introduction of Western medical technologies into China (cf. Huang Qichen 1998, 174). It would not be until 1849 that the "Jenner method" of vaccination was introduced into Japan at Nagasaki but soon became widespread throughout the country.

11. The "hidden" history of *cholera indica* was also entertained by Semmelink (1885) in his study of cholera in the East Indies before 1817, a work that also offers mortality statistics on Dutch East India Company ships and in Batavia hospitals.

12. Sourced from http://members.aol.com/magastodu/guahan/magalahi/hurao.htm (accessed December 1, 2002).

# 4

# Catholic Cosmologies

In this chapter, we seek to identify the fount of, arguably, the most de-terminedly powerful ideological missions of post-Columbian history: the attempt by European missionaries—Jesuit, Dominican, Franciscan, and many other orders—following in the train of Iberian traders and con-quistadores to convert, convince, or sway the elites as well as the popula-tions of Oriental empires, not even excepting the most powerful on earth in terms of bureaucratic controls and surveillance, those of the Middle Kingdom and Japan under the Tokugawa shoguns. Such is what Rafael (1993, 1–22) has described of early Spanish rule in the Philippines with reference to the semantic associations between conquest, "translation," and conversion. The Jesuits, in particular, armed themselves with the highest scientific and philosophical knowledge available in Europe to demonstrate the superiority of an alternative cosmology that, ultimately, few in Asia outside the Philippines and Vietnam embraced but, within the strict ambit of our 1500–1800 time frame, sowed the seeds of gradual change (China), irreversible cultural assimilation (the Philippines), and rejection or at least selection (Japan). We also seek to explore the complex cultural and ideological alterities sown by the missions, especially as their cosmological religious worldviews came to be received by elite and, in some regions and circumstances, mass audiences. Needless to say, there was no one method of proselytization and no one pattern of acceptance of alternative cosmologies across the vast Eurasian terrain. Neither were the missionaries bereft of internal contestation. At issue were not only the souls of millions but also the fabric of social values and political systems.[1]

## JESUITAS NA ASIA: THE JESUITS IN ASIA

Until they were expelled from Brazil in 1759 and from Spanish dominions in 1767, there is no question that the Jesuits were the single dominant group of missionary-intellectuals ever to embark from the shores of Europe in search of new worlds and new souls. Founded in 1540 by the Navarre-born Ignatius Loyola (1491–1556), the Company of Jesus, or Society of Jesus as they are known today, was recognized the same year in a papal bull. Part of the Catholic Reformation of the sixteenth century, itself a reaction to the Protestant challenge, the Jesuits took rigid discipline and education as the most important instrument of reform. In Europe, they addressed themselves to the great mass of common folk, although in Asia their approach would be different, often in the way of targeting elites, princes, and emperors. Jesuit schools and colleges founded throughout Europe laid down a rigorous curriculum in classics, logic, mathematics, and natural philosophy, a pattern also replicated in Asia.

A devoted follower of Loyola, Francis Xavier armed himself with letters of recommendation from King John III of Portugal (r. 1521–1557) and Pope Paul III (1534–1549) and departed Lisbon for Goa in 1541. Arriving in Japan in August 1549, following evangelization in India, Malacca, Ambon, and Ternate, Xavier vested most hope in Japan and China, a view shared by Allesandro Valignano, Xavier's successor as head of the mission after the latter's death en route to China in 1552. In 1601, the Jesuit Matteo Ricci was the first of the Jesuit missionaries to arrive in Beijing, where he stayed until his death in 1610. Together with their Chinese counterparts, the first generation of Jesuit Sinologists entering China from Macau actively promoted a two-way cultural exchange. Not only did they collaborate in introducing Western sciences to China, but they introduced Chinese philosophy to Europe. Via their Portuguese merchant and patrician connections, they also introduced to Europe Chinese medicine, tea, porcelain, lacquerwork, architecture, and other cultural attributes (Ngai 2000).

The large body of Jesuit letters written from Asia have been described by Lach (1965, 314–51) as representing for their time the most extensive cumulative store of knowledge on *Asia extrema*, a Jesuit term embracing India, Indochina, Japan, and China along with the East Indies and the Philippines. As such, they combined secular as well as religious knowledge, extending to ethnography, hydrology, geology, zoology, botany, climatology, astronomy, seismology, and terrestrial magnetism, among other inquiries. While certain letters and manuscripts were published, earning their place as important image-forming texts in Europe on Asia, others remain in manuscript form until this day.[2]

The reception of the Christian missionaries, whether Jesuit, Franciscan, Dominican, or other, across diverse parts of Asia is an important question in establishing the nature of the cultural encounter (facts taken up in chapter 7), but we seek in the following pages to explain the major medium of religious propagation, namely, the uses of print culture, including the effort to translate European books into local languages, along with the employment of visual arts, meant to explain as well as to awe. But just as Europe consumed knowledge of the New World via the medium of the rising vernacular press, the Jesuits went further by introducing or at least reintroducing the typographic method of printing in Asia. Allowing that printing, especially woodblock printing, along with the production of paper and inks, was obviously highly developed in China, Korea, Vietnam, and Japan at the time of the arrival of the Europeans, it is also the case that the Gutenberg revolution offered certain improvements and refinements in movable, including metal type, print. The installation of a typographic press at Goa in India, at Macau and Beijing in China, and at Nagasaki in Japan owed directly to the Jesuits. Each of these sites became major loci of East-West interchange, not only intellectual and scientffic but also at the level of architecture, urban planning, painting, music, literature, and even gastronomy and popular culture, albeit as by-products of mercantile and religious zeal on the part of European missionaries.

## THE GOA PRESS

The first of the Jesuit presses to be established in Asia was sited at the College of St. Pauls in Old Goa in 1556, although originally intended for Ethiopia. By 1573, three presses had been established in Goa, two belonging to the Church and one secular press operated by an Italian and a German printer. Two of the presses printed in Latin letters and one in an Indian script. In short time, presses were established at such other southern India coast locations as Cochin, Ambalacate, and Punicale, printing variously in Malayalam and Tamil and later in Hindi, Marata, and Gujurati.

The first book printed by the College of St. Pauls press was *Conclusiones Philosophicus* (Philosophical Conclusions; 1556), attributed to Francis Xavier. His pamphlet *Catecismo da Doutrina Crista* (Catechism of the Christian Doctrine) was also printed in October 1557. Aside from religious and philosophical works, the second Jesuit press at Goa also published Garcia da Orta's celebrated *Coloquios . . .* (1563), a pioneering work of early European Enlightenment studies on Asia. Few other secular studies followed. Exceptions were works on language and, importantly, before the press went into 150 years of hibernation, the first Latin translation of the Confucian classic *Sinarum Scientia Politico-Moralis* (Political and Moral Science of China), a hybrid production of thirty-six leaves struck in Chinese characters printed in Guangzhou and twenty leaves in Latin and

Konkani, an Indo-Aryan language, printed in Goa in 1669 (Gonçalves 1968, 242–69). The importance of these linguistic and philosophical studies are taken up in a separate chapter.

To be sure, in Goa as in other parts of Asia, the Portuguese did not enter a civilizational vacuum. Subrahmanyam (1997, 39) observes that pre-1500 Goa was a heavily contested area between local warrior clans, the Hindu rulers of Vijayanegara, and remnants of the Bahmani sultanate. Undoubtedly, such a mosaic of dividing influences facilitated Portuguese conquest. In seeking to wipe the slate clean of Indo-Persian influences, Albuquerque sought the conversion of Brahmins followed by lower castes, soon accomplished in the *Ilhas Conquistas* (Old Conquests). With the introduction of the Inquisition in Goa in 1560, "horrific and violent images of Hinduism and Buddhism were produced for consumption in Europe in contrast to the earlier cliché of the peaceful *gentio* (non-believer)." Concessions were made to win allies against Marathi and Mughal attacks, but with the acquisition of the *Novas Conquistas* (New Conquests) in the last quarter of the eighteenth century, a new vigilance was mounted against contamination from Hinduism.

While the Jesuit beachhead in Goa and on the Malabar coast of southern India remained contestatory, the most dramatic and fruitful of the Jesuit enterprises in the interior, as described by Lach (1965, 275–81), were three missions of 1580–1583, 1591, and 1595–1605 to the Mughal court of Akbar (r. 1556–1606), located variously in Agra or Delhi. Akbar believed that Christianity might provide the basis for a new eclectic religion. The missionaries, especially the Persian-speaking Jerome Xavier (1549–1617), a nephew of Francis Xavier, had a close relationship with Akbar, albeit at times suspected of being a political agent of the Portuguese. To the disappointment of the mission, Akbar did not personally accept Christianity, although he allowed his subjects to convert. Nevertheless, the hostility of the Islamic faction in the court forced the Jesuits to beat a cautious retreat. Still, Lach muses, as in China and Japan, far from the centers of Portuguese power, the Jesuits were obliged to learn the ways of others and to actively penetrate alien cultures. While the Jesuit focus stayed on Japan and China in the sixteenth century, commencing in 1581, the mission established a presence in the Philippines and launched their activities in Cambodia and Cochin China from 1615, in Tonkin from 1627, and in Macassar from 1617 to 1618.

## THE MACAU PRESS

The arrival of the Jesuit press in Macau, following its Portuguese foundation in 1557, was preceded by the long tradition of xylographic press in

China, items of which soon arrived back in Goa and Lisbon. The first book printed in Macau was also done by the xylographic, or wood-engraving, method, namely, a Chinese-language catechism by the Jesuit Michele Ruggiero and Chinese collaborators in 1581 or 1582. This was *Tian-zhu shilu* (The True Story of God and the Holy Religion; 1581), also reprinted in Zhaoqing in 1584. According to Barreto (1997), this was "the first Chinese book of the modern era, with Western ideas." But while xylographic printing was well adapted for the printing of Chinese characters, it did not suit reproduction of Latin letters. Accordingly, the mission ordered a movable-type press from Portugal. This was achieved, and the first work published in Macau using the typographic method was that of Giovani Bonifacio on Christian education titled *Christian Pueri Institutio Adolescenti* (The Education of Christian Children; 1588).

The next book to be printed in Macau was *De Missione Legatorum Iaponensium ad Romanum* (The Japanese Mission to Rome; 1590), an account of the celebrated Tensho-era mission to Europe in 1585 by four young Japanese Christian acolytes and their experiences. As well documented, the four young "princes" from Kyushu departed Nagasaki in February 1582, learning Latin and European music during a stopover in Macau from March to December before departing for Lisbon, where they arrived in 1584. Feted in Portugal and Rome, the "ambassadors" arrived back in Macau in 1590 before sailing to Japan, where attitudes had turned hostile to the Christian presence. Believed to have been written by Jesuit Duarte Sande and the Italian Jesuit Father-Visitor Alessandro Valignano, who accompanied the press from Europe, the text was intended for translation into Japanese for "students of the Japanese seminaries." Written as a dialogue, as discussed in chapter 8, it also stands as a crossover text, introducing both elements of European civilization and governance as well as a richly nuanced account of China (cf. Barreto 1997; Teixeira 1988, 3–10).

## THE NAGASAKI PRESS

Around 1591, following up on early successes achieved by the missions in Japan, Valignano had the press removed from Macau to Kyushu, where at three locations—Katsura between 1590 and 1592, Amacusa between 1592 and 1598, and Nagasaki between 1598 and 1611—some fifty books were printed. Classics of the Jesuit press in Japan include *Doctrina Christiana* (Christian Doctrine; 1600); *Vocabulario da Lingua de Japon* (Dictionary of the Japanese Language; 1603); *Arte de Lingoa de Japão* (Japanese Grammar; 1604), compiled by João Rodrigues; and *Sacramento Ecclesião Ministranda* (The Administration of Church Sacraments; 1605). Using both metal typeface for Latin letters and wooden (later metal) typeface for hiragana and characters, the works included dictionaries, grammars, works on religion, and literature. In a major innovation, certain combined *romaji,* or Roman letters, with kanji, or Chinese characters. Other texts were published in Latin. Another innovation, a first in Japan, was the use of both red and black inks in the printing of *Sacramento.* Boxer divides these works into three groups: first, those translated from European languages into Japanese (with the exception of Aesop's fables, all were devotional works); second, works adopted from Japanese originals, such as the medieval heroic epic *Heike Monogatari* (Tale of Heike); and, third, linguistic works, grammars, and dictionaries. Notably, one branch of the printing enterprise established in Kyoto was placed in Japanese hands from 1610. Antonio Harada and Thomas Goto Soin are the most renowned of the Japanese printers (Boxer 1951, 189–98; Koda 1939, 42–53). Reissued by a Kyoto bookseller in 1659, Aesop's fables (*Isoho-monogotari*) was the only publication to survive the anti-Christian edicts beginning with Hideyoshi's edict of July 25, 1587.

While the question of readership and circulation of these texts, some twenty-three of which are extant, remains unstudied, there is no question that the Jesuit press in Japan served to deepen and consolidate the Christian mission, just as the number of Christians in this country swelled to over one million. Nevertheless, setting aside the many manuscript texts produced by the Jesuits and others, especially before the arrival of the printing press, a body of indigenous Japanese Christian writing also existed inside and outside of the Church. Paulo Yoho-ken (1510–1596), the "father" of Japanese Christian literature, wrote passion plays besides grammars, catechisms, and stories on the Portuguese black ships (cf. England 2001). Gracia Tama Hosokawa (1563–1600), the Christian convert daughter of a recalcitrant warlord and wife of a *daimyo,* or feudal lord, wrote a series of letters to a European missionary along with poems. As revealed by documents recently discovered in the National Library of Vienna, under the rubric "*Gratia: Regni Tango Regina,*" Gracia's noble Christian role was immortalized in a seventeenth-century European musical play.

The other side of the coin to the persecution of Christians in Japan, which involved tortures, executions, deportations, and tests of loyalty, was the impact on Europe, especially the church. Early church writings on Japan from Francis Xavier to Luís Fróis to Lope de Vega's *Triunfo de la Fee en los Reynos del Japon, por los Años de 1614 y 1615* (Success of the Faith in the Kingdom of Japan from 1614 to 1615; 1618) had built up a reasonably praiseworthy picture of Japan and its intelligent people. But with the persecutions, Portuguese, Spanish, Latin, and even English editions and translations of works on Japan produced a veritable genre

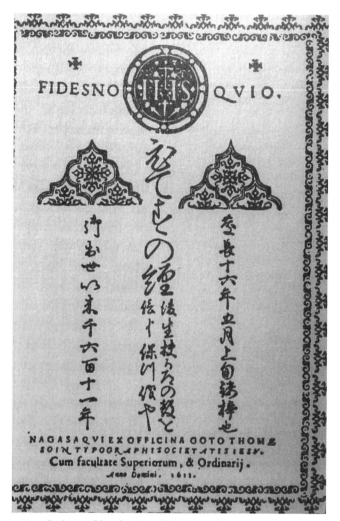

FIDESNO QVIO.

Figure 4.1.   Frontispiece of book printed in Nagasaki in 1611 by Goto Soin, taken from *Review of Culture* (2nd ed.), no. 17 (1993): 52.

of martyrology. Just to list these works would require a small catalog.[3] One was Pedro Morejon's *A Briefe Relation of the Persecution Lately Made against the Catholike Christians in the Kingdom of Japonia* (1619), in turn a translation of the Spanish original done in Mexico. With the final exclusion acts against Portuguese traders enforced in 1639, the image of Japan in mainly Catholic Europe had turned from laudatory to wary in the extreme.

## THE BEIJING PRESS

In 1611, with the enforcement of strict exclusion laws against the promulgation of Christianity in Japan, the press was taken back to the safety of Macau, where at St. Paul's College it was used to print João Rodrigues's pioneering linguistic study *Arte Breve da Lingoa Japoa . . .* (Short Japanese Grammar . . .; 1615). After 1624, the press either went into eclipse or was again removed to Manila or likely into the interior of China. In any case, the mission in Beijing published in Chinese on Chinese presses some 125 books before 1640. To achieve this feat, it is known that the missions in China gained imperial permission to strike copper matrices of Chinese characters (Braga 1942a; Matos 1988). While the Jesuit impact also extended to the importation and circulation of religious and other works printed in Europe, it is noteworthy that the letterpress technology introduced by the Jesuits appears not to have been emulated in Japan or China in that age and was adopted only in the early modern period, when mass printing became imperative. Nevertheless, a lively woodblock print culture on both religious-ethical and secular subjects continued in both countries, with Japan continuing to import a range of Chinese books through the centuries.

## THE MANILA PRESS

In general terms, the rise and development of the Spanish press in Manila was an outgrowth of the development of the press in the New World. Assisted by the Cromberger printing dynasty of Seville, Archbishop Zumárraga, who first arrived in Mexico in 1528, obtained the Spanish king's monopoly license to print in Mexico City. Between 1555 and 1601, under the supervision of Juan Pablos, the first printer to operate a press in the Americas, the Spanish press in Mexico evolved from printing, under viceregal patronage, religious tracts to such secular works as books of law and medicine but also grammars and dictionaries. It is notable as well that missionary texts were also printed in Nahuati (Aztec) and other indigenous languages.[4]

Similarly, in the Philippines it was the missionary press that pioneered printing, notably the Augustineans who arrived with the fleet under Legaspi in 1565, the Franciscans in 1577, the Jesuits in 1581, and the Dominicans in 1579. From their base in the convent of St. Domingos inside the Spanish fortress of Intramuras at Manila, the Dominicans fanned out to Macau, China, and Japan. It was also the Dominicans who were responsible for introducing the xylographic press in the Philippines and for producing the first books.

First off the new press was *Doctrina Christiana en Lengua Espanola y Tagala* (Christian Doctrine in Spanish and Tagalog), dated 1593 and printed by Juan de Vera (Veyra), a Chinese Christian convert. Based on the catechism of Jesuit theologian Cardinal Bellarmino, *Doctrina Christiana* is regarded as the first book printed in the Philippines. It also carried Vera's woodcut engraving of St. Dominic. Another book printed the same year, although undated, was *Doctrina Christiana en Letra y Lengua China* (Christian Doctrine in the Chinese Language), printed by Keng Yong (Juan de Vera?).

Also of great interest was the *Bian zhengjiao zhenchuan shilu*, or the *Apologia de la Verdadera Religion en Letra y Lengua China* (Testimony of the True Religion in the Chinese Language), dated 1593 and printed at the University of São Tomé. This was authored by Juan Cobo (1546–1592), a Spanish Dominican who also served in 1592 as envoy of the Spanish governor to the Japanese shogunate. Written in Chinese, the *Shilu* records discussions between a Spanish missionary and a group of Chinese scholars on philosophical and religious matters. According to the Beijing-based scholar Liu Dun (1998), Cobo's *Shilu* contains "important information about European ideas concerning geography . . . all of which was new to sixteenth and seventeenth century learned Chinese." Inter alia, this work carries a number of woodcut maps, one of which superimposes a rudimentary delineation of the Pacific on a zonal map framework including depictions of Mexico, China, Japan, and the Luzon Sea (Suárez 1999, 177).

The first established product of the movable-type method in the Philippines was the Spanish Dominican Francisco Blancas de San José's *Libro de los Cuatro Postrimerios del Hombre,* printed by Juan de Vera in Binondo in 1604. Better known was Blancas's *Arte y Reglas de la Lengua Tagala* (Grammar and Rules of the Tagalog Language; 1610), held up for the next century as the most comprehensive codification of Tagalog. As Rafael underscores, through its use of Latin and Castilian as the principal points of reference, Blancas's *Arte* fitted with sixteenth-century Spanish notions of translation "whereby vernaculars were decoded in terms of master languages and placed in a hierarchical relationship to one another" (Rafael 1993, 27).

All together, some one hundred texts dating from 1593 to 1640, deemed incunabula in the Philippines, were printed in Spanish, Chinese, Tagalog, Latin, Bisaya, Pampamgan, Ilocano, and Japanese, dominated by religious texts and catechisms. For example, an Ilocano version of *Dotrina Cristiana* was printed in 1621 by Francisco Lopez at the Convent of St. Pauls, Manila, and reprinted many times with a final edition in 1895. While the first press was a partnership between Chinese print workers and the Dominicans, in short time a group of Filipino printers emerged.

The first Filipino printer of renown was the *ladrino,* or bilingual, Tomas Pinpin, who established his reputation as the printer of Blancas's *Artes.* Pinpin was also the author and publisher in 1610 of *Librong Pagaaralan Nang Manga Tagalog Nang Uicang Castila* (The Book with Which Tagalogs Can Learn Castilian) (Santos 1996; Vallejo 2000). Rafael explains that, uniquely, Pinpin's book dealing with the language of the dominant is "richly instructive for what it tells us about the interests that animated Tagalog translation and, by implication, Tagalog conversion." Ostensibly a guide to Castilian language, Rafael reads Pinpin as more concerned with acoustic fit than meaning, more concerned with numbers than arithmetic, suggesting that the work "undermines the missionaries totalizing claims to political and linguistic authority." While Pinpin appears to embrace the colonizer, he stops short of total subjugation. As these examples reveal, his apparent enthusiasm for Castilian as the language of power is hedged by resistance to its political and linguistic constraints (Rafael 1993, 82–83).

The São Tomé College in Manila gained extra work publishing works on the martyrdom in Japan but also secular works and histories. Another printed by Tomas Pinpin was *Vocabulario de Japon Declarado,* a Spanish-Japanese adaptation of the original Portuguese-Japanese grammar authored by João Rodrigues and others at Nagasaki in 1603–1604. The last of the Manila incunabula was *Historia de . . . de la Orden de Predicadores en Philippinas, Japon y China* (History of the Order of the Preachers in the Philippines, Japan, and China; 1640) by the Dominican Diego Aduarte (1569–1636). A less well known work is that of the Jesuit chronicler and pioneer educator in the Philippines, Pedro Chirino, *Relación de las Islas Filipinas* (History of the Philippine Islands; 1604). In any case, by the end of the sixteenth century, the Manila press went into eclipse.

There is a sense, however, that despite the flowering of a Spanish press in the Philippines, this was a religious press, and the circulation of print material in the Philippines was even more closely circumscribed than in Mexico. Early ordinances given by the Spanish king specified that no secular literature was to sail to the new colony. This regulation was strictly enforced through searches of arriving vessels in Manila harbor ensuring the exclusive circulation of religious books. Obviously, there were exceptions to this rule, but such libraries that existed outside of state control were the preserve of bishops and clerics (Hernandez 1999).

## THE CHURCH CANON ON ASIA

The other side of the coin to active proselytization through print and visual media was the creative production of knowledge in Asia by the Jesuits and other missionaries, leading to the creation of a veritable church canon on

Asia, a body of knowledge unassailed in Europe until pierced by Enlightenment challenge and the needs of secular science and commerce.

## China

As discussed in chapter 8, the pioneering church-sponsored work on China was Gaspar da Cruz's *Tradado as Cousas da China* (Treatise on Things Chinese; 1569), especially in introducing to Europe basic knowledge on Chinese livelihoods as well as such secular pursuits as the art of tea drinking. But we can agree with Lach (1965, 743; 1991, 4) that one of the most notable of the early church works on China was by the Spanish Augustinian Juan Gonzalez de Mendoza (1545–1618) titled *Historia . . . del Gran Reyno de la China* (History of the Great Kingdom of China), published in Rome in 1585, going through many editions and translations. This work was derived from a digest of the Chinese compendiums brought back from China by the Spanish mission from Manila that visited Fujian in July–September 1575. Mendoza's work soon became a classic and was superseded only by Jesuit works of the eighteenth century. Also rich in material on Central and South America, Japan, the Moluccas, and the Philippines, the mapmaker Ortelius acknowledged the text as a major source of information.[5]

But while Mendoza had never set foot in China, the Italian-born missionary Matteo Ricci (1552–1610), who sojourned twenty-seven years in China, supplied Europe with the most authoritative source of knowledge on Chinese civilization, including descriptions of Ming life, laws, religion, and government. Ricci's biography was compiled from manuscripts by Frenchman Nicholas Trigault (1577–1628) and published as *De Christiana Expeditona Apud Sinas* (History of the Christian Expedition to China) in Augsburg in 1615. While this work introduced Confucius and Chinese science to Europe, Ricci is also remembered as pioneering knowledge of Archimedes, Euclid, and even Copernicus to China alongside, as mentioned in chapter 5, his contributions to cartography.

It cannot be overemphasized that, until the first Jesuit texts entered print, Europe's understanding of Cathay, or China, was pretty much derived from the Poloean stereotype of the Mongol court of the great khan. While numerous modern interpreters have pointed out that Polo never mentioned tea drinking, Chinese calligraphy, cormorant fishing, bound feet, and the Great Wall, among other ellipses (cf. Spence 1998, 12), and that he may not even have visited China (Wood 1995), the point is that the Poloean legend built up a powerfully positive image of China that persisted in European circles through Renaissance times. Early Jesuit accounts, laudatory in the extreme, confirmed a form of benevolent authoritarian rule, striking great resonance in Europe among a curious literati, a theme to which we will return in chapter 7.

One of the most sensational texts of the period, at least as evidenced by the large number of reprintings and translations, was that of the Trente-born Jesuit Martinus Martini (1614–1661), *De Bello Tartarico Historia . . .*, first published in Rome in 1654 and quickly translated into English as *The Conquest of the Great and Most Renowned Empire of China, by the Invasion of the Tartars* (1654). Having resided in Hangzhou during the period of the Manchu conquest (1634–1635), Martini was well placed to write this text. Martini's work was combined with Alvaro Semedo's *Imperio de la China* (1642). This was published in Lyon (1667) as *Histoire Universelle de la Chine* (Universal History of China).

As serving bishop in Mexico and acting viceroy of Spain, Juan de Palafox y Mendoza was well placed to command access to church as well as official Spanish records on China. A prolific author, Mendoza published his *Histoire de la Conqueste de la Chine par les Tartars* (History of the Conquest of China by the Tatars) in Paris in 1670. A work touching on religion and customs of the Chinese peoples, it was still being reprinted over fifty years later. Another influential text entering English in this period was the Jesuit missionary J. Gabriel de Magalhaes's (1609–1677) *A Nova Relação da China* (1688), translated in the same year as *A New History of China*.

A half century later, however, the new standard was Jean-Baptiste du Halde's (1654–1743) *Description Geographique, Historique, Chronologique, Politique de l'Empire de la Chine* (1735) or, in the English version, *The General History of China . . .* (1735). A French Jesuit, du Halde served as chaplain to Louis XIV (1638–1715) and then to the regent for Louis XV (1723–1774). Meticulously compiled from Jesuit sources sent to Europe, du Halde's encyclopedic work, ranging from Chinese life, flora, government, and astronomy, became the "bible" on things Chinese in Europe, the most comprehensive then published. As discussed in chapter 6, this was a seminal text in debates among Enlightenment philosophers over Asian governance. Besides carrying engravings of Chinese costumes and court life, including a famous picture of the Jesuits in Chinese mandarinal attire, the book also carried single maps of Tibet and Korea and was one of the first European books to discuss Tibet.

Also germane to Enlightenment discussions on China was an understanding of Confucianism. The first Latin translation of the works of Confucius is attributed to the Jesuits Philippe Couplet, Prosper Intorcetta, Christian Herdtrich, and François Rougement, *Confucius Sinarum Philosophus . . .* (Confucius, the Philosopher of the Chinese), published in Paris in 1686. It also carried an introduction to Chinese history and theology and a biography of Confucius. Commanded by Louis XIV, their book remained the main source of study of Confucian philosophy in Europe for over one hundred years. By 1706, a French translation of Confucius had been achieved, attributed to Louis Cousin or Jean de la Brune. The first discussion of the *Yijing* (Book of Changes) and the *Shujing* (Book of History) was by Joseph de Guignes in *Le Chou King: Un des Livres Sacrés des Chinois* (1770). This was based on a manuscript sent to Paris from Beijing by French missionary Antoine Gaubel.

Possibly the last of the great Jesuit Sinologues before the age of Orientalism was Joseph Anne Marie Moyriac de Mailla (1669–1748), French author of *Histoire General de la Chine, ou Annales de cet Empire . . .* (General History of China, or Annals of This Empire), published in Paris in 1777. This multivolume work of dynastic and religious history, drawn from a Mongolian-language version of the *Tong-kien-kang-mou,* covered the

**Figure 4.2.** Frontispiece of *Tian zhu shilu,* an engraved book by Jesuit Michele Ruggiero, printed in Macau in 1584, taken from *Review of Culture* (international edition), no. 2 (2002):15.

period from 2953 B.C. to A.D. 1730 and ranged over present-day Cambodia, Vietnam, Thailand, and China. Although the manuscript was completed in 1730, its publication was delayed because of the political climate in France against the Jesuits. Mailla had participated in the cartographic survey of China and had been appointed mandarin for his services.

## Tibet

The first eyewitness account of Tibet offered to Europe was by Portuguese Jesuit António de Andrade (1580–1634), who set out from the Mughal court in 1624 and crossed the Himalayas. His first visit was described in *Novo Descobrimento do Gram Cathayo, ou Reinos de Tibet . . .* (New Discovery of China and Kingdoms of Tibet), published in Lisbon in 1625. An account of a second journey took the form of a *relation,* or letter-missive, sent from Tsaparang on August 15, 1626. This was also published in Segovia the same year. While the Portuguese Jesuit Benedict Goes had earlier pioneered the land route to China from India in his path-blazing journey of 1602, an account, *The Travels of Benedict Goes . . .,* was published in London only in 1811. But it was the Italian Ippolito Desideri, traveling from Kashmir, who successfully established the first mission in Tibet. He reputedly was the first European to learn Tibetan language, and his *Travels* (1711–1727) was published only in 1904 in Italian from a manuscript source discovered in 1875. A pioneering publication was Francisco Orazio de la Pena's *Relacion del Reyno del Gran Tibet* (Account of the Great Kingdom of Tibet; 1742). A member of the Capuchin order, Orazio was part of a group of missionaries dispatched to Tibet by his ecclesiastical supporters. Arriving in 1721, the Capuchins were issued a passport by the authorities in Lhasa and permitted to found a mission but were expelled in 1745. Tibet was closed to Europeans for decades. His book carries basic information about the life and religion of the Tibetans.

## Japan

The sociological writings of Luís Fróis and João Rodrigues on Japan claim special attention, even though their audience may have been restricted to church circles. We refer to the unpublished late sixteenth-century manuscript of Rodrigues, titled *Historia da Igreja do Japão* (History of the Church in Japan). One authority, Castelo (1993), hails this as "the chief analysis of Japanese society and culture undertaken by a Westerner during the first century of Euro-Japanese contact." Compared to those who analyzed Japanese society solely as an aid to missionary endeavor, Rodrigues's concerns were the dissemination of knowledge. We are also referring to *Tratado das Contradições e Diferenças de Costumes entre a Europa e o Japão*

(Treatise by Luís Fróis on the Difference between European and Japanese Customs) only rendered into print from a manuscript version in 1955 (Fróis 1993). We shall return to a detailed discussion of this text in chapter 8. Even so, the new church standard on Japan became François-Xavier de Charlevoix's *Historie . . . du Japon* (History of Japan), published at Rouen in 1715. Anticipating Kaempfer's classic *History of Japan* (1727), a revised version of Charlevoix's work published in Paris in 1736 compares unfavorably to Kaempfer given its undue attention to religious issues and general lack of sociological insight.

### Indochina

Iberian merchants from Malacca and Manila began to enter Vietnam, Cambodia, and Laos in the sixteenth century. The pioneering work on Laos and Cambodia was by the Dominican Gaspar da Cruz, who spent over a year in Cambodia before returning to Portugal, where, as mentioned, he published his *Treatise*. But, by the early seventeenth century, Jesuits arriving from Macau also began entering the two warring and competing states of Cochin China and Tonkin. Half a century later, French secular priests of the Paris Mission Society also entered Vietnam, spurring a conflict within the Catholic Church back in Europe. The result of all this activity was the successful conversion of a large percentage of Vietnamese (Lach 1991, 25).

The expansion of European knowledge about the Indochinese states was also reflected in European publications. The first may have been a work printed in Macau in 1626 by Guilano Baldinotti (1591–1631), *La Relation sur le Tonkin. . .* (Account of Tonkin), subtitled *An Account of a Voyage to the Newly Discovered Kingdom of Tonkin.* A better-known missionary study of southern Vietnam, one still mined by historians, is the work of the Italian Jesuit Christoforo Borri, *Relation de la Nouvelle Mission . . . au Royaume de la Cochinchine* (Account of the New Mission to the Kingdom of Cochin China; 1631). Borri (1583–1632), a Milanese mathematician and cartographer, first arrived in the Cochin China region in 1618 and sojourned there for four years. Quickly entering French, Latin, Dutch, German, and English translations, Borri offered a fascinating account of Vietnamese history, geography, nature, language, and culture, which he clearly admired.

Early Jesuit writings on Vietnam owe much to Frenchman Alexandre de Rhodes (1591–1665) and his Vietnamese collaborators. Rhodes first arrived in Tonkin in 1627 and was active in the Hue-Danang area between 1640 and 1645. As discussed in chapter 9, Rhodes, a pioneer in the making of a new Vietnamese orthography, also wrote *Histoire du Royaume de Tunquin . . .* (History of the Kingdom of Tonkin; 1651) and *Relation . . . au Royaume de la Cochinchine* (Account of the Kingdom of Cochin

China; 1652), among other works, including those touching on China and the archipelago.[6]

Other important texts included Metello Saccano's *Relation de Progrez de la Foy au Royaume de la Cochinchine* (Account of the Progress of the Faith in Cochin China; 1635), Pierre Martiny Romain's *Relation Nouvelle et Curieuse des Royaumes de Tunquin et de Lao* (New and Curious Account of the Kingdoms of Tonkin and Laos; 1666), and Gio Filippo de Marini's *Historia et Relatione del Tunchino e del Gaiponne . . .* (Historical Account of Tonkin and Japan), published in Rome in 1665, treating especially Tonkin and Laos. Nevertheless, as discussed in chapter 7, missionary influence went beyond mere cultural contact and even came to reinvent Vietnamese written code and its civilizational link through writing with China and Japan.

## Siam

Just as European knowledge of Laos, Vietnam, and Cambodia came to be increasingly filtered through Jesuit sources, so the exchanges between the French and Siamese courts spawned a large specialist literature. At a time when France sought to dominate trade in the Bay of Bengal, as touched on in chapter 6, King Narai (r. 1656–1688) briefly entertained an alliance with France to neutralize the Dutch threat. This was carried in the report of the embassy sent to Siam by Louis XIV, headed by Chevalier Alexandre de Chaumont and penned by the French missionary-eccentric François Timoleon Choisy. Writing in the style of letters to a lady, the report was published as *Journal du Voyage de Siam fait en MDC.LXXXV. et MDC.LXXXVI* (Journal of a Voyage to Siam in 1685 and 1686; 1687). Needless to say, Choisy was unsuccessful in his attempt to convert Narai in return for the alliance. The violent events in Siam in 1688 leading to a rupture with European traders also spawned a small literature. Such was Marcel de Blanc's *Histoire de la Revolution de Royaume de Siam arrivé en l'année 1688* (History of the Revolution in the Kingdom of Siam in 1688; 1692). Yet another was that of François-Henri Turpin (pseudonym for Henriques Pangrapho), *Histoire Civile et Naturelle du Royaume de Siam, et des Révolutions qui sont Bouleversé cet Empire jusqu'en 1770* (Civil and Natural History of the Kingdom of Siam and the Revolutions Which Sundered This Kingdom until 1770; 1771). Written from church sources, the work was suppressed at the request of the Vatican-appointed vicar apostolic of Siam because of its alleged distortions.

## The Archipelago

Dominican writings excelled where their missions were strongest, namely, in the eastern archipelago, particularly on Solor, the fortified island base of the sandalwood trade with Macau. Such are Miguel Rangel's *Relaçam das Chrisrandades e Ilhas de Solor, etc.* (Account of Christianity in the Solor Islands; 1635) and Antonio da Encarnação's *Breve Relaçam das Cousas, que nestes annos proximos, fizerão os religios da Ordem dos Pregadores, e dos prodigios, que succedeaõ nas Christandades do sul, que correm por sua conta na India Oriental* (Brief Account of the Recent Activities of the Order of Preachers among the Christians in the East Indies; 1665), offering a detailed account of the mission on the islands of Timor, Solor, and Flores from 1638 to 1662. Yet another within a broader Portugalized imperial context was Luis de Sousa's *Historia de S. Domingos* (History of Saint Domingos; 1767). The most detailed work on Macassar on the island of Celebes written during the seventeenth century was Nicolas Gervaise's *Description Historique du Royaume de Macaçar* (Historical Description of the Kingdom of Macassar; 1688). Divided into three parts, it offers a discourse on geography and natural history, customs and government, and religion.

## THE VISUAL ARTS IN RELIGIOUS PROPAGATION

Whereas the Jesuit mission in Paraguay famously used musical form as a bridge to the indigenous population and whereas in China the Jesuits impressed courts and mandarins with their science and technology, the visual arts was also a tool in religious propagation. Especially where printed reading material reached a restricted or elite audience, the Church in Asia, as indeed in Europe, looked to printed images among other forms to aid mass proselytization.

When missionaries arrived in China—Matteo Ricci among them—they brought works of European art, ranging from devotional paintings and illustrated books to engravings of biblical and secular themes. Chinese were particularly impressed with Renaissance techniques of perspective, light, and chiaroscuro. Chinese artists were also fascinated, leading to some emulation and reproduction in Chinese books, especially of illustrations and engravings, some thousands of which probably entered China by way of the sea route from Europe. Italian-born Jesuit Giuseppe Castiglione (1688–1766) won special favor with Emperors Kangxi (r. 1662–1722), Yongzheng (r. 1723–1735), and Qianlong (r. 1711–1799) for his skills in architecture and painting and his ability to combine Western geometrical techniques with Chinese washing effects. The longest-serving missionary painter under the Qing, he produced vivid paintings of the emperors and imperial concubines along with paintings of plants and animals. Followed by such missionary painters as Jean Denis Attiret, Ignaz Sichelbarth, Louis de Poirot, and Giuseppe Panzi, the new hybrid "Tai Xi painting style" exerted a major influence on imperial painting in the middle period of the Qing dynasty for almost a hundred years.[7] Gradually, as Mungello (1999, 27–33) explains, the process of Sinicizing European techniques moved forward.

Beautiful pictures, images, and other icons were all used by the missions in the Philippines (Hernandez 2000). By introducing Western painting techniques to artisans in the Philippines, the Spanish friars extended the concept of patronage, replacing communal traditions and indigenous forms. In a word, through co-option and stricture, the Church, particularly the friars, became the new patron of the arts. While the publication of books obviously awaited the arrival of a print-literate audience, restricted even in vernacular, images eased communication problems with an essentially illiterate mass by displaying and dramatizing the concepts behind Christianity, the story of Christ's life and passion.

Indios or Tagalog artists proved good students of the Spanish friars in taking up two-dimensional art, especially in the reproduction of religious icons. The legacy of such enterprise can still be seen in the portraits of saints and religious scenes. The unsigned Christ figures of the Visayas island of Bohol are superlative in this sense. The first and best-known artists of this genre were Josef Luciano Dans (1805–ca. 1870), celebrated for his "Langit, lupa at impierno" (Heaven, Earth and Hell; ca. 1850), displayed in the church of Paete, Laguna. Nevertheless, it was sculpture in which the Tagalog artists excelled. This genre included church doors, pulpits and *carrozas* (floats that carry the saints in procession), church facades, and the art of transforming *anito* (spirits or souls of the dead) into *santos* (saints), used primarily for church altars, or *retablos*. While the earliest artists are unknown, the earliest known sculptor of religious images is Juan de los Santos (ca. 1590–ca. 1666) of San Pablo, Laguna. Numerous copper etchings were also achieved by Francisco Suarez (1690–ca. 1762) and Nicolas de la Cruz Bagay (1702–1765), who signed their works with terms such as "Indios Tagalo" or "Indio Filipino." Known for their collaboration in the production of the Murillo map, Suarez and Bagay also illustrated the *payson* (passion play) written by Gaspar Aquino de Belen titled *Mahal na Passion ni Jesu Christong Panginoon natin na tola* (The Holy Passion of Our Lord Jesus Christ in Verse) (Hernandez 2000).

The first recorded example of the introduction of religious art into Japan stems from the arrival of St. Francis Xavier in Kagoshima. He also took note of a demand for such paintings from local *daimyo*. But as demand outstripped supply, the mission saw to the insertion of painting and engraving in the curriculum of the newly established seminaries alongside music and religious subjects. Boxer has shown that connected with the Jesuit mission in Japan was the use of copperplate engraving, especially in the title pages of the books, and oil painting. But as the Flemish school of painting was then in vogue in Portugal, *retablos*, votive, and altar pictures painted in this style were introduced into Japan. The most influential teacher of European artistic style and technique was the Neapolitan missionary Giovanni Niccolo, who established an atelier operating, successively, at Shiki (Arima), Nagasaki (1603–1613), and Macau (1614–1623). But it was Japanese who proved the most apt pupils, especially in turning out "slavish" copies of European originals. Some dozen exemplars still exist and are preserved in Japanese art galleries.

Even so, as Gutiérrez (1993) offers, the Japanese artists were also able to combine the new European techniques with the vitality of the Kano school of Japanese painting, such as in a series of *emaki-mono*, or picture scroll portraits, generically called The Mysteries of the Rosary. The finest example of *emaki-mono* was discovered only in 1930, that of the color-on-paper portrayal of Xavier and Loyola, executed some years after their canonization in 1623 along with a single-colored portrait of Xavier. *The Great Martyrdom of Nagasaki* (1622; copies in Rome and Macau) is another example of a European-style painting influenced by the Kano school perspective (Boxer 1951, 200–1).

A uniquely Japanese innovation was the production of *Namban-byobu*, or southern Barbarian picture screens, painted by Japanese Christian acolytes. The best known of this genre were painted by masters of the Kano, Tosa, and Sumiyoshi schools, mostly depicting the arrival in Nagasaki of the *kurofune* (lit. "black ships"), or great Portuguese ships. After a 1614 edict proscribing Christianity, churches or religious figures no longer appear on the screens. Employed as decorative pieces, the *byobu* offer rare glimpses of European–Japanese transactions, along with such depictions as Portuguese dressed in baggy *bombacha* pantaloons, exotic animals, and even acrobatic black slaves. Another genre was the production of picture screens depicting world maps after the style of Abraham Ortelius's *Theatrum Orbis Terrarum*, a copy of which was brought from Rome in 1590. Boxer allows that they were not slavish copies with respect to the Asia area but far more accurate than the original, having been corrected by using indigenous sources (Boxer 1951, 200–1; Gutiérrez 1993).

A formalist religious style of art also developed among Japanese acolytes offering pseudoclassic renditions of European life. Nevertheless, this genre never survived the persecutions in Japan, although no doubt it continued in Macau, Mexico, and Manila. One survivor, however, appears to be a mid-sixteenth-century wool tapestry, presumably of Iberian provenance that, with the revival of the ancient (ninth century) Gion festival in Kyoto in the early Edo period, became incorporated into the festival format as a foreign icon. Still extant, the tapestry offers a multihued scene from the *Iliad* of European kings and courtiers. Other rare survivors of this age include temple screens depicting Iberians, also to be found in Kyoto.

Church publications on Japan expanded in pace with the persecution. Graphics lent a special quality to these books. Such was the illustration by

Theodore de Bry in *De mirabelaa SVA peccata confitendi ratione*, or "balance des actes," a Christian martyr hanging in the scales of divine redemption at the hands of Oriental torturers. Illustrations added to António Cardim's *Fasciclus e Japonicus Floribus* (1646) offered graphic detail on the martyrdom of Julian Nakamura, one of the four Japanese ambassadors to Europe, "hanged at the pit" in Nagasaki on October 21, 1653. Julian's portrait had been painted by famed cartographer Urbano Monte (1544–1613) in July 1585, when the Japanese embassy passed through Milan.

Mughal India also fell into the pattern, although at the court of Akbar, the great Mughal himself actively commanded court artists to reproduce images of Christian saints in the style of late Renaissance Europe. Akbar's son and successor, Jahangir (1605–1627), ordered murals of devotional images to be painted on the walls of imperial throne rooms, gardens, villas, and tombs. But the Mughal court was more interested in European art, aesthetics, and religious debate than conversion. As Bailey summarizes, this was a case of Michelangelo over Christ. The result was a new eclecticism blending Persianate forms with European techniques in perspective, light, and color. While secretly perverting Christian iconography, the Mughal emperors were also giving a free plug to the new religion. On the other hand, the Jesuits at the Mughal court uniquely accommodated to local form, even adopting Sufi imagery and metaphor to explain Christian tenets. Such was the *Mirat al Quds* (Mirror of Holiness; 1602), composed by Jerome Xavier, the first Christian tract in Persian, the language of the Mughal court (Bailey 2000).

## ALTERITIES, HERESIES, AND HYBRID COSMOLOGIES

Observing the florescence of a missionary press in Portuguese Goa and Macau and under the Spanish in Manila, we have remarked that this was a controlled press, under the double censorship of the state and the Church. No text that challenged the orthodoxy of the times saw print in such circumstances. The parallel can be made with Spanish America before the dissolution of empire between 1808 and 1830 where controls and seclusion limited the number of Spanish presses on the entire continent to fewer than six. Given the near monopoly of the religious press in Goa, Nagasaki, Macau, and Manila, even at the expense of secular publishing, was any challenge to the orthodoxy possible?

We speak here of the Holy Inquisition in its Oriental version. Established in India in 1560, the Inquisition was formally abolished only in 1812, with a temporary cessation in Portugal from 1774 to 1778, stemming from the efforts of Marquez de Pombal, chief minister in Portugal from

1750 to 1777. With its headquarters in Goa, the jurisdiction of the Holy Office of the Inquisition extended to all Portuguese possessions in the East. But its excesses were by far the most extreme in Goa. For example, on April 2, 1560, Viceroy D. Constantine de Braganca issued an order instructing the removal of Brahmins from Goa on pain of confiscation of property. Indian Hindu nationalists today see this history as an all-out assault against Hindu religion and culture (cf. Gupta 1999). Hindus were not the only victims of the inquisition in Goa. One victim who survived was Frenchman Gabriel Dellon, author of *Relation de l'Inquisition de Goa* (Account of the Inquisition in Goa; 1688).

In Mexico, where Zumárranga had introduced the typographic press, the bishop himself was appointed inquisitor in 1535. In 1571, an Office of the Inquisition, administered by the Dominicans, was established in Mexico City. While the main victims of the Holy Inquisition in the colonies were crypto-Jews, blasphemers, bigamists, alleged witches, and so on, "pagan" natives were not always immune. In 1558, the great inquisitor appointed an inquisition for Mexico with jurisdiction over all of New Spain, including the Philippines. Inquisitional methods applied in the Philippines generally led to the proscription of many popular beliefs, including shamanism, as heretical. Needless to say, teaching and learning in the newly founded Catholic universities and schools in Mexico and the Philippines was rigidly Catholic and not without major impact on native tradition, language, and cultural orientation.

Bankoff (1999) has drawn attention to the creation in the Philippines of hybrid cosmologies, "neither wholly indigenous nor wholly exotic." The first-arriving Spanish not only were alarmed at the activities of native priestesses, shamans, or spirit mediums but also held them responsible for instances of apostasy. Squared with theological doctrine then obtaining in Spain, such activities were tantamount to witchcraft. As the great witch-hunts of the sixteenth and seventeenth centuries reached a climax in Europe between 1575 and 1650, so the missions in the Philippines confronted the contradiction, as in the New World, of thriving idolatrous practices alongside an apparent enthusiasm in the new faith. In line with Hispanic Christian notions of patriarchy, the association of shaman and devil was easily accommodated. Such was the celebrated case of Seberina Candelaria laid before the bishop's representative in the town of Obando on June 4, 1808. But by this age, Enlightenment views, as percolated down to the provincial Philippines, held that Seberina was more a victim of the devil's entreaties than possessed. And so, by reconceptualizing the possessed as mentally deluded, the cosmological distance between demonizing Spanish and indigenous adepts of local belief that had incorporated Hispanic and Christian symbols actually broadened.

But while the repression of heretics in Europe and Goa was the order of the day, as Boxer records, heresy was written out of the first books printed in Japan so as to boost the campaign of missionization. In any case, rivalry between Jesuits and Franciscans in Japan became an aspect of state rivalry between Spain and Portugal in the East and generally poisoned attitudes against the Church in the eyes of the wary shogunate (Boxer 1951, 226–30).

The religion continued, but only in the *kakure*, or underground, tradition, a highly syncretized Christian-Buddhist form that offered protection from persecution across many generations but that became so devoid of meaning over time that even the best anthropology is hard put to give Christian meaning to obscure expressions and form that may have survived until the present (Whelan 1994). Nevertheless, the *kakure* tradition has bequeathed specific examples of indigenous Christian folk craft, most famously, as can be viewed in museums in Nagasaki today, ceramic images of Maria-Kannon, the Madonna and child in the form of Kannon (Guanyin), the Buddhist goddess of mercy, in some versions marked with a cross and sometimes holding a lotus flower bud instead of a child.

It is some irony that, palpably, the most enduring monument of the Jesuit encounter with the Orient is that written in stone, favorite backdrop of tourists, at the facade of the Jesuit church of St. Pauls in Macau, known locally as Sam Ba Sing Tsik. Built in 1602–1603 on a site adjoining the Jesuit College, where missionaries such as Matteo Ricci and Adam Schall studied before serving in the Ming court as astronomers and cosmographers and where the Japanese ambassadors to Rome reposed and studied, the church was destroyed in 1831 and never rebuilt, leaving only the imposing stairway and even more imposing facade. Built over a number of years by Japanese Christian exiles and local craftsmen under the direction of Jesuit architects, it combines, in the words of Macau historian Manuel Teixeira, elements of medieval, classical, and Oriental forms. Meant to impress, the soaring carved stone facade built around four colonnaded tiers, topped by a pediment, not only is an alien structure piercing a quintessentially urban Chinese landscape but, for over four centuries, has also presented its bas-relief as a didactic message for believers and nonbelievers alike to behold, thus going far beyond the interior message of hoary books, manuscripts, and pious homilies. In the center of the pediment is a bronze dove, symbol of the Holy Spirit, spreading its wings between carvings of the sun, moon, and stars. Here we behold statues of virgins and saints, symbols of the Garden of Eden and Crucifixion, angels and the devil, a Japanese chrysanthemum, and a three-masted Portuguese sailing ship battling stormy seas. But the figure of the devil, pierced with an arrow, has a women's body, symbolizing the temptations of the world, as Chinese characters warn, "Because of the devil, man became sinful." Another pious warning struck in Chinese characters reads, "The Holy Mother tramples on the Dragon's Head." On another panel is a skeleton and sickle, the symbol of death bearing the Chinese inscription, "Remember death and you shall never sin." An inscription over the main doorway reads "Mater Dei" (Mother of God) and over the two other doors "I.H.S." (The Holy Name of Jesus). Still visible at the base is the cornerstone signed, "Virgin Magnae Matri, Civitas Macaensis, Libens Posuit AN. 1602" (To the Great Virgin Mother the City of Macau willing placed this in the year 1602) (Teixiera 1979b).

As an allegory in stone, St. Pauls has its parallels in the baroque churches of Goa and the Philippines, but for its positioning, its *feng shui* in Chinese geomancy, St. Pauls is peerless and is recognized as such in local Macau as well as Chinese lore. Acknowledging the facade as a unique piece of art rich with cultural overtones representing one aspect of the Portuguese-Jesuit attempt to acculturate the Chinese with Christian faith, Christina Cheng finds the iconography often misinterpreted. Even the dragon motif, she explains, is endowed with "contrasting semiotics in Chinese and Christian cultures," especially as the dragon has different cultural symbolism in Chinese and Christian culture. To wit, the "symbol-saturated relief" comes across as a "bricolage of cross-cultural elements and architectural expressions . . . a meeting point of different civilizations and an

**Figure 4.3.** "Because of the devil, man became sinful." Christian exhortation in Chinese characters matching an Orientalized devil/dragon image alongside a Portuguese carrack carved in stone on the facade of St. Paul's church, Macau, today a major tourist destination for foreign, including mainland Chinese, tourists. (Author's collection)

ethnic mosaic per se." Far from being a mere "sermon in stone," as often described, the hidden symbolism of the facade is foreign not only to non-Christians but also to many Christians outside a religious elite (Cheng 1999, 83–100).[8]

## THE RITES CONTROVERSY

Nevertheless, it was the so-called rites controversy that became a major point of internal disputation facing the church, impacting on its work in China and even Vietnam. As Mackerras (1989, 29–30) explains, in the seventeenth century, as such Catholic orders as the Dominicans and Franciscans began working in China alongside the Jesuits, all became embroiled in the rites controversy. While the Jesuits held to the view that ceremonies in honor of Confucius and one's ancestors were compatible with Christianity in certain circumstances, the Dominicans and Franciscans adopted the alternative view. In 1702, Pope Clement XI dispatched his legate, Charles Thomas Maillard de Tournon, to China to engage the rites issue. But Maillard's rejection of Christian accommodation with Confucian practices led the Chinese authorities to banish him in June 1707 to Macau along with his followers. Placed under house arrest by soldiers dispatched by the Portuguese governor, the affair brought the Portuguese state into a collision course with the Vatican (Gu Wei-min 2002, 94–95). Pope Benedict XIV affirmed the ban on accommodation of Chinese "rites" with the additional rider that further debate on the issue was prohibited. Eventually, the Jesuit's patronage by the Kangxi emperor was lost with his death in 1722. According to Mungello (1999, 114), bickering over the rites controversy contributed to Kangxi's disillusionment with Christianity, although he continued to patronize individual Jesuits at court. The Kangxi emperor also regarded the rulings in Rome as foreign intrusion in internal matters.

In eighteenth-century Europe, the rites controversy also reverberated. In 1740, the Swiss priest Pierre-François Favre published in Neuchtael his *Lettres . . .*, or letters, on an apostolic visit to Cochin China. Sent by the Holy See to Indochina as part of a group of French missionaries, Favre offered a stinging critique of Jesuit practices in Indochina, notably in accommodating pagan rites. As a result, the book was placed on the index and publicly burned in April 1746 in Fribourg, a Catholic stronghold in Switzerland that remained Catholic through the Reformation.

In fact, the Jesuit order would soon fall victim to its own success not only from Calvinist rivals but also from its orthodox adherents. In Portugal, the Jesuits were blamed for fanning revolt by Indians in the *Reduction*, or reservations, they founded in Paraguay. In 1758, the marquis of Pombal, justifying his actions in the language of the Enlightenment, sequestered Jesuit assets in Portugal and the colonies and had the Jesuits expelled to the Papal States. Pombal's edict was enforced in Macau in 1762. Such action opened a ten-year breach between Portugal and Rome in which Pope Clement XIII defended the Jesuits. But in 1764, Louis XV (1715–1774) declared all Jesuit schools in France closed, and in 1767, Spain, under King Charles II (1665–1760), expelled the Jesuits from Spanish domains. Even José Basilio da Gama, the Jesuit-trained author of the Brazilian epic poem *O Uraguai* (1769), an account of the Portuguese-Spanish expedition against the Jesuit-controlled *Reduction* of the Uruguay River basin, emerged as a Pombal protégé. The tide turned against the order when, in 1769, it was ordered liquidated by Rome, leaving individual Jesuits destitute and their rich libraries abandoned. Only a popular demand for education and missionary work forced Pope Pius VII to restore the order in 1814. To add some perspective, it should also be observed that, by the eighteenth century, the pendulum of Jesuit activity had swung away from China to the Americas. Where in Asia there had never been more than thirty Jesuits active at any one time, their work concentrated in China, by the 1750s there were over 600 active in Brazil alone.

But by this age, Protestant missions were active in Asia (Malacca and Macau, where the English East India Company gained a foothold, were so transformed), injecting a vastly new contestatory ideology into Asian cultural space. There is much to be said of Mungello's (1999, 7, 94–97) contention that the first cycle of the Asian encounter with Europe, beginning with the arrival of the Portuguese, rang down with the visit by British ambassador Earl Macartney to the court of the Qianlong emperor in 1793 and the death of the emperor in 1799. Again China became a major arena of Christian missionary activity in the last half of the nineteenth century. Portuguese Macau, from where the missionaries sallied forth, was hardly to blame, but the hugely destructive anti-Qing peasant rebellion of the pseudo-Christian Taipings, led by Hong Xiuquan, or "God's Chinese Son," as termed by Spence (1996), had its wellsprings in misplaced Western missionary endeavor.

## CONCLUSION

The Jesuit and missionary enterprise in launching the typographic press in various parts of Asia, as well as adapting the press to long-established typographic methods, as in China and Japan, merits attention as one of the key ideological and institutional components of the first globalization. Such was the acknowledged expertise of the missions in this realm that states, trading companies, and merchant marines simply abdicated their role, at least until the age of high imperialism. But as we reiterate, this was also a two-way, even multivalent, traffic. Just as the binary figures of Jesuit mandarins interpreted Renaissance learning and Christian doctrine to Asia, so they emerged as the major conduit for European knowledge in Asia, at least before the age of imperialism. In any case, state and church were partners in European aggrandizement. Conflicts of interest could always be mediated. The traders needed the missionaries as linguists, cultural brokers, and intermediaries with Oriental potentates and others. Nevertheless, with notable exceptions, such as in linguistics and regional histories, church writings were simply Christian cosmologies that had to be read alongside more hardheaded letter books and treatises. But with the case of the Philippines in mind, there was also a deliberate censorship of non-Catholic books in a suffocating intellectual environment where even the temptation of secular knowledge was seen as potentially heretical to church teachings. Even so, the Jesuits played a key bridging role in interpreting the Orient for European audiences and seeking to change it through demonstration of "superior" cosmology.

We have also seen that the Catholic worldview met with a wide variety of responses across various cultures. In the Americas and the Philippines, the Iberian model of missionary discourse was confrontational, but it was also accommodating. The witch-hunts of Europe and the persecution of crypto-Jews may have found their echo in Mexico and the Philippines, but this was a pale echo. As Rafael (1993) demonstrated of the Tagalog experience, there was often a disjunction between missionary discourse and native assimilation. Simply stated, pre-Hispanic beliefs were overriding, and there is a great body of evidence to adduce that new hybrid cosmologies emerged in this encounter. Outside of the protection of Iberian fortresses and power, the missions were obliged to be even more accommodating. The rites controversy in China was a monumental case in point. Similarly, the Church in Japan was bound to disavow heresy at home in order to stay credible to believers. But even the Jesuits outlived their usefulness to the crowns of Spain and Portugal. In a word, the church canon in Asia remained canonical until breached by the scientific discoveries and knowledge gathered by the great Enlightenment-era discoverers and the voyages of Cook, Banks, Bering, La Perouse, and others.

As taken up in chapter 7, Western assumptions of modernization reaching back to the Renaissance, along with conviction in the progressive transfer of European science and Enlightenment ideas, were sorely tested by the missionary "visionaries" in the first age of globalization. This was especially so given that a great deal of obscurantism and mystification clouded the transmission and reception of religious doctrine and philosophical concepts from India to China to Japan, many widely contested and soon to be discarded in the Europe of the Reformation and Counter-Reformation.

## NOTES

1. Here we recall Said's (1983, 226–47) traveling theory or concept of the migration of ideas across time and space, including the conditions of acceptance or resistance to a new theory or idea, and the possible accommodation or incorporation of the new ideas. The general corpus of postcolonial studies has developed out of the intersection of traveling theory, culture, and locational identity.

2. The catalog of the Jesuita da Asia collection in the Ajuda library in Lisbon runs to tens of thousands of entries in some sixty codices, spanning China, Japan, Tonkin, Cochin China, Cambodia, Laos, Malacca, Manila, Goa, and Macau. The *cartas annuas,* or annual letters, of the College of Macau is another source lode. One important published compilation was *Cartas de Japão,* short title of "Letters Written by Fathers of the Company of Jesus from Japan, 1549–66," published in Coimbra in 1570. Inter alia, this work offers examples of Japanese kanji with explanation. Another example of a published compilation is the *Letter* by the Jesuit Luís Fróis (1589).

3. Kapista (1990) provides an exhaustive chronological bibliography of texts on or touching on Japan printed in Europe or by Catholic presses in Asia.

4. Also notable was the printing of Bernandino de Sahagun's *Psalmodia Christiana* (Christian Psalmody in Mexico; 1583). As a psalmody, his work represented a church-sanctioned continuation of the preconquest use of song and dance as part of the learning process in a highly oral society. But with the end of the Cromberger/Pablos monopoly, other job printers of various broadsheets, including *hojas volantes* (lit. "flying pages" or "news bulletins"), were attracted to Mexico City.

5. An Italian version of Mendoza (1586) was viewed by the author in the Southeast Asia Research Center Library, Nagasaki University.

6. Rhodes's Vietnamese collaborators include the former Buddhist monk Joachim and the scholarly catechist Ignatius, while Minh Duc, concubine of Nguyen Hoang, was an important patron (England 2001).

7. Examples of the art from the Palace Museum in Beijing were exhibited from December 16, 2001, to March 17, 2002, by the Macau Art Museum in the exhibition "The Golden Exile: Pictorial Expressions of the School of Western Missionary Artworks of the Qing Dynasty Court."

8. The bricolage effect is actually celebrated publicly in postcolonial Macau, at least in secular forms. Such is the drama "Macau Bride," a joint mainland China–Hong Kong–Macau production staged at the Macau Arts Festival in March 2001. Set in seventeenth-century Macau, it describes—in an unlikely role reversal given the historical absence of Portuguese women—the love match of a Macau (Chinese) sailor and a Portuguese girl.

# 5

# Mapping Eurasia

In this chapter, we seek to explain how, at one level, map and graphic images of Asia reflected geographical knowledge in late Renaissance Europe but also, reflexively, paved the way for European expansion, providing Cartesian empowerment to later generations of colonizers-imperialists. No other medium as well anticipated the creation of a sixteenth- and especially seventeenth-century European-dominated world system in the making. But at another level, map images reified, distorted, disguised, and even falsified terrestrial representations and the new discoveries in line with enduring Christocentric prejudices and the weight of Ptolemaic tradition as much as the need for secrecy. Nonetheless, as this chapter explores, map production cannot be seen outside of cultural blinkers, just as maps remained cultural products of their creators and their age. None of this is to deny rich traditions of indigenous Asian, including Chinese, Japanese, and Islamic, mapping, but it was the Europeans who were literally the first to depict the sphericity of the globe, to include the new discoveries, and to globalize the new representations.

## THE RISE OF EUROPEAN MAP CULTURE

To be sure, the evolution of woodblock printing techniques for print in Europe is inseparable from the early development of graphics reproduction, including maps and the science of cartography. As in China and Korea, where printing was perfected long before its mastery in Europe, innovations in the production of paper were also a prerequisite for

advances in printing. Beginning in Europe in 1460, we find the development of "block blocks" text and illustrations cut into woodblock, a practice that became common in Germany after 1470 and Italy after 1490. The
earliest maps printed by the new technology appeared in Ptolemy's *Cosmographia* in 1478, done by Arnold Bukinck at Rome. The Latin version of
Columbus's *Epistola de Insulis Nuper Inventis,* published in Basle in 1493,
also carried maplike woodcut images of his expedition. From around
1570, the engraving method began to replace the woodblock method in
European map production, especially in the hands of Italian engravers.

Before 1560, McIntyre confirms, maps were mainly handmade, few in
number, expensive, and hard to obtain and, in any case, reached only the
governing classes, the maritime classes, and the very wealthy. But thereafter, maps commenced to be mass-produced to satisfy the hunger of educated people for geographical knowledge. Engraved and printed, their
number multiplied. With the establishment of map shops and a class of
mapmakers usually dominated by family businesses, the international
circulation of maps began. First based in Venice, these artist-businessmen
also held high office as royal geographers. Besides Venice, German cartography also flourished in the fifteenth and early sixteenth centuries, including such eminent practitioners as Martin Waldseemuller, Sebastian
Munster, Theodore de Bry, and the Homen family (McIntyre 1987, 132).

The two nations most active in pioneering the new discoveries, Portugal and Spain, were also the most secretive in guarding the knowledge. In
Portugal, an office known as the Casa da Mina e India produced and revised maps and issued them to pilots on condition that they be returned
at the end of a mission. Similarly, in 1503, Spain organized the Casa de la
Contratacion de las Indias, combining trade and hydrographic questions.
It also produced a master chart called the Padron Real. Such cartographic
intelligence fed each nation's respective ambitions as to ownership of the
globe as divided by the Treaty of Tordesillas (1494). Nevertheless, leakage
from this system of royal controls led to the production of ever more sophisticated world maps, not only by Iberians but also by other centers of
map production, some of them engaging Iberians in their service.

As alluded, Gutenberg's innovation was preceded by centuries in China
and Korea, from where the methods of paper manufacture and woodblock
printing were exported to Japan, Korea, Vietnam, and Tibet. The practice
of using engraved boards for printing in Vietnam dates back to the twelfth
century (Anonymous 1977, 99). Some of the earliest surviving examples of
woodblock printing are from Japan. In thirteenth-century Korea, wood,
copper, iron, and lead were all used in the manufacture of type. Early in
the Yi dynasty (1392–1910), large quantities of copper type were used in
the production of both Buddhist scriptures and Confucian state documents. But just as the Jesuits introduced a movable-type press in Japan in

1591, so almost simultaneously Shogun Ieyasu imported Korean movable-type technology, leading to an albeit short-lived coexistence of the metal- and wooden-type press in Japan. However, Ieyasu's successors did not develop this medium, giving way to the revival and refinement of wood-block printing, or *ukiyo-e*, part of a brilliant, "information-oriented" Edo culture, a reference to the blossoming of printed booklets, Chinese reprints, maps, and images produced and consumed in the flourishing urban centers of Japan. As alluded, the movable-type press using metal typeface reappeared in Japan only in the modern period as a European import.

## OVERCOMING PTOLEMY/POLO

In his monumental study of the cartographic "construction" of India, Edney (1997, 1–16) has observed that, in the fifteenth and sixteenth centuries, Europeans conceived of Asia as a vaguely defined series of exotic and fabulously wealthy entities, notably Cathay (China), Cipangu (Japan), and the "Indies." In the Hellenistic conception, *India intra gangem* comprised lands lying between the Indus and the Ganges, while *India extra gangem* comprised all lands further east, specifically what became modern Indochina and Indonesia. It makes sense to heed Edney's understanding of how India (and other regions of Asia) came to be, sequentially, "framed" both ideologically and cartographically in line with, essentially, imperialistic ambitions.

Yet it is remarkable that the Alexandrian astronomer, mathematician, and geographer Claudius Ptolemy (A.D. 87–150) came to exert such a profound influence over the way that Europeans perceived Asia spatially long after the discoveries produced new empirical data. The Ptolemaic view of the world, it should be mentioned, introduced a three-continent picture that demarcated and framed Europe, Asia, and Africa as distinct yet connected landmasses. Besides introducing the terms for latitude and longitude, it is understood that Ptolemy collected data from merchants and travelers in the attempt to document and make sense of their tales in a spatial sense. But until his *Geographia* was published in Italy in 1477, it was the Arabs who preserved and transmitted this knowledge in manuscript collections. All together, four Ptolemaic world atlases were published in the fifteenth century, three printed from copperplate in Italy and one from woodcuts. The next three Ptolemaic atlases were published north of the Alps (Waldseemuller's in 1513, Lorenz Fries's in 1522, and Sebastian Munster's in 1549). But one major problem with so-called Ptolemaic maps was in delineating the region between the Ganges and what Ptolemy called Sinnae, or China, otherwise termed the *Aurea Chersonesus*, or Golden Peninsula, the alleged source of gold and riches. Not only did this designation and the myth of gold confuse early mapmakers, and even travelers (Columbus), it also emboldened them. Further reinforcing the Ptolemaic view, Savage has written, was the perception by the first European visitors that Solomon's Ophir was also located here. But even when the Golden Cheronese was logically identified with the Malay Peninsula loosely dividing the maritime coast between India and China (Crawfurd 1820), the myth of Ophir, Solomon, and the Golden Cheronese came to be perpetuated by even later-arriving colonial empire builders (Savage 1984, 30–32).

It is instructive in this respect to examine the world map of Henricus Martellus of 1489–1490. A German working in Florence, Martellus revised the Ptolemaic world map on the basis of Marco Polo's information on Asia and incorporated recent Portuguese voyages to Africa, including the voyage of Batholomew Diaz around the Cape of Good Hope in 1487–1488. But the 1489 Martellus map extends from the Canaries to the east coast of China, exaggerating East Asia and, according to Davis, setting the trap for Columbus. He used one version of this map to confirm his idea that Japan was only ninety degrees west of Lisbon. Famously, Columbus sought to convince European monarchs that Cipangu could be reached by sailing west as opposed to the difficult Poloean land voyage east across central Asia, although Polo also left a description of his return journey by ship from China to Aceh on the island of Sumatra to India. The Martellus world maps, then, along with Martin Behaim's globe of 1492, represent, according to Davis, "the last view of the old pre-Columbian world as perceived by Western Europe before the great expansion" through the subsequent twenty years (Davis 2001).[1]

## INCORPORATING NEW
## CARTESIAN GEOGRAPHY

Just as the Waldseemuller map set a new standard, so it was undoubtedly derivative of one or more of the planispheres leaked from Portugal. As a representation of a sphere or part of a sphere on a plane surface, the production of planispheres reached a new level of development in Portugal, especially as new knowledge produced by the discoveries came to be synthesized. The one that merits particular discussion is the Cantino world map of 1502, currently held in the Biblioteca Estenso in Italy. Inscribed in Portuguese as "chart for the navigation of the islands lately discovered in the parts of India," the 218- by 102-centimeter map drawn in color on parchment by an unknown artist was smuggled out of Portugal soon after its production by Alberto Cantino on behalf of the duke of Ferarra. Lost for a long time, it resurfaced in Italy in 1859. According to one interpretation (Davis 2001), the Cantino planisphere is "the earliest surviving Portuguese map of new discoveries in the East and West." As such, it represented a summary of knowledge of the known world at that date. Drafted just after the epochal voyages of da Gama (1497–1499) to India and Cabral (1500–1501) to Brazil, Africa is well represented, including, by name, Mozambique, Soffala, and Melindi and (unnamed) the island of Madagascar. The peninsular shape of India is represented, and the island of Ceylon is drawn to proportion. Cambaya and Calicut are named. East of India on a southward-stretching peninsula, Malaquais (Malacca) is marked as opposite the large island of Taperbane (Sumatra). Malacca is also captioned: "In this city there is all the merchandise which comes to Calicut. . . . The great majority of them comes from outside, from the land of the Chinese" (Anonymous, n.d., *Macau*, 29). Further east, "Bar" Singapore and China Cochin (Cochin China) are marked. It is plausible, as Davis (2001) postulates, that the Cantino map squeezes the longitudes east of Malacca to accommodate the Moluccas into the realm, as defined in the Treaty of Tordesillas.[2] Importantly, the Cantino planisphere is the first chart of Asia that did not follow the Ptolemaic tradition. It is also the first to show the equator and the tropics.

Magellan's circumnavigation provided a wealth of new knowledge for European cartographers. In 1529, the official mapmaker for Spain, Diego Ribeiro, assimilated this new information into his world map, albeit still an example of early *portolan* cartography, or charts derived from the empirical observation of mariners. The Ribeiro map is a landmark production in introducing the Pacific Ocean along with the names of prominent islands. But it is to Sebastian Munster that we owe the first generalized map of Asia. As featured in his *Cosmographia*, printed in Basel in 1544, this map covers a vast terrain from Arabia in the west through, as named, India to Cathay in the east. While the Indian Ocean is illustrated with a giant fish and mermaid, the archipelago off the coast of China, plausibly the Philippines and the East Indies, previously mentioned by Polo, is identified as "Archipelagas 7448."

The great contribution of the European mapmakers, according to Lach, was to gradually eliminate the Ptolemaic and Poloean conventional picture of Asia, replacing it with maps based on empirical data. Even so, the Ptolemaic version died hard. Notably, this author finds a divergence between maps up to 1570, still swayed by Ptolemaic conventions, and the more accurate and practical information reflected in *portolans*, albeit in manuscript form (Lach 1969, 218). *Portolan* maps, or maps showing sailing directions, appeared at the same time that Europeans began using the magnetic compass. First drafted to assist coastal navigation in the Mediterranean but rapidly adapted for blue-water sailing in the Atlantic, the maps offered scale of distances along with a compass rose. Ptolemy's great influence can be seen in Columbus's belief that Asia extended far further east than it does and also in the way that, until disproved by James Cook in 1755, the Indian Ocean was considered as bounded by a southern continent. Still, as alluded, Ptolemy introduced India of the Ganges River, the island of Ceylon, and even the Malay Peninsula.[3]

Despite Portuguese and Spanish activity in the Southeast Asian region stemming from the Portuguese conquest of Malacca in 1511 and the Spanish circumnavigation in 1521, information about the discoveries was only slowly incorporated on maps of the region published in Europe. Doubtless, as Fell elaborates, this state of affairs stemmed from elements of secrecy as much as inertia, as, by the 1550s, mapmaking had begun to catch up with their pace of discovery. He also explains that while few indigenous maps of Southeast Asia survive, importantly Malays and Filipinos also contributed their knowledge to these European productions (Fell 1988, 9). As discussed later in this chapter, mapmaking in, respectively, China, Korea, and Japan owed to indigenous traditions, although in the case of China in the early Qing, it came to be influenced by Jesuit conventions.

Of particular interest is Francisco Rodrigues's *Livro da Geographia Oriental* (Book of Oriental Geography; ca. 1513), a manuscript compilation unpublished until the modern period. In conjunction with Abreu's voyage from Malacca to the Moluccas, Rodrigues collected a mass of information on the East Indies, southern Asia, and China and produced several charts of the Spice Islands and the China coast founded on direct observation. These are the first European representations of China's coastal profile. In addition, it was on his chart of 1519 that the name "China," as opposed to Cathay, first appears. Even so, it was the *portolan* chart of Portuguese mapmaker Lobo Homen of 1554 that first offered a surveyed rendering of the coast of China. This was also the first chart to render Cipangu as "Japam," or Japan. The first cartographer to include Macau, founded as a Portuguese city-state in 1557, was Fernão Vaz Dourado (1520–1580) in his *Atlas de vinte folhas* of 1570. An official cartographer in the employ of Portugal, Dourado assimilated and revised data collected by the Jesuits in the east.

Rodrigues's charts were evidently used by official Portuguese mapmakers, that is, Pedro and Jorgé Reinel, in their unsigned maps of 1517–1519, revealing the eastern archipelago in some detail along with Indochina and the China coast to Guangzhou (Canton). Gaspar de Torreno (1552) also outlined the Philippines for the first time, derived from information probably acquired from survivors of the Magellan circumnavigation. The Pacific hemisphere thus entered world knowledge (Lach 1969, 217–28).

The Rodrigues tradition of direct observation and incorporating local knowledge became well established among Portuguese seafarers in the China Sea area. Such is "Mapa Topografica da região de Macao e Cantão," attributed to Jorge Pinto de Azevedo, drawn between 1630 and 1646 and compiled to alert King John IV of Portugal of difficulties in entering into commercial relations with China. According to a modern interpreter, Rui d'Avila Lourido (1994), it is probably the first known example of Portuguese cartography offering detailed information on the coast of China from

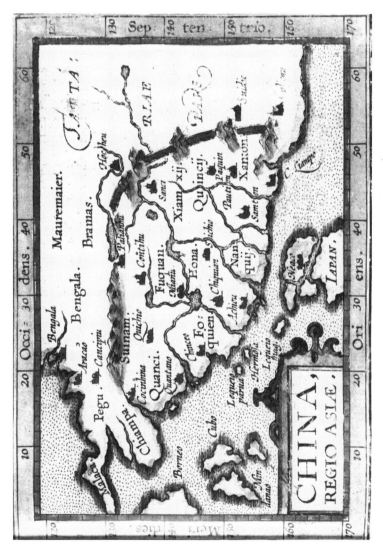

Figure 5.1. *China Regio Asiae* in Abraham Ortelius (ca. 1575). An early post-Ptolemaic map of Asia squarely placing China at the center. Japan, the Ryukyus, the Vietnamese coast, and other features could not be represented without incorporation of knowledge derived from the Portuguese voyages. It is believed that Matteo Ricci used a version of the Ortelius map to produce his own China-centered world map. (Courtesy of the Macau Historical Archives)

Hainan to the Pearl River with detailed descriptions of the Guangzhou and Macau areas, including architectural and military features. Lourido observes that some seventy-seven European maps from the sixteenth century depicted the China coast, although the majority was *mappa mundi.*

Lach also explains how the cartographers of the day were drawn into discussions by their respective protagonist-patrons, culminating in the Treaty of Saragossa of 1529, which arose out of the contest between Spain and Portugal over "ownership" of the Moluccas and the Philippines. Lach argues that between 1529 and 1548, new literary material entering maps was few. Only when the Jesuits began to operate in Asia did new materials start to circulate in Europe as cartographic documentation. Around midcentury, as explained later in this chapter, even information derived from Japanese-made maps began to arrive in Europe (Lach 1969, 217–28). Nevertheless, as Fell advises, Portuguese and Spanish maps tended to either be in manuscript form or issued only in limited numbers (Fell 1988, 8–19).

## ATLASES AND GLOBES

From about 1570, reflecting the commercial shift in gravity away from the Iberian Peninsula, globe and mapmaking came to be dominated by the Low Countries: Belgium and Holland. In about 1575, Abraham Ortelius (1527–1598) brought out *Theatrum Orbis Terrarum* (Theater of the World), a collection of maps and the forerunner of the modern atlas. We observe that Ortelius's *China Regio Asiae* incorporates information on the China area from the mid-sixteenth century. Macau, founded in 1557, is not indicated, but such Portugalized toponyms as Aracao (Aracan), Hermosa (Formosa), and Iapan (Japan) are recorded. Ortelius not only produced the most detailed charts of China of his age but, in his *Maris Pacifica* of 1589, literally put a new spin on Eurocentricity. Bordered by the Americas to the east, this map takes as its base an undifferentiated southern landmass titled "Terra Australis," while its western boundary is framed by a huge "Nova Guinea," the Philippine islands, the coast of China, and a poorly defined Japan.

Gerhard Mercator (1512–1594) was responsible for developing the well-known projection that bears his name. Jodocus Hondius (1563–1612), a notable engraver of maps, inherited the Mercator family collection, including *Insulae Indiae Orientalis.* His map of *America Meridionalis,* as published in the Purchas collection, also heralded the existence of the *Mare Pacifica.* In turn, the Hondius family business was taken over by notable mapmaker Jan Janson (1588–1664). His contemporary, Willem Janszoon Blaeu (1571–1638), founder of another mapmaking dynasty, was particularly prolific (Fell 1988, 15). Blaeu's *Atlas Novus* was completed by his son

Jean and published as *Atlas Maior* in 1642 along with numerous other lavishly executed editions produced by the Blaeu family.

Importantly, the first of the Blaeu atlases incorporated the *Novus Atlas Sinensus* by Jesuit Martinus Martini (1614–1661), first published in Amsterdam in 1655. Based on Chinese sources collected by Martini during his eight-year sojourn in Macau and China, this work was considered superior in its day. Besides separate maps of China and Japan, revealing Korea as a peninsula, the richly illustrated *Atlas* offered maps of fifteen individual provinces of China plus one good map of *Imperii Sinarum Nova Descriptio* and one *Japonia Regnum*. In this, Martini critically used Chinese sources, probably including sources taken to Italy by the Florentine merchant Francesco Carletti and, above all, as revealed recently, the cartographic work of Jesuit Michele Ruggiero (Bencardino 1998, 31). As part of the *Atlas Maior sive Cosmographia Blauiane,* it was often translated and, in 1655, came out in French, Dutch, Spanish, and German translations.

While there were many other Dutch mapmakers of renown whose names are associated with Southeast Asia, by the second half of the seventeenth century, France emerged as a new center of mapmaking, especially associated with the Sanson dynasty founded by Nicolas Sanson d'Abbeville (1600–1667). Notable, as discussed later in this chapter, was the achievement of Jean Baptiste d'Anville (1697–1782) in producing the path-blazing *Nouvel Atlas de la Chine* (1737), superseding the work of Martini. In 1752, Anville also constructed the *Carte de l'Inde,* the first modern "framing" of India. Jacques Nicolas Bellin (1703–1772), official hydrographer of the French king, emerged as the most important French cartographer of his age. His *Le Petit Atlas Maritime,* published in Paris in 1764, included reproductions of many of his earlier charts in smaller format along with fresh material amounting to 580 charts of Asian, African, and American locations. Bellin also introduced to European audiences maps of cities of China, such as *Plan de la Ville et du Port de Macao* (1748), as well as maps of Beijing, Guangzhou, and so on, most of which were printed in Prevost's *Histoire Générale des Voyages* (1746–1770).

The most renowned of the early mapmakers in England was John Speed, publisher in 1627 of *Prospect of the Most Famous Parts of the World* (Fell 1988, 17). Notable also was the enterprise of Sir Robert Dudley (1573–1649), an Englishman working under the patronage of the grand duke of Tuscany who published his own atlas, *Del Arcano del Mare* (Secrets of the Sea), in Florence in 1646 and 1661. Another was Herman Moll, an immigrant, probably from Bremen, who arrived in London in the mid-1670s. As mentioned, Moll made a number of maps that were printed in the works of such friends and confidants of geographical knowledge as Dampier, Funnell, and Rogers. Moll's crowning achievement was the folio atlas *The World Described* (1715–1754), comprising thirty large two-sheet maps of all parts of the world, inter alia heralding the dawn of the British Empire (Reinhartz 1997). Moll's *West Part of India, or the Empire of the Great Mogul,* published in his *Atlas Geographicus* (1717), offers, in the opinion of Edney (1997, 7–8), "one of the first maps to show India in is modern conception."

The rise of the atlas was also accompanied by the production of globes, useful for representing the distance between any two places on earth. Columbus, Magellan, and Del Cano were evidently armed with globes. All the big names entered this science, including Waldseemuller (1509), Mercator (1541), the Italians, and, by the very early seventeenth century, the Dutch school, including the van Langren, Hondius, Blaue, Jansen, and Goos families. We have mentioned the Martin Behaim globe of 1492 as marking a watershed between the pre-Colombian world and the age of discovery. Even so, Behaim, a Nurenberg-based explorer-cartographer, embellished the Ptolemaic picture of Asia not only with Poloean interpretations but also with knowledge gained from his stint in Lisbon as member of the mathematical junta or council. As Davis summarizes, Behaim's globe was designed to demonstrate to European kings and patrons the ease by which Europe could reach Japan and China by sailing west. Following the pattern set by Martellus, the coast of China is portrayed as eighty degrees west of the Canaries (Davis 2001).

The European production of globes expanded after Behaim, in part as navigational aids, although, as discussed later in this chapter, heliocentricity was propounded by Copernicus only in 1530 and would be long resisted by the "flat-earthers" of the day. Stevenson (1921) demonstrates that only in the second quarter of the sixteenth century, globe and plain maps mirrored the general acceptance that the New World was but a prolongation or eastward extension of the Asian continent. Hitherto, the newly discovered lands were represented as having no geographical connection with the Old World. However, by the third quarter, Mercator again led the push at representing a large body of water separating Asia from the northern continent. But by the first half of the eighteenth century, celestial and terrestrial globes were superseded for shipboard use by flat maps. As with the sequential "framing" of Asia Minor (Turkey), the Holy Land, Persia, and India, so, as elaborated later in this chapter, Japan, Korea, "Tartaria," the vast unknown inner Asian perimeter of China, the East Indies, the Philippines, and the "Indian" and "Pacific" oceans all became incorporated into the ideological compass of European maps, such as those produced by Munster, Ortelius, Mercator, and Blaue, building on and improving the Ptolemaic type. In the following pages, we sketch the successive framing of discrete regions of Asia by European cartographers.

## MAP REPRESENTATIONS OF
## SIBERIA AND CENTRAL ASIA

The Russian conquest of the vast lands extending from the Ural Mountains to the Pacific, along with its mapping, offers an intriguing perspective on the Eurasian encounter. Beginning with the Cossack campaign of Ataman Yermak in 1581 (1579 in some accounts), opening the Irtysh valley to the Russians, the Siberian khanate came to an end with the defeat of the khan Kuchum in 1598. From 1661, Irkutsk became the center of a vast region comprising Cis-Baikal and Trans-Baikal, with the frontiers progressively extended to natural boundaries by the beginning of the eighteenth century. The area around the Amur River had acquired special importance with the conclusion of the Treaty of Nerchinsk between Czar Peter the Great (r. 1672–1725) and the Kangxi emperor (r. 1662–1723). Czarist designs on Tibet also date back to the early eighteenth century, albeit restricted to encroachments on Lamaist communities on the frontier with China.

Eventually, new evocations of continental Asia, including "Tatary," broadly defined as central Asia including Siberia and Manchuria, began to appear, as in Anthony Jenkins's (Jenkinson's) *Russaiae, Moroviae, et Tartarie Descripto* (1562), a production arising out of the author's travels in Russia and Asia. The form of Tartary-Siberia was improved with Abraham Ortelius's *Tartariae Sive Magni Chami Regni Typus*, done at Antwerp in 1570. Appearing in the *Teatrum Orbis Terrarum* atlas of 1570, it was also the first printed map of the region. *Tartariea Iodocus Hondius* (1600) also assimilated results of the expedition of Willem Barents to Novaya Zemlya (1595–1597). Even so, this map still reflected Ptolemy's conception of a north shore of Asia washed by a "quiet sea of Russians." Another version of Tatary appeared in Jan Janssen's *Tartaria Siva Magni Chami Imperium*, published in Amsterdam in 1647.

Still, it would take a century before the old conception of Tatary would be radically revised. This was accomplished in 1687, when Nicolas Witsen (1641–1717), the enterprising burgomaster of Amsterdam, subsequently published his *Noord en Oost Tartaryen* (North and East Tartary; 1692), in part as a text-guide to a map published seven years earlier comprising Siberia, Mongolia, China, and Persia. But by the early decades of the eighteenth century, far more exact maps of the Russian Empire were compiled using geodic survey methods. Commenced in Russia in 1721, the survey assimilated new materials derived from, for example, the expeditions in 1728 and 1741 of Danish-born explorer in the employ of the czars, Virus Bering, to Kamchatka and the strait that bears his name. Notably, it was Bering who announced that Asia and America were separate. Maps and atlases produced by the St. Petersburg Academy of Sciences, along with those drawing on intensive expeditionary and survey activity, were as much concerned with setting down boundaries as with framing Russian space in its sprawling Asian Far East, not excepting Russian America, a reference to Alaska. By the eighteenth century, the northern and eastern borders of the Asian continent were defined and mapped, the correlation between the Asian continent and North America had been established, and the sea route linking Okhotsk, Kamchatka, and Japan had been established (Prolova 2000).

## MAPPING CHINA

Building on the Ptolemaic and Poloean traditions, the general image of China had been built into the first of the great European atlases. But the detailed mapping of interior China would await the passage to Beijing in 1601 of Matteo Ricci. Until his death in Beijing in 1610, Ricci produced several Chinese versions of the European *mappa mundi*. One of the treasures that Ricci brought to China in 1601 had been a copy of *Typus Orbis Oriental* from Ortelius's 1570 *Atlas*. In modifying Ortelius to place China near the center of his world map, Ricci also sought to accommodate Chinese pride of place as the Central Kingdom. Ricci's revolutionizing contribution was to introduce the concept of the five-continent spherical earth to the Chinese, who since antiquity had held to a flat-earth view even though acknowledging the existence (as proven by the great Ming voyages) of outlying continents. Neither had the Chinese cartographic tradition grasped the importance of longitude and latitude, such as conveyed on the European charts. According to one student of Chinese cartography, Richard J. Smith, the fact that the Jesuit picture contained the pre-Copernican notion that the sun revolved around the earth was of no particular consequence. In any case, the legacy of Ricci and his successors in China was limited. As discussed in chapter 7, not only did they face the opposition of cultural conservatives, but the Christian mission itself was formally banned in 1724. Smith (1996, 46–47, 54–59) concludes that from the late seventeenth to the early nineteenth century, the vast majority of Chinese mapmakers ignored Jesuit constructions of the world almost entirely. One exception is that names of distant places first coined by Ricci continue to be used in Chinese cartography.

Smith (1996, 3) has also reflected that, whereas from about 1500 on cartographers in the West viewed space as "bounded, static and therefore measurable," traditional Chinese concepts of space emphasized dynamism and fluidity, investing physical space with "deep, multivalent cultural meaning." But central to China's self-image in its dealing with foreign countries (*waiguo*) was the Sinocentric tributary system and the conceit of Chinese superiority over other peoples of the world. Not only did the Chinese record textual descriptions of aliens from an early period, but they also produced visual images. Smith (1996, 19–22) observes that the most comprehensive illustrated account produced over many centuries was the *Huang qing zhigong tu* (Illustrations of the Tribute Bearing People of the Qing), produced in 1731. The list included not only ethnic minorities but also such overseas tributaries as Korea, the Liuqiu islands, Annam, Siam, Sulu, Laos, Burma, and even, in confused manner, European countries. Chinese maps also reflected Sinocentricity with China occupying center place.

To be sure, from Roman times on, all imperial powers positioned themselves at the center of their respective spheres of influence. Obviously, China's sense of its centrality evolved through its long dynastic history, especially with its own discovery of the world. As Needham (1954, 179; 1959, 490) reveals, small Chinese merchant ships had been sailing to the Malacca Straits area by A.D. 350, reaching Ceylon by the fourth century and Aden by the following century, even entering the Red Sea and Persian Gulf. However, from the eighth century on, Arab traders dominated the sea routes from East Africa to the southern China coast, just as, by the early fifteenth century, the Arab world was preeminent in its geographical knowledge of Africa from north to south. Waley-Cohen (1999, 37–38) demonstrates that Sung China (960–1276) made a series of major technical advances related to geography, astronomy, mapmaking, and shipbuilding. They invented the compass, and every ship carried one. Arab or Muslim colonies on China's coast, especially Quanzhou or Zayton in Polo's description, were important centers of transmission of knowledge.

Building on Song Chinese knowledge of the maritime trade routes gained through Islamic contacts, Mongol control of the terrestrial "silk roads" led to the introduction of new knowledge. Notably, in 1267, Persian astronomer Jamil al-Din established a new calendar for Kublai while also introducing a Persian-style terrestrial globe and other astronomical instruments. Guo Shoujing (1231–1316) later adopted these instruments for Chinese needs at the Beijing observatory, such as witnessed by the first-arriving Jesuits. While Jesuit astronomers would eventually find favor in the Ming court, it is important to remember that, building on Islamic knowledge, Mongolian mapmakers had already acquired a conception of a world that also embraced Africa and Europe (cf. Waley-Cohen 1999, 42–43).

Not even the introduction of Islamic cartographic influences during the Mongol Yuan dynasty (1280–1368), along with mathematical principles, could dislodge the tradition of Chinese cartography to produce maps based on general knowledge acquired in voyages. Even so, the great Ming voyages, reaping vast new geographical information, as discussed in a following chapter, did not profoundly alter traditional mapping, even if they led to the production of sailing charts for practical purposes. Aside from the Jesuit interlude, Chinese mapmakers simply saw no need to establish a purely mathematical cartography even to modern times. Smith (1996, 60–75) cites a number of Qing productions that combine cartography with cosmology. Even so, neo-Confucian critics of Chinese geomancy began to find allies in the Jesuit visitors at the court.

It was under the Qing (1644–1911), however, that Jesuit cartographers achieved preeminence at the court, especially in the actual surveying of large tracts of China and otherwise accumulating hard data in the production of even more accurate Chinese maps. The project commenced in 1700 under the Kangxi emperor (r. 1662–1722), who commanded the Jesuits (Bouvet, Régis, and Perenin) to survey the environs of Beijing. For the Qing, both surveying and mapping were viewed as a tool for the consolidation of the empire (including the newly incorporated Formosa/Taiwan) and vast stretches of Siberia acquired under the 1689 Treaty of Nerchinsk and as the prerequisite for good interior defenses. To this end, in 1708, Kangxi commanded the Jesuits to chart the length of the Great Wall. The following year, Manchuria and eastern Siberia were mapped, followed in 1713 by Shanxi and Shaanxi. Other missionaries had been dispatched to Mongolia in 1710. Notably, the emperor sought to extend strategic bases in the vast area inhabited by the nomadic Mongol tribes. Mapping the Amur River was charged to the Jesuits Regis, Jartoux, and Fridelli, part of a strategy to consolidate diplomatic gains with Russia. According to the account of French missionary Jean-Baptise du Halde, "Tho' it was empty enough—the emperor was well pleased with [it]." Finally, in 1721, the Jesuits completed their work in the sense of determining the longitude and latitude of hundreds of points within the Chinese domain as well as measuring distances between key points. Kane observes that the vast holes in their surveying, including off-limit areas in Tibet and Korea, were met by Chinese sources of information (Kane 2000).[4]

The results of the Jesuit survey were published in the *Huangyu quanlan tu* (Map of Comprehensive View of Imperial Territory), printed from woodblocks. First presented to the throne in 1718, additional copies printed between 1717 and 1726 added maps of Tibet and Korea. Versions of the "Kangxi," or Jesuit atlas, reached French King Louis XV in 1725 (Kane 2000), allowing, as mentioned, Jean Baptiste d'Anville to produce in his *Nouvel Atlas de la Chine* (1737) the first reasonable conception of the "Celestial Empire." Only exploration and actual survey work would lead to revisions of his rendition, or "framing," of Qing China. In turn, du Halde republished the maps, including the rare Tibet map and the first map depiction of part of Alaska, in his four-volume *Description . . .* (1735). He also offered a description of Mongolia.

Elliot (2000, 626) also explains that, by the early nineteenth century, Chinese, Japanese, and European maps superseded "Tatary" altogether. This new "framing" occurred in tandem with the Qing court's desire to substantiate its territorial claims and, at the same time, to firmly establish Manchu identity. Seen in this light, according to Smith (1996, 54), the most important Qing bequest to modern China was simply its geography. By harnessing Renaissance cartographers to imperial ambition, the Kangxi emperor expanded the bounds of the Middle Kingdom to encompass Tibet, Manchuria, and large swathes of central Asian frontier lands. Undeniably, Jesuit endeavor assisted this imperial project. Notably, the *Huangyu qualan tu* remained the primary source of geographical information on China until the twentieth century.

Overall, Needham is more equivocal as to the superiority of European techniques, asserting that China was actually ahead of all other countries in mapmaking. Besides, the Jesuit, Mongol, and Manchu travelers all made their contributions to Chinese geographical knowledge. But even between East and West, as Needham interprets, there was an interweaving of influences, a one-way transmission of Renaissance cartography to China and the reverse transmission of geographical information from East Asia to Europe (Needham 1959, 583–90). It is also true, as discussed by Smith (1996, 54–59), that at the end of the day Jesuit cartographic influence remained limited in China. In part, this was due to the fate of the Jesuit mission in China, as discussed in chapter 4, but was also linked with the rise of a tradition in Chinese scholarship of drawing only selectively on Western scientific knowledge. From the late seventeenth to the early nineteenth century, the majority of Chinese mapmakers discarded Jesuit constructions and mathematical principles entirely by returning to Song-dynasty models. If mapmaking is strictly defined in positivistic terms with a concern for scale and measurement, then the Europeans were possibly ahead, but if we appreciate maps, as in the Chinese tradition, that were grounded in cultural aesthetic, allowing written commentary and moral maxims to take over, then Needham is probably correct.

## THE EUROPEAN MAPPING OF JAPAN

The European mapping of Japan took slow form, even though the depiction of Cipangu reached back to the Middle Ages. In 1528, the Venetian cartographer Benedetto Bordone (1460–1531) produced his *Isolario,* or atlas of islands, including a woodblock map of Cipangu, presumably echoing Polo's Cipangu. Martin Waldseemuller's *Tabula superiorus Indiae & Tarteriae maiorus* of 1522 advanced on Ptolemy by adding knowledge derived from Polo. The result was that Japan appeared on this map in the form of a trapezium-shaped island. It would be some time before the three main islands of Japan—Honshu, Kyushu, and Shikoku—were separately represented and even longer before the northern frontier island of Japanese expansion, Hokkaido, was depicted.

No advance on the cartography of Japan could have been made without reference to indigenous material. Japanese cartography has its origins at least back to the *gyogi-zu*-type maps of A.D. 805 but remained stereotyped over 800 years. As described by historian Charles Boxer (1951, 133–34), these maps are characterized by the round or oval form given to each of the sixty-six provinces. Boxer is adamant that certain data in maps by Fernão Vaz Dourado, Luis Teixeira, and other Portuguese cartographers, usually compiled in Goa, were derived from *Gyogi-zu*. One such hybrid Portuguese-Japanese map, dated 1585, as examined by the Japanese scholar H. Nakamura, has been located in archives in Florence.

With the appearance of a map in a work by Ramusio in 1553, the term "Giapam" first makes an appearance. Early representations of Japan included that by Lazaro Luis in 1563 and then, in 1568, by Fernão Vaz Dourado. Contacts between the Jesuit Luis Teixeira and Abraham Ortelius led to the production in Antwerp of *Iaponiae Insulae Descriptio* (1595), the most accurate map of Japan extant from the sixteenth century, entering Ortelius's *Theatre de l'Univers* in 1598 and *Theatro d'el Orbe de la Tierra* in 1612. Korea is still represented as an island, but good form is given to the three main islands of Japan. The fact that the map includes toponyms related to parts of Honshu not conceivably visited by Europeans suggests that Teixiera and Ortelius, who had never visited Japan, benefited from a range of information supplied secondhand by Japanese informants. Linschoten also included in his *Itinerario . . .* (1596) a map of Japan, Korea, the Luchu (Ryukyu islands), and the China coast engraved by Arnold van Langren, apparently a copy of a map by Portuguese cartographer Bartolomeu Lasso. Such toponyms as Firanso (Hirado), Kagoshima, Tanaxuma (Tanegashima), and Nara appear. *Minas da prata* (silver mines) are also marked, just as "Hiwami" (Iwami) silver mines appear on the Ortelius maps. Korea begins to make an appearance, albeit as an island, while Honshu is not yet optimal. Neither was there an agreed European standard on orthography, as nations and individual authors continued to offer their own versions (cf. Michel 1993, 48–50). Honshu long appeared in European maps as a turtle-shaped image bereft of even a hint of the large northern island of Hokkaido, not yet part of Japanese imperial domain. In the period before the Dutch and English gained a toehold in Japan, Jodocus Hondius produced a map of Japan in 1606 based on Portuguese sources. Also drawing on Portuguese (and Dutch) sources was the map of the Formosa-Ryukyu area by Sir Robert Dudley. This was *Carta Particolare d'una Parte della Costa di China con lInsola de Pakas, e Altre Isole* (1646) from his *Atlas*. Tanegashima is marked as "Tanez," the Anami islands as "Lequeio m[a]gg[o]re," and Ryukyu as "Leque Minore."

Dutch cartography on Japan gained second wind with the designation of Batavia as a second cartographic center for the Dutch East India Company under Hendrick Brouwer's administration in 1632. This initiative, too, was linked with exploration and the quest for new sources of gold and silver. Such was the impetus behind the expedition of 1643 under the command of Maerten Gerrits Vries along the hitherto unexplored eastern coast of Japan, including the unknown Hokkaido and Sakhalin. Eventually, the "discoveries" of the Vries expedition were disseminated in

Figure 5.2. Map of Nagasaki port and town by Jacques Nicolas Bellin (1744). The port of Nagasaki, revealing the fan-shaped artificial island of Deshima, was the single European window on Japan during the *sakoku*, or closed country, epoch of the Tokugawa despotism. (Author's collection)

printed form as part of the 1645 world map by John Blaeu and the *Nova et Accurata Japaniae* done by Johannes Janssonius in 1652 (cf. Sieboldt 1859). While this reproduction led to new distortions—notably, the failure to distinguish Hokkaido as an island—the influences of this interpretation persisted into the nineteenth century (Michel 1993, 38–39).

Michel also explains how the annual Dutch journeys to the court in Edo (Tokyo) found their counterpart in the Arnoldus Montanus map of 1669, followed by Jean-Baptiste Tavernier's map of the Tokaido (great north road) of 1679 and François Valentijn's of 1726. Both Montanus and Tavernier reveal the sea route around the northern side of Kyushu. Valentijn, for the first time, signals the land route between Nagasaki and Kokura. But it was Engelbert Kaempfer who (ca. 1716), secretly using a compass, mapped the entire route, naming all places from Nagasaki to Edo (Michel 1993, 37).

## MAP PRODUCTION IN JAPAN

Having alluded to the longevity of *gyogi*-type maps in Japan, we should also acknowledge that the Tokugawa accomplished major countrywide mapping and surveys. Beginning with the construction of *han*, or domain maps, complete maps of the country were achieved as the era progressed. As Yonemoto (2000, 648) has revealed, far more spectacular was the rise of indigenous Japanese map publishing commensurate with the expansion of a market economy and the rise of a thriving urban culture. She cites the singular example of mapmaker-artist Ishikawa Ryusen (?–1713), who specialized in maps of urban Edo. Kaempfer also illegally exported Ishikawa's maps of Japan. We could also offer the example of the *Tokaido bunken ezu* (1690), a map of the Tokaido by Ochikochi Doin, later celebrated in woodblock print by Hiroshige Ando (1797–1858). Yonemoto describes such aesthetic productions as conforming to a "spatial vernacular" otherwise associated with cultural practices before the advent of standardized geographical practices. Citing Mathew Edney (1993), Yonemoto offers Tokugawa Japan as a case of "cartography without progress" in contrast to the Western teleological sense of scientific progress. Map production in Tokugawa Japan, she argues, did not "trump" other forms of knowledge and, as such, entered a "process of cultural and political exchange, debate and contestation." This is true, but considerable local initiative was also made on several fronts, namely, in the production of world maps and in the mapping of Japan's expanding realm.

The importation into Japan in 1603 of Ricci's world map, as created for the Chinese court, set the stage for the Japanese study and eventual production of world maps, literally revolutionizing geographical awareness, even though, as explained in chapter 7, Buddhalogical cosmographies also prevailed. The earliest "modern" world map published in Japan is the *Bankoku sozu* (Complete Map of the Peoples of the World), printed from woodblocks in Nagasaki and disseminated in 1645. Meant for popular education, this map was inscribed with place names written in katakana. It was more than just a map, as it included a considerable amount of astronomical information. Ricci taught not only the concept of the sphericity of the earth but also the concept of climatic zones, continents, longitude, and latitude (Ayusawa 1964; Frei 1984).

Derivatives of the Ricci map remained popular until the early nineteenth century. Meanwhile, however, other maps in European languages came to be imported via Deshima. Joan Blaue's world map of 1639 was one that was translated into Japanese in 1786 by *rangaku* scholar and physician Katsuragawa Hosho (1751–1809). A Nicolas Sanson atlas of 1692 was another source. English world maps followed by Russian world maps also became sources by the early 1800s. In 1794, Shiba Kokan produced a map projection featuring western and eastern hemispheres, reproductions of which even reached street vendors in Edo, where demand was high. Copper etched maps eventually succeeded woodcut maps, but hand painting and coloring were also in vogue. As with European maps, explanatory text or images were often added (Ayusawa 1953, 123–27).

Even so, there is evidence of a great deal of borrowing and assimilation of world knowledge stemming from Japanese contacts with the Dutch at Deshima and during their annual procession to the shogunal court. For example, in 1639, Nagasaki-born Nishikawa Joken, a student of astronomy and calendar making, produced *Ka-i tsûchô*, a compilation on the geography of the "known" world. Part I covered China, while part II covered Korea, Ryukyu, Taiwan, Southeast Asia, and Western countries. A 1708 revision offered expanded information on Indochina, the East Indies, England, Africa, and Oceania.

Initiative and progress was also made in Edo Japan in expanding geographical knowledge, especially in the part of the world that concerned its immediate interests. Notably, in 1794, Katsuragawa Hosho published the fruits of his independent research on the expanding Russian frontier in Siberia in *Hokusa bunryaku*. This he accomplished by interviewing Daidokuya Kodayu, a seaman from Ise who had drifted to Russian-held territory and had returned to Japan with critical geographical information. Katsuragawa also incorporated maps brought back from Russia by Daidokurya inscribed with toponyms in Russian and Japanese scripts. But Russian-Japanese contacts reached back to 1697 from the time when Japanese explorer-adventurer Denbei was marooned on the Kamchatka coast, then being explored by Ukrainian-born Cossack Vladmir Atlasov. In Moscow in 1702, Denbei served as a source of information on Japan for Czar Peter, then expanding trade and settlements in the Russian Far East, leading to the foundation of Okhotzk in 1722 (cf. Sansom 1977, 212–19).

According to Ayusawa (1953, 124), the world map of Takahashi Ayusawa, the *Shintei bankoku zenzu* (New Universal Map), reached the highest standard yet in Japan from a scientific point of view. Among other sources, Takahashi used English mapmaker A. Arrowsmith's map of 1780. Observing that Sakhalin was not indicated on European world maps, Takahashi dispatched his agent to explore the region. Having discovered its insular character, the agent entered this information on Takahashi's map of 1810, thus filling in gaps in the new world maps then being produced in England. Just as informal Japanese-Russian contacts increased, so the Russian presence in Kamchatka and the Kuriles expanded. In 1739, the second expedition by Bering to Siberia was sighted off Shimoda. In 1770–1771, Count Mauritius Augustus de Benyowsky, a Hungarian political refugee, called at the Ryukyus, warning the Dutch at Nagasaki and alerting the Japanese of Russian expansionism (cf. Sansom 1977, 212–19).

In any case, as woodblock printing techniques improved during the Edo period and as new countrywide geographical knowledge came to be assimilated, domestic mapmaking became more sophisticated. For example, in 1775, the geologist Nagakubo Sekisui compiled the first latitudinal map of Japan, the *Kaisei Nihon yochi rotei zensu*. The first complete map of the Japanese archipelago including Hokkaido and the southern Kuriles, mirroring an expanded framing of the Japanese nation, was initiated in 1800 by Ino Tadataka and Takahashi Kageyasu and completed twenty years later. By 1821, the country was mapped for the first time using European survey techniques. To strike a comparison, the Great Trigonometrical Survey of British India was launched only in 1802 and was not completed until many decades later.

## KOREA MAPPED

Known vaguely in Europe since the time of Marco Polo, Korea (or Corea) was rediscovered by the Portuguese from their trading posts and networks in Malacca, Macau, and the island of Hirado in Japan. However, it was the Dutch who offered the first descriptions of Korea following attacks on Dutch shipping straying into Korean waters, as occurred in 1622 and again in 1653 with the shipwreck of Hendrik Hamel and associates on Cheju island. First appearing on European maps as an island, in *Iaponia* (1633) Jodocus Hondius added a note expressing doubt. The European mapping of Korea, however, reached maturity only with the *Atlas Sinensis* map of Blaue and his "Hanging Island of Corea or Chaosien," derived from the Jesuit Martinus Martini, who, in turn, gained his information from Chinese or Korean maps. To be sure, cartographic information pertaining to Korea increased dramatically in Holland after Hamel and company made their dramatic escape from captivity in Korea to the Dutch trading post on Nagasaki. Hamel bequeathed no map, but his depiction of Cheju as Quelpaert endured on European maps for the next two centuries. Notably, by the eighteenth century, Korea was depicted on the map of Nicolas Witsen (1641–1717), as attached to his study of Tatarie (cf. Savenije 2002). But the Jesuit contribution is explicitly acknowledged by J. N. Bellin in his *La Chine . . .*, printed in Paris in 1748.

One of the traditions Korea shared with China was in mapmaking, along with a shared sense of geomantic conceptualization of land and space. In other words, cultural elements were combined with empirical knowledge. As with China, Japan, and Ryukyu, Koreans gained geographical knowledge of Asia through direct trade contacts. Thus, the *Ch'onhado* (Map of All under Heaven), a representation originating from the sixteenth or early seventeenth century, was copied with little change into the nineteenth century. Japan, the Ryukyus, and the "islands" of Cambodia and Thailand were included, along with Korea and the Chinese landmass. While the central landmass (the China area) and islands combined real with mythological places, an outer ring of land on the mandela-style map features entirely fictional places. Not only was the insularity of Cambodia and Thailand, Suárez (1999, 50) interprets, a cultural spin on other lands, but, as with early Western portrayal of Korea as an island, Koreans may have also misrepresented these distant destinations as islands. Even so, Suárez believes that the map did not reflect the best societal knowledge of the region at the time, suggesting that the traders and sailors knew more.

## MAPPING VIETNAM AND SIAM

As heir to the Sinitic tradition, Vietnam, like Korea, not only figured in Chinese maps but also drew from the Chinese tradition of mapmaking. The Sino-Vietnamese–style map of Dong Do (Hanoi) executed in 1470 is a case in point (Anonymous 1977). Other imperial geographies include *Thien nam tu chi lo do thu* (Book of Maps of the Four Cardinal Points of the Southern Country), first drawn in 1630. We can say that indigenous representations of space in Vietnam began to change only with the colonial cadastral survey of central Vietnam conducted in 1814 (Nguyen 1993, 117–27). Suárez has drawn attention to *Regnu Annam*, a separate map of Vietnam from Alexander Rhodes's (1650) *Relazione de' Felici Successi della Sante Fede nel Regno di Tunchino*. Situating Hanoi in relation to Macau and Hainan as well as boundaries with Laos, Cambodia, and Champa, Rhodes's map of Tonkin is striking for the depiction and names of rivers. Another map of the entire Vietnamese coast from this period is by the Dutch merchant Daniel Tavernier, first published by his brother Jean-Baptiste in 1679. Richly annotated in Dutch, it mixes fact with fiction. Doubtless, William Dampier, who visited Vietnam in 1687, added to English cartographic knowledge of this country, especially Condore (Con Son) island, which he charted (Suárez 1999, 216–17). More accurate renderings of parts of the Vietnam coast appeared only in the eighteenth century. Such was J. N. Bellin's *Carte du Cours de la Riviére de Tunquin depuis Cacho Jusqu'a la Mer, Levée par un Navigateur Anglais,* appearing in Prevost's *Histoire Générale des Voyages* (1746).

Although Siam had been visited by the Portuguese shortly after they arrived in Malacca, the kingdom made an appearance only on Ramusio's map of 1554, the Linschoten map of 1595, and, together with Pegu, on the Vaz Dourado map of 1570. With expanding knowledge brought to Europe by traders, missionaries, and others, Siam came to be better represented on the maps of Blaue, Jan Jansonn, and others, with the usual rider that the coastal areas were better represented than the interiors (Fell 1988, 73). Even so, the relative positions of Siam, Laos, and Cambodia featured on seventeenth-century French maps only in the most impressionistic style. We discuss "Buddhalogical" concepts of space in chapter 7.

## MAPPING THE EASTERN ARCHIPELAGO

Island Southeast Asia entered European geographical knowledge with the passage of the first caravels through the Straits of Malacca. Notably, a map of Java and part of Sumatra appeared in the first edition of João de Barros's *Decadas da India* (1552). Even so, Arab travelers and traders amassed a corpus of texts on Asian lands, including the Southeast Asian region, beginning from the early seventh century (Tibbetts 1979). In his 1154 *Book of Delights,* Al-Idrisi mentioned sites that can be identified with Java, Sumatra, Brunei, and Luzon, among others. However, over the centuries, Arab mapping of Southeast Asia assimilated many mythological elements not improved even by Ibn Batuta's firsthand observations. Nevertheless, reflecting Arab maritime activity in the region, navigational texts were superior even if, in the opinion of Suárez (1999, 51–53), "they are often ambiguous and inconsistent." The earliest surviving Arab pilot texts, replete with compass bearings and latitudes, are those of Ahmad bin Majid (a figure linked by tradition to Vasco da Gama's voyage to India) and Sulamein al-Mahri, dating from the fifteenth century. The focal points of these guides are Malacca, Singapore, Java, and Zaitan (Quanzhou) in China, with Timor identified as the easternmost destination.

However, as Suárez (1999, 51–53) summarizes, when Portuguese explorers reached the East Indies, the Arab geographical concept of Southeast Asia had stagnated for three centuries, at least alongside the rising Persian and Turkish geographies. By the seventeenth or early eighteenth century, Arabic mapping of Southeast Asia was beginning to utilize European sources. Ottoman knowledge of Asia was crystallized by Halifa Mustafa bin Abdullah (Katip Celebi) (1609–1657), whose atlas *cihannuma* (Mirror of the World), printed in 1732, was based primarily on Arab cartography but was also influenced by Mercator's *Atlas Minor*, which he examined in 1648. An example of his synthetic approach is his map of the southern Philippines and Borneo, part of a larger work covering India and Southeast Asia.

Even so, the question of indigenization of Arab and Ottoman geographical knowledge in the Malay world remains problematic for the modern historian, especially given the paucity of surviving indigenous mapping from this part of the world. Indeed, European observers denigrated Malay geographical knowledge and navigation. Referring to the people of the Malay sultanate of Patani, which he visited in 1662, Dutchman Nieuhoff (Churchill and Churchill 1704, vol. 2, 220) offers, "When we named some countries to them, they laughed at us, affirming we only talked about some town or village, their geographical knowledge of the coast reaching no further than Siam, by reason of the little traffic they have with strangers further from them." Yet Patani was a place connected by trade with the Ryukyu kingdom, Malacca, and beyond, suggesting that Nieuhoff was deceived or that Patani's memory of its former splendor faded. An even more negative view of "Malay" geography entered the writings of Crawfurd (1820, 317–26), who declaimed, "The figure of the earth, and the relation of the parts to each other, are wholly unknown to them."

Also arriving in the archipelago from the Indian Ocean, as with the Portuguese, the Dutch first mapped the Maldives and Ceylon (the Langenes map of 1599), Sumatra, the straits, Java, and Bali. The earliest printed map devoted to any island of the archipelago that was derived from firsthand information was that of Sumatra prepared by the master copperplate engraver Gastaldi. But the quest for control over the source of spices in the Moluccas awaited advanced cartographic knowledge of hitherto uncharted regions. Two fragments of the archipelagic charts of Francisco Rodrigues were reproduced in *Atlas do Visconte de Santarém*. One delineates eastern Java, Madura, Bali, Lamboque (Lombok), and Sumbawa and the other Cabo das Frolles (Flores), Solor, and Ceram (Leitão 1948, 39–52).

But it was not until the Magellan expedition brought back to Europe detailed knowledge on the Philippines, the Moluccas, Brunei, and Timor, including crude map images, that this zone became part of Western geographical imagination. As a zone of intense competition between the Iberian countries and, in turn, Holland and England, it is not surprising that the Moluccas also became subject to intense political and cartographic intelligence, such as represented in the Atlas Miller in 1519, the Pedro Reinel map of 1520, the Diego Ribeiro world map of 1529, and, in turn, the so-called Dieppe maps, or *mappe monde*.

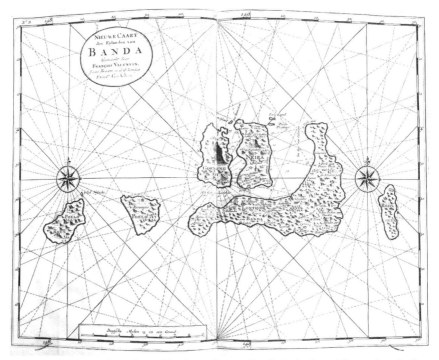

**Figure 5.3. Map of Banda archipelago, from Valentijn's *Oud en Nieuw Oost-Indien*
(1724); Banda map. As with maps of the Sumatra/Malacca Straits area, early zones of
exploitation and navigation were the best mapped. (Reproduced with permission of Nagasaki University Library)**

With the production of the Pierre Descalier map of 1530, the eastern archipelago from Flores to Timor is well delineated. Aside from its famous
reference to "Cypangu," the somewhat confused map offers up names of
such kingdoms and ports as Cochin China, Camboya, Syam (Siam),
Malacca, Muar, Aceh,[5] Sunda, Banca, Madura, and Tuban, along with Cy-
ombaia (Surabaya) on Java. Sumatra (Taporobana) is named, but Borneo
(Brunei) is marked on, as designated, the island of Java Menore. The
Moluccas are named, as is Malua and Timor, the last two probably derived from information supplied by the Magellan expedition.

By 1602, with Pieter Bertius's *Moluccae Insulis,* part of a miniature atlas
done in Amsterdam, Celebes (Sulawesi) and the islands east of Borneo
are well delineated, probably the best to date. The identification of Insula
Borneo and the Celebes is made on Jodocus Hondius's *Insulae Indiae Orientalis* (ca. 1635). But while the relative size and shape of Borneo is captured, the shape of the Celebes is not yet optimal. Singapore is identified
as an island. But as with the islands of Ceram and Gilolo (the Halme-
hares), the size is disproportionately large. Even more fine-grained charts

of the Moluccas appeared with W. J. Blaeu's *Moluccae Insulae Celeberrimae* (ca. 1630). Here, the location of Dutch forts and settlements is clearly illustrated.

Timor, along with a host of island toponyms, is marked on *Terra Ostro Tavola*, the map derived from Portuguese information published in Ramusio's 1556 book. Timor's famed crocodile shape is even captured in Pigafetta's word portrait: "All this island is inhabited, and it is very long from east to west, and very wide from south to north." One of the first large-scale map images of Timor was "Mapa de Solor e Timor, 1613," entering Manuel Godhinho Eredia's manuscript *Declaraçam de Malaca*. Still, the form of the island is only approximate with Solor, long the major port of call for Macau Chinese and Portuguese traders, vastly exaggerated in size relative to Timor. Timor is marked with the toponyms of some dozen *reinos*, or kingdoms.

As revealed by a map published in Valentijn's *Oud en Nieuw Oost-Indien* (1724), the Dutch had achieved a relatively detailed grasp of the basic features of Timor and the Sunda islands by that date. However, it was only in 1760 that the Dutch East India Company produced a large-scale map in what might have been the first attempt to cartographically demarcate Dutch from Portuguese territory on the island. In any case, it was clear by this age that the Portuguese capacity to match Dutch mastery in this science had badly flagged (Gunn 1999b, 144). But the shape of Timor was hardly improved on by British mapmakers Laurie and Whitle in their eastern archipelago chart of 1798. While the traces of the Dampier and Cook voyages to Timor are offered, Lifau, which the Portuguese vacated in 1789, is falsely named as the Portuguese seat of government. As with the Dutch chart, the eastern part of Timor remains poorly defined. Nor have any extant eighteenth-century Portuguese maps of Timor been recovered, perhaps, by this date, reflecting a total lack of state resources rather than any deliberate policy of secrecy.

In a map published in 1554, Ramusio includes not only such islands as Cebu, Negros, and Mindanao but also one titled Filipina, a name given by Villabos in 1543 that quickly became the official designation for the archipelago (Lach 1969, 625). Situated east of the Moluccas, the large island of New Guinea was, as mentioned, a later Spanish discovery and appears in exaggerated size in Ortelius's *Maris Pacifica* of 1589. But the first detailed map of the northern coast of New Guinea and the Solomon Island group (as named), along with *las Islas Filipinas*, appeared in Antonio de Herrera's *Descripcian de las Indias Occidentales* (Description of the West Indies), published in Madrid in 1601. Herrera offers a key to ten toponyms relating to the Philippines, including Manila and one nonnative name for an island east of Mindanao, dubbed San Juan. Japan (Xapon) and the southern islands, including Luchu (Lequio), are well indicated. Major provincial cities on the coast of China are named. Timor is absent. In his *Nova Guinea et Ind Salomonis Description de la Novelle Guinee*, printed in Amsterdam in 1616, Petrius

Bertisus shows part of the Solomon Islands attached to the northern tip of *Terra Australis Incognita*.[6]

Local mapmaking took a new turn, however, with the royal order directed in 1733 to the Spanish governor of the Philippines, Fernando Valdes y Tamon, to produce an official map of the islands. The task was given to father Pedro Murillo Velarde, professor of canon law at the Jesuit College in Manila. Author of *Geographia Historia* (History of Geography; 1749), Murillo produced the commissioned map within twelve months, having it printed in Manila in 1734 by Nicolas de la Cruz (Nicholl 1986). Serving as a standard for the next century, the map is also, as mentioned later in this chapter, a treasure trove of nautical interest.

## IMAGINING ASIA

As alluded, it was Ramusio's *Navigationi* (1556) that pioneered the incorporation of maps with text. But firsthand images of Asia from the sixteenth century were rare. Artists seldom accompanied voyages, with the result that the genre is, to a great extent, one of imagined images. Shipboard artists also may not have contributed much to the illustrations accompanying *De Eerste Schpvaart* (First Ship Sailing; 1598), an account of the expedition by Cornelis de Houtman in 1595–1597, aside from the stylized images of the fleet off Banten and the map of Bali. Otherwise, the Dutch engraver's images of gamelan, games, suttee, and sailing craft are wooden, even though Asian faces begin to take on life. Contemporaneous was Theodore de Bry's *Grand Voyages*, published around 1590–1634, offering a wealth of engraved images. De Bry accumulated a mass of drawings and original works relating to the New World, including many re-created from the source documents. For example, the narrative of van Noort's voyage was illustrated with twenty-six engravings. Reprints of Linschoten's *Itinerario . . .* (from 1610) were likewise illustrated by de Bry, including classic although highly stylized scenes of native life in Goa. In truth, de Bry's engravings ran the gamut from the highly fanciful albeit celebrated image of Macau to the realistic bird's-eye view of Manila to the highly evocative depictions of Spanish atrocities in Central and South America. De Bry's engravings of central American Indians are still of ethnographic interest, and, as with many in his Asian portfolio, there is simply often no substitute visual image. The importance of de Bry's engravings is suggested by the fact that they were often reproduced without attribution centuries later. Many relating to the East Indies, for example, appear in Valentijn's work from 1724.

A rather different aesthetic came into play, however, in the richly baroque productions of, especially, the Iberians. Such would describe "Gente do reino de Pegu, Gentios Cahaman-de Pegus," among other graphics from the Codice Português da Biblioteca Casanatense. The superbly rendered charts and images found in the *Livros das Plantas das Fortalezas, Cidades* . . . (Book of Plans of Fortresses, Cities . . .) evoke city plans of Goa and Malacca along with many other fortified outposts of the *Estado da India* in the seventeenth century. Specifically, the fortifications and defenses of Aceh are beautifully albeit fancifully captured in the colored illustration of Dourado in his *Demonstração* of 1568. The Aceh fortification is only slightly more realistically rendered by Manuel Godhino da Eridia in his 1602 work. We also recall the map by Pedro Barreto de Resende offering designs in gouache by Andreas Beeckman of lifestyle scenes and figures of the Moluccas in the seventeenth century (Scalliet 1997). Portuguese and Dutch *portolano* dating from the early sixteenth century frequently carried views and figurines. A Dutch *portolano* of 1661 surviving in the British Museum contains forty-nine colored maps and views of, inter alia, Neira, Amboyna, Bouro, and Ceram in the Moluccas. From another quarter, copper engraved prints of Persia and Russia, drawn by Dutch adventurer John Struys, appeared in *The Voyages and Travels of John Struys* (1684).

Still, we may wonder as to the role that Asian artists played in literally bringing home these images. A striking visual rendering of Timor from the early eighteenth century is the *Planta da Cailaco* (ca. 1727), a vivid Bayeux-like tapestry design of Portuguese *topasse* forces struggling to overcome, as labeled, the Timorese *inimigo* (lit. "enemies") in the formidable *pedras* (lit. "stones"), or mountains, of East Timor. Believed to have been executed by a Goan or Macau Chinese artist, this image is the earliest on Timor. The detail on this map is so fine that it has been used by those with botanical knowledge to identify certain trees (Cinatti 1959; Gunn 1999b, 99).

One of the finest evocations of the early eighteenth-century Philippines, the Pedro Murillo Velarde map, was a work of collaboration with two Indio or Tagalog artists, undoubtedly trained in European techniques. Twelve vignettes placed on both sides of the map were executed by Francisco Suarez (ca. 1690–1762), while the engravings were executed by Nicolas de la Cruz Bagay (1702–ca.1765). These miniatures include depictions of Chinese, Africans, mestizos, Japanese, Persians, and Indians; a lampoon of high Spanish officials; a street scene; two rare rural, rather ageless scenes; a typical house; a farmer plowing his field with a water buffalo; a man cutting bamboo; a coconut tree and various animals; and inset maps of Guam, Manila, and Zamboanga (cf. Suárez 1999, 247–49). In addition, in fascinating detail, the Murillo map offers depictions of sailing boats of the time, including finely drawn Spanish, Portuguese, Macau, and indigenous sailing vessels (Nicholl 1986). As alluded, Indio artists were also known for their illustrations of *pasyon*, or passion plays (Hernandez 2000).

But artists also accompanied the shipboard voyages, and by Enlightenment times the ability to record images became an obligatory skill for the elite classes. Edney (1997, 59) elaborates on the fine distinction between the ostensible "scientific gaze" of the Enlightenment artist who merely recorded the facts of the external world and the "picturesque gaze," an aesthetic view blending Roman pastoral poetry with Italianate landscape. Just as the scientific gaze was embedded in its own cultural constructs of reality, so the picturesque gaze became in the hands of the English "a perfect intellectual tool for imaging the landscapes of South Asia."

Macau, the European gateway to China, became a favorite object of imaginative images through the centuries, gaining in fame only following three failed Dutch expeditions to conquer the territory. Exemplary are the "naive" sketches of Macau life by Peter Mundy, who arrived in 1637 with the fleet of English captain John Weddel, offering perhaps the first European sketches of Chinese junks, Chinese attire, Macanese women, and even Japanese exiles in Macau. Also befitting the scientific gaze was Isaac Commelin, who produced a series of small engravings and maps derived from firsthand drawings made by the captains or crew of Zeiger van Rechteren's and Cornelis Matlief de Jonghe's voyage to the mouth of the Pearl River in 1607 to engage the Chinese in trade. These included depictions of a Chinese temple and junks and a rare image of the mandarin's palace on Lantau island (later Hong Kong territory) as well as more schematic views of, respectively, Macau and Fort Zeelandia on Taiwan, reprinted frequently in many other editions. Van der Aap's "View of Macau," reproduced in Nieuhoff's *An Embassy from the East India Company* . . . (1669), offers a vista of Dutch ships pounding Macau's fortifications, answered back by deadly Jesuit fire, a fanciful rendering of an historical event. Offering over 200 engravings of scenes of China, Nieuhoff's book had a lasting influence over subsequent illustrated works on China.

Singular among Dutch images from South and East Asia were special views commissioned by the Dutch East India Company and adapted into full-scale paintings for viewing by the office of directors. Notable were the productions by mapmaker Johannes Vingboons (1616–1670). Known also for his 1639 map of Manhattan (the earliest known), Vingboons, who had not traveled outside Europe, drew from imagination a view of Ayutthaya, offering a city worthy of comparison with Amsterdam, as well as a detailed rendering of the formidable Osaka castle.

By the eighteenth century, China, Japan, and the archipelago entered the scientific gaze of Europe through such illustrated works as those of Nieuhoff, Montanus, Kaempfer, Jacob de Meurs, and Valentijn. For example, Andreus Everard van Braam-Houckgeest, the second-in-command of the Dutch embassy to China in 1794–1795, returned to Holland and later America with a massive portfolio of drawings and images of China, some sketched by himself but mostly contracted out to various Chinese artists. These included seven volumes or 368 drawings of general views and landscapes; two volumes concentrating on Guangzhou, including mythology, games, music, and ships; and a separate collection on natural history, including botanica. As his English publisher R. Phillips commented on this collection, the interest lies not so much in the accuracy of the drawings or the coloring "what European eyes are accustomed to seeing" but that of a China as represented by Chinese artists. In commenting favorably on this method, Phillips remarked, "The resemblance gains a great deal that it might have been robbed of by the more delicate hand of an European" (van Braam 1798, 302).

The "Company School" had its counterpart in the visual images commissioned by the British East India Company, a term that was also used to describe works by Malay, Indian, or Chinese artists for British patrons. For example, William Farquhar (1774–1839), who served as resident in Malacca from 1803 to 1818, commissioned a range of natural history drawings. Other European artists were attracted to Calcutta. One was the Flemish artist François Balthazar Solvyns (1760–1824), who, during his sojourn in the Indian city between 1791 and 1803, produced a veritable ethnographic survey of Hindu castes in Bengal.

Just as the Jesuits had introduced Western painting techniques into Macau and China in the early seventeenth century, some 200 years later Macau had also become a haven for European artists, the doyen of which, Irish-born George Chinnery (1774–1852), an exile from Calcutta, came to be acclaimed in his life as an exponent of picturesque scenes of Macau (Cheng 1999, 135). Chinnery, in turn, schooled a group of local Macau Chinese artists in Western landscape and portrait techniques. Commencing in the mid-eighteenth century, scenes of the foreign settlement in China executed in oils or gouache were actively exported from Guangzhou and Macau, a genre eclipsed only with the arrival of photography on the China coast.

Imaging the "hermit" kingdom of Korea came last chronologically. Only with English Commodore Basil Hall's naval survey of the west coast of Korea was the country introduced to the English-speaking world. Hall used tinted drawings of Korea executed by W. Havel from sketches made on the spot to illustrate his popular *Account of a Voyage of Discovery to the West Coast of Corea and the Great Loo-Choo Island* (1818). But within decades, the *Illustrated London News* would be printing an expanding series of wood-engraved prints of eastern scenes, offering a new visuality on an expanding British Empire.

## CONCLUSION

The act of mapping and imaging has seldom been neutral. While not denying the contribution of the ancients in framing a three-continent view of the world, it is also true that the revival of Ptolemaic atlases in the late fifteenth and early sixteenth centuries perpetuated a vainglorious sense of

Eurocentricity when even the evidence from sailors disproved the orthodoxy. To be sure, the European flat-earthers of their day had their counterparts in Oriental court astronomers and other guardians of cosmological verities. But royal geographers and cosmographers-general in the
employ of European monarchs were no less custodians of vital intelligence, the equivalent of modern notions of state secrecy. Just as commercial and military espionage continued in new guise, so the Iberian pioneers guarded their trade secrets with their lives. As with printing, so
developments in cartography and the production of visual images cannot
be dissociated from the rise of new centers of political and commercial
power in such production and distribution centers as London, Frankfurt,
Paris, and Amsterdam and, along with it, a rising secular European commercial bourgeoisie, displacing the courts of Europe as the major consumer of the grand collections and travel literature.

Cultural studies also help us understand Enlightenment views as to the
unquestioning acceptance of maps as unproblematic and truthful statements of reality (cf. Edney 1997, 16–17). In reality, as the age of discovery
shaded into the age of imperialism, the production of maps based on more
and more rigorous scientific techniques served to definitively "frame" the
mental and physical boundaries of empire. Even so, as we shall see, there
was no even progression in the way that ideas traveled or in the way they
were received at either a mass or an elite level. Countries with developed
cartographic traditions, not to mention alternative cosmographies
(namely, the Middle Kingdom and its satellite tributaries), were better positioned both to control and to influence European intelligence gatherers.
Japanese cartography simply progressed as a reflex of its own burgeoning
urban culture and its own expanding sense of frontier. If the East Asian
cartographers lagged in their representation of the globe, it is because their
prime commercial and diplomatic contacts were strictly within the orbit of
the millennium-old East Asian tributary-trade system. But equally, European cartographers and their agents came to influence the way that indigenous cartographers positioned themselves in the world as local awareness of geography and the earth's sphericity dawned.

## NOTES

1. This information is sourced from www.henry-Davis.com/MAPS (accessed
March 25, 2002), a rich site on the history of Renaissance cartography that also has
the merit of offering online maps.

2. Nevertheless, because of the scale and resolution of the Cantino planosphere
on this and other sites, I cannot verify the identification of place names as mentioned by Davis.

3. With specific reference to Southeast Asia, Ptolemy's *Geographia* has been the subject of much analysis and some deconstruction. See Meuden (1974, 1975) and Wheatley (1961).

4. Notably, Tibet was not part of the Jesuit survey. Separately, the Kangxi emperor had ordered his newly appointed imperial representative in Lhasa to draw up a map of Tibet. His rough sketches were in turn presented in 1711 to Régis, who incorporated them into the Jesuit atlas of China. Newer material on Tibet was incorporated into the thirty-two-sheet Jesuit atlas of 1721.

5. The map imaging of Aceh is discussed in some detail in Reid and Takeshi (1999). The superior Dutch map of Aceh (ca. 1645) discussed in this article has its provenance in the "Castello collection," comprising eighty-two Dutch aquarelles depicting the East and West Indies. Having passed into the hands of Cosmo II de Medici in 1667, it is currently held in Florence's Biblioteca Medicea Laurenziana.

6. Arriving in the western Pacific islands in 1597, Spanish navigator Alvaro Mendana de Negro named them after King Solomon. He also named Ysabel (after his wife), Guadacanalar, and San Christoval, names that have endured.

# 6

# Enlightenment Views of Asian Governance

The irony should not be lost that, in the time when Hugo Grotius (1583–1645) was penning his *De Jure Belli Ac Pacis Libri Tres* (The Rights of War and Peace; 1626), Europe was a major arena of cruel and lawless religious and national warfare. Religious intolerance went hand in hand with tyrannical state power. I am also amazed that when Europe was in a state of near permanent war, China under the Qing experienced a prolonged peace throughout the long eighteenth century, though the Qing also greatly extended the scope of empire through military conquest on northern and western peripheries. I have described how the Jesuit mission in China actually assisted the Kangxi emperor in mapping his expanding domains. With the notable exceptions of Hideyoshi's invasion of Korea in the late sixteenth century and the violence surrounding the Ming–Qing transition in the seventeenth century, including the ouster of the Dutch from their factory on Taiwan in 1661, the Central Kingdom could be viewed from Europe as a model of powerful order and industry. This understanding was reflected in Jesuit scholarship on China. Just as interpretations of Confucianism began to disseminate throughout Europe, so an appreciation of Asian, especially Chinese-influenced, systems of governance began to grow, notably in prerevolutionary France, among Enlightenment thinkers and philosophes. With the recovery of Aristotle's *Politics,* so the term "despotism" reentered European intellectual vocabulary not only to describe the medieval Church but also to be linked with negative conceptions of the Ottoman Turks and other caricatures of Islamic polities. Such analyses were not extended to China and Japan at the time.

The intellectual movement known as the Enlightenment also sought to critique the senselessness of wars fought between the powerful nation-states of Europe by offering schemes to establish peace on a permanent basis. It is all the more striking that, in the seventeenth and eighteenth centuries, Europe vented its aggression not only in the New World *conquista* but also in facing down new challenges from other colonial powers. Intramural Dutch-Portuguese-Spanish-English conflict over Brazil, the Caribbean, and the East Indies; piracy and profit associated with European trading company rivalry over the India and China trade; and conflict over British and French colonies in North America, often fought out on the high seas or as running raids on isolated colonies, reached new lows in savagery. Bringing an end to the destructive Seven Year Wars (1756–1763), the Treaty of Paris of 1763 also confirmed Great Britain as the leading European colonial power at the expense of France. In this chapter, then, we seek to answer the question, How did Enlightenment Europe behold forms of governance in Asia, albeit running from the more familiar Islamic to the lesser understood Hindu-Buddhistic to the seductive "enlightened despotism" of Qing China and Tokugawa Japan?

## ENLIGHTENMENT VIEWS
## OF GOVERNANCE IN CHINA

As alluded, the formative image-making texts on China on which Europe drew its impressions included such missionary writings as those of Athanasius Kircher, Jean-Baptiste du Halde, Louis Daniel Le Comte, Joaquim Bouvet, and Charles Le Gobien. It was du Halde's *Description . . .* (1735) that long remained preeminent. A virtual summation of European knowledge of China in the eighteenth century, the text was widely consulted by a range of Enlightenment philosophers. Significantly, the French philosophes were foremost in Europe in translating China. This owed to the patronage by the French king of the Jesuit China Mission from its establishment in 1700 to the dissolution of the Jesuit order in 1773. But in France, four illustrious names came to be associated with the reception of China—Montesquieu (1689–1755), Voltaire (1694–1778), Quesnay (1694–1774), and Rousseau (1712–1778)—albeit views ranged from Sinoskeptic (Montesquieu) to Sinophile (Rousseau, Quesnay, and Voltaire).

Drawing on the generally favorable Catholic observations on China, the European public continued to admire China's industry, inventiveness, philosophical strengths, and cultural richness until at least the middle of the eighteenth century. While appreciation of Chinese classics first gained ground with their translation and publication in prerevolutionary France, it was in England that the aesthetic cult of Chinoiserie blossomed. But all Europe soon shared this penchant for things Chinese and Asian in general, especially in decor and design, porcelain (China), lacquerware (Japanware), silk, ornamental gardens, and mock pagodas. Chinese institutions, however, provided the context of much debate. The French Jesuits set the tone by presenting a laudatory picture of early Qing, especially appreciative of the role of the mandarinate and the teachings of Confucianism in appearing to check the despotism of the ruler. Nevertheless, China and the Orient became a kind of contestatory space in the hands of the philosophes, often at the expense of the Jesuit view of the world, but also at homegrown institutions. D. E. Mungello (1999, 87–88) has characterized this as a contest besetting Jesuits, representatives of received religion, and the deistic (sometimes atheistic) framework that the philosophes sought to establish. In a word, the philosophes sought to replace Christianity (a religion of revelation) with deism (a religion of reason). Even so, through the eighteenth century, the Jesuits continued to dominate sources of information on China, while practically none of the philosophes had visited Asia.

Mungello (1999, 88) points to the first Enlightenment thinker to extol the Chinese system of government as the German Christian Wolf (1679–1754). For his efforts, Wolf was charged with atheism, a victim of the reaction by religious fanatics (the Pietists). But Wolf had also been influenced by the German philosopher Gottfried von Leibniz (1646–1716), a figure credited with the invention of binary mathematics supported by his study of the *I Ching,* or the Chinese Book of Changes. As Leibniz wrote in *Novissima Sinica* (Latest News from China; 1697), "I almost think that Chinese missionaries should be sent to us to teach the aims and practices of natural theology, as we send missionaries to them to instruct them in revealed religion." Still, Mungello (1999, 90) views Leibniz's "polyhistor model" as closer to the (Jesuit) proto-Sinological approach, "serious and scholarly," as opposed to the broad intellectual project of the philosophes who succeeded him.

In any case, it soon became clear that the philosophes worked to their own cultural agenda as opposed to the serious study of Oriental cultures. Unlike the Jesuits with their culture of Scholasticism, the philosophes were also prey to intellectual fashion. In *Les Lettres d'un Persan* (Persian Letters; 1721), Baron de Montesquieu offers fictional exchanges between Persian traveler-exiles to France who discover the customs and institutions of Europe. Obviously, this is the reverse of the typical Oriental travel narration. Not only does Montesquieu satirize Parisian life and mock Louis XIV, but he also critiques the tyrannically male-centered Turkish harem. In this encounter between two civilizations, Europe is made to look seductive, but much ambiguity also exists.

Montesquieu is better known for his understanding of despotic government as especially capricious, based on organized fear and, geographically, most likely to be found in large, arid, agrarian regions. Especially, Montesquieu found in du Halde's *Description . . .* powerful ammunition to defend his classic and influential text on how governments should best work. This was *De l'Esprit des Loix* (The Spirit of the Laws; 1748). Observing three types of government—monarchical, republican with elected leaders, and despotic under a dictator—Montesquieu defended an elected government and the separation of powers, such as would become the basis of the U.S. Constitution. The examples of China and Japan, then, offered confirmation to Montesquieu as to the despotism of Oriental institutions. On China, Montesquieu observed, "Our missionaries inform us that the government of the vast empires of China is admirable. . . . But I cannot conceive what this honor can be among people who only act through fear of being Batinadoed" (a punishment described in chapter 8). Taking a snipe at the Church, which looked to the favors of princes and rulers with a view to winning mass conversions (the book was indexed in 1758), Montesquieu asked rhetorically, "Might not our missionaries have been deceived by an appearance of order?" Indignant, Montesquieu declared, "In China fathers are punished for the crimes of their children." Echoing du Halde (1748, 134), who summarized, "It is the cudgel that governs China, " Montesquieu concludes, "China is therefore a despotic state, whose principle is fear."

But the idealization of China in France reached its pinnacle with François Quesnay (1694–1774), intellectual leader of the Physiocrat school of political economy. In *Le Despotisme de la Chine* (The Despotism of China; 1767), Quesnay presents a glowing picture of China clearly derived from Jesuit sources. Arguing that a truly enlightened despotism would benefit the people as a whole rather than a privileged minority, he found in Confucianism a moral restraint on abuse of power. Quesnay was even instrumental in convincing the son of Louis XV to adopt the Chinese emperor's practice of ritual plowing of sacred land as emblematic of the government's benevolent interest in agriculture.

But for the most famed of the Enlightenment philosophes, François Voltaire, China most closely approximated Plato's idea of rule by a philosopher-king. As Mungello summarizes, Voltaire believed that the cultural spirit of the Chinese Confucian scholar-officials offered "an ethical and political model for Europe (Mungello 1999, 89). In *Orphelin de la Chine* (Chinese Orphan; 1733), a play that Voltaire adapted from a Chinese play translated into French in 1755, he sought to prove the superiority of Chinese art and culture in its triumph over the barbarism of the Mongols. In so doing, Voltaire was responding to Rousseau's theories on the innate goodness of simple human nature. As Jonathan Spence (1999, 134) has commented, Voltaire's praise for Chinese institutions appeared in a cultural context that was intensely sympathetic to China. Yet the China cult, in both its aesthetic and its intellectual versions, faded swiftly with the advent of the age of imperialism. In turn, Voltaire's enthusiasm for "enlightened despotism" came to be the object of sarcasm or mockery, assailed by both Rousseau and Montesquieu, who emphasized the despotic character in Chinese institutions over the benign.[1]

China suffered a parallel decline of image in England. Influenced by *Persian Letters*, English playwright Oliver Goldsmith (1730–1774) produced a spoof on English manners through a fictional Chinese gentleman, Lien Chi Altangi, in his "Chinese Letters," published as *Citizen of the World; or, Letters of a Chinese Philosopher, Living in London, to His Friends in the East* (1760–1761). According to Chen Shouyi, a modern literary critic, "They not only assured Goldsmith's literary fame, but also marked the culmination of English interest in Chinese culture and things Chinese." Voltaire, Le Comte, and du Halde all served as source material for Goldsmith, yet, for all that, the Englishman was only indifferently enthused by Chinese culture (Chen 1998, 283). In 1742, Samuel Johnson wrote two essays in praise of du Halde's book but ultimately deemed the rage for China but a "novelty" (Qian 1998, 120, 135). He was right because not all sentiments in England were favorable to du Halde or China. Such can be seen in Daniel Defoe, China's "severe critic," especially in consideration of the second and third parts of *Robinson Crusoe* (1719), where Defoe offers a "contemptuous opinion of China" (Chen 1998, 216).

Others have noted the waning infatuation with China in eighteenth-century English letters just as the wave of public infatuation with Chinoiserie peaked. Quan Zhongshu writes from a detailed survey of articles, periodicals, and books that "the English literature of the eighteenth century is full of criticisms of Chinese culture in general and the prevailing fashion of Chinoiserie in general." Quan exposes a world of difference in attitude between Peter Mundy's sympathetic portrait of China in *The Travels of Peter Mundy* . . . (written as a diary in 1637, though not published until 1919) and the next book by an Englishman to experience China firsthand, namely, George Lord Anson's *A Voyage round the World* . . . (1778), "the most cocksure unfavorable opinion of the Chinese character" (Qian 1998, 118).

## ENGELBERT KAEMPFER
## AND JAPANESE DESPOTISM

We have already remarked on the uses made of Engelbert Kaempfer's *History of Japan* (1727) as a probable source for Jonathan Swift, among others, but Kaempfer's text was a major source lode for such Enlightenment thinkers as Montesquieu, Rousseau, Voltaire, Raynal, Diderot, and Kant, especially in reflecting on Japanese society and governance. This is all the more remarkable as Kaempfer spent only two years in Japan and was unsuccessful in his lifetime in publishing his original German manuscript. Arriving in Nagasaki in 1690, the German-born Kaempfer was already a seasoned traveler and observer of Russia, Persia, Batavia, and Siam. As medical doctor in the employ of the Dutch East India Company at Nagasaki, Kaempfer was fortunate in gaining the assistance of the cultured Japanese translator Imamura Gen'emon in amassing knowledge and documents concerning Japanese history and culture. But as the first major published text on Japan by a Protestant author, it is notable that Kaempfer stepped back from the long line of Catholic writings on Japan that set the tone in Europe of an almost demonic empire that would go as far as even sacrificing their children seemingly in defense of culture and nation.

Already known in Europe for his botanical studies of Japan, Kaempfer's manuscript (Japanese Life) was acquired by London antiquary Hans Sloane and translated into English by his secretary as *History of Japan* (1727). A dozen editions and translations appeared in the following decade. A German edition based on a different manuscript source appeared only in the late 1770s. New editions and reprints appeared in the nineteenth and twentieth centuries. Only with the opening of Japan and the writing of new histories was Kaempfer finally superseded, although he had his detractors in the pen of the French Jesuit historian of Japan L. P. Charlevoix (1736). Michel (2000a) has observed that Kaempfer was appreciated in Enlightenment Europe as a non-Catholic source, but also his writings found resonance especially as they addressed three grand intellectual issues: the place of religion in society, state power and policy, and the aims of human history. Notably, his account of harsh Tokugawa state laws directed against stubborn regional lords in the interest of national unification stimulated much debate in Europe.

What did Kaempfer have to say concerning the state and laws in Tokugawa Japan? A virtual prisoner on the artificial island of Deshima, Kaempfer nevertheless could witness life in Nagasaki, then an imperial town governed by a governor who answered direct to the shogun. Recalling the history of the expulsion of the Portuguese from Nagasaki and the suppression of Catholicism, Kaempfer recalled how the "reigning secular monarch" (the shogun) severely reprimanded the errant "Prince" (*daimyo*) of Omura in privileging the Iberians. He also described the practice of *Jefumi* (figure treading), or the compulsory act of trampling over images of the Virgin Mary, a device used to flush out crypto-Christians. He also witnessed other strict acts of social control, such as a system of internal passports, house registration, and the legal principle whereby certain people are led to suffer for the crimes committed by others. On the matter of dogs, he declared, "no body dare touch an errant dog except the Public Executioner and nor even he without order of the Emperor," a reference to a shogunal edict protecting dogs. Needless to say, the executioner was a busy person in clearing the *Roja,* or city jail: "By so many strict regulations, and so many troublesome offices to be personally served, it cannot be denied that the inhabitants of Nagasaki are kept at a very great degree of slavery and submission, which indeed is scarce to be paralleled; but on the other hand they are not overburdened with taxes as the subjects of a European prince."

Contrary to Montesquieu's position on an inevitable Asiatic despotism, the group around Voltaire held that in Japan "the laws of nature have been transformed explicitly into civil law." Specifically, as Montesquieu read in Kaempfer's *History of Japan,* "Eastern punishments may even corrupt a despotic government; of this we have the instance of Japan." In Japan, "the question is not so much to correct the delinquent as to vindicate the authority of the prince." In *Candide ou l'Optimisme* (1757), Voltaire's argument against optimism and the existence of evil in a less-than-perfect world, he has one character utter, "Death and zounds! I am a sailor and was born at Batavia, and have trampled four times upon the crucifix in as many voyages to Japan; you have come to a good hand with your universal reason."

It is of more than interest that, during the eighteenth century, several copies of the Dutch edition of Kaempfer's *History of Japan* (1729, 1733) reached Japan and, along with other *rangaku* texts, attracted the attention of the local officials. A number of partial translations of Kaempfer's writings into Japanese were also executed. According to Jansen (1989, 88), the term *sakoku* (closed country) entered the Japanese language only in 1801 with a translation of Kaempfer's defense of the system by Nagasaki interpreter Shizuki Tadao.[2] More than that, we might interpret, Japan's seclusion-on-pain-of-death policy, a key concept explaining the Tokugawa polity (Michel 2000c), entered late Renaissance and even Enlightenment Europe imagination as a master narrative. In truth, however, Japan's intellectual and commercial exchanges with especially China and Korea continued just as Tokugawa forged its own version of a brilliant urban culture.

Kaempfer's explicit support of Japan's isolation policy also met with approval from German philosopher Immanuel Kant (1724–1804) in his *Perpetual Peace: A Philosophical Sketch* (1795). "China and Japan (Nippon), who have had experience with such guests [a reference to European intruders], have wisely refused their entry, the former permitting their approach at the shores but not their entry, whereby the latter permit their approach to only one European people, the Dutch, but treat them as prisoners, not allowing them any communication with the inhabitants." But Diderot had earlier defended a similar position in his contribution to Abbé Raynal's multivolume history (1770) declaring Europeans "too dangerous as guests."

## HENDRIK HAMEL'S KOREA

First known to the Portuguese as the island of "Coria," the peninsular character of the country was first attested in print by Portuguese Jesuit Luís Fróis around 1590–1594, appearing in Richard Hakluyt's *Voyages Traffiques & Discoveries of Foreign Voyagers* (1928, 300–46). Although Fróis did not visit Korea, he offered a sketch of the country drawn from his Japanese sources, observing, importantly, Korea's tributary status to China: "And albeit the inhabitants in nation, language, and strength of body (which maketh the people of China to dread them) be different to the king of China, and exercise traffique with his subjects, they do after a sort imitate the Lawes, apparel, customes, and government of the Chinians." Even so, a long time would pass before a firsthand account of Korea reached Europe.

Eventually, Choson-dynasty Korea became known to Europe in the seventeenth century through the accounts of shipwrecked Dutch sailors who managed to escape captivity. Dutchman Jan Weltevree, who arrived in Korea in 1628, was forbidden to leave and died there some decades later. A similar fate awaited thirty-six more Dutch sailors who were shipwrecked on Cheju island in 1653 en route to Nagasaki. The escape of a party led by Hendrik Hamel brought to the Dutch authorities in Nagasaki and eventually to Europe new information about the "Hermit Kingdom." Hamel's original manuscript account of his hazardous open boat escape, "Account of a Shipwreck," eventually entered text editions in Amsterdam and Rotterdam (1668), followed by a French edition (1670) and, from the French, entering the Churchill and Churchill collection (1704). Besides introducing the tribute-trade connections between Korea and, respectively, Beijing and Japan and even Siam, Hamel also brought to Europe the basic contours of the Korean system of governance: "Corea is subject to a King, whose power is absolute (tho' he pays an acknowledgment to the Tartars) and he disposes of all things he pleases, without asking anybodies advise. There are no Lords of peculiar places, that is who are proprietors of Towns, islands or villages. . . . In martial affairs, the King keeps abundance of soldiers in his capital city, who have no other employment than to keep guard upon his person, and to attend him when he goes abroad."

Hamel also remarked on a king's council comprised of senior officials that met every day at court, a reference to a kind of mandarinate, although as an educated but untrained observer the Dutch sailor does not press the Chinese Confucian model. Additionally, he observed, a tax on production and imports also served to raise revenue. To support this system, storehouses were situated across the countryside. As taken up later in this chapter, justice was strictly upheld and enforced, especially the crime of rebellion. As Hamel remarked, "He that rebels against the King is destroyed, with all his race, his houses are thrown down, and no man does ever rebuild them, and all his goods forfeited and sometimes given to some private person" (cited in Churchill and Churchill 1704, vol. 5, 589).

All in all, Hamel offered confirmation to Europe of a highly functional and serviceable despotism in Korea. But Hamel's was virtually the only source on Korea for the next hundred or so years. It is of more than interest that text versions of Hamel's account, the Churchill and Churchill collection version included, carried graphic descriptions of imagined man-eating crocodiles in Korea, in some editions actually illustrated. Needless to say, such an embellishment was serviceable to the image of a Hermit Kingdom rejecting foreign overtures. But, as mentioned, some, such as Kant, saw merit in self-imposed isolation.

## ISLAMIC COURTS

In modern Indian historiography, Montesquieu's idea of despotism is viewed as authenticating eighteenth- and nineteenth-century images of Mughal and Brahmin India.[3] Does this view also hold for the myriad princelings and sultanates that made up the map of premodern India and Southeast Asia? Such would tend to be the case of European writing on, especially, the Islamic courts of Southeast Asia, doubtless filtered by stereotypes of Islam reaching back to the Crusades. That is to say not that attitudes were necessarily condescending but, in the circumstances, that they were tempered by needs to treat with religious rivals as equals on matters of trade. While prerevolutionary Europe was dominated by absolute monarchies (France, Spain, Portugal, Russia, and Sweden), we recall that the English civil war led to the overthrow in 1647 of absolute monarchy and the execution of Charles I. Holland was already a republic in the hands of an oligarchy of merchants, although it is of interest that, in dealing with Oriental potentates, the Dutch merchants often invented a monarch to appear to be worthy of honor. Alfons van der Kraan (2000), writing of the justice meted out in 1636 by the court at Ayutthaya against an errant Dutch East India Company servant, argues that Asian despotism provided a rising European bourgeoisie one more weapon in the ideological struggle against Europe's traditional monarchical order. It remains to be seen how this assertion is borne out by Europe's engagements with the court polities of Southeast Asia.

But Islam also provided Enlightenment Europe with a special variant of despotism. As ancient adversaries, European travelers in Oriental Islamic

courts were on relatively familiar terrain. Such works as Ogier Ghiselin
Busbecq's *Itinera Constantinopolitantum et Amasianun* (Journey to Constantinople and Amasia; 1582), by Emperor Ferdinand's ambassador to the
Porte, alerted Christian Europe to the ruthless efficiency of the Turkish
army. A no less serious work touching on Islam and governance was Paul
Ricaut's *Histoire de l'Etat Present de l'Empire Ottoman* (History of the Present
State of the Ottoman Empire), published in Paris in 1670. Ricaut had been
secretary to the British ambassador in Constantinople. The French
artist-traveler to Constantinople, Guillaume Grelot, exoticized the sultan
in his desire to please his monarch in *Relation Nouvelle d'un Voyage de Constantinople* (1680), or, in the English edition, *A Late Voyage to Constantinople*,
published in 1683, coincidentally the year of the Turkish siege of Vienna.

Islam followed the trade routes, Arab knowledge guided the Portuguese seafarers to Malacca and beyond, and Magellan brought along a
Malay interpreter on his globe-girdling voyage, useful—actually fatal—
when he arrived in the Philippines. Following the practice pioneered by
the Portuguese on the coast of Africa, the Persian Gulf, and the Indian
coast, the Portuguese captured key Islamic trading centers in a zero-sum
game to wrest control over the spice trade routes and an even more
deadly game in the early sixteenth century when the Iberians zeroed in on
the spice trade at the source. But the spiceries were also zones of contest
in civilizational terms. While the Dutch and English were less concerned
with missionary activity in maritime Southeast Asia, they soon came to be
bogged down in military campaigns (Bantem, Mataram, and Macassar)
and wars of pacification (Aceh) against Islamic enemies.

## JEAN-BAPTISTE TAVERNIER'S TRAVELS IN INDIA

Singular in its influence on a French and European public were the travel
writings on Persia and India of Jean-Baptiste Tavernier (1605–1689), the
French diamond merchant and traveler extraordinaire. Author of *Nouvelle
Relation du Serrail du Grand Signier* (1675; published in Paris), or, in English
translation, *A New Relation of the Inner Port of the Great Seraglio* (1667) and *Les
Six Voyages* (Six Voyages; 1676–1677), among other works, Tavernier's fame
in Europe spread as his major works appeared in many editions and translations. Notable is his account of a personal meeting with Shah Jahan (r.
1628–1658) at Agra in 1640, including a vivid description of the Taj Mahal
then under construction; his meeting on another journey with Shah Abbas II
(r. 1642–1666) at Isfahan in 1657; and his audience with the great Mogul Au-
rangzab (r. 1658–1707), at Jahanabad, whom he described as "the most powerful and richest monarch in Asia." Tavernier's baroque account of the riches
of the great Mogul is no doubt unsurpassed, just as his rambling account of
passing off diamonds in various Oriental courts, not excluding the court of

Louis XIV, defies belief. But breathless description of journeys through Kabul, Delhi, Agra, Surat, Goa (where he encountered the Inquisition), Dacca, and elsewhere undoubtedly ensured Tavernier a special reception in Europe, much in the way that a modern travel writer delivers his next best-seller on cue. Doubtless Tavernier's special trade, namely, the diamonds and gemstones business, gave him reason to temper his language and moderate his views on the Asian (and European) potentates he encountered, much in the way of modern diplomats and arms traders eager to please. The French-man also left some valuable advice: "So true is it that those who desire to do business at the courts of the Princes, in Turkey, as well as in Persia and In-dia, should not attempt to commence anything unless they have consider-able presents ready prepared, and almost always an open purse for divers officers of trust of whose services they have need" (Tavernier 1889, 141).

In any case, Tavernier had been preceded to Mughal India by English merchants John Newbery and Ralph Fitch in 1583–1584, their accounts en-tering, respectively, the Hakluyt and the Purchas collections. Another source was Joannes de Laet (1593–1649), a Flemish geographer and natu-ralist who had been entrusted by the Dutch East India Company with their early reports. His book *De Imperio Magni Mogolis . . .* (The Empire of the Great Mogul) was published in Leiden in 1631. Tavernier was also rivaled by Sir John Chardin, author of *Travels in Persia 1653–1677* (1686). A French Hugenot, Chardin himself was commissioned by Shah Abbas II to create jewelry and witnessed the coronation of his successor, Shah Safi (r. 1666–1694). Yet another image-creating source was François Bernier, who worked as a physician to the Mughal court and also published his *Histoire de la Dernière Revolution des États du Grand Mogul (1670–1671)* (History of the Last Revolution of the States under the Great Mogul 1670–1671; 1671–1672), dealing with the wars through which Aurangzib came to power.

Compared unfavorably in France with the writings of Thevenot (as in-troduced in chapter 1), Bernier, and Chardin (Voltaire for one was con-temptuous), as his modern biographer Ball (1889, xxxxii) has written, Tav-ernier was preferred by the reading public for his facts and observations as opposed to "the philosophical speculations which were added to his facts by his rivals." In this vein, Montesquieu used both Tavernier and Chardin as source material, especially in the preparation of *Letters of a Per-sian.* Rousseau, likewise, had recourse to these sources.

## AUGUSTIN DE BEAULIEU AT
## THE SULTANATE OF ACEH

Marco Polo, who plausibly sojourned in Aceh on his homeward journey by the sea route from China to India, flagged an Islamic center on the northern tip of the island of Sumatra. But from relatively obscure origins,

Aceh had achieved prominence by 1540, especially as a result of the westward export of pepper and spices to the Red Sea. Because of this activity, Aceh's reputation also reached as far as Constantinople, to which it sent an ambassador (Boxer 1969b). The pepper trade linked Aceh to Java and further afield in the archipelago while, at the same time, acting as a powerful disseminator of Islam (Lombard 1967). Needless to say, the Portuguese were drawn into commerce and war with Aceh, and it is to Portuguese sources that we look for the first writings on Sumatra. As chronicled by Jorge de Lemos (1585), Aceh was sieged on numerous occasions, especially in the late 1560s and 1570s.

The young French captain Augustin de Beaulieu penned one of the most detailed accounts of early seventeenth-century Aceh. A product of the early French Enlightenment, Beaulieu studied sciences and navigation before making a first voyage to Gambia. In 1616, he was appointed captain of one of two ships fitted out for the East Indies by merchants of Paris and Rouen, his hometown. He died of "fever" in September 1637 at the age of forty-eight following an illustrious career in the French navy. Arriving in the precincts of Aceh in early January 1621, Beaulieu learned that the English and Dutch (and before them the Portuguese) had been expelled from the trading port two years earlier. Nevertheless, he sought to achieve an audience with Sultan Iskander Muda (1607–1636) to obtain a trading license and to erect a factory. At stake was a slice of Aceh's command over precious pepper deliveries. Beaulieu (in Harris 1745, vol. 1, 728–31) writes that on January 8, 1621, he was conducted to an audience with the king (sultan) by the *shabandar,* or chief harbormaster, and four of the principal *orangkaya,* or leading merchants. He recounts the following ceremony redolent of civilizational elements found across the Malay Islamic kingdoms:

> Upon a great elephant sat one of the principal orangkayas in a covered pulpit, who sent me a great silver dish covered with a cloth, embroidered with gold and silver of diverse colors, in which I put the letter, and then gave it to him.
>     The other two orangkayas rode upon Arabian horses before the elephant that carried the letter. Before them were 14 or 15 men each of them carrying a piece of the present covered with yellow cloth, without which nothing could be presented to the King. Six trumpets, six drums, and six hautboys led the van, which sounded till we arrived at the castle, about a league off. In the rear followed three s[h]abandars, and all the officers of the Albandeque on foot.

The Frenchman vacillated between awe for the splendor of the court and the material civilization it supported and horror at the unchecked despotism of the sultan.

On his part, Montesquieu (1748) had no doubts as to the despotic character of Aceh, especially the institution of slavery. From his reading of the

English navigator Dampier, the French philosophe observed, "At Achim everyone is for selling himself. . . . In these states, the freeman being over-powered by the government, have no better recourse than that of making themselves slaves to the tyrant in office." Elsewhere, under the rubric "Of the Vanity and Pride of Nations" (book XIX), Montesquieu finds support in Dampier to describe the people of Aceh as "proud and lazy" in the way they used their slaves even to carry a quart of rice a hundred paces. In an aside on what we would now describe as status considerations, he declared, "They would be dishonored if they carried it themselves."[4]

## MONTESQUIEU, THE SERAGLIO, AND THE SLAVERY OF WOMEN

We have commented on Montesquieu's jibe at the Turkish seraglio, or harem, in *Persian Letters*, but the French philosopher, whose source materials included most of the great voyages of the ages, ranged widely on the question of "slavery of women" in *Spirit of the Laws* (book XVI). In part, this discourse turns on his own version of climatic determinism, finding "natural inequality" between the sexes in "hot climates," where, from his reading of a vast travel literature, he confirms women are marriageable at eight, nine, or ten years of age. Rampant polygamy at the sultanate of Bantam on Java and at the seraglio in Morocco offers Montesquieu further confirmation: "The slavery of women is perfectly conformable to the genius of despotic government, which delights with treating all with severity." In particular, Montesquieu searched the literature to find examples of female confinement, deemed virtuous, or lack of it, deemed corrupt. In the empires of Turkey, Persia, Mughal India, China, and Japan, Montesquieu responds, with what can be only bitter sarcasm, that "the manners of the wifes are admirable." In this logic, "the greater their wealth, the more enlarged is their ability of keeping their wives in exact confinement, and of preventing them from entering again in society." The contrast, he argues, could not be greater than with India (East Indies) with a multitude of islands, infinite petty states otherwise ruled by despots. Here, where wealth is more moderate and corruption abounds, "the confinement of women cannot therefore be very strict."

Characteristically, Montesquieu never interrogated much less doubted his sources, confirming the sense that the writers of travel narratives and their editors contrived to solicit evidence of even more bizarre and despotic practices if only to feed the cravings of an educated readership in Europe with the staple to which they had been habituated. An exception was Mary Worsley Montague's *Letters of the Right Honourable Lady Mary Worsley Montague* (1763), a compilation of erudite epistolary travelogues by the wife of the British ambassador to Turkey in 1717–1718. Sympathetic to Turkish culture, Montague (1689–1764) ventured where men failed, notably, the harem and bathhouse, and in so doing overturned many male stereotypes of Turkish women. Unlike Montesquieu, whose literary and philosophical depictions of Persia and the Orient set up deliberate distinctions, the English lady found many elements of commonality in Turkish society with Europe.

## HINDU-BUDDHISTIC KINGDOMS

The Theravada Buddhist kingdoms of Southeast Asia, some of them retaining Hinduized ceremonial trappings, also came under the critical gaze of Enlightenment Europe. Even so, Oriental pomp and divinity could even be harnessed to European notions of court ceremonial, such as instanced later in this chapter with reference to the visit to Versailles by representatives of the court of Ayutthaya. But mostly, such encounters were not intellectualized but merely conducted by hastily appointed European "ambassadors," Christian missionaries, Dutch East India Company officials, travelers, or merchant-adventurers. Still, the entry into the arcane world of the sixteenth- to seventeenth-century Southeast Asian court culture was fraught with peril, just as the protocol of obeisance and gift giving was a tedious fact of life facing the would-be European supplicant.

As widely understood, the classical Indian concept of governance, such as confronted by early-arriving Portuguese at the Hindu court of Vijayanegara in southern India, lingered on in Southeast Asian polities until profound European influence forced them to abandon or attenuate practices in the nineteenth century. Traditional Hinduized or Indianized Southeast Asian states were defined not by rigorous control over boundaries but by the exultation of a mandala center. Typically, the center demanded loyalty or fealty from peripheral states over which theoretical rather than actual control was exercised. Typically, sacred centers were located in fertile areas, river valleys, or plains, where control over irrigation and rice production became the sine qua non of temporal power (cf. Suárez 1999, 70). Kingship was vested in a sacred monarch, a *deva* or *Buddha-raja*, at the apex of a steeply hierarchical court system. Certain paraphernalia, such as the sacred parasol, the color yellow, royal titles, and the concept of *negara*-state, known for its ostentatious displays of power, were even carried over into Malay Islamic political systems.

### GASPERO BALDI AT THE COURT OF PEGU

Entering Portuguese knowledge around 1506, the Portuguese established direct relations with the king of Pegu (in today's Burma) in 1519, in the form of a mission led by António Correa (Caetano 1990, 23–26). Pegu figured along with Siam and Bengal in the Vaz Dourado map of 1570. In November 1586, Englishman Ralph Fitch sailed up the Irrawaddy River to Pegu, having arrived by boat from Bengal, observing a grand city of gilded towers of which the king's house was the most sumptuous (Fitch 1921, 30–31).

Three years prior to Fitch, the Venetian merchant Gaspero Baldi also visited Pegu. Baldi, who received an audience with the king, was greatly impressed, observing also a "street of Portugals," testament of prior Portuguese contact with the kingdom. In an intriguing inquiry into European governance, the king of Pegu commanded Baldi to explain as to "what parts Venice was seated and what King governed it." Baldi recalled his reply and the king's response: "It was in the Kingdom of Italie, and that it was a Republik or free state and not governed by any King. When the King heard this, he greatly wondered, so he began to laugh so exceedingly, that he was overcome with the cough to which made him that he could hardly speak to his great men."

Looking back at Baldi's account, Montesquieu (1748) entered under the rubric "Of laws in relation to the principles which form the general spirit, mores and customs of a nation" (book XIV), "What legislator could propose a popular government to a people like these?" In any case, within fifteen years of Baldi's encounter, Pegu, Burma's Toungoo Empire for most of the sixteenth century, fell to rebels, pending the transfer by stages of its capital up the Irrawaddy River. As a footnote to all this, just as various evocations of Portuguese activities in Burma entered dynastic chronicles, the same reveal that the Portuguese were not always remembered kindly, especially in their encounter with Buddhist institutions (cf. Guedes 1998, 215).

## HENRY HAGENAAR
## AT THE CAMBODIAN COURT

The record of a Dutch East India Company voyage to Phnom Penh in 1637 throws further light on the Cambodian, or Khmer, kingdom, actually sited at Lovek. Together with the following account of the Dutch in Ceylon, it also offers some insights into the ways that European travelers and faux emissaries deported themselves at Oriental courts. Although not the first account of Cambodia, it is the best documented. In fact, over Portuguese opposition, the Dutch first took an interest in Cambodia from 1620. In command of four vessels, Dutch Ambassador Henry Hagenaar, accompanied by his deputy, van Galen, was charged with presenting Company letters to the older and younger kings of Cambodia. On May 12, the squadron entered the Bassac River and proceeded to navigate up the Mekong with great difficulty. On May 28, they made first contact with an interpreter of the king, arriving finally on June 10 at Phnom

Penh, where they observed a "golden tower." They departed Phnom Penh for Japan on July 11.

According to the Dutch account, a *nampra*, or court official, was dispatched by the court to receive the Dutch letters and presents. Letters for the two kings were borne by the *nampra* under a parasol and placed on an elephant. Hagenaar himself was borne on a golden cart, van Galen on a second, another court official in the third, and the captain of the vessel in a fourth along with the presents. Duly presented to the king in the audience, these included two harquebuses, ten Spanish rifles, two pistols, and two sabers. The letters were read in Malay and translated into Khmer. The king offered various remedies for the ambassador's maladies, and they were also plied with fruits and *arack*, or local alcoholic drink. Attended by musketeers and trumpeters, the Dutch party was pampered by a solicitous king, eager to acquire cannon. As observed, a group of Japanese enjoyed special privilege at the court. The king's interpreter spoke in Portuguese. For the most part, the procedures were repeated in attempting to gain an audience with the young king. Located sixty leagues upstream, "Camboei" was described as hosting Japanese, Portuguese, Vietnamese, and Malay communities. "It is a fertile country, but little peopled. There is a quantity of creeks, rivers, of flowing and stagnant waters, which becomes (in a reference to the Tonle Sap) a great lake, a kind of internal sea." Observing that Cambodia could mobilize between twenty and 30,000 men, it was also understood that their hosts were at war with the king of Siam, against whom they had rebelled. The Buddhist clergy were also observed as being close to the king, "with whom they speak more familiarly" (Hagenaar 1725, 430–73).

In the event, the Dutch succeeded in establishing a factory at Phnom Penh, although its importance began to decline from 1655. Willy-nilly, Cambodia began to appear on Dutch maps from this time, just as more verifiable knowledge of Cambodia entered Europe, filtered through Dutch sources. Even so, as discussed in a following chapter, it would be the European "discovery" of the famed Angkorian kingdom that would confirm the fallen grandeur theme in European versions of Asia history.

## GERALD HULFT AT THE COURT OF KANDY

Standing outside the conventionally bounded histories of Southeast Asia, the kingdom of Kandy was never so treated by the Portuguese and the Dutch but, rather, was smoothly integrated into their interlocking system of fortified trading posts. In 1656, the Portuguese and the Dutch were squared off on the island from the fortresses at, respectively, Galle (today's Gale-face); Jaffna, from 1619; and Colombo, the political capital of modern Ceylon (Sri Lanka). In this struggle, the Dutch commander Gerald Hulft, going by the title commander-in-chief of all the sea and land forces sent to Ceylon, sought an audience at the court of Raja Singha II. The reconstruction of this event by Philip Baldaeus, a Dutch minister in Ceylon, appears authentic. It is also a more or less representative account of the way that European agents presented themselves or were received at Oriental courts, at least when they were not at war:

> About noon, just as the General was at dinner, we heard a noise of drums, trumpets, and other music on the other side of the river and soon after saw some of the chief courtiers of the Emperor with three of the choicest horses of the stable, adorned with most magnificent saddles, bridles and other accouterments, to advance in very good order towards us, some persons of the best quality marching before to invite his Excellency to Court. The General ordered immediately his Guards to pass the river with the presents, with an intention to follow them in person with his whole train.

He then describes how they proceeded to the Imperial Palace, about which was ranged a number of musketeers, in a procession accompanied by elephants, horses, and musicians:

> The Doors being shut after them, all the Hollanders there present were conducted through a large square into a spacious hall (called by them Mandonoe) on the West side whereof they found his Majesty seated in great pomp upon a Chair of State, mounted some steps from the ground. No sooner had they entered the Hall, but all the great courtiers paid their reverence by falling flat with their faces upon the ground, and the Dutch upon their knees, till his majesty was pleased to order them to rise by a nod. Then they began to approach the Imperial Throne, adorned with most precious tapestries of gold (called by them alcatives) coming to the middle of the hall, they fell upon their knees a second time, according to the customs of the Eastern nations, till his Majesty was pleased to arise from his seat and commanded the General to come nearer who made the following speech.

We defer to offer the speech, but it commenced thus: "Most Potent Monarch! Your most humble servant approaches your Imperial Throne with a most violent passion." Making it clear that he came to renew and confirm their alliance, Hulft then commenced to deliver up his presents, including Persian horses, Japanese gowns, sandalwood, and so on. Confirming English philosopher Thomas Hobbes's famous axiom as to the ephemeral character of life in situations of weak government, scarcely had the Dutchman departed the place when he was felled by a Portuguese musket shot (Baldaeus 1704, 745). Hulft is remembered today in the name of a suburb of Colombo.

## EUROPE AT THE COURT
## OF SIAM—SIAM AT THE COURT OF EUROPE

Alone among the Southeast Asian kingdoms, Siam stands out in not succumbing to direct colonial rule and, as with China and Japan, Europeans
traded on sufferance. Not surprisingly, the first European visitors to the
Ayutthayan court were Portuguese, especially as Albuquerque had received an envoy from Siam even prior to the conquest of Malacca. A river
port on the Chaopraya River, connecting with the Gulf of Siam, Ayutthaya was the capital of the Siam kingdom from its foundation in the
mid-fourteenth century until its eclipse at the hands of the Burmese in
1767. In large part because of the steady stream of books published on
Siam during the seventeenth and eighteenth centuries, the kingdom was
well known, if little understood, in Enlightenment Europe.

Ayutthaya, first visited by the Dutch in the last years of the sixteenth
century, dispatched a mission to The Hague in 1609. In this visit, a delegation of five Siamese, including two ambassadors of King Ekathotsarot
(r. 1605–1611), traveled to the United Provinces aboard a fleet of ships
commanded by Admiral Cornellis Matelief de Jong. They visited a number of Dutch cities, taking a keen interest in shipbuilding as well as the
newly European-invented telescope, before returning home via the East
Indies. Not far behind the Dutch were the English, who, from 1612, established trading factories at Ayutthaya and Patani. However, it was the
French who made the greatest political impact, dating from the visit in
1662 by the French missionary Pierre de la Motte-Lambert, followed up
by a mission to Ayutthaya led by Alexandre de Chaumont in 1685 and the
dispatch of an embassy from Siam to Versailles in the same year. A previous embassy dispatched by Ayutthaya in 1681 had been lost at sea off the
African coast. For King Narai (r. 1656–1688), the French served as a coun-
terweight to occasional bullying of the Dutch merchant contingent. In
this, the French gained the services of Constantine Phaulkon, a
Greek-born adviser to Narai who also served as commissioner of trade
and finance.

The gap between the rituals of European courts and their Asian analogues
could not have been wider. This was apparent from Marco Polo on and
sorely tested by the English, Dutch, and others in the Central Kingdom
through the rituals of the kowtow and, in Japan, through the annual ritual
of the journey to the shogunal court, as performed successively by the Portuguese and Dutch through the centuries. In Asia, interstate relationships
demanded strict hierarchy between tributary and tributor, whereas in Europe the concept of equal sovereign states and *raison d'etat* was developing
as signaled by the Peace of Westphalia in 1648, ending the Thirty Years' War.
But how were Oriental visitors accommodated in European courts?

The audience granted by Louis XIV on September 1, 1686, at Versailles to three ambassadors of King Narai is illustrative. But what made the reception in Versailles unique was the way in which the Sun King emulated as nearly as possible the outward forms of Siamese court ceremonial. According to Love (1996), not even the reception of the sultan of Morocco or the czar of Muscovy could equal the display of pomp in the newly constructed Hall of Mirrors by Louis XIV, himself robed in a gem-studded suit and seated on a diamond-encrusted cushion in emulation of the king of Siam. Still, the envoys were underwhelmed by the lack of protocol alongside the standards of Asian despotism where the king could not be gazed on much less approached. While, in part, the affair passed off as a comedy of errors or faux pas, at least the Sun King could assert his absolutist claims and magnify his image as French monarch extraordinaire.

As Simon de la Loubère, envoy of the French king to the king of Siam in the years 1687 and 1688, related in his 1691 work *Du Royaume de Siam* (Kingdom of Siam), when three elephants (presents from the king of Siam to Louis XIV) were dispatched to France, the royal elephant keepers whispered the following words in their ears: "Go; depart cheerfully. You indeed be slaves,—but slaves to the greatest monarch in the world, whose sway is as great as it is glorious." No doubt, as British empire builder Sir John Bowring (1857, 222–23) acerbically commented on this anecdote, the Siamese certainly treated elephants as "reasonable beings," but no less, "this sort of invention was suited to the taste of the Grand Monarque, and the temper of the times."

French missionary fantasies that the Siamese king might convert to Catholicism were soon to be allayed. By 1688, King Narai and Constantine Phaulkon were dead, victims of palace intrigue. The new king Pethracha (r. 1688–1693) signed a commercial treaty with the Dutch, who, with some interruptions, carried on in Siam until 1767. Although deploying forces numbering in the hundreds, the French prudently withdrew from their base in the swamps of Bangkok, no match for the manpower and levies that the Oriental monarchs could command. As John Wills has written of this bloody event, "The fundamental stability of the Siamese kingdom had never been in doubt." Moreover, the Siamese polity had long been open to participation of individual foreigners in the management of trade and finance, notably Chinese residents who had long managed Siam's tribute trade with China (and Japan) (Wills 2001, 87–92). Inconceivable in a European context, Chinese and Portuguese merchantmen based in Ayutthaya flew the Siamese flag on foreign forays.

Although hardly matching China or Japan in the fascination of Enlightenment thinkers, Siam nevertheless caught the attention of English philosopher John Locke (1632–1704) in his celebrated *Essay concerning Human Understanding* (1690). Here Locke cites Abbé de Choisy's *Journal du*

*Voyage de Siam* . . . (Journal of a Voyage to Siam; 1687) to the effect that "the theology of the Siamites profoundly owes to a plurality of gods, or consists properly in acknowledging no God at all." He also offers a now much-cited anecdote whereby, in a reported conversation with the Dutch ambassador, the king of Siam defies reason by refusing to believe that ice formed on water. In so doing, however, Locke affirms that the grounds of probability are guided either by one's own experience or by the testimony of others. Of course, as Voltaire notes in *Traité sur la tolérance* (A Treatise on Toleration; 1763), if there was real Christian tolerance, then Europe would treat Chinese, Jews, Turks, and Siamese as equals or as brothers.

Interestingly, Siam was profiled in Harris's *Navigantium* . . . (1705), not from the pen of a European visitor but by a "native of China . . . bred up on letters" who may never have visited. The account of Dionysius Khoo, a Jesuit convert, is all the more interesting for its own "Orientalist" spin. Siam, he observed, a very large kingdom, formerly subject and tributary to the Chinese Empire, had, because of distance and upheavals in China, "shook off the yoke." "This is a Kingdom of very wide extent, but the land is waste, untilled and uninhabited; and its people living mostly in Woods and Wildernesses, behave themselves rather like Wild beasts than reasonable creatures."

## VOLTAIRE ON BRAHMIN INDIA

In 1756, Voltaire challenged the dominant European Christian-centric view of India through his essay "Dialogue Entre un Brahmane et un Jesuit sur le Nécessité et l'Enchainement des Choses" (Dialogue between a Brahmin and a Jesuit on the Necessity of the Sequence of Things; 1961, 311–16). In this exchange, the dialogue not only is a fiction contrived by the philosopher of the Enlightenment but is presented through the eyes of a local agent using Western discourse. Specifically, Voltaire sets up a conversation between a learned Brahmin and a councilor of the government of Pondicherry, from 1673 a French enclave on the Coromandel coast of India until its temporary loss to the British in 1761. Essentially, the question posed to the much-traveled Brahmin is, "Under what sort of government would you choose to be born?" The Brahmin finds little content among a populace ruled by rajas, *omrahs,* and nabobs, wishing an end to the great Mogul's rule. Allowing that laws, unlike religions, are climatically determined, ultimately for the Brahmin the ideal state is where the laws are obeyed. Mystically, he replies to the councilor, to find that country, "we must look for it" (Voltaire 1924).

Over the following decades, Voltaire was increasingly convinced that Western astronomy and astrology had its origins in the Ganges River region of India. For Voltaire, India came to replace China as the ideal civilization. To be sure, Voltaire may have been handicapped by his sources, as translations from Hindu texts were still fragmentary at best in his time. But church sources were accessible. We recall the writings of Macau-born Franciscan Jacinto de Deus (1612–1681), who spoke of the Orient as a counterpart of Europe: "We must evaluate the place [India] by the substance and by the natural endowment. The endowments give the place greater dignity because there God planted his earthly paradise. . . . There started the first politics, as well as the first learning and science, that the Greeks had learned from the Hebrew, Phoenician, Magus and Brahmins. Here started the elucidation of science, both Testaments and sacred Theology" (Deus 1690, 2–3, cited in Ramada Curto 1997, 69).

As Voltaire (1924) himself wrote, "Is it probable that the Brahmins were the first legislators of the earth, the first philosophers, the first theologians?" Even if the sacred books were full of contradictions, then "figurative meaning, allegories, symbols, express declarations of Birma, Brahma and Vishnu, which should close the mouths of all who reason." In his eightieth year, Voltaire returned to an Indian theme in his *Fragments sur l'Inde et sur Le General Lalli* (Fragments of India and on General Lalli; 1773). *Fragments* not only was a critique of the French justice system as applied to the general blamed for losing Pondicherry to the British but also offered a forum for Voltaire to expand on a civilization older than China. This he illustrated with reference to the little kingdom of Bishnapore, a part fictional and part utopian gesture.[5]

## DUTCH JUSTICE IN ASIA

Native despotism was one thing, but, willy-nilly, the Europeans brought their own standards to Asia. Such was carried in the Dutch massacre of the English (and Japanese) at Ambon in the Moluccas in 1623. The details of the "Amboina massacre," as it was known, were graphically carried in such publications as Beaumont's *Emblem of Ingratitude*, subtitled *A True Relation of the Unjust, Cruel, and Barbarous Proceedings against the English at Amboyna in the East Indies, by the Netherlands Governor and Council There . . .* (1672), becoming a best-seller in England and running to many editions. Fifty years after the event in 1673, the English poet John Dryden (1631–1700) published his prose tragedy *Amboyna, or the Cruelties of the Dutch to the English Merchants*, otherwise written to prod the English to prosecute the Third Dutch War (1672–1674).[6]

Enemies, in European legal discourse of the age, were fairly dispensable. So were renegades, such as witnessed in the 1680s by the Englishman Christopher Frykes in Batavia. He observed that a mixed bunch of European

"pirates" and renegade Dutch, possibly survivors of one of the Company attacks on the northern Java trading port of Bantam, were "examined" in
Batavia. As a result,

> one part was broke upon the Wheel, some were Quarter'd, some were
> W'hipt, some had their Ears and Noses cut off, and some were burnt in the
> forehead. The three Hollanders were hang'd. The two Danes beheaded; and
> a great number of others were sent to several islands; to burn lime, Hew
> Stones, &c and there remain Slaves all their Lives. Their Wives and Children
> were served after the same manner, that it might more effectively prove a ter-
> ror to others. (Fryke and Schweitzer 1997, 133, 146)

Less than fifty years later, a "very extraordinary affair" came to the attention of Dutch sea captain Roggewain some months before his arrival in
Batavia in 1722. This was news of a plot by Batavia-born Eurasian Christian Peter Erberfeld and comrades to overthrow the Dutch establishment.
In this affair, he was alleged to have conspired with certain Muslim
princes, only to be undone by one of these gentlemen who feared that his
plot would not stop at assassinating the governor-general but other emi-
nences as well. From the tersely written judgment handed down by the
Dutch court in Batavia,

> The two criminals, Erberfeld and Catadia, otherwise styled Rading shall be ex-
> tended and bound, each of them on a crop where they shall each have their
> right hands cut off, and then their arms, legs and breasts, pinched with red-hot
> pincers till pieces of flesh are torn away. They shall then alive their bellies
> ripped up from the bottom to the top, and their hearts thrown in their faces, af-
> ter which their heads shall be cut off, and fixed upon a post, and their bodies,
> being torn to pieces, shall be exposed to the fowls of the air without the city in
> whatever place the government shall please to direct.

Brought down on April 8, 1722, the sentence was executed as pronounced on Wednesday, April 22, 1722. Another four were similarly "broken alive," albeit without receiving the coup de grâce, then left to the prey
of the birds. Finally, their effects were confiscated to pay for the executions. Peter Erberfeld's house was pulled down and a "Column of In-
famy" erected on the site. This was embossed with a death head and inscribed in Dutch, Portuguese, Malay, Javanese, and Chinese, "In this place
heretofore stood the house of that unworthy traitor Peter Erberfeld"
(Roggewain in Harris 1745, 283). Very clearly, Christian mercy or, for that
matter, the application of reason to justice as advocated by Grotius one
hundred years earlier had not traveled far in European domains. But
Christianity was also invoked in the sentence pronounced on Nicolo, a
Venetian caught flagrante delicto in the act of sodomy with two boys on a
Dutch ship in the 1680s. In this case, and a more or less standard sentence

for this act in this age, the threesome were bound together and flung into the sea "the next after morning prayers" (Fryke and Schweitzer 1997, 113).

## CONCLUSION

We have viewed how Asian forms of governance offered a sounding board for European Enlightenment thinkers. The model of Islam was always close at hand, whether the Barbary coast, the Ottoman Turks, or the Moors of the Magellan circumnavigation as encountered on the other side of the earth. But just as Jesuit and other texts relating to Persia, Mughal India, Qing China, Tokugawa Japan, and the Choson court gained a wide reception in Enlightenment Europe, so in the hands of the French philosophes the debate on Oriental despotism was launched. While, to be sure, the enlightened-despotism view of Voltaire faded fast by the nineteenth century, assailed by liberals as much as by the new discourse opened up by the French Revolution, there is a sense that Asia was condemned in this debate or at least its sequels. Here we are referring to Kant, Hegel, and especially Marx, who denigrated Asian regions as not only despotic but also fossilized, incapable of progress and offering obstacles to capitalist development. Famously, Marx described such societies as conforming to an Asiatic mode of production. Even until the 1950s, thinkers such as Karl Wittfogel saw in agrarian China a perfect fit with Oriental despotism.

Our examples of European images of Southeast Asian courts do not detract from the Enlightenment perspectives of Asian despotism, at least as summarized by Montesquieu, but with the added sense of tyrannical justice unmediated by legal institutions, as in China, such as was respected, if not greatly admired, in Europe.[7] From our selective survey, it can also be argued that the courts and cosmopolitan trading kingdoms of India and maritime and mainland Southeast Asia failed to impress the Europeans as to either governance or military prowess. But warfare in Asia was more often than not over control of manpower. The struggles between the Buddhist kingdoms of Ayutthaya, Vientiane, and "Burma," as witnessed by the first European visitors, often led to the relocation of the capital (Ayutthaya to Bangkok) or in offering dual allegiance (Luang Prabang and Phnom Penh, respectively, to Bangkok and Hue), yet there was cultural continuity as well.

One of the major trends of the early modern period was for the disappearance or at least consolidation of princelings into kingdoms. Whether termed *chaomuang* (lord of the realm), raja or sultan, or other appellations, the number of princelings in our bounded Asian region undoubtedly numbered, according to definition, into hundreds or even thousands in the premodern period. In significant ways, European expansion as much as dissemination of new military technologies hastened this consolidation and eventual homogenization. European expansion, even in the age of the first globalization, both accommodated to and disrupted age-old Asian forms of diplomatic communications between these royal centers long before a nation-state system of equals came to be accepted either by European interlopers or by Asians themselves.

While the focus in this chapter has been on the intellectual reception in Europe of especially narrative accounts of Asia, particularly China, we reserve for a separate chapter understandings of Europe in Asian courts and centers.

## NOTES

1. Another exemplar is Victoire Antoine Hennequin (1849), who adopted the literary conceit of having a Chinese mandarin, Kao-Tseu, observe with distaste the 1848 Paris commune. The fictional mandarin solicited information on communism from workers he interviewed.

2. Recent scholarship on Kaempfer's original manuscripts reveals that certain of his translators and editors distorted his text. Nevertheless, Kaempfer's views on the seclusion policy were already published in his *Amoenitatum Exoticarum* (1712). See Michel (2000c).

3. Bhabha (1994, 93–101).

4. The major study of Aceh during this period is Lombard (1967). See also Lombard (1996) for an account of Augustin de Beaulieu's travels to the East Indies.

5. For a scholarly study on Voltaire and Indian philosophy, see Halbfass (1998).

6. The Ambon massacre has also been told with verve by Milton (1999, 309–42).

7. In an interesting observation, Woodside (1998, 121–34) argues that contemporary postmodernism, while criticizing the "othering" embraced by Orientalism, consistently ignores Chinese thought. Contrariwise, China-based scholars are conversant with Western thought, including the Enlightenment and classical thinkers. As we discussed, Montesquieu, Rousseau, and the French philosophes certainly took China seriously, but, as Woodside reminds us, the same cannot be said of Derrida and Foucault. For Woodside, the Western and Chinese "theory worlds" are less reconciled than they were in the seventeenth and eighteenth centuries. As Woodside unequivocally states, the blame lies with Western provincialism.

# 7

# Civilizational Encounters

The first Europeans arriving in the Orient were obviously confronted with vastly different and even perplexing renditions of time and space. Local dynastic cycles used for measuring eras, such as those that still prevail in Japan, struck them as idiosyncratic. Attempts to impose or even observe the Christian calendar in China and Japan were not tolerated. Christian-Catholic Iberians, basically familiar with Arab science and Islamic lore, clearly entered a long learning curve in their encounter with Hindu, Buddhist, and Confucian civilizations. While elements of contestation between adherents of these religions also entered the picture (the expulsion of Christian missionaries from Japan in the late sixteenth and early seventeenth centuries being perhaps the most dramatic example of rejection), the major momentum of this activity was obviously the attempt to convert, usually, rulers and ruling classes, followed by their subject peoples (though relatively few conversions from Islam, Hinduism, or Buddhism were in fact achieved), or the conversion of animist peoples, a process that continues today. Islamic conversions on the island of Borneo and Christian conversions of animist Timorese in East Timor are cases in point. In this chapter, we survey the variety of civilizational encounters between the first-arriving Europeans and local bearers of power in the various court polities and royal centers of Asia. As should become clear, the term "encounter" implies a number of readings, from curiosity to reception to accommodation and rejection. It also implies a good deal of mutuality, as the intellectual and cultural exchanges in the age were truly two way, as perhaps best exemplified in the binary figure of the Jesuit mandarin.

## THE MONGOL EXCHANGE

The Mongol conquest of a vast Eurasian zone evoked both fear and awe in Europe. On the side of awe, as discussed in chapter 1, the international character of Mongol administration under Kublai Khan (1215–1294) in his new capital in Cambuluc (now Beijing) offered opportunities for Europeans, including Dominican and Franciscan friars and Genoese and Venetian travelers, Marco Polo among them. The unification of disparate ethnic and religious groups stemming from the Mongol conquest of the central Asian region brought Europe and China into direct contact for the first time in 1,000 years. It also brought security for the terrestrial Silk Road trade. In describing the place of the Mongols in the thirteenth-century world economy, Janet Abu-Lughod (1989, 154) argues that their major contribution was "to create an environment that facilitated land transit with less risk and lower protective rent," opening a route for trade through central Asia that briefly broke the monopoly of southern routes.

Nevertheless, the inhospitable arid lands, long traversed by Jewish and Muslim traders, especially the Transoxiana region, came to be incorporated into Muslim empires. Muslim Samarkand was one such key node and caravansary in an age-old web of "silk roads" connecting China with the Mediterranean zone from Roman times. As Abu-Lughod (1989, 159–60) emphasizes, medieval European knowledge of the vast Asian system it wished to join in trade was scant, at least until the accession of Kublai Khan in 1260. Real testimony of the great central Asian route to Cathay from the fourth decade of the fourteenth century, at the point when this pathway was to close, comes from the merchant handbook of Francesco de Balducci Pegolotti (ca. 1340), although Marco Polo also described the great Mongol commercial centers of Hangzhou and Guangzhou along with the splendors of the great khan's empire.

The rapid collapse of the Pax Mongolia and the shift of Mongol interest from the conquest of Eurasia to the conquest of Song China and the establishment of the Mongol Yuan dynasty (1279–1368) coincided with a Mongol religious-military alliance with Tibet. But Mongolia simply dropped off the agenda of European interest, at least until Jesuit mapmakers in the employ of the Qing had occasion to visit in the first decades of the eighteenth century. While the Manchu were clearly dominant in their alliance with the Mongols, the latter nevertheless provided the Qing with important military support, especially on China's vast inner frontier. Notably, the Mongol Turgut of the Oirat confederation moved into the Volga region of Russia, followed by the Dorbet tribe, together forming a Kalmyk settlement. Stung by onerous czarist taxes and fleeing ahead of pursuing Russians, Kyrgyz, and Kazaks, the Mongols made a narrow and "heroic" escape. Alone in Europe, it was the Russian scholars, politicians, and others who engaged the Mongol remnants and ethnic-cultural "contamination." Historian of the Mongols Uradyn Bulag, in a communication to the author, stated, "The importance of the Kalmyks should not be understated. European biologists/anthropologists got their racial knowledge about the Mongols from European travelers to Kalmykia. It is perhaps not unfair to say that the Kalmyk Mongols provided the 'concrete' sample for the racial type Mongoloid."[1]

## THE SINIC VIEW OF THE UNIVERSE

The Sinic view of the universe, at the core of the neo-Confucian orthodoxy, long held to the concept of the universe as a harmonious system. The cosmos was seen as a moral and social order, and, as Goodman (1986, 87–88) has elaborated, European investigations into sciences were undoubtedly viewed with much suspicion by the mandarinal authorities. Of greatest concern to Confucian scholars, he elaborates, was that somehow the westerners were tampering with the "laws" of heaven, threatening to create serious disharmony. This held as much in Japan as in China, but, as discussed later in this chapter, the attitudes of these two East Asian civilizations toward Western science, as much the intellectual outcomes in terms of assimilating and adopting the new learning, were nevertheless poles apart.

Obviously, the great Ming voyages between 1405 and 1433 to the Indian Ocean zone under the Muslim admiral Zheng He (1371–1433) reinforced tributary relationships over a broad area, just as it expanded Chinese geographical knowledge of the Afro-Asian maritime trading routes derived from Song times. There is not a little irony in the fact that the great Ming sea voyages into and across the Indian Ocean, or what Waley-Cohen (1999, 48) terms "the most extensive maritime explorations in world history," preceded the Portuguese by generations, although it also might be said that the outcomes were entirely different (cf. Chaudhuri 1985, 34–62). Prior to the age of the great European discoveries, the African world below the Sahara, much less its shape, was largely unknown in Europe. But the "Oceans of Darkness," otherwise much feared in Europe, had already entered Chinese understanding. Chang Kuei-sheng (1970, 21) confirms that Sino-Arab trade and intellectual exchange not only manifested itself in an emerging world concept of

Chinese cartography, such as in Mongol-dynasty maps, but also served to facilitate Chinese maritime entry into the Indian Ocean.

Importantly also, as Needham (1959, 490) explains, unlike the Portuguese, the Ming did not seek to establish fortresses and strong points to mark their advance; rather, their mission was pacific, diplomatic, and even "protoscientific" in the manner of collection for trade and consumption. The scope and scale of these state-sponsored voyages was vast. In terms of scale, the first expedition reaching Sumatra on the outward voyage and Java and Siam on the return comprised sixty-two large junks, 225 smaller ones, and a crew of 27,000 mariners, including gunners. The sixth voyage established official relations with such places as Malindi, Mombassa, Zanzibar, and Dar es Salaam. By the seventh voyage, Zheng He's fleet had cemented commercial and diplomatic ties with some thirty-five states in the Indian Ocean, the Persian Gulf, the Red Sea, and the east coast of Africa.

Suárez confirms that maps and information were collected before each of Zheng's voyages and that charts were compared and corrected for compass bearings and guiding stars, while drawings of islands and water bodies were also compiled (Suárez 1999, 48–49). Modern scholarship identifies 715 Chinese toponyms used in the *Ying-yai shenglan*, a 1433 chronicle of the Ming voyages written by Ma Huan (1997). But with the death of Emperor Yong-lo in 1424, the death of Zheng He a decade later, along with the shift of China's capital from Nanjing in the south to Beijing in the north and the Ming prohibition on overseas trade, China's push into the southern seas was not repeated on such scale. Although the junk trade continued in significant ways to Malacca, Batavia, Manila, Nagasaki, and other destinations (Hung 2000), the Indian Ocean trade continued to be dominated by Muslim merchants until the Portuguese themselves entered the arena not only as traders but also as conquistadores. Still, as Chang Kuei-sheng (1970, 30) has demonstrated, the long era of contacts with the Arab world irreversibly modified the traditional view of Chinese geographical understanding.

## THE JESUIT RECEPTION IN CHINA

We have discussed the Jesuit push into China, remarking on their role as cultural brokers in the reception of China in Europe, but it is equally appropriate to examine the Jesuit reception in China. The Jesuits at the court of late Ming China not only labored hard to win converts to Christianity but also won the admiration of the court mandarins for their skills at mapmaking, clock making, and other sciences, veritably presenting an alternative cosmology at that time and place. We also observe that Jesuits worked hard to accommodate local cosmological views in order to win access to the court. Such compromises with Confucian practice and even doctrine would, as discussed in chapter 4, led to the "rites controversy."

As Mungello (1999, 14) has explained, in China the Jesuits favored a "top-down" approach. Unlike the more uncompromising Spanish Franciscans who gained some success in mass conversions of ordinary Chinese in Shandong Province, the Jesuits came to understand that only by accommodation with the Confucian elite was it possible to make headway in China. In so doing, the Jesuits eschewed popular Buddhism and Daoism and, controversially, blended Confucianism with Christianity. Early Jesuit success was marked by the conversion of a number of prominent Ming scholar-officials. The original Jesuit reception, Mungello explains, was also eased by a late Ming liberalism in experimenting with different philosophies, an attitude to be contrasted with a "closing of Chinese minds" after the Manchu conquest of 1644.

In 1629, the Jesuit Adam Schall had been allowed to form the Board of Calendrics in Beijing, offering him a privileged position to influence the Chinese court on a range of astronomical, mathematical, and geographical questions. According to Jesuit texts transcribed in Purchas (1905–1907, vol. 12, 275), also revealing of the way that Ricci sought to accommodate the Chinese sense of centrality,

> They had a cosmological map in European characters, hanging in their hall, which the learned beheld with great pleasure, much desiring to see it in Chinese characters, little knowing, as little having to do with the rest of the world. They had maps pretending a description of the world but presented only their fifteen provinces, with the sea and a few lands, and the names of such kingdoms as they had heard, all which kingdoms scarcely equaled one province of China. They now wondered much to see themselves straightened in an Eastern corner of the world. Ricius at the governor's request, published it in China characters: They have a conceit that the heavens are round, the earth square, and their empire to be seated in the midst thereof, he therefore so projected his Description, that he presented China in the midst.
>
> They that before thought barely of other men, as if elsewhere were no king, nor Republics, nor books, began to be better conceited of Europeans and to be better prepared for the need of the Gospels, and also less fear European forces so remote from them.

Even so, after initial successes, imperial regents turned against the missionaries, reviving the old charge that they were preparing a Portuguese invasion of China. Some were sentenced to death and many taken prisoner. Matters changed only when the fourteen-year-old Kangxi emperor was befriended by the Jesuit Ferdinand Verbeist (1617–1688) and began to intercede in favor of the missionaries. Documentation on the ambiguous imperial rescript tolerating Christianity was published in China in 1671 by the Portuguese vice provincial Antonio de Gouvea (1592–1677) following his release from prison.

In 1668, the young emperor had challenged Verbeist to prove the superiority of European mathematics through a series of contests with his detractors among the mandarins, such as in determining the absolute and relative positions of the sun and planets on a given date. Victorious, Verbeist rescued the imperiled Jesuit mission and was offered the presidency of the Bureau of Mathematics. Reputedly, the emperor became Verbeist's devoted pupil in mathematics, geometry, topography, and other disciplines. In 1673, Verbeist even managed to persuade the Kangxi emperor to pull down the celestial globe and armillary sphere erected in the palace in Beijing in 1274 by the Mongol emperor's astronomer and to replace it with new ones of his contrivance (Stevenson 1921, 128, 132). But as bearers of superior knowledge of astronomy and mathematics, the Jesuits themselves were not yet fully reconciled to the Copernican view of the universe.

## CHINESE ETHNOCENTRICITY?

Just as we witness a resurgent Sinocentrism or at least Sinicizing trend on the periphery of present-day China, at least as concerns Hong Kong, Macau, and Taiwan, so some Sinoskepticism has emerged in the West, paradoxically arising out of China's strength, not weakness. But the Middle Kingdom syndrome was also the bane of early Jesuit missionaries, just as Jesuit ethnocentricity also shone through, at least in their personal letters. Jesuit concerns with Chinese disinterest in the science of Europe in favor of studies that led to official preferment were expressed from the outset. As Jesuit missionary-scholar Nicolas Trigault revealed, "It is evident to everyone here that no one will labor to obtain proficiency in mathematics or in medicine who has any hope of becoming prominent in the field of [Confucian] philosophy." As Jean-Baptiste du Halde stated the matter in his canonical *Description* . . . (1741), "The great and only Road to Riches, Honor, and Employments is the study of the *ching* (or canonical books), History, the Laws and Morality." In particular, as de Bary (1960, 563–6) interprets, the capabilities of the educated class were narrowly controlled by the type of examination system screening entrance to official life.

Figure 7.1.   Armillary sphere and celestial globe, from Ferdinand Verbeist, *Ling tai yi xiang zhi* (1673). This is but a selection of the European astronomical instruments recreated in China by the Jesuit Verbeist, in turn reproduced in this Chinese woodblock production. (Courtesy of the Macau Historical Archives)

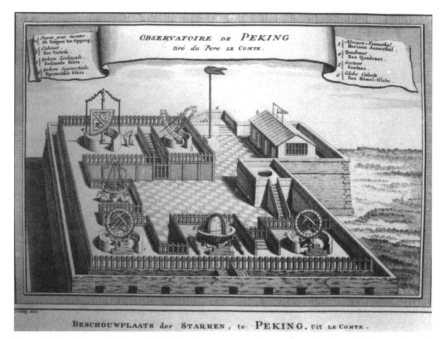

**Figure 7.2.** General view of Beijing observatory after adaptations made by Ferdinand Verbeist, from Dutch engraving in Louis Lecomte, *Nouveaux Memoires sur l'Etat present de la Chine* (1696) after Verbeist, *Astronomia European sub Imperatore Tartaro Sinico Cam Illy* (1674 [1697]). Still extant, the famous Jesuit observatory in Beijing not only served the transmission of post-Renaissance European scientific knowledge but actively serviced the calendrical needs of the neo-Confucian establishment, albeit short of China's own scientific revolution. (Courtesy of the Macau Historical Archives)

As signaled by Jesuit Father Chavagnac in a letter to his superiors in France from Fuzhou, dated February 10, 1703, on the obstacles facing missions in China, "The contempt with which the Chinese look upon all other Nations is one of the greatest, even among the meaner people. Having to a great Conceit of their own country, their manners, their customs and their Maxims, they cannot be persuaded that anything which is not of China deserves to be regarded." As the Chinese literati answered back, "Your religion is not to be found in our books." Indeed, he continued, "They often ask us, whether there are towns, villages, and houses in Europe." But nothing surprised the father more than the doubt expressed by the literati when he showed them his *mappe monde.* "This I said is Europe, this Africa and this is Asia, in Asia, here is Persia, here India, and here Tartary. They all cried out, then where is China? It is this small spot of land, said I, and here are its bounds." Amazed, they replied, "Ciao te kin [It is very little]." Several years later, as revealed by the Jesuit Pierre Jartoux, the Jesuits were engaged by the emperor to produce a "Map of Tartary," an exercise that afforded them the leisure of wide-ranging travel and observation (*The Travels of Several Learned Missioners* 1714, 180–81).

Even so, as Mungello (1999, 39) summarizes, opposition on the part of the literati to Western culture and Christianity was based less on ethnocentricity than on the strength of the neo-Confucian orthodoxy that saw in Christianity, as with Buddhism and Daoism, a heterodox challenge. Unlike historical Confucianism, which the Jesuits favored and even exalted in their writings, neo-Confucianism, with its embrace of spirits and transcendent concerns, had explicit religious dimensions. Moreover, the European missionaries added to a general fear of subversion, especially on the part of the Qing.

## CHINESE REJECTION OF WESTERN SCIENCE

Joining Korean, Mongol, and Manchu emissaries at the Qing court in Beijing in 1794, after a long overland voyage via Guangzhou, André Everard van Braun, second in command of the Dutch embassy, offered very positive comments on Chinese accomplishments, including agriculture, architecture, and bridge making, but in reflecting on the "superstitious" practices of the court, for example, in observing lunar eclipses, he commented, "It is evident that the scientific knowledge possessed by the Chinese is of very ancient date, and they obtained it long before the sciences were known in Europe. But everything has remained in its primitive state, without their even seeking like the Europeans, to make further progress, or to bring their discoveries to perfection." "We have consequently far surpassed them," he further mused, yet the Chinese could not perceive, nor would they acknowledge, it (van Braam 1798, vol. 2, 38). During the first half of the Qing, the state further extended its patronage of Confucian scholarship, including classical studies. De Bary (1960, 564) declares that the great contribution of the Qing was to indirectly foster a "Chinese feeling of self-sufficiency in intellectual matters" at a time when the empire was peaceful and prosperous. Even so, the Europeans—the Jesuits included—had to struggle to overcome the prejudices of the age, especially when Christian dogma stood in the way.

According to Nathan Sivin (1995), Chinese rejection of modern science as introduced by the Jesuits should not be seen as some intellectual failure but owed to the garbled transmission. Simply stated, the Jesuits were forbidden to openly discuss the concept of a sun-centered planetary system after 1616. But in their intellectual efforts to honor Copernicus, they characterized his world system in misleading ways. The first Chinese text on the discoveries of Galileo is illustrative because, as Ricci had recognized, science, and especially astronomy, was a powerful tool to influence the elite, especially by demonstrating superior methods for the calculation of the Chinese calendar. This was *Thien wen lueh* (Explicatio Sphaerae Coelestis), printed in Chinese characters on woodblock in 1615. The author was the Portuguese Jesuit Emmanuel Diaz (d. 1659). Diaz enthusiastically related how he had recently been informed that a famous Western scientist had observed the heavens through a telescope, a reference to Galileo's discoveries in 1609. Despite the 1616 injunction of the Holy Office prohibiting Galileo from publicizing the Copernican doctrine on the motion of the earth, the Jesuits in China continued to work with the telescope and to transmit the discoveries while careful not to play up the ecclesiastical controversies (Needham 1972, 444). Again, as Sivin (1995, 72) argues, the Copernican episode in China demonstrates the need for care in understanding the interaction of the two systems of science and how one culture accepts or rejects the scientific ideas of another.

## VIETNAM AND THE CHINESE MODEL

Vietnam, which secured its independence from China in the tenth century (like Ryukyu/Okinawa in the eighteenth and nineteenth centuries), developed with varying success a tributary or, rather, subtributary diplomacy on the Chinese model. For Vietnam, this was a means of organizing power, preserving order, monopolizing a dynamic maritime trade, and establishing hierarchy. The Chinese, too, frequently imagined tributary principles of subservience where doubtless others saw mostly economic gain or other advantage.[2]

The complexity of the Vietnamese approach has been identified by Li Tana (1998) in her monograph on Nguyen Cochin China. Her story traces the rise in the early seventeenth century of Dang Trong, a new political center in the south of Vietnam around the Nguyen dynasty, at first offering up tribute to the more powerful Le-Trinh in the north but by 1621 resisting. A shallow model of the north, the breakaway regime of the Nguyen penetrated a frontier where Confucianism was unknown and local traditions were permeated with the legacy of the Hindu Cham *negara*. Complicating the picture, a third center of power emerged around Hue in the center of the country. Despite elaborate attempts to rebuild a civil administration based on the Chinese model, the Nguyen, more Buddhist than Confucianist, were unsuccessful in gaining Chinese approval to become an independent vassal. The end of the Le-Trinh dynasty (1428–1788) also coincided with major social and political upheavals leading to the rise in 1771 of the Tay-Son movement with its roots in the south. In 1801, taking advantage of the Qing invasion of 1788–1789, the Nguyen restored themselves in the north as Gia-Long, the last dynasty in Vietnamese history. Splits in the ruling Nguyen family opened the way for progressive French intervention, leading to gunboat diplomacy (1847) and eventually full-scale imperialist intervention (cf. Marr 1971, 15–27).

As Alexander Woodside has brilliantly summarized, up to the nineteenth century, the Vietnamese court successfully maintained the internal consistency of the Chinese model in its geographical conceptualization of Asia. This is seen in the way that Vietnam adopted Sino-Vietnamese variants of Chinese names for regional toponyms (for example, "Ai Lao" for "Laos," a Chinese term since late Han times). In 1815, Emperor Gia-long published a list of thirteen countries deemed vassals of Vietnam, including Luang Prabang, Vientiane, Burma, France, England, Tran Ninh (a province of Laos), and the Jarai, or montagnard kingdoms, termed "water haven" and "fire-haven." From the perspective of the court in Hue, these countries conceded the legitimacy of Sino-Vietnamese diplomatic laws relating to the management of distant peoples and even "border barbarians." But the presumption to collect tribute from most of these countries or regions at Hue was more than often fictional. By 1802–1847, only the relatively weaker courts of Luang Prabang, Vientiane, and Phnom Penh could be called true vassals of Vietnam. Woodside summarizes that "the Vietnamese tributary system was a frame of reference for mediating Vietnamese adaptations to the external world. But it was a culturally borrowed frame of reference." Vietnamese ambivalence to the model in its pure Sinitic form was also manifested in the way that, by Minh-mang's time (r. 1820–1841), Southeast Asian toponyms came to be Vietnamized in *quoc am*, not classical Chinese (Woodside 1971, 234–46).

In the opening decades of the seventeenth century, European missionaries and adventurers joined Japanese and other Asian traders in the thriving cosmopolitan trading port of Hoi An in central Vietnam (Anonymous 1993). In general terms, as Li Tana (1998, 173–79) has written, westerners were confused over the identity of the "king of Cochin China," the seat of government, as much the political complexion of the realm. Notably, through the seventeenth century, the Dutch confounded the governor of Quang Nam, an important economic center, with the king himself, even misleadingly terming the country "Quinam." Vexed by their reception in Quang Nam, in 1643 the Dutch sided with the Trinh in, unsuccessfully, launching a joint expedition against the southerners.

A second wave of Europeans was attracted to Than Long (Hanoi) from the early seventeenth century. In 1648, the British established a trading post in nearby Ha Khau, followed by the Dutch in 1683, attracted by the trade in, especially, silk but also rice and sugar. As related by Peter Auber (1834, 140), in 1672 an English ship was sent to Tonkin to revive trade but some fourteen miles upriver was subject to "unreasonable imposition," namely, being forced by the mandarin and his armed body to sail against wind and tide, obviously incomprehensible to a mariner. Over the protests by the English ship, the mandarin replied in Chinese characters, "We were come to a great country of good justice and government and that if we would do all things that he would have us it would be well for us." Moreover, he lectured, "the King was king of Tonquin before we came there, and would be after we departed." No less incomprehensible to the ears of the English "supercargo" or shipborne commercial agent was the retort by the mandarin that his country had no need of foreign things, although that statement was belied by craft and trade traditions. Not only did the English merchants deem the journey unprofitable, but they left much chagrined at their inexplicable reception.

Even so, Italian missionary J. P. de Marini, who sojourned in Than Long in the early seventeenth century, was one who drew attention to the capital's famous specialist craft quarters. Writing of his visit in 1688 some nine years before the English trading post was closed, Englishman William Dampier (1699, 29–30) was clearly impressed by the industry of the ancient capital: "Shoing-smiths, turners, weavers, tailors, potters, painters, money changers, papermakers, bell varnishers." Nevertheless, foreign trade was strictly controlled, and a 1746 edict forbade foreign traders to stay overnight in the capital (Anonymous 1977, 79).

There is a sense that the Vietnamese literati entered a long contestatory ideological zone stemming from the first missionary encounters, leading to a deepening crisis during the epoch of French colonialism. In chapter 3, we noted the presence of Portuguese mathematician and naturalist Juan de Loureiro at the Nguyen court. While the Nguyen remained fundamentally opposed to the Christian mission, nevertheless the practice of employing Jesuits at the court, especially as doctors but also as mathematicians and astronomers, continued generation after generation until the 1820s. To be sure, as Boxer has written, Jesuits arriving from Macau were also useful suppliers of guns and gunners (Boxer 1984, 37, cited in Li Tana 1998, 72). Overall, the Jesuit presence at the Nguyen court has to be seen alongside the tradition of religious syncretism established in Cochin China—no apparent contradiction in the attempt to re-create a pale version of the Chinese administrative model but also no major deviation from the model as far as the reception of Western science was concerned. Linguistically, however, as explained in chapter 9, the first European encounter with Vietnam would have a lasting impact on Vietnam's civilizational identity.[3]

## THE JAPANESE RECEPTION OF EUROPE

While Japanese traders and pirates were also drawn into the Southeast Asia trading networks at least until the seclusion edicts forbade their activities, and while the island kingdom of Ryukyu traded to such maritime destinations as Malacca and Java, prior to the European intrusion, the neo-Confucian state in Japan remained wedded to a three-kingdom cosmography that privileged Japan, China, and India, sometimes expressed in so-called Buddhist world maps, or Gotenjiku (five Indias). Such maps were inspired by pilgrimages to the land where Buddha was born dating back to the Tang dynasty. While derivative of a broad cosmographic tradition shared by China and Korea in the production of so-called wheel maps (cf. Needham 1959, 565), the prototype Buddhist world map drawn in Japan was by the Buddhist Hotan and published in 1710. According to Ayusawa (1953, 124), the special feature of these maps is the representation of an imaginary India and the illustration of the religious world as expounded by Buddhists, typically featuring the equivalent of a Mount Meru. In these maps, the real world, albeit not the world depicted on the then-available European world maps, is connected with the spiritual world. Derivatives of Hotan's map were reproduced through the Edo period, even though new geographical knowledge was being assimilated through the accumulation of empirical data.

Early-arriving Europeans in Japan were undoubtedly perplexed as to Japan's cosmological traditions. In a letter of 1552, St. Francis Xavier (1506–1552) wrote of Japan, "There is as yet no one who knows of the shape of the earth and its movements" (cited in Goodman 1986, 90). As recorded in Jesuit Luís Fróis's letter of July 12, 1560, he was asked many questions by Oda Nobunaga (1534–1582) about the geography of India, the characteristics of hot and cold climates, and customs and manners of foreign countries. But just as the first Portuguese visitors to Japan brought knowledge of Europe, Africa, and the Americas, so the Europeans looked to Japanese cartographers to expand their knowledge of the Japanese archipelago and Korea, long misrepresented on sixteenth- and seventeenth-century European maps as an island.

It should not be forgotten that in embracing neo-Confucian doctrine, the Tokugawa also dropped the practice of mounting direct tribute embassies to the Chinese court. Rather, the Japanese developed their own version of subtributary diplomacy, expanding geographical knowledge and economic links throughout the Asian region. This was especially the case with Ryukyu when, from 1601, the Tokugawa brought the island kingdom into its tributary orbit, albeit not in a way to prejudice the island king's valuable intermediary tribute-trading role with China alongside its active trade with numerous Southeast Asian ports. In fact, until the kingdom was absorbed by Japan in 1879, Ryukyu paid dual tribute to China and Japan. The complexity of the system is also exemplified by Tsushima island in the straits of that name, which sent envoys to both the shogun in Edo and the Korean court while in turn serving as an intermediary for Korean tribute missions to Japan and, from the early 1600s, Japanese envoys to Korea, thus both officializing and ceremonializing a two-way trade between the two countries (McCune 1946). The point is that within the vast Chinese-centered tribute-trading system, as described by Hamashita (1994), the Japanese were supremely confident in their commercial and political knowledge.

Obviously, the voyage to Europe and back (1582–1585) by a Japanese delegation offered Hideyoshi (1536–1606) certain validation of global geography, especially as they returned with such gifts as the first edition of the atlas of Abraham Ortelius, scenes of which entered Japanese folklore as painted screens. Tokugawa Ieyasu (1542–1616) learned geography directly from the Englishman Will Adams, who was shipwrecked in Japan in 1600. By 1610, Ieyasu had also inaugurated direct Japanese contacts with New Spain (Mexico). A mission dispatched to Rome via Acapulco by Date Masamune (1566–1636), *daimyo* of what is now Miyagi Prefecture, returned from Europe in 1620 with new knowledge and documentation. Portraits of the envoy, Hasekura Tsunenaga, a veteran of the invasions of Korea, rest in Rome's Borghese Palace and the Quirinal, or former Papal Palace, testifying to the reception of a surviving band of twenty-eight members. In any case, Japan was already part of a global bullion trade network connecting Nagasaki-Macau-Guangzhou-Manila-Acapulco and even Europe (Gunn 1999a).

Western science made its entry into Japan through the Japanese interpreters and their studies of Dutch language, especially after they could read Dutch books. After Shogun Yoshimune's (1634–1719) 1720 edict allowing the importation of Western books, reversing the ban imposed by Shogun Iemitsu of 1630, the interpreters began translating European works on medicine, botany, astronomy, geography, mathematics, physics, and military sciences, among other fields. This became known as the Dutch school of learning, or *rangaku*. Strictly confined to the trading post of Deshima, although allowed to participate in the annual procession to the seat of the shogunate, a restricted circle of European officials in the employ of the Dutch East India Company facilitated this transmission of Western scientific knowledge. Preeminent were Engelbert Kaempfer, Charles Peter Thunberg, and Philip Franz von Siebold (Plutschow 1991, 195–201; see also Goodman 1986, passim).

In Nagasaki, the interpreters gained high social status, and the profession even become the monopoly of certain families. Besides having proficiency in Dutch, Kaempfer (1727, 226–27) observed specialist interpreters in such languages as Portuguese, Vietnamese, Siamese, and three dialects of Chinese, indicative of a range of cultural influences and contacts. While Kaempfer was not impressed with their proficiency as interpreters, decades later Thunberg (1796, 294–95) commented that, ranked into classes according to skill, they "speak with more or less accuracy the Dutch language." He also observed their fondness for European books and their inquisitiveness as to European customs and science. Thunberg obtained a Latin-Portuguese-Japanese dictionary from an old interpreter handed down from the time of the Jesuits in Japan.

Goodman (1986, 6) contends that the grasp of Western science in Japan followed two main lines of development: medical-botanical and astronomical-calendrical. While the revelation of Western astronomy was particularly controversial, *rangaku* developed rapidly by the end of the eighteenth century. But to comprehend the intellectual revolution that fermented in Edo Japan, it is important to grasp, as Goodman emphasizes, the contemporaneous rise of urban society and the growth of trade and commerce. Even so, and in counterpoint to Nathan Sivin's caution as to the complexity of transmission of science across civilizations, the shogunal authorities long saw in the neo-Confucian orthodoxy a useful tool for social control, and few of the new scholars risked alienation from the powerful establishment.

Taking medicine as a standard, the Jesuits first established a hospital in Funai in 1549, but little progress was made in Japan in medicine until the mid-Edo period. In any case, European practice came to a halt with the expulsion of the Jesuits in 1614. European concepts of the body—especially the tradition of surgery and dissection—never challenged the dominance of Chinese concepts of cosmic harmony in Sino-Japanese medicine. Chinese medical texts continued to be imported in large numbers through Nagasaki during the so-called seclusion period. Importantly, Dutch physicians attached to the Deshima trading post progressively introduced European medical concepts into Japan through the seventeenth century. All together, 150 Dutch physicians were appointed to Deshima between the opening of Dutch trade and its closing in 1858.

One of them, Engelbert Kaempfer, who arrived in Nagasaki in 1689, even gained the attention of the shogun. Kaempfer's students included interpreter Narabayashi Chinzan, who went on to author *Koi geka soden* (The Origins of European Surgery). Another was botanist Charles Thunberg, who arrived in Nagasaki in 1775. Thunberg's pupils included Kogyo Yoshio (1724–1800), a Japanese pioneer in introducing surgical techniques, and interpreter-mapmaker Katsarugawa Hoshu, instructed by Thunberg during his single sojourn in Edo. However, it was the German-born Siebold, arriving in Deshima in 1823, who made European medical knowledge accessible to a large number of Japanese. Establishing his school of medicine in Nagasaki, Siebold's first pupils were the interpreters, some becoming his confidants and collaborators. Author of the wide-ranging scholarly study of Japan, *Nippon*, published in Leiden in 1832, Siebold achieved primacy in Europe in Japanese studies. Although Siebold was eventually expelled in 1828 for cartographic espionage, his legacy in Japan also ranged wide, from botany (he established a botanical garden in Deshima) to pharmacology to zoology, among other contributions.

It also happens that the first work translated from Dutch into Japanese was a book on anatomy. This was *Ontleedekundige Tafelen*, a Dutch translation from the German-language *Anatomische Tabellen* (Anatomical Tables), a widely circulated text on anatomy originally published in Latin in 1722 by the Danzig physician Johann Adam Kulmus (1689–1745). Translated by pioneering Japanese physician Sugita Gempaku and Maeno Ryotaku over a period of four years, the work appeared in 1774 under the title *Kaitai shinsho* (The New Book of Anatomy). Not only were the authors obliged to gain the shogun's approval for the enterprise, but they had to overcome the difficulty of discovering meanings, finding equivalents, and inventing terms for the organs unknown to Chinese tradition (Plutschow 1991, 102). For Japan, this was a revelation, as the dissection of bodies was the work of outcasts, and the tradition of anatomy was practically unknown.

In Japan, the Buddhistic cosmological view of the world combining cultural-religious elements was not really challenged until, as mentioned, such world maps as those produced by Mercator, Ortelius, and Blaeu, brought by the Dutch, came to be examined and copied. Goodman (1986, 51–52) explains that in 1770, Yoshimune permitted the importation into Japan of a number of Chinese-language texts by Ricci and others on geometry, mathematics, astronomy, and so on, many dating back one hundred years. According to Needham (1959, 447), unlike in China until the arrival of Protestant missionaries, Copernican ideas were fully admitted into Japan because of Dutch influence. Notably, Shizuki Tadao's (1760–1806) translations of a Dutch text, a ten-year labor leading to its publication in 1798 as *Rekisho shinsho* (New Impressions of History), introduced Newtonian physics and the theory of gravitation. In 1772, another interpreter, Yoshinaga Motoki, introduced the heliocentric theories of Copernicus from a translation of a Dutch source and published treatises on astronomy and geography (Plutschow 1991, 98).

Even so, Goodman (1986, 224, 233) is more agnostic as to the smooth transmission of European science into Edo Japan. Notably, he states, Dutch scholars in Japan were simply unable to grasp the significance of chronology in Western culture. Translations from the Dutch largely ignored the major European languages of English, French, and German and were haphazard as to choice and date of publication. The failure to draw on major European languages and such randomness with respect to chronology suggested to Goodman that the Japanese failed to understand the unfolding of a veritable scientific revolution in Europe. Rather, Western knowledge in the hands of the *rangaku* scholars was treated as a "Confucian-type" immutable scholarship. While sowing a tradition of curiosity about the West, he concedes, important when Japan began its modernization drive in earnest, in their time Dutch studies in Japan were "a superficial phenomenon" conducted by a small coterie of devotees and constricted by a powerful neo-Confucian establishment.

One example is indicative of the tension and caution in the Japanese encounter with Enlightenment Europe. The German Japanologist Wolfgang Michel recounts a terse exchange between Tokugawa inquisitors and Schaep, captain of one of the Dutch vessels, part of the voyage of discovery of 1643 by Vries from Batavia to chart the waters of northern Japan, Hokkaido, Sakhalin, and the southern Kuriles. Having navigated eastern Honchu as far north as Sakhalin by skirting the coast of Ezo (a term referring to Hokkaido, Sakhalin, the Kuril islands, and Kamchatka), only to be detained on the return journey to Taiwan, the Dutchman was interrogated as to how he presumed to know Tatary without a map. He replied that the Dutch had adduced the existence of Tatary from general information found in books and that, in any case, he was intending to produce a map. Moreover, he explained to the doubtful official, exact maps could exist only for regions that they had already visited, and his was the first European ship to visit the region. In this exchange, the counselor was assisted by a naturalized foreign missionary who produced his own "flat globe" map lacking any conception of Hokkaido and parts farther north (Michel 1993). In due

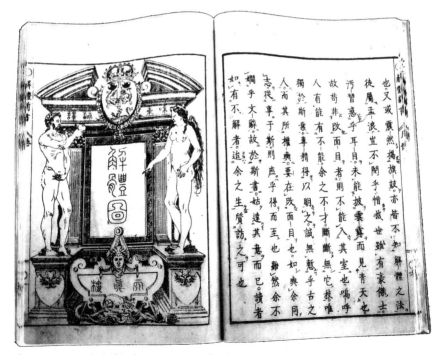

**Figure 7.3.** *Kaitai Shinsho,* **or New Book of Anatomy (1774). Replete with anatomical drawings, the original of this Japanese crossover text is a small masterpiece of translation and woodblock printing and remains well known today to Japanese schoolchildren tutored in the standard educational curriculum. (Reproduced with permission of Nagasaki Prefectual Library)**

course, information obtained from the Vries expedition (1643) entered Johann Janssonius's (1588–1664) 1652 *Atlas Novus* as *Nova et Accurata Japoniae.*

## AN EXAMPLE FROM KOREA

Enduring over 500 years, the Choson court, or Yi dynasty (1392–1910), adapted neo-Confucianism as its state ideology. An elaborate Chinese-style bureaucracy supported a royal center and system of government with powers over taxation, trade, and military affairs. The period of contact with Europe coincides with Middle Choson from the end of the fifteenth century to the end of the dynasty in the early twentieth century. The Choson court was, in turn, a tributor to the Central Kingdom, to which it sent regular missions and from which it returned with rich borrowings from the Chinese tradition. Korea shared many elements of Chinese religious cosmography. Needham (1959, 565) writes that, even alongside China, Buddhist "wheel maps," supposedly archaic, were frequently reproduced in Korea in the seventeenth and eighteenth centuries.

But just as the Choson court dispatched frequent envoys to the Ming court, so they came into contact with the Western learning, promoted by such Jesuits as Matteo Ricci and his countryman Guilo Aleni (1582–1649). From discussion with the Korean envoy Yi Su-gwang, Ricci was able to add Korea to his world map. In turn, Ricci presented Yi a copy in Chinese of his *Doctrine of the Lord of Heaven.* According to Tennant (1996, 177–88), Ricci's work was incorporated into Yi's monumental collection of essays on astronomy, mathematics, and geography, striking a new critical objectivity in his interpretation of history that broke with traditional metaphysics. By 1644, with the Manchu capture of Beijing, exiled members of the Choson court were allowed to return home. Notably, Crown Prince Sohyon brought with him a globe, books of Western learning, and a copy of the Gregorian calendar produced by the Jesuit Adam Schall.

While, as indicated, Korea became known to Europe through the accounts of various Dutch visitors, the Portuguese in Macau better understood early Choson Korea. As related and illustrated in the annals of the Choson dynasty for 1592–1599, Portuguese soldiers or military specialists were integrated into Chinese imperial forces and dispatched to the battlefront to help the Korean monarchy thwart the series of invasions mounted on the peninsula by Japanese forces under Hideyoshi. Known in Korea as the Im-Jim war, the Haegui, or *demonios do mar* (demons from the sea), deployed alongside the Ming forces can be viewed in the *Chujo Jangse Jeonbeoldo* found in the *Sae-jeon-wha-cheo* book (Neves 1994).[4]

As Henry Hamel and his band of shipwrecked mariners observed of the erstwhile hermit kingdom of Korea during his long sojourn between 1653 and 1666, "When we named some countries to them, they laughed at us, affirming we only talked of some town or village; their geographical knowledge of the Council reaching no further than Siam, by reason of the little traffick they have with strangers farther from them." He continued, "They believe there are but twelve Kingdoms or countries in the whole world, which once were subject and paid tribute to China," albeit freed since the Tatar or Manchu conquest of China. The Dutch castaways were no less struck that natural phenomena could even influence matters of state security. Observing that, at the latter end of 1653, "a blazing star appeared and, after that two at once, the first was seen on the southeast for about two months, the other in the southwest, but their two tails were opposite against one another." Hamel continued that "the Court was so alarmed of it, that the King caused all the guards to be doubled at all his posts, and aboard his ships . . . he expected nothing more than an invasion from some of his neighbors" (Hamel 1745, 584, 631).

Tennant continues that, with time, the importation of Western learning came to challenge traditional scholastic preoccupations. In the early 1780s, a number of Korean literati in contact with Western learning in Beijing had themselves baptized, signaling the arrival of Catholicism in Korea among a select group seeing in this faith a liberation from traditional tenets. By the end of the century, their ranks had reached the thousands (Tennant 1996, 194–95). As alluded, the Korean court was also drawn into the Tokugawa polity's version of subtributory diplomacy, dispatching elaborate embassies, such as the one witnessed by the Dutch in February 1712, actually linking Japan with the continental trade in silver exchanged for furs and ginseng (van der Velde and Bachofner 1992, 143).

## SYMBOLIC SPACE IN INDIC COSMOGRAPHY

The reception of Europeans in the "Indianized" states of Southeast Asia must be viewed against certain civilizational verities. Needless to say, misunderstanding on both sides, along with European transgressions, led to sometimes grotesque outcomes across the centuries. This we seek to examine with reference to European encounters—and collisions—with forms of symbolic power and symbolic space in Indic cosmography. Here we refer to the classical Indian concept of geopolitical space that lingered on in Southeast Asian polities until abandoned under profound European influence in the nineteenth century.

The use of symbolic power by a state to maintain legitimacy was not unknown to courts of Europe, but in Hindu Bali, Dutchman Cornelis de Houtman, leader of the first Dutch voyage of 1597, found a friendly kingdom. The island of Bali and the Hindu raja, or king, is illustrated in Houtman's (1598) book to deliberately set it apart from Islamic Java. The raja, borne in a chariot and shielded by a parasol, emblem of sacred power, is portrayed as majestic (Vickers 1989, 12–13). Cultural anthropologist Clifford Geertz (1981) would later describe the *negara*, or state, in Bali as a "theater state," a reference to the courtly display and aesthetic associated with an "exemplary" Hinduized politicoreligious center. Geertz (1981, 8–9) expounds a theory of endogenous development of Balinese culture between the fourteenth and nineteenth centuries, especially as the island avoided the twin revolutions of Islamization and intense Dutch colonization. "Bali in the later half of the nineteenth century," he observes, "may not have been a mere replica of Bali in the middle of the fourteenth, but it was at least fully continuous with it."

Writing of "Buddhalogical space" of the Siam/Thai kingdoms, Reynolds (1978, 197) holds that despite the universalism of the major Siamese cosmological texts, particularism can also be discerned in the sphere of architecture and socioreligious patterns. Notably, the capitals of the various premodern Siam/Thai kingdoms were laid about a central representation of Mount Meru, often in the form of a stupa. Typically, the reigning monarch of each kingdom would be symbolically and ritually associated with the various divine rulers in the heavenly realms, the court with lesser heavenly beings, and the ordinary people with ordinary human beings. As Reynolds sees it, important elements of the universal cosmic symbolism were appropriated to undergird the civil religious base of each particular Theravada kingdom.

In his masterful analysis of indigenous space and ancient maps of Siam, Thongchai Winichakul (1994, 20–36) expands on the meaning of Buddhist (Traiphum) cosmography. Rather than offering geographical reality, such sacred topographies offer a picture of religious space, imaginative to us, and so a space that does not correspond to the earth's surface. Needless to say, he adds, the effect could be dramatic when people stopped imagining space in terms of orderly relations of sacred entities and began conceiving of it according to new classificatory systems and signs, such as offered by European geography.

Thongchai does not broach the matter, but the weight of especially French Jesuit influence at the Ayutthayan court of King Narai (r. 1656–1688) was particularly intense. Narai, as mentioned, was the monarch who dispatched three missions to the French court of Louis XIV, only one of which was successful. While the thrust of these missions, encouraged by Constantine Phaulkon, were opportunistic in the sense of seeking out a French alliance against the Dutch, they also revealed a precocious understanding on the part of the Siamese court of temporal geography outside of Buddhalogical concerns. Another of Narai's court favorites was a Persian, Aqa Muhammad (Smithies 1990).

We recall that Kosa Pan, Narai's emissary to France in 1686, avidly collected European maps. Back in Ayutthaya four years later, visiting Dutchman Engelbert Kaempfer attested that Pan openly displayed the maps in his official quarters. Moreover, as part of their diplomatic push, the French king dispatched increasingly large delegations to Siam in 1682, 1665, and 1687, the last accompanied by 1,400 French soldiers and 300 skilled craftsmen. The French expedition was also endowed with a virtual laboratory of instruments prepared in advance for observation of the eclipse of the moon to more accurately gauge the longitude of Siam. Narai was witness to this erstwhile demonstration of superior French science and cartography from his palace in Lopburi (Smithies 1990; Suárez 1999, 30–31). To be sure, an anti-French and anti-Catholic mood within the Siamese court also coincided with Narai's illness, leading to the usurpation of the throne by the master of royal elephants and the slaying of Phaulkon and the dying king's brothers. But whether Ayutthaya shut itself off from European influences after the 1688 "revolution" has been disputed by some (Dhiravat na Pomberja 1993, 252–53).

The greatest of the agrarian court centers of pre-European contact in Southeast Asia was undoubtedly Angkor before its "fall" in 1431 and the shift of political power toward the Mekong River delta. No longer a living center, Angkor's awe was nevertheless recounted by the first Europeans to learn of, if not actually to witness, this monument, setting a Western tradition of ascribing fallen grandeur to Asian civilizations. David Chandler declares that the first European to write in detail on Cambodia was Tomé Pires in *Suma Oriental* from a manuscript written between 1512 and 1515. But Pires was relying on hearsay, and, as mentioned, the first eyewitness account from a European is that of Portuguese missionary Gaspar da Cruz, who visited the new site of the Cambodian kingdom, Lovek, in 1556 before its siege by Siam in 1587. Angkor came to be written into Spanish accounts, following their disastrous interventions in the kingdom in the last decades of the sixteenth century. In a striking display of ethnocentricity, as related by the Dominican Gabriel Quiroga de San Antonio in his *Brève et Véridique Relation des Envénéments du Cambodge* of 1604, the first Spanish adventurers believed that Angkor, which they compared to Seville beside the Guadalquivir River, was built by Jews arriving from China leaving the ruins abandoned on their departure (Cabaton 1914, 101).

From his study of Cambodian toponyms in ancient Khmer texts, Chandler (1976) found that the Cambodian realm was a sacralized topography of places looked after by local spirits. As such, the arrangement served as an indigenous map of the realm before the advent of modern geography. But, as discussed in the previous chapter, the post-Angkorian trade-oriented Khmer capital of Lovek also accommodated foreigners of various nationalities, suggesting that the world was closing in on a kingdom obviously a shadow of its former glory. Chandler (1993, 89–94) is equivocal as to the effect of Europeans on Cambodian ideology, albeit allowing that Siam and, subsequently, Vietnam would make their mark on cultural affairs. Still, seventeenth-century Cambodia was relatively independent. Very traditional Buddhalogical rules for monarch and people prevailed—not only correct behavior and language fitting one's status but also, as revealed in local versions of the Ramayana, Indianized conceptions of the universe.

Even though the kingdom of Pegu, located on the lower Irrawaddy basin, had already entertained contacts with Portuguese, Muslims, and others (both at home and abroad via an active trade policy), by 1599, Pegu, Burma's first Toungoo Empire for most of the sixteenth century, fell to rebels, pending the progressive transfer of the capital in early 1635 to Ava. Lieberman argues that this transfer of the capital was made on domestic geopolitical and cultural grounds and had little to do with European threats, marginal until the early nineteenth century. While Portuguese and Muslim mercenaries of the sixteenth century had been pressed into service of the kingdom, Pegu still called the shots by keeping European and other rivals at bay. Cosmologically, Lieberman finds a trend toward Buddhist orthodoxy through the seventeenth century, as the Ava court continued to grow at the expense of animist, Hindu, syncretic, and nontextual elements. In the restored Toungoo period, Hindu or non-Buddhist traditions were rewritten to provide the monarchy with a more explicitly Buddhist charter (Lieberman 1993, 214–49).

As Anthony Reid (2000, 171) has written in an essay on categorizations of Europeans in Southeast Asia during the early period of contact, the tradition of tolerance of Theravada Buddhist societies to the religious practices of others was breached by the bloody interventions of the Spanish invaders in Cambodia and by the actions of Portuguese soldiers in Burma. Burmese chronicles from the sixteenth and seventeenth centuries have nothing good to say about Europeans. Notably, Philip de Brito, the Portuguese captain who seized the port of Syriam (opposite modern Rangoon) on behalf of the king of Arakan in 1599, was denigrated in Mon chronicles in Buddhist language as lacking "merit" and denounced in the chronicles of the Toungoo, who recaptured the port and executed Brito in 1613 as a "destroyer of religion." Still, we have instanced King Narai of Siam as a Buddhist monarch who was very receptive to the overtures of the Europeans.

## *DARUL ISLAM:* THE WORLD OF ISLAM

Three great Islamic empires embraced most of the Muslim world outside of western Africa and Southeast Asia at the time of the first European expansion. With the capture of Constantinople in 1453, the Ottoman Empire under Suleyman I (1520–1566) was well known and feared by Europe, even though the power of the Sublime Porte, as the government was called, was in decline by 1600. Under Akbar (1556–1605), the Mughal Empire was fully extended, although the Deccan, or southern India, was never conquered. Until being absorbed into British India, the ruling Mughal Muslim minority had adroitly accommodated the Hindu majority. More short lived than these two empires was the Safayid Empire based on Persia from its foundation in 1501 to its eclipse in 1722. Each of the empires communicated and traded with each other, at least after peace between Suleyman I and the Safayids in 1555, and each left important legacies, whether in commerce, architecture, governance, or warfare.

The true world of *Darul Islam* (lit. "world of Islam") undoubtedly eluded the Iberians, at least until the Magellan circumnavigation, although, as mentioned, the Portuguese thrust into the Indian Ocean brought them into conflict with Muslim power from Mombassa to Diu to Aceh. Manila was a Muslim outpost at the time of its Spanish "foundation." The Moros of Jolo and the sultan of Brunei resisted constant Spanish attempts at subordination, while the Moluccas were always contested before the rise of Dutch hegemony. Even so, where they failed to conquer, Christian Europe was also capable of diplomacy, such as in the Portuguese modus vivendi with the Mughal emperors, the Franco-Ottoman alliance/treaty of 1536, or the Portuguese relationship with the sultan of Brunei.[5]

Nevertheless, disbelief, feigned disbelief, or ethnocentricity all around was, no doubt, matched by ignorance at certain levels in the Christian encounter with Islam in the first wave of globalization. We could say that in the peripheral zones of world civilization, or at least outside the myriad little worlds of animist culture, such as those discussed later in this chapter, European Christocentrism collided with Islamocentrism, though engagement and religious debate was not entirely precluded. Apostasy was also not unknown of recent Christian and even Muslim converts from "paganism."

Certainly, the "Middle East"–centered Islamic world was far better connected in terms of spatial awareness of Asia than the Christian Europeans, facts reinforced by age-old trade networks; knowledge of Arab navigation and maritime lore; knowledge of the hajj, or Muslim pilgrimage; and the wider *ummat*, or Islamic community of believers, in general. We could multiply examples, but such is implied in the two Safayid Persian world maps from the late seventeenth century, discovered in 1989 and derived from earlier models. Both place Mecca at the center and offer practical information for would-be pilgrims from China to Andalusia as to the distance and direction to Mecca. Reflecting high Muslim achievement in mathematics and cartography, the maps offer a sophisticated longitude and latitude grid (King 1999).

The Europeans also interacted with the Islamic empires. The Augustinean missionary Antonio Gouvea tells how in 1608 the shah of Persia and family greatly appreciated the music of the Portuguese mission, notably a Christian performance including an ensemble of harpsichord and zither. In this account, one of the princes extravagantly expressed his delight, saying that he felt he was in paradise (Brito 1996,

13). But Gouvea, who sought an alliance for Portugal with Persia in their war against the Turks, was undoubtedly a welcome and privileged guest. As Sanjay Subrahmanyam has written, from an early period, Portuguese images of Islam became more subtle acknowledging differences between Mamaluk and Ottoman Sunnis and Persian Shiism. Such distinctions were drawn, for example, in the writings of Tomé Pires. To be sure, such awareness did not thwart Portuguese designs in wiping out the legacy of the Indian-Persian sultanate in early Goa, nor did it nullify the myth promoted by Albuquerque of freeing subjects from Muslim rule (Subrahmanyam 1999, 36–38).

It may be slightly apocryphal, but as an example of the tightrope walked by the early Catholic missions in the first civilizational encounters, the pioneering Jesuit translator of Persian texts, Jerome Xavier, a favorite at the Mughal court and, as mentioned, author of *Mirat al Quds* (The Mirror of the Holyness; 1602), was answered back in print by one Lin El Abeden of Isfahan in a volume titled *The Mirror Repolished.* Rome determined it necessary to offer a correction to the latter work and commissioned Jesuit Philip Guadagnot to undertake the task. This he did with such apparent zeal and abuse of the Prophet that, fearing for the survival of the Jesuit mission, he was ordered to rewrite. This he did with "so strong an encomium on Mahomet" that, in turn, he was dealt a severe reprimand (La Loubère, cited in Bowring 1857, 343).

An extraordinary crossover figure in the Mughal court under Bahadur Shah (r. 1707–1712) and his successor, Jahander Shah (r. 1712–1713), was Donna Juliana Dias da Costa, a Portuguese lady who wore her Catholic identity in the form of crucifix as costume jewelry. A daughter of a Portuguese doctor who served at the court of Aurungzeb, Donna Juliana rose to become a veritable governess of the harem. There was no question that this stylish lady was held in high esteem in the women's world of the court but also in the favor of the emperor himself. As recorded in some detail by Valentjin (1724–1725, 284), in 1710–1712 she also facilitated the Dutch at Surat in gaining commercial favors from Bahadur Shah and his successor.

In general terms, according to Reid (2000, 166, 169, 178), while the Europeans were often astonished by what they found in Southeast Asia, the surprise was not always reciprocated in the early period of contact, especially as the major Muslim trading ports of the region had long welcomed outsiders of a variety of ethnic groups and religions. Further, he argues, even Portuguese military victories could be written into early Malay chronicle sources with some neutrality. Nevertheless, when religious polarization set in around 1550, especially with the arrival of Catholic missionaries and the militant trend established by the sultanate of Aceh throughout the sixteenth century, neutrality turned to hostility. By con-

**Figure 7.4.    Donna Juliana Dias da Costa at Mughal court, from Valentijn's** *Oud en Nieuw Oost-Indien* **(1724). (Reproduced with permission of Nagasaki University Library)**

trast with the early-arriving Portuguese, Dutch empire builders are not remembered well at all in Malay *syair,* or epics.

An example of collision, albeit without dire consequences, was the well-documented report concerning the visit by Portuguese envoys to the Brunei court, where Islam was well entrenched. Generally, Bruneian traders were well received at Portuguese-controlled Malacca, and Brunei welcomed Portugal as traders and as an ally against the Spanish. In 1526, the Portuguese captain of the Moluccas, Dom Jorge de Meneses, dispatched a vessel captained by Vasco Lorenzo to Brunei to pioneer a northern route to Malacca. Arriving in Brunei, the party sought to present the sultan with the usual gifts but included a tapestry from Portugal on which was represented the marriage of Henry VIII of England and Catherine of Aragon as well as depictions of men and women. Believing the images to portray devils, the sultan threatened to kill Lorenzo and was pacified only when the party had the tapestry destroyed (Teixiera 1961–1963, vol. II, 170).

Macassar, where Christianity may well have preceded Islam, offers another example where religious apostasy worked against the missions, although offering the example of a Portuguese-speaking sultan, willing to debate theology with entreating missionaries. Macassar, under the cosmopolitan ruler Karaeng Pattingalloang (r. 1634–1654), was also possessor of an impressive library containing, besides books in Malay and Turkish, Blaue's four-volume atlas as well as a specially commissioned 130-centimeter globe. Alexander de Rhodes, who was received by the chief minister of the court in 1647, reported of his host that he knew "all our mysteries very well [and] read with curiosity all the chronicles of our European kings." Moreover, he avidly studied European science and mathematics (Suárez 1999, 250). A Jesuit notice from the seventeenth century reported of the Macassar sultan that "he always spoke favorably of the Pope and of the saints and so could easily be taken for a Catholic" (Jacobs 1988).

## THE ANIMIST WORLD VIEW:
## AN EXAMPLE FROM THE MARIANAS

We wonder how the Tupi Indians, the "Indios" of the Philippines, the "Tetums" of East Timor, and all the other aboriginal peoples apprehended the bearers of new religions and other "civilizational" agents coincident with the European conquest. Outside the centers of literacy, such representatives of tribal, lineage, or little cultures bequeathed few contemporary records, in any case entering the domain of twentieth- and twenty-first century ethnography and anthropology.

A rare insight into the thinking of the Chamorro people of the Mariana Islands strategically located athwart the Acapulco-to-Manila Pacific galleon trade route is offered by the French Jesuit Charles Le Gobien (1671–1708). Pejoratively dubbed the Ladrones, or robber islands, by their discoverer Magellan in 1521, it was not until June 1668 that a band of six Jesuits arrived at Guam to initiate the Christian conquest of the Marianas. What transpired over the next two decades at the hands of the missionaries and the Spanish military rivaled only the massacres of Mexico and Peru, although disease and cultural conflict may have been the major cause of drastic population loss in especially the Chamorros case. A Spanish census of 1710 revealed a surviving population of Chamorros of 3,739, one-tenth the original size (Hezel 1982). Gobien, author of *Histoire des Isles Mariannes* . . . (History of the Mariana Islands; 1700), a skilled and sympathetic interpreter, bequeathed a speech-lament by the Chamorro chief Maga' Lahen Hurao from 1671:

> The Spanish would have done better to remain in their own country. We have no need of their help to live happily. Satisfied with what our islands furnish us, we desire nothing. The knowledge which they have given us has only increased out needs and stimulated our desires. They find it evil that we do not dress. If that were necessary, nature would have provided us with clothes. They treat us as gross barbarians. But do we have to believe them? Under the

excuse of instructing us, they are corrupting us. They take away from us the primitive simplicity in which we live.[6]

The lament has a contemporaneous ring about it from the perspective of Fourth World, or indigenous, peoples in today's globalized world. But early colonizers repeated the error of the conquistadores, only to be met with redemptionist and millenarian, as much as antitax and antiforeign movements from across the planet earth. Today, as our Internet source reveals, Chamorros take pride in the pre-Hispanic culture, just as Mexicans and other peoples of Central and South American origin in their North American diaspora rediscover their pre-*conquista* roots and identities outside the Latino label.[7]

But it would be a mistake to believe that in their encounter with technologically superior outsiders, native peoples and recent converts to Catholicism were passive actors. For example, in 1769 on the island of Timor, the notionally Catholic mixed-race descendants of Portuguese, Chinese, and islanders, dubbed Larantuqueiros, pushed the Portuguese governor and entourage into the sea, forcing a relocation of the capital to the present site in Dili (Gunn 1999b, 99–103). In Mexico, the slogan of the *independistas* at the end of the eighteenth and early nineteenth century was "Long Live the Virgin of Guadalope! Death to the Spaniards," harking back to the historical revelation of the Virgin Mary in 1531 to the Indian Juan Diego. In 1638 on the peninsula of Shimabara near Nagasaki in Japan, 30,000 Christian peasant antitax rebels under the leadership of sixteen-year-old "Amacusa" Shiro perished in a doomed standoff against 200,000 Shogunal forces assisted by Dutch warships (Gunn 1999a, 87–99). In the Philippines, where *illustrados* were denied entry to the priesthood, one Apolonario de la Cruz established a native religious order, the Confradia de San José, and, in 1841, led an armed attack against the Spanish. We could multiply examples of active responses by newly converted natives from peripheral zones in the first centuries of European contact, although these examples also show that the victims could answer back in the language of the conquistadores.

## CONCLUSION

In this chapter, we have highlighted the first major encounters between Europe and China since the arrival of Venetian and other European travelers at the Mongol court. We have offered numerous other examples of early encounters between Europeans and Asian civilizations. How do we evaluate the encounter in its full range of interpretations? Across the first two centuries of the Eurasian encounter, what legacy was bequeathed by Catholic missionaries in the core Asian civilizations even alongside the peripheral zones of contact? Related to that, what conclusions can be drawn as to the overall impact of the secular teachings and practical science that the Jesuits taught in the various Asian courts and centers of civilization?

The truth is that, by 1800, Goa, Malacca, and Macau, the major beachheads of Jesuit mission in Asia, remained creolized Christian enclaves in, respectively, Hindu, Muslim, and Chinese oceans. At the end of the day, the Jesuit "top-down" approach did not bring mass conversions. In Vietnam, conversions were often matched by persecutions, although the Nguyen also proved their tolerance. Japan, which offered such promise to the missionaries through the sixteenth century, had seen massive reversals of fortune with the exclusion (or sequestration) of Christians enforced by blood in the early decades of the seventeenth century. Japan's window on the world in Nagasaki was still open to Chinese and, exclusively among the Europeans, Dutch commercial enterprise.

Mentally and ideologically, the mass of Buddhist peoples within its various traditions were tolerant yet indifferent to the new faith. This we have illustrated with reference to conflicting Western and Indic representations of symbolic space, perhaps best represented in the culturally multivalent exchanges between the French court of Louis XIV and King Narai of Siam.

In this age of civilizational contest, at least as concerns Christians and Muslims, Muslims resisted Christian incursions. By seeking to outflank the historical cores of the Islamic empires on the Eurasian landmass, the first-arriving Europeans nevertheless entered Islamic seas in the Indian Ocean and the Malacca Straits area. Although conquest of sultanates from Diu to Malacca was the order of the day, opportunistic alliances were also entertained, such as between Portugal and the sultanates of Brunei and Macassar. But generally, the arrival of the Christian interlopers in the archipelago sharpened ideological contestation to the level of warfare. The Moros "problem" in the Philippines dates from this epoch, and communal conflict in the Moluccas and elsewhere is another legacy. In any case, European conversion of Muslim masses was never seriously ventured.

The European impact on the animist worldview, which remains embedded in many Asian societies even alongside ritualized courtly culture and the religions of the book, remained even less. Even today, many Asian peasant societies are circumscribed by local space and ascribed worldviews in settings governed more by agricultural and seasonal cycles than by theological, much less scientific, understandings.

But while European missionary activity made relatively few inroads in the core Asian civilizations, Western science had a far more complex reception. Even those most intellectually disposed to study the new doctrines, the Confucianized literati of China and Japan and, to a lesser extent, Korea and Vietnam wavered between acceptance and rejection. Where China under early Qing pronounced itself "self-sufficient" in the face of multivalent religious and secular messages conveyed by the Jesuits, by rejecting Christian overtures absolutely, Japan was far better positioned to screen out religious from secular learning. The Western learning movement in Japan, in the context of the Edo social revolution, provided the right mix of conditions for selective reception and adaptation of the scientific laws and the principles that underpinned them. Japan (unlike Korea, largely isolated from direct Western contact) had the luxury of evaluating, and, in such fields as medicine, actually applying the new Western sciences, even though traditional Chinese learning and books continued to be imported through the "seclusion" period. There is a sense that Jesuit influence at the Nguyen court was never allowed to interfere with the major project of implanting a Confucianized state order on a shifting frontier at a time of considerable civil strife.

Nevertheless, we would be mistaken to view identities and mentalities in absolutist terms and in error to set up dualities, especially where hybrid or syncretic ways of internalizing new philosophical systems had a long history. Understanding that the penetration of seventeenth- or eighteenth-century mentalities by twenty-first century research is problematic, we nevertheless seek out in a following chapter certain empirical views of Asian lifestyles at least as bequeathed by wide-eyed European travelers and adventurers.

## NOTES

1. Communication with author, 2000.
For a major study on Mongolian "hybridity," see Bulag (1998).
2. I am obliged to Mark Selden for the tenor of this formulation.
3. Of 134 titles written in Nom or Sino-Vietnamese characters in the Bibliotheque Nationale in Paris, many are works on religion by indigenous writers. For example, *Sam truyen ca* (To Teach Repentance) by Lu Yi Duan (1670) used Confucian and Buddhist imagery. Although rejected by missionaries, it was used by Vietnamese Christians in the underground until 1810. It was translated into *quoc ngu*, or Romanized form, in 1818. The anonymous work *Ho dong tu giao* (ca. 1796), reprinted in Saigon in 1959, presents a summary of exchanges by leaders of four religious traditions (Confucian, Buddhist, Christian, and Taoist). See England (2001).
4. Copies of the relevant passages of the Choson annals along with the Chunjo Jangse image can be viewed in the Macau archives under "iconography."
5. Reid (2000, 15–18) also offers an accessible account of the Islamicization of Southeast Asia.
6. From http://members.aol.com/magastodu/guahan/magalahi/hurao.htm (accessed December 1, 2002).
7. Arrillaga (2001).

# 8

# Livelihoods

The first European travelers not only stood agog at elements of high culture and court rituals but also were deeply moved by the variety and color of the myriad societies they encountered. There is no end to such observations, ranging from music, dance, theater, festivals, marketplaces, food, fashion, gender, and sexual mores, among other social and cultural attributes. No selection can be representative, but still there is room to impose order on these essentially male Christian accounts written for an ever-expanding, albeit restricted, literate European audience drawn not only from the Church and new centers of learning but also from the rising bourgeoisie. But also, as the case of China famously reveals, the tantalizing picture of Confucian order and benign despotism presented by the French Jesuit school to eighteenth century Europe, along with the public fascination with Chinese aesthetics, came to be intellectually contested in the decades prior to the French Revolution. Even so, we should not conflate the "naive" observations of the first late Renaissance Iberian visitors to the Orient, whether religious or secular, with the harder-nosed raw empirical accounts of the traveler-merchants and navigator-buccaneers of which the figure of William Dampier is emblematic. Again, a distinction must be made between the primary source texts on the Orient, such as were entering the great travel collections, and their literary embellishments by the "historical confabulators" as viewed in chapter 2 or by Enlightenment philosophes as discussed in chapter 6.

## IBERIAN VIEWS OF
## SIXTEENTH-CENTURY CHINA

The revelation of Cathay to Europe by Marco Polo and the first confirmation of China by visiting Iberians at some 300 years remove clearly
represented major defining moments in the Eurasian encounter. While
the veracity of Polo's account of his travels in China continues to be discussed, no such controversy attaches to the Dominican Gaspar da Cruz's
*Treatise on Things Chinese* (1569). The impact of the first book devoted to
China published in Europe was no doubt amplified with the republication of extracts in the Purchas collection of 1624. Da Cruz's was one of a
handful of Iberian accounts of southern China that together formed the
basis of sixteenth-century European knowledge and images of China.
Chronologically, the first was the account of Galeote Pereira, a Portuguese merchant-adventurer captured and imprisoned in 1549. Published in Italian in 1565, Pereira's upbeat account of China, including its
legal system, achieved some circulation in Europe. Another was Martin
da Rada, a Spanish Augustinean priest who wrote on his visit to Fujian
in 1575. Although derived in part from his reading of Pereira, the value
of da Cruz's work lies in his own observations drawn from his sojourn in
China of several months (Boxer 1953, passim). In the view of Mackerras
(1989, 25), da Cruz was "a most observant and honest traveler," as with
Polo, much impressed with what he saw.

Chinese cuisine particularly impressed the Portuguese visitor, who
observed of an exquisite banquet hosted by two local notables that
"there were many daintees they eat at one table, fish and flesh, and the
base people dress it some time altogether." All together, he observed,
China was a "well husbanded country . . . well inhabited, and people in
abundance." This is a theme to which we shall return. The Chinese, he
found, were big spenders on food and other items, "using themselves
very deliciously in eating and drinking, and apparel, and in other services of their houses especially that they are very great eaters." They were
also great workers, "every one laboring to get a living, and every one
seeketh ways to earn their food, and keep and maintain their great ex-
penses." Da Cruz was not only impressed with the food but also much
taken by the fine porcelain and presentation. Chopsticks he described as
"two small sticks very fine and gilt for to eat with, holding them between the fingers, they use them instead of a pair of pincers, so that they
touch nothing of that which is on the board with their hand." He was
equally amazed that even grains of rice could be adroitly handled with
chopsticks. But where Pereira (and Polo) failed to mention foot binding
and the practice of drinking tea, da Cruz does not disappoint (cf. Spence
1998, 16–17).

Da Cruz (in Purchas, 1905–1907, vol. 11, 474–569) was also enthusiastic about trade and industry in China, observing, "There are in this country many workmen of all trades and great abundance of all things necessary for common use, and so it is requisite for their people are infinite." For example, he remarked on the supply and demand for shoes, finding in Guangzhou two streets of shoemakers but also goldsmiths, silversmiths, ironsmiths, along with many "perfect workmen" and "great abundance of things of every trade and very perfect." Such included silk and cotton goods along with pottery and ceramics sold but not manufactured in Guangzhou.

Yet another sixteenth-century Iberian, actually Jesuit, source full of admiration for Chinese technological accomplishments is *The Japanese Mission to Rome*, as mentioned in chapter 4, first printed in Latin in Macau in 1590. But for the suppression of the mission in Japan, a Japanese-language version would have seen the light of day. A copy of the book reached England following the capture of the Portuguese ship *Madre de Deus* off the Azores in 1592 (Barreto 1997). An excerpt relating to China appeared in translation in the second edition of Hakluyt (1599) under the rubric *An Excellent Treatise:*

> Their industry does no less appear in the founding of guns and in the making of gun-powder, whereof are made many rare and artificial fire-works. To these may be added the art of printing, albeit their letters be in manner infinite and most difficult, the portraitures whereof they cut in wood or in brass, and with marvelous facility they publish a huge multitude of books.

The Jesuit observers also wrote approvingly of learning in China, including the presence in China of universities and the Chinese love of literature. Added to that, they also remarked on high skills in navigation (sailing as far as India) and an impressive countrywide system of military garrisons to protect the country against the Manchus.

But as mentioned in chapter 4, *The Japanese Mission to Rome* stands as a crossover text also meant to inform Japan about the remarkable things that the four young Japanese ambassadors had seen in Europe. A collective work, based on the diaries of the Japanese, it sets out to compare China with Europe while also offering some asides on Japan. Especially, the work runs to detail on the forms of government in Europe (monarchical, aristocratic, or democratic), their ways of carrying out war on land and sea, the splendor of their courts, and the manners and customs of the nobility alongside common people. It also offers descriptions of the towns and cities they visited, notably Lisbon, Evora, Madrid, Pisa, Florence, Rome, Milan, and Genoa. It singles out the Republic of Venice for special discussion, but, as a Christian tract, it also praises the power and authority of the pope in Rome (cf. Kaempfer 1727, introduction).

## LUÍS FRÓIS'S JAPAN

European accounts of sixteenth-century Japan are hard to come by out-side ecclesiastical and trade concerns. One such rarity, as signaled in chapter 4, is the *Treatise on the Difference between European and Japanese Customs* by Lisbon-born Jesuit Luís Fróis (1532–1597). Penned in 1585 at Katsura, a missionary center and Portuguese trading port in Arima on the Japanese island of Kyushu, Fróis was a veteran of some twenty-two years' sojourn in Japan. In the words of his modern editor (Garcia 1994, 38), *Treatise* might justifiably be described as one of the first works of "comparative cultural anthropology." Remaining in manuscript form until the modern period and therefore not an image-shaping text, at least outside church circles, Fróis's *Treatise* offers rare insights into late Renaissance European as well as pre-Tokugawa Japanese mentalities and livelihoods.[1] Undoubtedly contrived to educate arriving missionaries, at the same time Fróis tapped into a Renaissance tradition of comparing the known world with the unknown and exotic.

Fróis's treatise runs to fourteen chapters under the following Braudelian rubrics: (1) men, their character, and their clothes; (2) women, their character, and their mores; (3) children and their mores; (4) monks and their mores; (5) temples, images, and things that touch on their religion; (6) the manner of drinking and eating in Japan; (7) offensive and defensive Japanese weapons of war; (8) horses; (9) illness, medicine, and doctors; (10) on Japanese writing, their books, paper and ink, and missives; (11) houses, workshops, gardens, and fruits; (12) embarkations, practices, and naval accessories; (13) composition, farces, dances, songs, and musical instruments; and (14) various extraordinary matters that defy categorization.

Offering many hundreds of paired examples, Fróis commences each observation with the phrase "In Europe" or "chez nous" matched by a comparative remark on Japan. Europe, for Fróis, was undoubtedly the aristocratic world of court culture that he experienced in Lisbon or the transplanted version in Goa where he sojourned. The Japan he describes also tends to mirror the privileged circles of the Christian *daimyo* and aristocratic classes who offered him patronage in western Japan.

Fróis's observations on gender are striking in their contrast with Catholic Europe and confirm Japanese accounts of the freedoms and accomplishments of Japanese women in aristocratic circles of this age. In Europe, he wrote that, "according to their natural corruption, it is men who repudiate their spouses; in Japan it is often the women who repudiate their man." Whereas women in Europe do not leave the house without the permission of their husband, "women in Japan have the liberty to go where they wish without their husbands even knowing." On alcohol, he observed, "In Europe it is improper that women drink wine; on festive occasions in Japan women sometimes drink until they fall to the ground." On women's literacy, he observed, "In Europe, it is rare that women know how to write; a woman of honor in Japan would be held in low esteem if she could not write." Fróis also expressed surprise at the frequency of abortion and infanticide in Japan.

Fróis's observations on Japanese cuisine are no less important as they remind us not only of certain essentializing, time-transcending features, namely, that Japanese eat rice and use chopsticks, but also of the less sophisticated practices of sixteenth-century Europeans. "We eat with our fingers, Japanese, men, women and children, eat with chopsticks." Moreover, "In Portugal we eat salted rice as medicine to fight dysentery; among Japanese rice is cooked without salt and eaten as daily food just as we eat bread." To that he added, "In Europe people like pastries, in Japan they appreciate salted things," and, "Our wine is made of grapes, theirs of rice." Sake, or rice wine, survives as a Japanese cultural product even within modern Shinto practice. Even within present-day Japanese cultural lore, it was the Portuguese who introduced their sweet cakes, namely, *castella* and *bolo*. By the seventeenth century, the Dutch were driving a flourishing trade in Nagasaki in sugar from Java, destined for the new sweets industry, such as for cakes served at O-bon or the festival for worshiping one's ancestors.

On medical practice, Fróis declares, "In Europe, our doctors must submit to examination or be sanctioned; in Japan, any person can declare himself doctor just to make a living." Added to that, he continues, "Our doctors examine urine to better understand the illness; Japanese never do this." "We use enema and injections, they don't follow this practice," he observed. "Our doctors," he explains, "prescribe medicine from a pharmacy; in Japan they dispatch a doctor to the house." Whether it is a comment on extracting teeth or the question of venereal disease, Fróis is at least as much concerned with describing cultural practices as opposed to clinical or technical practices where they differ with Europe. As such, Fróis offers a striking matter-of-factness in his account.

On writing and printing, Fróis observed, "We write with 22 letters; they with 48 alphabetized in *kana,* and with infinite characters in various kinds of letters." Doubtless reflecting his own difficulty in mastering Japanese, Fróis offered, "Our books are read for their arts and sciences, they spend their entire lives just to know the characters." As mentioned, printing techniques were certainly known in Japan, but mostly of the xylographic method. As Fróis commented, "We use a printing press for something distinguished; they almost always write manually, because their printing press does not always have their letters."

On weapons, he observed, "We have bombards; among them are those who have not even used muskets"; "Our arrows are of wood, theirs as well, but of bamboo"; and "We use epées, the Japanese *katana* (sabers)." Unlike the Japanese, "we go to war with fifes, drums, and royal trumpeters"; "We fight on horse, the Japanese on foot"; "Our weapons are heavy; theirs are light"; and "Our kings and captains pay a salary to their soldiers; in Japan in time of war each soldier must account for his own food, drink and clothing." Aside from the reported edge in musket power, a technology soon to be emulated by his Japanese hosts, Fróis's account highlights more of a cultural divide separating Japanese from European military practices than one of technical inferiority.

There is much naïveté and even error in Fróis's observations but, for their age, they are a revelation unmatched in European writing until the Enlightenment, when seventeenth-century Japan, at least Nagasaki, came to be well documented in such European writings as those of Kaempfer. But continuing into modern times, European missionary writing on Japan was deeply reactive to the real persecutions of Christians in Japan, as perhaps best symbolized by the crushing of the Shimabara rebellion of 1637–1638, a doomed stand by Japanese Christian peasant converts against Tokugawa despotism (Gunn 1999a, 87–99).

## URBAN SOCIETY

Early European travelers to China, Vietnam, and Japan were deeply impressed by the sheer scale and dynamism of city life in Asia. This should not completely surprise because Ming China was far more populous than all of Europe combined. Especially the lower Yangtze delta area of Jiangnan experienced a rapid growth in size and density from the sixteenth century on (cf. Marks 1998, 309–11). Precisely, as we have examined in chapter 3, New World crop introductions in coastal China played their part in supporting a steady demographic expansion, notwithstanding perennial natural disasters. Agricultural prosperity fueled the emergence of regional and national markets at a time when the use of money, particularly silver, became prevalent. As Waley-Cohen (1999, 58) relates, such developments actively contributed to the trend in urbanization in China. Urbanization, in turn, went hand in hand with the expansion of commercial culture, including an indulgence on the part of the upper classes in luxury goods—imported and local—along with the spread of literacy and an increased availability of books. We may add that Japan's precapitalist transformation under the Pax Tokugawa was mirrored by the development of a brilliant information revolution based on woodblock printing, such as glimpsed by the European traders who made their annual tribute mission to the seat of the shogunal court and as can still be seen on reproductions of *ukiyo-e* woodblock scenes.

For example, the Spanish governor of the Philippines, Rodrigo de Vivero, described Edo at the time of his visit in 1609 as a city of 150,000 inhabitants, dwarfed by Kyoto with over 800,000 people, although these could only be estimates. A decade later, Englishman John Saris (1941) described Suraga (modern-day Shizuoka) "as large as London, with all the suburbs," while Hakata and Osaka were described "as bigge as London within the walls."[2] Modern demographers calculate Japan's population in 1500 as sixteen million versus Europe's combined population as sixty-eight million (cf. Frank 1998, 170), so the comparisons with English cities are compelling. Over a century later, Engelbert Kaempfer was also struck by the degree of urbanization in Japan. His block-by-block description of Nagasaki is a pioneering study of a small Asian city; from execution grounds, to pleasure quarters, to daily life, little escaped his eye. Generally, Kaempfer (1727, 263) drew a picture of a bustling city, with streets teeming with people. These ranged from "merchants, shopkeepers, tradesmen, handicraft men, artificers, brewers, besides the numerous retinue of the Governors of the town and the people employed in the Dutch and China trade." To be sure, Kaempfer was hardly a naive observer but, as mentioned, a hard-nosed product of Enlightenment Europe.

We lack comparable studies of Vietnamese cities, but the Italian missionary J. P. de Marini, who lived in Than Long (Hanoi) in the early seventeenth century, described a single district of the capital as being as large as a medium-size Italian city (Marini, cited in Anonymous 1977, 79). Writing of Bangkok in the early decades of the nineteenth century, Crawfurd (1820, 394–95) estimated the population at around 300,000. As he describes it, Bangkok was largely a Chinese city or peopled by descendants of Chinese, with Siamese being a narrow minority. Such strong demographic growth is all the more surprising, as Bangkok (actually Thonburi across the Chaophraya River from the modern city) emerged as the center of power of the reestablished kingdom of Siam only in 1782, following the sacking of Ayutthaya by Burmese armies.

Then, as now, China and Chinese cities dwarfed those of Japan and Europe. Martin da Rada described China as a "a veritable ant-hill of people," "a country of 9,676,246 households totaling 60,187,047 tributors, minus certain aboriginal people" (Boxer 1953, 243). The acknowledged rigor of Chinese census methods adds credence to these figures, at least for "tributors," although modern demographers would place China's population in 1500 at one hundred million. Even so, by 1800, China's population would rise to over 300 million people, vastly outstripping Europe with 173 million. Generally, in the period from 1400 to 1800, population grew much faster in Asia, and especially India and China, than in Europe (cf. Frank 1998, 171).

Writing of the walled city of Guangzhou, Gaspar da Cruz declared "the streets of the city are all drawn by a line very straight, without any of

[them] making a nook or winding, all the crossings are straight on the streets." With its paved streets and triumphal arches, he described Guangzhou as a "beautiful and ennobled city." Houses of the ruling classes were sumptuous, but even those of the common people were "much to be admired," at least the interiors. Echoing da Rada, da Cruz declaimed Guangzhou as "very populous, and the people is as much, that at the entering of the gates at the riverside, you can scarce get through." No less, he gushed, the river at Guangzhou supports "so great a multitude of shipping that it is a wonderful thing to see them, and that which is most to wonder is that, that the multitude never decreased nor failed almost all the year, for if thirty or forty or a hundred go forth one day, as many do come back in again the next" (da Cruz, in Purchas 1905–1907, vol. 11, 328, 494).

We should not neglect the rise of new urban centers across maritime Asia, a reference to Goa, Malacca, Macau, and Manila, to name the more important of these profoundly creolized societies, standing in the vanguard of intense cultural exchange. With the permanent establishment of Dutch and British imperialism, a second tier of colonial cities emerged, even within our 1500–1800 framework, the more important being Batavia

**Figure 8.1.** Batavia viewed from shipboard, from Argensola's *Histoire de la Conquete des isles Moluques par les Espagnols, par les Portugais & par les Hollandais* (1707). Although Batavia was built along a Dutch model, its subimperial status as capital of the Dutch East Indies masked its profoundly hybridized Asian character. (Author's collection)

(Jakarta), Calcutta, Colombo, Bombay, and Penang. Characteristically, the new centers of administration and commerce attracted a range of mercantile classes and groups. Typically, European concepts of governance, urban planning, and architecture masked profoundly Asian patterns of social organization, as Chinese, Arab, Armenian, Indian, or other ethnic or religious groups set down their roots alongside indigenous peoples, thus injecting a new level of hybridity into social relations. Still, in our time frame, large numbers of Asian cities and court centers remained outside European influences, although like Edo or Beijing, Delhi or Jogjakarta on Java, or indeed the new Bangkok, Europeans were visiting as missionaries, bearers of tribute, or traders.

## MUSIC, DANCING, AND FESTIVALS

Just as the systematic study of oriental music, dance, and theater awaited the high tide of Orientalism and continues to occupy scholars (e.g., Mackerras 1975) and doctoral candidates alike, descriptions entered the first European writings on Asia. Gaspar da Cruz was fortunate to witness the first day of the year or "Chinese New Year" in Guangzhou in the early decades of the sixteenth century. His was also a rare description of music in China for its age:

> All the streets and doors are very richly dressed, and chiefly they do endeavor and labor to deck the triumphant arches, covering them with many cloths of damask and of other silk, with many lanterns. There is much playing of sundry instruments, and singing, and jointly with this great store of meat of sundry kinds and great abundance of wine.
>
> The instruments they were to play on are certain Bandores [guitar] like ours, though not so well made, with their Pinnes to tune them, and there are some like Gitternes which are smaller, and others like a Viall de gamba [bass violin], which is less.

If less impressed with the instruments, da Cruz was nevertheless pleased with the effect: "They play many instruments together sometimes concerted in few voices which make a very good harmony." Writing of actors and performers, he observed, they sometimes go to the ships to play "that the Portugal may give them money" (da Cruz, in Purchas 1905–1907, vol. 11, 516–17).

As advised, Fróis (1984, 107) entered theater, dance, and music in his "Treatise on Japan," observing that, whereas plays in Europe were staged at night, those of Japan could equally be staged in daytime or nighttime. English Captain John Saris was witness to a "great feast" in Hirado island off Kyushu on the occasion of the establishment of the British trading post (Saris 1941). Writing of Macau, where he arrived on August 4, 1695, the

Italian traveler and Habsburg official Giovanni Francisco Gemelli Careri (Churchill and Churchill 1704, vol. 4, 290) related,

> I went to see a play acted upon after the Chinese manner, it was represented at the cost of some of the neighbors for their diversion in the middle of a small square. There was a large stage to contain 30 persons, men and women actors, and tho I understood it not, because they spoke mandarin, a Court language, yet I perceived the manner of it, that they acted with life and skill. It was partly recited and partly sung, the music of several instruments of wood and brass harmoniously answering the voice of him that sung. They were all well enough clad, their garments adorned with Gold, which they changed often. The play lasted 10 hours, ending by candle light. When an act is done, the players sit down to eat, and very often the audience does the same.

A near contemporaneous report by Dutch Commodore Roggewain on the Chinese of Batavia is of no less interest:

> They [the Chinese inhabitants] are uncommonly fond of shows, and of entertainments. The feast of their New Year, which they celebrate in the beginning of March, lasts commonly for a whole month. During this time, they do nothing but divert themselves principally in dancing, which they do in an odd way, running round to the sound of bassoons, flutes and trumpets, which makes none of the most agreeable concerts! They make use of the same music at their comedies and other theatrical diversions, of which they are very fond. Yet there is no great matter in this comedy of theirs, which is, in fact, a mixture of play, opera and pantomime; for they sometimes speak, sometimes sing, and sometimes the whole business of the scene is performed by gesture only.
>
> They have none but women players, who bred up to this trade from their infancy; but many of them act the part of men; and for that purpose change their dress, and disguise themselves.
>
> Whenever a comedy is acted, the city receives the sum of 50 crowns for a license. They erect their theater in the street beside the house of him who is at the expense of the play. (Roggewain, in Harris 1745, 281)

Observed almost everywhere in the archipelago was cockfighting, which had its ritual as well as social entertainment values. Often, cockfighting was a form of disguised gambling where commodities in lieu of money changed hands. The Dutch were quick to capitalize on a local, especially Chinese, penchant for gambling by creating a lottery. As visiting Englishman Christopher Fryke (Fryke and Schweitzer 1997, 128) observed of the lottery in Batavia in the 1680s, it was mostly full of Chinese, the "greatest gamesters in the world." He continued, "Whoever is the loser there, the Company is sure to be the winner; for there is a Money-Changer appointed by them . . . and every throw that is thrown with Dice, there is two pence paid."

## FASHION, STYLE, AND ATTIRE

Then, as now, fashion and attire was a subject of mutual Eurasian interest. The black hats and baggy trousers of Portuguese seafarers in Nagasaki helped spawn a virtual genre, that of *byobu-e*, a few examples of which survive in Japanese and European museums. Costume, or lack of it, likewise became an object of interest to the first European engravers of Asian images. But in certain locales and among certain classes, especially where Europeans and Asians mingled, a new hybrid attire was already evident during the time frame of the first globalization.

Englishman Peter Mundy, who arrived in Macau in July 1637 aboard the East India Company fleet captained by John Weddel, sojourned in the area for six months, observing of *fidalgo,* or aristocratic, culture,

> This place affords many rich men, clad after the Portugal manner. Their women like those at Goa in Sherazzes or (?and) lunghees, one over their head and the other about their middle down to their feet on which they wear low chapines. This is the ordinary habit of the women of Macao. Only the better sort are carried in hand chairs like the sedans at London, all close covered, of which these are very costly and rich brought from Japan [*norimono* or *kago*]. But when they go without it the mistress is hardly known from the maid or slave wench by outward appearance, all close covered over, but that their sherazzez or (?shawls are) finer. . . .
>
> The said women when they are within doors wear over all a certain large wide sleeved vest called in Japan kimono because it is the ordinary garment worn by the Japanese, there being many dainty ones brought from thence of died silk and of others as costly made by the Chinese of rich embroidery of colored silk and gold. (Mundy, in Boxer 1993, 67–68)

No doubt, Mundy was commenting on the forms of attire required of Portuguese Catholic patriarchy among the creolized women of Macau, in fact a form that lingered on into the middle of the twentieth century. His observation of the Japanese kimono suggests a unique hybridization of Oriental and Western fashion in seventeenth-century Macau.

Gemelli Careri, Italian visitor to Spanish Manila in 1697, also observed a hybrid fashion imposed by both patriarchy and local circumstances on the local wives of Spanish metropolitan males:

> The women of quality in Manila go in the Spanish habit; the common sort have no need of tailors, for a piece of Indian stuff called saras wrapped around their middle serves as petticoat, and another they call Chinina for the waist upwards, for a waistcoat. The legs and feet stand in no hose and shoes by reason of heat.
>
> The Spanish are clad after the Spanish fashion, only on their feet they wear wooden clogs. The Indians are forbid wearing stockings, and they must of necessity go bare legged.

Those that live well have always a servant to carry an umbrella to save them from the sun. The women have fine chairs, or hammocks, being nets hanging by a long pole carried by two men, in which they are carried in their ease. (Careri, in Churchill and Churchill 1704, vol. 4, 417)

But as Abbé Raynal commented, albeit secondhand, on bourgeois society in Batavia in 1780,

Luxury has maintained its ground more successfully than concubinage. . . . The ladies who are universally ambitious of distinguishing themselves by the richness of their dress, and the magnificence of their equipage, have carried the taste for fineness to excess. They never stir out without a numerous train of slaves; and either ride in magnificent cars, or are carried in superb palanquins. They wear gold or silver tissues, or fine Chinese satins, with a net of gold thrown over them, and their headdress is loaded with pearls and diamonds. In 1738 the government attempted to reform these extravagancies, by prescribing a mode of dress suitable to each rank. These regulations were received with contempt. (Raynal 1780, 289)

As English navigator Sir Thomas Cavendish (1560–1592) observed of the peoples of the island of Capul during his passage through the strategic strait south of Luzon via the Pacific Ocean in 1586, "They wear a square piece of linen woven out of plantain leave as about their waist, and another coming down their backs, and so under the twist which is fastened to their girdles" (Cavendish, in Harris 1745, 14).

In a rare observation of Islamic attire in the southern Philippines in the late eighteenth century, Englishman William Dampier wrote,

Their clothings are a turban tied once round the head with cloth, the ends fringed or laced, tied in a knot and hanging down. They wear also breeches and frocks over them; but neither stockings nor shoes. The women tie their black and long hair together in a knot, hanging down behind. They are smaller featured than the men, and have very little feet. Their garments are only a piece of cloth sewed together at both ends and a frock reaching a little below the waist. (Dampier, in Harris 1745, 106)

Writing of early sixteenth-century Laos, Dominican traveler Gaspar da Cruz observed,

This people are not very brown . . . they go naked for the middle upward, and from the hips downward, they wear certain cotton-clothes girt about them all white: the women so covered from the breasts to the hip lege: they have their faces some which like the Chinas...the priests of their idols do wear yellow clothes got about as the rest of the people. (da Cruz, in Purchas 1905–1907, vol. 11, 483)

Figure 8.2. Japanese woodblock in *Nagasaki-e* style of Dutch lady visitor to Japan (late Edo period). The first to defy the ban on the presence of European women in Japan, the stylish Dutch lady visitor to Nagasaki was obviously the center of much attention for her demeanor and fashion. (From a postcard reproduced courtesy of the Nagasaki Prefectural Art Museum)

William Funnell, mate to Captain Dampier, also offered a description of the inhabitants of Ambon but suggested the imposition of a dress code:

> They are middle stature and tawny; but the women are of a brighter tawny than the men, and have long black hair, which reaches down to the calves of their legs. They have round faces, small mouths, noses and lips. They wear a linen waistcoat, which reaches no further than the lower part of their breasts; and about their middle, they wear a piece of cloth, about four yards wide, and a yard deep. This they roll around them, and it serves them instead of a petticoat; for none are allowed to wear petticoats, but the Dutch women only. Neither are the Malayan men allowed to wear a hat, excepting only for the King. (Funnell, in Harris 1745, 131–50)

Still, it was Luís Fróis (1994, 41–44) alone who observed that in sixteenth-century Japan there was no fashion. Unlike Europe, style was unchanging. "Almost every year we invent a new manner of dressing; in Japan the form is always the same and never varies." He also observed that unlike in Europe where clothing was strictly gendered, in Japan *kimono* (*katabira*) were worn equally by male and female. Still, he allowed, unlike in Europe, where dress was constant through the seasons, in Japan—in a practice that holds today—dress was strictly changed according to, respectively, summer, autumn, and winter. Fróis's observation on invariant fashion undoubtedly held for most of Asia outside the creolized zones of European contact, especially as costume remained (and remains in some societies) a marker of status and social and national identity.[3] Even so, we must allow that in Japan, merchant and especially aristocrat classes had a special eye for the consumption of luxuries, including the latest and richest silks, the major imported prestige item actually driving the Portuguese and Chinese trade with Nagasaki.

## CULINARY ENCOUNTERS:
## WILLIAM DAMPIER IN VIETNAM

Writing in 1688 of Tonkin or northern Vietnam, where a small community of English and Dutch traders resided, Englishman William Dampier (1699, 29–30), who had thrice circumnavigated the globe, could at least be relied on to enter a certain relativistic understanding of world cuisines. Vietnam's ubiquitous fermented fish sauce, or *nuoc nam,* he described as "a composition of strong flavor, yet a very delightful dish to the natives of this Country." To make it, he described, "they throw the mixture of shrimps and small fish into a sort of weak pickle made with salt and water, and put it into a tight earthen vessel or jar." Even the fish is not gutted, he remarked. "After a time, the fish is reduced to pap, they then draw off the liquor into fresh jars, and preserve it for use. The mashed fish that remains behind is called Balachan, and the liquor poured off is called Nuke-Man [and] is also very savory, after one is a little used to it." *Nuoc nam*, "is also very savory and is used as a good sauce for fowls not only by the natives, but also by many Europeans, who esteem it equal to soy." Dampier was also introduced to soy sauce in Vietnam and learned of its method of preparation in the Japanese manner.

But Dampier was also a man of his age. We have described him as being part of a circle of Enlightenment thinkers and creative writers including such contemporaries as Swift and Defoe. There is a palpable sense that Dampier traveled and recorded impressions with a view to European audience. "They dress their food very cleanly, and make it savory, for which they have several ways unknown in Europe, but they have many sorts of dishes, that would turn the stomach of a stranger, yet which they themselves like very well, as particularly, a dish of raw pork, which is very cheap and common . . . minced very small fat and lean together, which being afterward made up in balls, on rolls like sausages, and pressed very hard together, is then neatly wrapped up in clean leaves, and without more ado, served up on the table." Raw beef is another dish he described. Horse meat, elephant flesh, dogs and cats, great yellow frogs, and other eatables, "along with all sorts of roots, herbs and fruits," are matter-of-factly recorded by Dampier as having their place in the markets and kitchens of northern Vietnam. A daily scene that struck Dampier in marketplaces and villages was the presence of women "sitting in the streets with a pipkin over a small fire, full of chau (tea) . . . and is their ordinary drink." Dampier described a "delightful" countryside and a "generally healthy" population. As suggested, his point of reference was always Europe, but as one of the greatest world travelers of his age or any age, he had other continents and situations in mind.

## GENDERED VIOLENCE

No area of the New World encounter was as controversial as that of gender relations. A tradition of gendered violence literally began with Amerigo Vespucci's infamous description in his *Mundus Nouus* (Letter from the New World; 1504) of Amerindian women as capricious and lustful. As early as the 1570s, European map and book engravings began to allegorically personify America as a female archetype of the conquest.[4] The complexity and diversity of Asian cultures and societies hardly submitted to a single "conquest" stereotype, but the Iberian encounter also found its counterpart in the archipelago.

In many precontact animist societies, as Brewer (2001, 2002) found of the Philippines, bilateral kinship systems dominated, women actively participated in the economic realm, virginity was not valued, and "adultery" was not noteworthy. Moreover, indigenous constructions of gender departed substantially from the patriarchal models and gender behavior of Catholic Spain. Brewer's scrutiny of missionary texts revealed that a two-sex, two-gender model was enforced on the population. Such was the hegemony of the male-centered Hispano/Catholicism that, with the arrival of the Spanish, a tradition of shaman men identifying with the feminine in animist society was stripped away, and, by the late nineteenth century, even the broader tradition of female shamanism was suppressed.

While the Iberian "holy confrontation model," as elaborated by Brewer with reference to the animist realm, cannot be generalized to mission activities in the Confucian and Theravada Buddhist worldviews, it nevertheless alerts us to the pitfalls in discussing sex and gender in cross-cultural situations. As the following examples point out, bewilderment and confusion on the part of male European observers as to non-Christian sexuality is more than apparent. Cultural relativity awaited a modern age.

As Linschoten found of Portuguese creole society in Goa in the late sixteenth century,

> The Portugals, Mestiços, and Indian-Christian women in India, are little seen abroad, but for the most part sit still within the house, and go but seldom forth, unless it be to church, or to visit their friends, which is likewise but very little, and when they go abroad, they are well provided not to be seen, for they were carried in a Pallankin, covered with a mat or other cloth, so that they cannot be seen.

The image of gendered seclusion or retiring domesticity as demanded of the Iberian model, however, was somewhat modified by a notorious local practice:

> There are many men poisoned by their wives. . . . There are likewise many women brought to their ends by means of their husbands and slain when so ever they take them in adultere. (Linschoten, in Purchas 1905–1907, vol. 10, 239)

The notion that subordinate females could reverse roles was also not lost on the Dutch admiral Oliver van Noort, who sojourned briefly in Brunei in 1601. As he observed,

> The very women have so much soldier in their composition that, if they receive any affront, they presently revenge themselves with dagger or javelin upon him that gives it. This a Dutchman had like to have proved to his cost; for having some way disgusted one of those Bornean Viragoes she set upon him with a javelin, and had dispatched him if she had not been prevented by main force. (van Noort, in Harris 1745, 35)

Johan Nieuhoff was somewhat ambivalent as to the virtues of women of Ambon. Writing in 1659, he observed, Ambonese women are "very lascivious, and extremely desirous of Christians." He continued,

> If they find themselves disappointed in their expectation, or if they are left by their gallants, they have a way of infecting them with a certain potion, the operation of which is so slow, that they die a lingering death, neither can they cohabit with another woman unless they receive proper antidotes from the same woman who poisoned them. (Nieuhoff, in Churchill and Churchill 1745, vol. 2, 202)

In making this statement, we wonder whether Nieuhoff was identifying with the precontact status of the shamaness in animist society or a female archetype outside the gendered patriarchal holy Iberian model as identified by Brewer (2001; 2002). As William Funnell, mate of Captain Dampier, remarked, "The Malayan women [of Ambon] are said to be great whores, of which they are not ashamed. They are soon ripe, and often married by nine years of age, and many of them are said to have children by ten or eleven" (Funnell, in Harris 1745, 142). Whatever else, as viewed in chapter 7, it was such unadorned statements on "Indian" mores that informed and fed into Montesquieu's investigation of the "slavery of women."

As Cavendish (Harris 1745, 28) recorded of the peoples of the islands south of Luzon that he visited in 1586, beside the practice of circumcision,

> they make a perforation quite through the glans of the penis with a nail of tin split in the lower end, and riveted, which they order so as to take out, and put in again, as they have occasion. They invented this for a prevention of a certain unnatural crime which the men of the island were it seems horribly addicted to; and it was done at the humble petition of the women who laid the case before the magistrates, and obtained the remedy.

A similar theme was addressed by Nieuhoff (Churchill and Churchill 1704, vol. 2, 218), who sojourned in Patani in 1662. Ralph Fitch (1921) also observed the practice in Pegu in the early 1600s, although not with the same explanation.

As Careri observed in the Philippines in 1697, "These nations are much given to fecundity for their women either married or unmarried are seldom continent." He continued, "Formerly there were men that made it their trade to deflower maids that were to be married, and they were paid for it: because the maidenhead was looked upon as an obstruction to the bridegroom's pleasure. At present (as some Missions of the Jesuits told me) some of the Visayans, if they find when they marry their brides are maids, say they have got bad ones, because no man has a mind to, and debauched them" (Careri, in Churchill and Churchill 1704, vol. 4, 431).

Writing of foreign liaisons and even aristocratic patronage of such, Nieuhoff offers dispassionately this comment of women of Patani that he observed firsthand in 1662:

> Nothing is more common than if any foreign merchant come to Patane, to ask them whether they don't want some women for their convenience; and there is no want of young handsome women who offer their service, out of whom each may take his choice, and agree with her as best he can, as to what he is to allow her per month; which done she immediately repairs to his lodgings, where in the day she serves as chambermaid, and in the night for a bed fellow and during this agreement, the man must be as careful to avoid the commerce of other women as she is on her side unless he will expose himself to manifest danger. At parting the man pays her wages and so they are both free, and if she has a mind to change, he need not look far for one, it being as custom among the nobles here, to entertain many female slaves, whom they let out for such a life and gain great profit for them. (Nieuhoff, in Churchill and Churchill 1704, vol. 2, 218)

William Dampier, already notorious for the licentiousness of his crew, observed of the Muslim peoples of Mindanao:

> They covet the acquaintance and conversation of white men, and will be very free with them, as far as they have their liberty. One peculiar custom they have in the city of Mindanao, that as soon as any strangers arrive, the men of Mindanao come aboard, to invite them to their houses, where they are sure to enquire, whether any of them have a mind for a pagally (or innocent female friend). The stranger[s] in civility are obliged to accept the offer. (Dampier, in Harris 1704, 106)

As an anonymous British observer (Anonymous 1830) remarked on the Balinese, "the gratification of sensual lusts, seem to afford them their chiefest pleasures." He continued,

The women are sadly circumstanced and miserably ill-used in Bali . . . When marriageable, instead of being wooed and solicited as western dames are, or bought or sold like Turkish maidens, they are ravished and stolen away, by their brutal lovers.

In truth, Balinese women were coveted as slaves and concubines. Vickers (1989, 15) writes that Bali had sold slaves since the tenth century, but with Dutch hegemony established in the archipelago, the trade flourished, with Bali women being highly prized in colonial Batavia in Dutch and Chinese households alike.

Writing of marriage and infidelity in Confucianized Tonkin in 1627, pioneering Italian Jesuit missionary Alexander de Rhodes (1854) observed that their marriages were conducted with great ceremony in the presence of a magistrate. Contrariwise, clandestine marriages were outlawed with adultery severely punished. In the case of women who broke their marriage vows, the punishment was death by way of being trampled by an elephant.

Thunberg, in an aside on women in Japan (Nagasaki), wrote,

The Japanese, indeed, seem to pay little regard to female chastity; nor do they regard lasciviousness as a vice, particularly if practiced in such places as are protected by the laws of government. Houses of this kind, therefore, are not considered as infamous, or improper places of rendezvous. . . .

Some of them (women) paint themselves with a composition called bing; but this ornament is chiefly confined to the lips, which appear either red or violet, according to the quality of the paint that is laid on.

The married women are generally distinguished from the single, by having their teeth stained black, which in their opinion, is considered charm; but in the eyes of a European is very disgusting. (Thunberg 1809, 295–96)

Writing of his travels through China in 1697, Careri sought to set the record straight on the question of public prostitution: "The Chinese women," he asserted, "are much wronged in their reputation by the author of the Relation of the Dutch Embassy to Peking," a probable reference to John Nieuhoff's influential account. "In the first place," he continued, "he certainly dreamt that there were public whores in China, and that they were carried about Town" and actually touted. "I have never heard of so abominable traffick spoke of much less could I see any thing like it" (Careri, in Churchill and Churchill 1704, vol. 4, 414). It would seem that, in observing or failing to observe the exotic other, no two people, then as now, would always agree. But with Japan in mind, perhaps the Protestants were better trained in this field, given Dutch patronage of the pleasure quarters of Nagasaki.

**Figure 8.3.** Japanese woodblock in *Nagasaki-e* style of Dutchman and consort (late Edo period). (From a postcard reproduced courtesy of the Nagasaki Prefectural Art Museum)

## CRIME AND PUNISHMENT

Notwithstanding a predilection on the part of Europeans for violence, such as accompanied the *conquista*, codes of punishments as set down by various states in Asia never failed to astonish European visitors. We have viewed how such accounts fed into Enlightenment debates on Asian governance but also took on a life of their own in the sense of titillating a European public on the bizarre and unknown. China held a special fascination.[5]

Undoubtedly, one of the first commentaries on the Chinese legal system was that of Galeote Pereira, who, as mentioned, had been arrested and spent several years in detention in China. Pereira described beatings with bamboo whips, as discussed below, the sufferings of prisoners, and the impregnable castle-like prisons. Doubtless influenced by the favorable verdict eventually handed down in his own case, as Mackerras (1989, 24–25) interprets, Pereira believed that the Chinese system of public trials was fair. Gaspar da Cruz also followed Pereira in declaring that open trials made false testimony very rare but also elaborated on the savagery of the penal system as it prevailed in the late sixteenth century.

As already noted, Jean Baptiste du Halde's *Description* . . . (1748) was a seminal image-making text on China, including his ruminations on punishments. Du Halde introduced to Europe two notable instruments of Chinese punishment: the *bastinado* and the *cangue*. The *bastinado* was a thick cloven cane several feet long used to flay criminals on the order of a magistrate. The *cangue,* as it was known first to the Portuguese, was more infamous. This was a wooden collar composed of two pieces of wood hollowed out in the middle and placed around the neck of a criminal. Some three feet square or six inches thick, it commonly weighed fifty or sixty pounds. Other punishments included banishment or tattooing. While the law allowed execution on the spot for certain crimes, du Halde also acknowledged that capital cases were referred to superior tribunals. Reeducation in the Confucian classics could also be meted out for such cases as unfilial behavior.

As Hendrik Hamel observed in Korea following his enforced sojourn commencing in 1653,

> If a woman kills her husband, she's buried alive up to her shoulders in a highway that is much frequented, and by her is laid an axe with which all that pass by, and are not noble are obliged to give her a stroke on the head till she is dead.
> The man who kills his wife and proves he had cause to do so as for catching her in adultery, or any other heinous fault, is in no danger for doing so. (Hamel 1745, 589)

The interest in Hamel's account is that it is drawn from a hitherto unrecorded part of the world, finding its place in a celebrated collection of travel accounts.

In the words of the English supercargo aboard a mission dispatched from Bantam to establish a factory in Tonkin in 1672, on September 25,

> the mandarin told us, that nearby about three o'clock there was a gentleman to be beheaded, and several of his servants to have their hands cut off, who in the king's absence had asserted a pretended title to the kingdom and raised a considerable number of people. We were spectators of the execution. The principal suffered without the least apparent fear of death, sitting upon a green bank without anything before him to conceal the executioner preparing for the stroke. Next day several others were to suffer the same cause. (Auber 1834, 144–45)

As with the Korea case, this is a rare account of a little-recorded part of the world, albeit entering Dutch East India Company documents and therefore hardly a public account.

The Dutch at Deshima island in Nagasaki were also witness to, but never real victims of, the Tokugawa code of punishments. In 1691, they witnessed Chinese smugglers chained and banished. But executions in a designated place in the town were not infrequent. In December 1691, Dutch East India Company official Cornelis van Outhoorn wrote, "A strange message and an unheard-of order from the court, some criminals will be punished as a deterrent for the foreigners. We try to avoid this order in vain. Two criminals are brought onto the island." All Company officials were required to witness their execution. All complied except the head of the factory. In June 1693, it was observed that some imprisoned Japanese who were obliged to steal because of poverty had been released. But in the case of a personal servant of the governor who had put his adulterous wife and servant to the sword and mortally wounded another person, banishment was the punishment. In March 1695, the Dutch were advised to be careful with dogs. Across Japan, 70,000 dogs were supported by the shogun, costing 600 bales of rice daily. Several people had been executed because they violated the law on this matter (Vermeulen 1986). On August 24, 1700, H. Dijkman recorded in his diary that on a special island prepared for the purpose and in sight of assembled Chinese and Japanese merchants, the captain of a smuggler's barge was crucified while four sailors were beheaded after being taken around the town on horseback. Their heads were salted and placed on stakes (van der Velde and Bachofner 1992, 8).

In the Malay world, or, more specifically Patane, as witnessed in 1662 by Johan Nieuhoff,

> Those who by a time appointed do not pay what they owe the king, or private persons, are beaten twice or thrice a month on the shin bones, which is done till they can find means to discharge the debt. . . .
>
> After they have trampled upon the criminal, they pour vinegar on the putrefied carcass, which they then pour down the offender's throat through a funnel, and when he is full, they beat his belly with cudgels till it bursts. Thieves are trampled to death.
>
> If a single man is found in bed with a married women, he is stripped naked to a little pair of drawers, then daubing his face with lime, they ram an arrow thro' each ear, and fasten a little drum on his back, which they beat at all the cross-streets, to expose him to his shame. This punishment ends in 40 or 50 strokes of a cudgel on the man's bare buttocks, but the women receives 'em with drawers on. (Nieuhoff, in Churchill and Churchill 1704, vol. 2, 590)

But Aceh, or at least its image, was exceptional. As related by Frenchman Augustin Beaulieu in 1621, incensed that his large bird had lost to a smaller one in a cockfight, the sultan ordered the right hand of his *orang kaya* (lit. "rich man" or "noble") to be cut off "which was immediately put into execution." Added to that, Beaulieu witnessed the torture of five or six women blamed for plotting against the sultan's life. On his order, their "hands and legs were cut off, and their bodies . . . thrown into the river." He continues, "When the execution was over the King asked me what I thought of it? Though the spectacle was very mortifying to me, yet I dissembled upon the matters and answered, that, without the execution of justice no Kingdom could exist." Prudent answer, indeed, and first of a long line of European dissemblers in the East:

> In sine, the cruelty of this Prince is unparalleled.
> In sine, his cruelty is without a parallel; he takes advice from nobody, and never lived a day while I was at Aceh, without the execution of one and sometimes several of his people.

Still, there was justice: Beaulieu described the functioning of a grand court presided over by a man of great wealth as well as a criminal court under the jurisdiction of other *orang kaya*. Meeting daily, except on Fridays, this court heard "all the quarrels, murders, robberies. etc., committed in this city." "Yet," he continued, "there is never a day but the King orders a nose, eye, ear, hand, foot or testicle to be cut off from somebody or other." Beaulieu also witnessed an accused being bashed for stealing the value of a farthing and a man accused of peeping at a woman washing given thirty lashes. In yet another court, differences among merchants, "whether natives or foreigners," was adjudicated by the most senior official of the town (Beaulieu, in Harris 1745, 733–43).

Montesquieu (1748, book XXIV) likewise described a form of behavior, corresponding to the Malay loan word *amok:* "Among the inhabitants of Malacca where no form of reconciliation is established, he who has committed murder, certain of being assassinated by the relatives or friends of the deceased, abandons himself to fury, and wounds or kills all he meets." But for the French philosopher, this is an example of where religious law, in this case Islam, evidently failed to produce a way of reconciliation.

## CONCLUSION

Very clearly, European travelers of the sixteenth, seventeenth, and eighteenth centuries showed genuine interest as much as feigned surprise in the social habits and mores of different cultures. As examples, we have offered music, dancing, and festivals; fashion, style, and attire; culinary encounters; gendered relations; and crime and punishment. These are not necessarily Orientalist visions, even if that mind-set was germinating, neither do they invariably fall into the category of what Laborinho (1993) called the "trap of exoticism." Here we instance the comparative method of Luís Fróis, refreshing for its seemingly naive interpretation of Japanese society. But the most generous we can term these early modern impressions, especially those bequeathed by agents of the European trading companies, are "primitive cultural relativist" in an age before full-blown imperialism imposed its own ideological hierarchies and stereotypes. Primitive ethnography, we will see, later became part of the corpus of Orientalism.

Nevertheless, as we have viewed, from fashion to gender relations to sense of justice or injustice, the blinkers were hardly those of an enlightened age but bore all the features of, respectively, Catholic and Protestant Europe. While European geography, cartography, lexicology, natural science, and other developing sciences were evolving in the context of post-Renaissance humanism, it would appear that the science of society was not part of it. These early attempts at social observation more than confirm the modern origins of sociology and social science.

Here we must strike a distinction between the opening phase of the Eurasian encounter in the age of first globalization and the sequels. As certain of our examples drawn from seventeenth- and eighteenth-century Macau, Goa, and Batavia reveal, social mores from costume to cuisine were no longer the exclusive products of the mingling and mixing of Asians but increasingly came to assume a hybridity flowing from the Eurasian encounter. In the Philippines, the implantation of an Iberian Catholic model of "appropriate" gender behavior marked out profoundly new and enduring socioreligious conditions and forms.

## NOTES

1. A single surviving copy of Fróis's manuscript was discovered only in 1946 in the Royal Library of the Academy of History in Madrid. Unsigned, it is attributed to Fróis by its "discoverer," Jesuit Josef Franz Schutte, especially as internal evidence suggests a strong link between the manuscript and Fróis's *Historia de Japam* (1976–1984). See Fróis (1994, 31–32). Translations of Fróis are by the author from the French version.

2. This paragraph is drawn from Gunn (1999a, 182).

3. By the early nineteenth century, representations of oriental costume undoubtedly fed Orientalist images of the "Other." One of the masters of the genre was William Alexander, author of books on costume in Turkey (1802) and China (1805). Alexander, who accompanied the Staunton mission to China in 1792, became the first keeper of prints and drawings at the British Museum. But George Henry Mason (1800) accomplished the same, offering elaborate watercolor-on-rice-paper designs of Chinese attire, signaling rank and status. An example from India is a collection of etchings of ethnographic interest executed by the Calcutta-based Flemish artist François Bathazar Solvyns (see Anonymous 1807).

4. A major statement on this problematic can be found in Trexler (1995). Even so, the victims of Trexler's violence are less women than effeminate men.

5. The curiosity over Chinese punishments continued through the ages, as testified by a chronicle of books on this subject published well into the modern period.

# 9

# Language, Power, and Hegemony in European Oriental Studies

The other side of the coin to globalized dispersion of European languages was the need felt by the first European visitors to the East, from Marco Polo on, to learn Oriental languages. The first lexicographers were in fact the first visitors. We have seen as well that the Jesuit mission not only pioneered the production of books in vernacular languages but, as with the bicultural João Rodrigues, also led the field in linguistic studies. While longer-sojourning European traders, officials, and especially missionaries immersed themselves in these languages, those moving more quickly through the region by the sea route undoubtedly resorted to interpreters or made do with Portuguese or other European languages. Nevertheless, with the arrival of the Dutch, French, and English, linguistic, cultural, and literary studies meshed in an interlocking corpus that came to be glossed as Indology, Sinology, and more generally Orientalism. While such scholars as Said (1978) have enriched our understanding of the imperial pretensions of this science in its full-blown colonial form, we seek in this chapter to trace the school of Oriental studies to its roots. In so doing, we are making a distinction between Christian-Eurocentric attitudes that reach back to the Crusades and the now ideologized intellectual Orientalism, the science of Oriental studies that emerged as the handmaiden of early modern European colonialism.

## THE EUROPEAN STUDY
## OF ASIAN LANGUAGES

European humanism was long divided over the primacy of Latin and its appeal for cultural unity and the rise of vernacular languages. But the movement to grammatize vernaculars was upheld as a means to bestow on them the dignity and purity of Latin, the mother tongue. As elaborated in an essay by Ana Paula Laborinho (1994, 109–10), the European "language question" besetting purists, albeit defenders of a dead language, and the champions of colloquial languages also played itself out in the context of overseas expansion and evangelization. We have viewed the early missionary penchant for reproducing Christian texts in Latin, even though, from an early date, missionaries such as St. Francis Xavier had grasped the imperative to learn Asian vernaculars, a method soon taken up by the China mission. But in Europe as well, stemming from the publication by António de Nebrija (1444–1522) of his *Grammatica Castillana* (1492), the first printed grammar of a vernacular language, the Spanish state also came to understand the importance of language as an instrument of colonial domination. By presenting Queen Isabella with a tool for the unity and communication of the people under the Spanish crown, Nebrija anticipated the role of Spanish in other continents. Such verities were also understood by Fernão de Oliveira, who published his pioneering work on Portuguese language and orthography, *Grammatica . . .,* in Lisbon in 1536, followed in 1539 by João de Barros's *Grammatica da Lingua Portuguesa* (Grammar of the Portuguese Language). Accordingly, the Portuguese state not only adopted the language of Camões as language of state and commerce of its new seaborne empire but, to this day, jealously guards and endows the Lusophone heritage globally.

Setting aside the compilation of simple lexicon accomplished by the first Iberian visitors to the New World, by and large it was Catholic missionary enterprise that pioneered lexicology and the systematic study and scripturalization of non-European languages. Such enterprise bore fruit with the establishment of the first presses in the New World. The first dictionary printed in the New World and the first to codify an indigenous language was Alonso de Molina's *Vocabulario en Lengua Castelliana y Mexicana* (Vocabulary in Castilian and Mexican), printed in 1571. Molina, a Franciscan missionary arriving in Mexico on the heels of the Cortés conquest, served the Spanish policy of making Nahuatl, the language of the ancient Aztecs, the single language of communication in Mexico, below Spanish, the language of power, but over other Indian languages. Being understood in Nahuatl or other indigenous code also fit in with missionary enterprise and set the tone for numerous other dictionaries and translations not only in the New World but also in Africa and eventually Asia. In Africa, for example, Jesuit enterprise led to the publication in 1661 of a catechism in Latin, Portuguese, and Kimbundu, a language of Angola, while a description of language in Ethiopia was achieved in 1681.

By the seventeenth century, building on a long tradition of study of exotic languages, European publishing embraced more and more Asian languages in such native scripts as Tamil, Malayalam, Persian, Japanese, and Chinese.

Lach has written that early European humanists first looked for affinities among diverse Oriental languages to confirm prevailing doctrines based on classical and biblical precepts. Only later did they concede differences and turn to discover affinities among families of languages (Lach 1991, 10–11). A case in point was the gradual revelation of the Aryan family, of which Sinhala is an example, in turn part of an even larger Indo-European family embracing, on the one hand, Persian, Hindi, and so on and, on the other, modern German, French, and English, among other European languages.

Nevertheless, the Tower of Babel view of language, which accorded primacy to Hebrew, continued well into the eighteenth century to distort any scientific advance. As Said reminds us, Renaissance "Orientalists" were primarily specialists in the languages of the "biblical provinces." With the exception of the Jesuit advance on China, he asserts, "by and large, until the mid-eighteenth century Orientalists were Biblical scholars, students of Semitic languages, Islamic specialists." Indeed, until the eighteenth century, the Orient was nearly synonymous with the Islamic Orient (Said 1978, 50–51, 76).

The field of comparative linguistics awaited its discoverer. One of the pioneering works of comparative philology was by the Spanish Jesuit Lorenzo Hervás y Panduro (1735–1809), who published his *Catálogo de las Lenguas de las Naciones Conocidas . . .* (Catalog of the Known Languages) in Madrid in 1800–1818. This catalog, published in eight volumes, collected briefs on 300 languages and drew up grammars on forty, using data supplied by Jesuit missionaries from around the world. As acknowledged by Max Mueller in his *Lectures on the Science of Language* (1862, 139–42), Hervás made one of the most important philological discoveries by establishing the relation between Malay and Polynesian speech families, extending as far west as Madagascar. Hervás was a pioneer in emphasizing similarities in the grammar of different languages as opposed to resemblance of vocabularies.

## TRANSLATING THE ARABIC WORLD

Acknowledging that a tradition of Arabic-Latin translation reaches back to the Middle Ages and was well developed at Toledo from the twelfth century, we are concerned here with the revival of this tradition stemming from direct contact opened up by the great discoveries. Pioneering in this area was the role of Holland, virtually a new country following the Dutch revolt against the Spanish Habsburgs. As the rising European hegemon, capturing a larger share of global commerce at the expense of the Iberians, as discussed in chapter 1, the United Provinces also emerged as the European center of map and book production and a major consumer of new knowledge revealed by the discoveries. Even so, French, British, and other European nations upped the ante with respect to philological and other studies of the Arabic world commensurate with their deeper commercial and subsequent imperial interventions in the Middle East.

Founded in 1575, the University of Leiden soon emerged as the preeminent center of transmission of knowledge of the Arabic world in Europe, building on the dominance of the Dutch school in philology until well into the eighteenth century. There is much truth in the statement that Leiden laid the foundations of European Oriental studies, then defined as Hebrew and Arabic studies. Interest in Arabic not only stemmed from a desire to gain access to Arabic scholarship on mathematics and astronomy but also was linked with increasing trade with the Middle East. In turn, the study of Hebrew was motivated by theological and biblical purposes, especially linked with Dutch Bible translations of 1637 (Salverda 1990).

Preeminent individuals associated with Arabic studies at Leiden were such Renaissance "Orientalists" as Erpenius (Thomas van Erpen; 1584–1624) and his student and successor at Leiden, Jacob Golius (1596–1667). Both traveled widely on diplomatic missions, collecting manuscripts and studying languages. Importantly, they established an Arabic press at Leiden that, until 1650, was the only source of Arabic type in Europe. Appointed official interpreter of the states-general for Oriental languages, Erpenius had studied Arabic, Persian, Turkish, and Aramaic in Venice. Using the Arabic fonts crafted by Erpenius, the Leiden press produced such works as a collection of Arabic proverbs (1614), an Arabic translation of the Pentateuch (1622), and several editions of Elmacin, *History of the Saracens* (1625). Erpenius's own classic was *Grammatica Araba . . .* (1631). Golius, in turn, produced *Lexicon Arabico-Latinuum* (1635), a work derived from a classical Arabic source.

From 1623 to 1759, the Dutch East India Company was the most important trading firm in Persia, although not unchallenged. Dutch learning of Persia and its language made a hesitant start with the research of Leiden University professor Franciscus Raphelengius (1539–1597), who drew up a short list of Persian words based on a translation of the Persian text of the Pentateuch published in Hebrew letters in Constantinople in 1646. Notably, Raphelengius called attention to the similarities of certain Persian and Dutch words, in what might be hailed as the first attempt at comparative Indo-European linguistics. Persian studies continued in the Netherlands, especially as travelers returned from Persia with an increasing number of manuscript sources. Eventually, this work led to the publication by Lodewijk (Louis) de Dieu (?–1642) of *Rudimentae Linguae Persicae* (Rudiments of Persian Language) in Leiden (1639), the first Persian grammar in Latin (Floor 2001).

But France was also emerging as an incubator of Orientalist studies, as that nation also began to engage the enemies of its enemies in the Ottoman Empire. The first direct translation of the Holy Koran from Arabic into French was achieved in Paris in 1647 by André du Ryer, French consul at Alexandria and Constantinople, subsequently rendered into English by Alexander Ross as *The Alcoran of Mohomet Translated out of Arabique into French, by the Sieur du Ryer . . . And Newly Englished for the Satisfaction of All That Desire to Look into the Turkish Vanities* (1649). A Christocentric text to allow the French court to better know its enemies, du Ryer's work went through six more editions until 1856 and formed the basis of many other European translations.[1] Muslims long held the Koran to be untranslatable into European languages, and it would not be until the early decades of the twentieth century that "rightful" translations have been produced by Muslim interpreters. An accomplished linguist, du Ryer also authored *Rudimenta Grammatices Linguae Turcicae* (Grammatical Foundations of the Turkish Language), first published in Paris in 1630.

Laurent d'Arvieux (1635–1702), who spent many years in the Levant and at Aleppo, where he was French consul from 1679 to 1695, also contributed firsthand knowledge of the nomadic people of the Arabian Peninsula. Although long remaining in manuscript form, his *Voyage Fait par Ordre du Roy Louis XIV dans la Palestine, vers le Grand Emir, Chef des Princes Arabes du Desert . . .* (Voyage Made by Order of Louis XIV in Palestine to a Meeting with the Great Emir, Leader of the Desert Arabs) was published in 1728, also offering a translation of Sultan Ismael Abulfeda's account of Arabia. Almost contemporary was French historian Comte Henri d'Boulianvilliers's (1658–1722) *Histoire des Arabes, avec la Vie de Mahomed . . .* (History of the Arabs with a Life of Mahomed), published in Amsterdam in 1731. Although not versed in Arabic, Boulainvilliers expressed a rare admiration for Islam. The appearance in France in 1704–1717 of a translation by Antoine Gallard of the Arabic/Persian pastiche "Thousand and One Nights" is one important marker of the French exoticism of the Orient alongside scholarly attempts to understand (cf. Said 1978, 63–65).

Exceptional for his time was French Orientalist Abraham-Hyacinthe Anquetil-Duperron (1731–1805), author of *Législation Oriental . . .*, published in Amsterdam in 1778. A student of Hebrew, Arabic, and Persian, Anquetil-Duperron journeyed between 1754 and 1762 in the Near East, where he not only studied firsthand the systems of government and laws in Turkey, India, and Persia but also sought to prove that the nature of Oriental despotism—as abstractly presented by Montesquieu—had been misrepresented. Today, Anquetil-Duperron is better remembered for his introduction to Europe of Zoroastrian texts.

While Chinese language was being taught in the Collège Royale in Paris from the 1730s, French interest or intellectual priority in European Islamic world studies in the late eighteenth century was confirmed by the creation in Paris in 1795 of L'École des Languages Orientals. Foundation languages included Arabic, Turkish, Persian, and Malay. Though it was not until 1840 that a professor of Malay was appointed, the intertwining of French commercial and scientific interest was obvious. With merit, Said (1978, 51) describes Paris as "the capital of the Orientalist world" across the first half of the nineteenth century.

## INDOLOGY

We have described the establishment from the late sixteenth century of a Jesuit press in Goa. Jesuit preoccupation with missionary activities, however, was not to the neglect of the study of vernacular languages, especially the dominant language of Goa, Konkani (Canarim), and the dominant language of the Malabar coast (Malayalam). In 1640, for example, *Arte da Lingua Canarim* (Grammar of Canarim Language) was printed in Goa, composed by the Englishman Thomas Esteves (Tomas Estavdo) for the Jesuit mission, appearing in revised edition in 1649. Christian works, such as the much-published *Doctrina Christa* (Christian Doctrine), were also printed in Malayalam in Cochin in 1559 and in Konkani in Goa in 1561. *Catecismo* was also issued in Malayalam in Tamil script (1577), while various other texts were published in "Brahmana" (Gonçalves 1968, 256–57). A rare Portuguese study of Konkani from the seventeenth century was Diogo Ribeiro's *Vocabulario da Lingoa Canarina com versam Portugueza* (Vocabulary of Canarim Language with Portuguese Version), remaining in manuscript until published in Lisbon in 1973 (see Miranda 1985).

Following on from the first wave of Jesuit interest in India, a second wave might be signaled with the publication in Rome of two important linguistic texts on Indian languages in the late eighteenth century. One is the anonymously authored *Alphabetum Brammhanicum* (Alphabet of the Hindi Language; 1771), a work that deals with Hindustani grammar, pronunciation, and literature. Possibly one of the last of the Jesuit studies, at least until the dissolution of the order, was *Gramatica Indostana* (Hindi Grammar; 1778). Other second-wave linguistic studies were authored by the Austrian missionary Paulinus Bartholomaeo (1748–1806), pseudonym for Johan Phillip Wesdin. One of the inaugurators of Indian studies in Europe, following a ten-year sojourn on the Malabar coast, Wesdin was a prolific scholar. Besides composing a "Malabar" dictionary, in 1790 he produced the first-ever Sanskrit grammar to be published in Europe, known in modern translation as *Dissertation in the Sanskrit Language* (1977). Even so, Wesdin's work was based on the manuscript grammar of the Jesuit Haxleden.

Undoubtedly, the Portuguese and Jesuits were pioneers of European Indian studies, but the arrival of the English, Dutch, French, and Danish trading companies qualitatively and quantitatively upped the ante not only in linguistic studies but also in a range of scholarly works that might be glossed proto-Indology. Probably the first attempt to provide a systematic description of the Mughal Empire, at least outside of church sources, was Johannes de Laet's *De Imperio Magni Mogolis . . .* (The Great Mogul Empire; 1631). De Laet (1593–1649), a Flemish naturalist and geographer, based his work on a study of Dutch East India Company archives. Early works by the Dutch and English, joined by the Danes and the French, concentrated on coastal zones of contact.

For example, in 1638, William Bruton published the first detailed report on Orissa and Bengal, titled *Newes from the East Indies; or a Voyage to Bengalla.* In 1646, a detailed report on Gujarat and Bijapur by Johan van Twist, chief of the Dutch Factory in Gujarat, entered Isaac Commelin's collection. The Dutch missionary Abraham Roger (Rogerius), a long-term resident on the Coromandel coast, published his *De Open Deure . . .* (Open Door) in Leiden in 1651, a work that introduced an understanding of Hinduism to Europe. In 1672, another Dutch missionary, Philip Baldaeus, produced a celebrated work describing India's south coast regions along with Ceylon with much information on Hinduism and Hindu temples and rituals. This was republished in the Churchill and Churchill collection (1704) under the title "A True and Exact Description of the Most Celebrated East India Coasts of Malabar and Corromandel." In 1713–1715, the Danish mission at Tranquebar produced a locally printed version of the New Testament in Tamil. Sanskrit versions of the Bible or, at least, the Old Testament appeared in the 1840s, as did translations into Bengali and other vernaculars.

By the late eighteenth century, as British rule consolidated over the dismembered Mughal Empire, scholarly writings on such subjects as the Hindu calendric system, Indian music, ethnography, poetry, and history also began to appear in *Transactions of the Society Instituted in Bengal for Enquiring into the History and Antiquities,* printed locally by the East India Company's press. Three volumes of this journal had been published in Calcutta by 1782. While the Jesuits were the first to bring educated knowledge of Sanskrit to Europe, English studies on this language began in earnest with the emergence of the Asiatick Society at Calcutta and its journal, *Asiatick Researches,* in 1784. This was founded by the English jurist and East India Company official Sir William Jones (1746–1794), author of the multivolume *The Works of Sir William Jones . . .* (1799–1807). In 1786, Jones had proposed a common ancestor of Aryan languages—the Indo-European hypothesis—a major stimulus to the study of historical linguistics in the nineteenth century. As Said (1978, 78–79) has discoursed on Jones, while admittedly a brilliant linguist, classicist, and polyhistor, his vocation to know India better than any other European led him "to gather in, to rope off, to domesticate the Orient and directly turn it into a province of European learning." Even so, the figure of Jones remains central in debates as to his Orientalist presumptions versus an alternative

Figure 9.1. Frontispiece of Johannes de Laet's *De Imperio Magni Mogolis. . .* (1631).
One of the first European works on Mughal India feeding into the Leiden school of Oriental studies and a precursor of the Orientalism that was to follow. (Author's collection)

narrative that would acknowledge his contributions to the "renaissance" of classical Indian studies.[2]

The first translation into a European language of the Hindu holy text, *The Bhagavad-geeta, or, Dialogues of Kreeshna and Arjoon in Eighteen Lectures and Notes* (1785), was by another East India Company official, Sir Charles Wilkins (?1749–1836). A cofounder of the Asiatick Society and believed to be the first Englishman with a comprehensive knowledge of Sanskrit, Wilkins also edited, with David Hopkins, an abridged version of Richardson's *Dictionary* . . . of Persian, Arabic, and English, originally published in 1806–1810. But secular works in Gujarati, Marathi, and other vernaculars also appeared from this time. For example, Ferguson published his *Dictionary of the Hindustan Language* in London in 1773. In 1818, William Carey (1761–1834), English clergyman and professor of Oriental languages at Fort William, Calcutta, published his *Dialogues . . . of the Bengalee Language*. With the British takeover from the Dutch of Ceylon in 1796, a need was created for an English study of Sinhalese. This was achieved by the Armenian James Chater with his *Grammar of the Cingalese Language*, published in Colombo in 1815. The role of English alongside indigenous languages in British India is a theme to which we will return.

## *DUNIA MELAYU*: MALAY WORLD

The English school also had its parallel in those parts of India and the East Indies under Dutch domination. Founded in April 1778, the Batavian Society of Arts and Sciences (Bataviaasch Genootschep van Kunst en Wetenschappen) first looked to spread the gospel. But with the publication in Batavia on Java of the society's transactions in 1779–1781, the scientific study of "Malay world" antiquities, cultures, and languages had commenced with all the presumption of its metropolitan and other colonial counterparts.

It may not be obvious, but the *dunia Melayu*, or Malay world, and, more obviously, the "Indonesian" world, was from the outset a specifically European framing of the region. Englishman William Marsden, writing in 1812, correctly observed that the name of the Malay, as opposed to the Malaccan, Peninsula had only recently entered currency in the writings of Raffles, Valentijn, and so on and that it was not a name by which "chiefs of the various districts of the peninsula" referred to themselves (Marsden 1812, ix). But with the publication in 1869 by Lord Alfred Russel Wallace (1823–1913) of the evolutionary classic *The Malay Archipelago . . .*, the region had taken on a broader geographical identification. Even so, the identification of Malay as a language long preceded the study of the diverse peoples who spoke this language and the region they inhabited. The question of "Malayness" has always been problematic and subject to political mediation in colonial as much as postcolonial Malaya.[3]

The first understandings of the *dunia Melayu,* including the Philippines, were achieved by the Iberians.[4] With respect to Malay world linguistics, the task of lexicography, at least, was taken up avidly by Pigafetta (1969a), who, in 1521, compiled numerous word lists of Austronesian languages of the Philippines-Moluccas area, including a word list of the island of Tidor. Religious motive was undoubtedly behind St. Francis Xavier's attempts to learn and write religious tracts in Malay in Malacca in 1545 and subsequently in the Moluccas. Xavier also identified the language of Malacca and region as Malay "la lengua melaya, que es la que habla en Malacca, es muy general por estas partas" (Jacobs 1980, 35). In this era, it is highly likely that the Portuguese produced—but did not circulate—Portuguese-Malay word lists. As described by Thomaz and Lombard (1991), at least one has survived in manuscript form in the National Library in Lisbon. In 1599, the first Dutch navigators to visit Java and the islands (Ternate) also compiled and later published word lists of "Malay." In fact, unlike the Portuguese, the Dutch made systematic efforts to learn Malay, which became a lingua franca of the Dutch Company in the East Indies and complementary to Portuguese in many situations.

The pioneering philological study of Malay was that of Marsden (1812). Marsden (1754–1836) acknowledges a long line of Dutch predecessors in this endeavor, beginning with the first systematic dictionary, that of Frederik Houtman van Goud, *Spraeeck ende Woord-bieck in de Maleyasche Ende Madagascarsche Talen* (Dictionary of Malay and Malagasy), first published in Amsterdam in 1604 (republished 1673 and again at Batavia in 1707).[5] Houtman (1571–1627), son of Cornelis de Houtman, commander of the first Dutch voyage to Java and later Dutch governor of Ambon, acquired his knowledge of Malay while in captivity in Aceh between 1599 and 1602. By comparing some 2,000 Malay words with those lexified in Malagasy, the dominant code of Madagascar, he also demonstrated a linkage with what is now acknowledged as a broader Austronesin language family. A Latin translation of Houtman's dictionary was achieved in 1608 by the Dane Gothard Artus, in turn translated by Augustine Spalding, the English Company's agent at Bantam on Java, into English as *Dialogues in the English and Malaiane Languages,* published in London in 1624.

According to Marsden, the next original Malay dictionary is that by Caspar Wiltens (afterward improved by Sebastian Danckaerts) titled *Vocabularium, ofte Woorteboeck,* published in Holland in 1623 and reprinted in Batavia in 1706 and later translated into Latin and published in Rome by David Haex under the title *Dictionarium Malaico-Latinum et Latino-Malaicum . . .* (Malay-Latin and Latin-Malay Dictionary; 1631). It is of interest that the version by Haex also included a list of Portuguese (loan) words then in usage in the Moluccas, a list retained in a 1717 reprint. Wiltens offered an original and improved version published in

Amsterdam in 1650 and reprinted with improvements at Batavia in 1677 and 1708. There appear to be no indigenous attempts at Malay lexicology until the end of the nineteenth century.

Writing of Malacca under the Dutch, the navigator Nieuhoff also acknowledged the importance of Malay language in the archipelago and the importance of learning it. "The language used at Malacca," he announced, "is called the Malaya tongue from the natives of the country, being very famous throughout the East Indies." Composed of "best and choicest words" of many languages, he accounted Malay language "the neatest and most agreeable of the East Indies." He also acknowledged that "for the better encouragement of this language" and the benefit of officers of the Dutch East India Company, a Malay-Dutch dictionary had been prepared (Nieuhoff, in Churchill and Churchill 1704, vol. 2, 215). It is clear then that among the many regional languages in the archipelago, the Dutch and, in turn, the English privileged Malay as a lingua franca and, by developing a widely accepted Romanization system, ineluctably strengthened its dominance over other regional languages and dialects.

Another trend was also at work in the Malay world, namely, the introduction of European pedagogy outside strictly religious concerns, as was the bias of the Catholic missionaries. Nieuhoff observed the presence in Batavia of a Latin and Greek school "where the boys must divert themselves at certain times." While this school may have been the exclusive domain of the sons of Dutch burghers, Nieuhoff also commented on the presence of various other schools "for the instruction of young people in reading and writing, in which some of the natives, and especially the topasse are so ingenious, that they don't give way in that point to any other nation." He also observed that, from 1667, books not imported from Holland were printed locally (Nieuhoff, in Churchill and Churchill 1704, vol. 2).

From 1736, attempts at writing Malay grammars expanded, as did other endeavors at drawing up comparative word lists under the science of philology. Malay language vocabularies and grammars continued to be produced in the seventeenth century. Just as Batavia became a regional center for Dutch mapmakers, so, as Nieuhoff implies, it also emerged as a publishing center of dictionaries, grammars, and other materials. Marsden, who consulted many of these works, combined real knowledge of the language and culture with some sophisticated understanding of the principles of grammar along with a broad sense of the historical development of the language as well as an understanding of its links within a broad language family (Marsden 1812).

We should also acknowledge that early printing in *bahasa Melayu*, or Malay language, was almost synonymous with the missionary press. Batavia from 1746 and Singapore from the 1820s emerged as major centers of a missionary press directed at both China and the Malay world.

Specifically, translations of Christian tracts into Malay began in the eighteenth century, one from at least 1733. The British Free Bible Society's translation of the New Testament was printed in London in 1821. The first comprehensive dictionary of the Malagasy language also owes to British missionary enterprise, namely, J. Freeman's *Dictionary of the Malagasy Language in Two Parts*, published in An-Tannanarive in 1835. However, Frenchman Charles Nacquart missionized on Madagascar using his French-Malagasay catechism, published in Paris in 1657.

Attempts to collate other languages now considered within the Austronesian family lagged. The pioneering description of (Dutch) Timor and its languages was given by Willem von Hogendorp (1735–1784) in the first triple-volume edition of the Dutch-language *Transactions of the Batavia Society of Arts and Sciences* (1779–1781). One attempt to document Bugis vocabulary was that of the American seaman W. Vaughn, who attached six pages of vocabulary of this seafaring people to his *Narrative of Captain Woodward and Four Seamen . . . Surrendered Themselves up to the Malays, in the Island of Celebes* (1804). The systematic study of the ancient Kawi language of Java, however, was accomplished only in the early nineteenth century. Friedrich Wilhelm Humboldt (1767–1834) achieved this in his *Uber die Kawi-sprache auf der Insel Java* (On the Kawi Language of Java), published in Berlin in 1836–1839. Founder of the University of Berlin and an important figure in European philology, Humboldt had earlier demonstrated a philological commonality between Spain and North Africa.

The Latinization of Malay undertaken by the Europeans never displaced the language of the Holy Koran in questions of faith, even if it did on secular questions. Writing in Spanish from Ambon in May 1546, St. Francis Xavier regretted the general lack of writing systems in the islands with the notable exception of Malay ("la lengua en que escrivem es malays"), and the script it was written in was Arabic ("y las letras son arabias") on matters which Muslims were concerned ("Artes que se hiziessen moros no sabian escrevier") (Jacobs 1980, 35). From the late sixteenth century, Islamic writings increasingly began to appear in both Malay and Javanese scripts, signaling a trend toward the scripturalization of Malay manuscripts in Malayanized Arabic. Because of the loss of manuscripts in a tropical environment, the first documented evidence we have of Islamic writing in Malay is that of Hamzah Fansuri (d. 1590), a Sumatra-born mystic who studied in the Arabian Peninsula, returning to teach in Aceh (Riddell 2001, 104–5).

By the 1820s, a tradition emerged in Singapore of fixing Arabized Malay manuscript texts into print. The London Bible Society also saw to the printing of Christian tracts in Arabized Malay. The Orientalist-missionary presumption of Malay world studies may be taken for granted and, as we have seen, fits the prejudice of the age as mirrored by counterpart missionary translations of the Koran into European languages. The tide shifted in the mid-twentieth century, at least outside Islamic institutions and discourse, especially with the adoption of Romanized Malay as the basis of national languages in modern Indonesia and Malaysia. Today, independent Brunei Darussalam seeks to have it both ways in the sense of reviving and extending the use of Arabic script in official, including school, circles alongside Romanized form (Gunn 1997, 172–74).

## THE EXTINCTION OF TAGALOG SCRIPT

Hector Santos (1996), an energetic researcher on indigenous scripts in the Philippines, has commented that the early Spanish found that the people of Manila and elsewhere wrote on bamboo and especially prepared palm leaves in the ancient Tagalog script called *baybayin*. This was a syllabary of seventeen basic symbols using a diacritical mark called *kudit*. For good reason, Santos terms this "a simple and elegant system." Rather than signaling the existence of a priestly class, as was the norm in the Indianized states of Southeast Asia, he is of the opinion that the script was commonly used in personal communication, poetry, and so on. Although Pigafetta found no evidence of this script during his sojourn in the Cebu area, the generalized usage of the system is confirmed by the active publication of Christian texts in *baybayin* by Spanish missionaries.

Jesuit Pedro Chirino, who traveled widely outside Manila in the late sixteenth century, wrote in his *Relación de las Islas Filipinas* (Account of the Philippine Islands; 1604), "All these islanders are much given to reading and writing, and there is hardly a man, much less a women, who does not read and write." Still, he might have been remarking on the children of the schools he founded in Panay in 1593 and Iloilo in 1595, as from these years the first Tagalog and Ilocano Christian texts had been prepared in Roman script. In any case, the model had been pioneered in Mexico from the 1570s, whereon native languages were adapted to Latin and native script actively suppressed (Santos 1996).

Nevertheless, *Doctrina Christiana* was published in Tagalog script in 1593, and in 1620, Father Francisco Lopez issued an Ilocano version of *Doctrina Christiana*, also printed in the ancient syllabary. A 1621 revision (still extant) incorporated the cross *kudit*, a missionary innovation. This was a diacritic placed under a symbol, making it possible to vocalize final consonants, as in Spanish. We learn, however, that Tagalog script writers resisted this innovation, although conceding its utility in the case of Spanish, actually Castilian, borrowings. But in 1610, as mentioned in chapter 4, Tomas Pinpin published his *Librong Pagaaralan Nang Manga Tagalog Nang Uicang Castila* (The Book with Which Tagalogs Can Learn Castilian), a Latinized work in Tagalog, proving the ability to adapt the native language to the Spanish alphabet-based system. Even so, as Rafael (1993, 28) brilliantly summarizes, "that Tagalog should be organized around the matrix of Latin is a function of the Spanish belief in the proximity of Latin to the spirit of God's Word, a proximity that lent Latin its authority over the vernacular languages." In this sense, Rafael is musing on the question, Who controls translation: the missionary-as-agent-of-God or the language-as-divine-gift?

Santos (1996) allows that even though indigenous scripts have survived until the present in remote locations, by the end of the seventeenth century, the missionary-blessed script, whatever its acceptance outside church circles, had practically become extinct. As the Italian traveler, Careri observed in the Cavite-Manila area of the Philippines in 1697, "The Indians have almost forgot their way of writing, making use of Spanish." Even so, he observed a practice in the Philippines shared with the peoples of Siam, Pegu, and Cambodia (he might also have mentioned Java and Bali) of writing "on the smooth part of canes or on palm or rather coco-nut tree leaves with the point of a knife." He continued, "In the case of a letter that had to be folded, they use leaves" (Careri, in Churchill and Churchill 1704, vol. 4, 446).

Santos theorizes that the indigenous texts in the Philippines were not willfully destroyed by the Spanish, as happened in Mexico, but more likely lost ground because of the new prestige attached to literacy in Spanish, the language of power. Added to that, the disruption of traditional family activities also led to a decline in the production of indigenous texts. Moreover, the profusion of Spanish loanwords entering indigenous languages in the Philippines would have overwhelmed the ability of *baybayin* to adapt in recording the new sounds (Santos 1996). Even so, we observe the contradiction between an active church policy of scripturalization of indigenous languages in both Mexico and the Philippines and the destruction of texts in "lengua Mexicana," as transpired under the Inquisition, and the "mysterious" disappearance of parallel texts in native Filipino languages in more or less the same time frame.

The situation in the eastern archipelago, including the islands of Flores, Solor, and Timor, confronted by the Dominicans and later the Jesuits was rather different insofar as no literate tradition existed prior to European contact, especially as Hindu and Islamic influence was minimal. The lexification, much less the description, of languages and dialects spoken in Portuguese Timor likewise lagged, with the first comprehensive Portuguese-Tetum dictionary published in Macau only in 1889. This was *Diccionario de Portuguêz-Tétum* by the Portuguese missionary Sebastião Maria Apparicio da Silva. Dictionaries in other minor languages spoken on Timor, such as Galoli, followed in subsequent decades.[6] Even today, as East Timorese nationalists debate the choice of national and official languages, attempts to develop Tetum as a print language are embryonic.

## LEARNING CHINESE

Philological studies of China naturally developed with the arrival, especially in the Portuguese enclave of Macau, of the first European missionaries, part of a general trend that might be described as missionary Sinology. Gaspar da Cruz's *Treatise* (1569) offers perhaps the first description of Chinese writing, especially important in indicating that ideograms did not represent sounds as much as objects and that they were also understood by such peoples as Japanese and Vietnamese although pronounced differently. The Augustinean Juan Gonzalez de Mendoza restated in his *Historia . . .* (1585) that, though different Oriental peoples spoke in different languages, they could still communicate by writing ideograms. Specifically, in 1584, Ricci and Ruggiero compiled a Portuguese-Chinese dictionary. Ricci also worked with Nicolas Trigault to develop a system of Romanized Chinese. Writing in Chinese, it was Trigault who first presented a Chinese audience with the Latin alphabet as well as elaborating on his system of Romanization. This was titled *The Collection of Sounds and Writings of the Western Scholars* (1625).

One of the first—if not the first—works of Chinese philosophy to be translated into a European language was Juan Cobo's *Myong sim bo-gam . . .* (Mingxin baojian), rendered into Spanish as *Espejo Rico del Claro Coraz* (Precious Mirror of the Clear Heart). The book, published in Madrid in 1595, contains moral aphorisms selected from Confucian and Taoist texts.

A Chinese-Spanish grammar compiled by Franciscan missionaries in Fujian in February 1682 is recorded by Cordier (1883, 52), although he was unable to verify its existence. A pioneering text on the study of Mandarin was that by Francisco Varo (1627–1687), a Spanish Dominican missionary who arrived in China in 1654, namely, *Arte de la Lengua Mandarina* (Mandarin Grammar), printed on woodblock in Guangzhou in 1703. Varo's rare text written in Spanish and Latin may well be the first mention in print of what we today gloss Mandarin Chinese.[7]

Certain Jesuits also published in Chinese. One was the Bresnia-born Guilo Aleri (1562–1649), whose reputation was well known in China, especially Fujian, where he resided. A prolific author of some twenty-five titles, Aleri was also a figure attributed with introducing Confucius in Europe. Aleri authored the *Tchifang wai ki*, a geographical notice on all the supposed kingdoms of the world, as well as several texts on Chinese characters. Another Jesuit, Dominique Pairenin (1665–1741), authored the *Ki ho youen pe* (The Six First Books of Euclid). The Italian Luigi Buglio (?–1682) authored *Yu lan sifang yeo ki* (Memoir on Occidental Countries). The Portugalborn Ignacio da Costa, together with Prospero Intocetta, authored *Sapienta Sinica* (Chinese Wisdom), the earliest Latin translation of certain of the Confucian classics, printed in Jiangxi in 1662 and, as mentioned in chapter

4, *Sinarum Scientia Politico-Moralis* (1659). This is but a sample of Jesuit writings or translations in Chinese. Henri Cordier, author of *Bibliotheca Sinica* (1883), for its time the most complete bibliography of books on China in European languages, offers 194 titles from the Bibliotheque Nationale collection in Paris, albeit dominated mostly by religious issues.

Many theories on the origins of Chinese language and Chinese culture were bruited or put about in Europe throughout the seventeenth and eighteenth centuries, some of them entering print. Doubtless inspired by Jesuit writings that came to be known in England in the Hakluyt and Purchas collections, John Webb (1611–1672) produced his *HISTORICAL ESSAY Endeavouring a Probability That the Language of the Empire of China Is the Primitive LANGUAGE* (1669). According to Chen Shouyi (1998, 95), the best that can be said of this obscure work is that it was "Biblio-historic rather than linguistic." Even so, this work was consistent with the pre-Enlightenment attempt to seek biblical ancestors to exotic languages and cultures.

In chapter 2, we mentioned the faux description of Formosa by Psalmanazar (1704), but his ability to pass off his discourse on the language of Formosa (and Japan) without major dissent, at least outside Jesuit circles, tells much about the prevailing state of linguistic knowledge in Europe of Asia. "The language of Formosa is the same as that of Japan," he asserts, "but with the difference that the Japanese do not pronounce some Letters gutturally as the Formosans do." Japanese language has three genders, has no cases, use twenty letters in their alphabet, and so on. In Formosa, he continues, the "preterimperfect tense" is pronounced by raising the voice and the future tense by falling it and so on. To complete the deception, the impostor included a chart purporting to be the Formosan alphabet or, actually, syllabary (Penzer 1926, 235). In fact, from 1624, Dutch missionaries on the island had pioneered the Romanization of at least one indigenous language, now understood to be Austronesian, to facilitate conversion of the natives. Such manuscripts, known as "Sinkang Bunsu," were rediscovered only in the nineteenth century and could not have been known to Psalmanazar.[8]

Of a different order, albeit misguided, was Joseph de Guignes's (1683–1745) *Memoire dans Lequel on Prouve, que les Chinois sont une Colonie Egyptienne* (Note Serving to Prove That the Chinese Were a Colony of Egypt; 1759). As implied, this work, which was actually read before the French Royal Academy, attempted to prove that Chinese characters originated from Egyptian hieroglyphics via the Phoenician language.

But serious French Sinology had already been launched with the appointment by Louis XIV of Etiènne Fourmont to aid a young Chinese called Hoan-ji to compile *Meditationes Sinicae* (Chinese Meditations; 1737) and *Linguae Sinarum Mandarinicae Grammatica Duplex* (Grammar of Chinese Mandarin Language; 1742). Fourmont lectured on Chinese language and letters at the Collège Royale in Paris. In addition, a Sinological tradition was launched in Russia with the publication of Gottlieb Siegfried Bayer's *Museum Sinicum* . . . (1730), the first grammatical account of Chinese language to achieve currency in Europe. Bayer was professor of Greek and Roman antiquities at St. Petersburg Academy of Sciences (1726–1738). From another quarter, the St. Petersburg Russian Bible Society also entered the picture, producing in 1819 a Mongolian script edition of St. Matthew's Gospel in a collaboration between I. J. Schmidt and the Mongolian church.

Only with the lifting of the prohibition on publishing in the Portuguese colonies did the study of Chinese language make a rebound in Macau after a long hiatus left by the departing Jesuits. Notable was Joachim Afonso Gonçalves (1694–1738), author of such works as *Arte China* . . . (Chinese Grammar; 1829) and *Lexicon Magnum Latino Sinicum* (Greater Latin-Chinese Dictionary; 1841). A member of the Lazarista congregation, working out of St. Joseph College in Macau, Gonçalves not only used the college press to produce his dictionaries but also organized classes in typesetting, leading to the training of a cadre of local Macau printers whose skills would later be sought after by the Protestant missionaries. All together, Gonçalves was responsible for the printing of ten works on Chinese grammar, vocabularies, and dictionaries, including a translation of the New Testament (Braga 1942a, 42).

English Sinology developed in tandem with trade, commerce, and mission activity, leading to more serious work on Chinese language. Such was J. Hager's *Elementary Characters of the Chinese*, published in London in 1801. Forbidden to publish in Guangzhou, English Protestant missionaries also looked to Macau as a place to establish a press. Restrictions on publishing still applied to Portuguese until completely lifted in 1820, but the law was relaxed in favor of the London Missionary Society. While the renaissance of Portuguese language publishing in Macau belongs to the nineteenth century, we digress to mention the first works printed in Macau (and China) in English using the English East India Company press, later established in Guangzhou. These included John Francis Davis's (1795–1890) *San-yu-low, or the Three Dedicated Rooms. A Tale. Translated from the Chinese* (1815). Better known was Scottish missionary Robert Morrison (1782–1834), whose contribution to the East-West exchange, as acknowledged in China today, runs the gamut from translations of Chinese philosophy and pedagogy to lexicology. Notable was his typographically impressive multivolume *Dictionary of the Chinese Language* (1815–1823). Morrison also made the first systematic attempt to produce a Chinese version of the Bible. This he achieved by reworking an anonymous, presumably Jesuit, translation of the Gospels into Chinese discovered in the British Library. After years of labor, the Anglo-Chinese College in Malacca published this in 1823 as *Shentian shengshu*. In the same year, he published in Macau his Chinese-language *Yingguo wenyu fanli shuan* (Grammar of the English Language), anticipating an interest on the part of Chinese in learning the rising European language of commerce.

## *RANGAKU:* JAPANESE LEXICOLOGY

But Jesuit pioneers were always ahead. We have referred to the pioneering writings on Japan by João Rodrigues, namely, his *Arte da Lingoa de Japão* (Japanese Grammar), printed in Nagasaki in 1604, and, following his expulsion from Japan, *Arte Breve da Lingoa Japoa de Arte Grande da Mesma Lingua* (Shorter and Longer Grammar of Japanese Language), printed at the College of Macau in 1624. To this day, Rodrigues's dictionary is consulted by linguists and others and is otherwise esteemed for its renditions of seventeenth-century speech. Cooper (1994) states that, as Japanese had not hitherto made a systematic study of their own language, Rodrigues's grammars "mark the beginning of a methodical exposition of the spoken language." Cooper has explained that while lists of Japanese words obviously circulated among the missionaries in Japan, the decision to print a Japanese dictionary was made in 1590. The first fruits of this venture was the *Vocabulario da Lingoa do Japan* (Japanese Vocabulary) and its supplement printed the following year. All together, 32,798 entries are recorded with pronunciation of both the Kyoto and the Kyushu area, while poetic expressions and women's words are also noted. Even so, some conjecture applies to authorship, notably as to whether Francisco Rodrigues was principal editor or whether João Rodrigues also had a hand (Cooper 1994, 230–38). We observe also the efforts on the part of the mission in Japan and China to Latinize. Beginning around 1551, some sixteen texts of Latinized Japanese were prepared, although obviously Latinized Japanese never displaced the indigenous syllabaries, hiragana and katakana, or the use of kanji, or Chinese-derived characters.

Long years would pass before the revival of a European tradition of Japanese lexicology. Simply, Rodrigues was far ahead of his time in an age when not all European languages were lexified and when the compilation of bilingual dictionaries in European languages was in its infancy. But inevitably, the impatience of European traders to break into the China, Korea, and Japan trade led to an increasing penetration into East Asian seas by English, French, Russian, and other expeditions. In this context, one of the first descriptions of the language of the Ryukyus was achieved by Herbert John Clifford in his "Vocabulary of the Language Spoken at the Great Loo-Choo Island, in the Japan Sea . . ." annexed to Basil Hall's (1818) account of his voyage to Korea, part of the expedition accompanying Lord Amhurst to China. Missionary endeavor was another impulse. While working on Japanese language from his base in Nagasaki, Siebold also drew up a significant lexicon of Ainu terms derived from an array of sources dating back to early Jesuit contacts. This was published as an annex to his monograph on the discoveries of Gerrits Vries (1859). One rough attempt to codify Japanese in English was achieved by English missionary and Orientalist Walter Henry Medhurst in his *English and Japanese and Japanese and English Vocabulary,* printed in Batavia in 1830.

While, as mentioned previously, the Dutch were restricted in their dealings with the Japanese at Nagasaki by being obliged to work through the caste of interpreters, no such inhibitions restricted the Japanese side, especially when Dutch learning became the vogue. *Rangaku,* the study of European science through Dutch books, inevitably turned to the production of dictionaries. But contrary to the dictates of European Orientalism, it was actually the Japanese who took the initiative. In 1796, the Edo-based scholar and physician Inamura Sampaku (1759–1811) produced a first Dutch-Japanese dictionary. This was called *Haruma wage* after one of the French-Dutch and Dutch-French dictionaries of François Halma, first published in, respectively, 1701 and 1710. To place this work in comparative perspective, the first Dutch-English dictionary of any significance was produced only in 1637. A second dictionary, a work of Dutch-Japanese collaboration, *Zuufu haruma,* was compiled under the initiative of Henrik Doeff, Dutch captain on Deshima (1803–1817), but completed only in 1833. A manuscript version at least of a Russian-Japanese dictionary was also produced in the 1770s. But with a growing perception that the English were a rising power, especially after the Phoeton Incident of 1808 in which an English ship raided Nagasaki, the shogunate ordered the compilation of an English textbook (1811) and an English-Japanese vocabulary (1814), albeit for official use only. In 1856, using a newly imported Dutch printing press along with European type—the first such typographic press in use in Japan since the "Christian Century"—the authorities in Nagasaki reprinted a Dutch grammar, *Syntaxis, of Wordvoeging der Nederduitsche Tael.*[9]

By 1862, with the publication of an English-Japanese dictionary, Hori Tatsunosuke, the great age of Japanese lexicology of European languages had arrived, just as Japanese intellectuals began to desert *Rangaku* for English studies. The first French-Japanese dictionary issued by Léon Pages between 1862 and 1868, however, was heavily derivative of Rodrigues's masterpiece of 1590. Only in 1867 was the landmark Japanese-English dictionary by J. C. Hepburn produced, lending his name to the Hepburn-style Roman spelling system.

Aside from the first Jesuit contacts with Korea dating from the time of Hideyoshi's invasion of the peninsula in the late sixteenth century, we await the advent of Dutch contacts of the mid-seventeenth century before published descriptions of Korean language emerge. Such owes to the enterprise of Nicolas Witsen (1641–1717), who interviewed Matheus Eibokken, survivor of the shipwrecked Dutch party in Korea, and who is understood to have mastered the Korean *han'gul* alphabet during his long sojourn in the Cholla Namdo area of Korea from 1656 to 1666 (Vos 1975). As published in the 1705 edition of Witsen's *Noord en Oost Tartaryen* (North and East Tatary), a pioneering European study touching on Korea, Eibokken offered up from memory a vocabulary of 143 Korean words.

### THE JESUIT INVENTION OF *QUOC NGU*

Nowhere else did the impact of the Jesuits on linguistic form have such a far-reaching effect as in the court or courts of Vietnam, where Chinese-style characters were de rigeur in a governmental system that mirrored that of imperial China. For example, in the early age of trade contacts between Vietnam and Japan, state officials corresponded in Chinese characters. Styled *cho nom*, the Sino-Vietnamese writing system that had evolved from the tenth century on comprised two Chinese characters combined, one offering the meaning of a Vietnamese word with the other a guide to pronunciation. While the Latinization of *cho nom* awaited full-blown French colonialism, the invention of what later became known as *quoc ngu* (national language) had its origins in the first Jesuit contacts.

Stemming from the decision of the Macau-based Council of Bishops in 1615, a Jesuit mission was dispatched to Hoi An, the cosmopolitan trading port in central Vietnam, strengthened in 1617 with the arrival of Francesco du Pina, the first European speaker of Vietnamese and, in 1619, the Portuguese-Japanese Pedro Marquez and the Italian Christoforo Borri (1631), author of a famed book on Vietnam. Borri also bequeathed to Europe the first detailed description of "the language of the Cochin-Chinese," comparing and contrasting it with Chinese, "both of them using monosyllables, delivered in several tones and accents; yet they utterly differ in the word it self, the Cochin-Chinese being more full of vowels, and consequently softer and sweeter, more copious in tones and accents, and therefore more harmonious" (Borri, in Churchill and Churchill 1704, vol. 2, 736). After Borri, the third missionary to acquire Vietnamese-speaking ability was the celebrated Alexandre de Rhodes, who arrived in Dang Trong in 1624. Author of the trilingual *Dictionarium Annamiticum Lusitanum et Latinum* (Vietnamese-Portuguese-Latin Dictionary), published in Rome in 1631, along with a Latin catechism, Rhodes pioneered the Latinization of *cho nom.*

However, as Vietnamese historian Nguyen Van Hoan (1993, 176–83) has explained, the presence in the first Jesuit missions in Vietnam of a number of Japanese priests with Chinese character–reading ability undoubtedly proved invaluable to the Europeans as intermediaries. It should be recalled that Hoi An hosted a large Japanese community, including Christians banished from their homeland. Even so, in researching Vietnamese language, the missionaries were confronted with the problem of lack of unity between language, *nom,* and characters, a situation in which Vietnamese spoke one language and wrote in another. Building on their prior experience in Latinizing Japanese and Chinese languages, the missionaries in Vietnam set about first transcribing words and then inventing a script. The introduction of accents or tonic signs, absent in Borri's work, found appearance only in that of Rhodes, becoming a "new, regulated, theoretically-based and systematic script." In any case, it is now believed that the invention of *quoc ngu* was a collective undertaking made by Italian, French, and especially Portuguese missionaries. The influence of Portuguese pronunciation in the transcription of Vietnamese was profound. Rhodes is also generous in acknowledging the help of Vietnamese priests and others. In the opinion of Nguyen Van Hoan, the invention of *quoc ngu* was "the beautiful fruit of the fortuitous meeting between Vietnam's national culture and the European's Latin culture."[10]

Nevertheless, as Woodside (1988) elaborates, the Chinese cultural spell over the Confucianized Vietnamese literati persisted until the advent of colonial rule, even though hybridized Sino-Vietnamese forms of writing emerged, "a mosaic of adjustments and surprises" (50–58, 294). Moreover, many mandarins balked at the notion of accepting a script that would subvert the ability of the Vietnamese population to read either Confucian or Buddhist texts. But foreign ambitions of religious success became "fatally entangled" in Vietnamese court politics, and real persecution and execution of missionaries began in the 1830s. French gunboat diplomacy achieved the de facto creation of the French colony of Cochin China by 1862. Putting paid to the Confucian examination system (the last was organized in Hue in 1919), the French set about adopting the *quoc ngu* Romanization system, which eventually became the mode of instruction in village schools and accepted by Vietnamese reformists in the early twentieth century against traditionalist diehards (Chandler et al. 1987, 131–32, 262, 316).

Intellectually, the colonial project was anticipated by Jean-Louis Taberd, compiler of *Dictionarium Anamitico-Latinum er Latino-Anamiticum* (Vietnamese-Latin, Latin-Vietnamese Dictionary), printed in Serampore in India in 1838. His was the first comprehensive dictionary of Vietnamese, preceded only by Rhodes's imperfect Latin version. Taberd's dictionary included, for the first time, a double column of phonetically adapted Vietnamese characters and Latin.

## TRANSLATING BUDDHIST ASIA

With respect to Tibet and the Theravada Buddhist kingdoms of mainland Southeast Asia, we may speculate that indifference to conversion, as much as difficulty of penetration after early successes, retarded linguistic studies and the general translation of knowledge until the eighteenth and nineteenth centuries.

According to Cordier and Lenhart, writing in the *Catholic Encyclopedia* (1912), "The missionaries were the first Tibetan scholars." In 1716–1721, Jesuit Hippolito Desideri authored two Christian apologetic works on Tibet, and Capuchin Francesco Orazio della Penna (1681–1745) translated two Christian texts into Tibetan as well as translating into Italian the "History of the Life and Works of Shakiatubi, the Restorer of Lamaism." He also compiled the first Tibetan dictionary, containing 55,000 words in Tibetan characters with corresponding Italian translation. Still, all these works remained unpublished. The first printed dictionary and grammar of the Tibetan language is the *Alphabetum Tibetanum . . .* (Tibetan Alphabet), published in Rome in 1762 by the Italian Augustinean Antonio Agostino Giorgi (d. 1797).

British Tibetology had its tentative beginnings in the researches of an employee of the East India Company. This was Alexander Csoma de Koras (1784–1842), a Hungarian-born graduate of Gottingen University who studied Tibetan in Ladakh for nine years. Between 1834 and 1836, de Koras published a grammar book of Tibetan language and a Tibet-English dictionary. He also published a series of articles on Tibet in the *Journal of the Asiatic Society of Bengal*. Csoma de Koras's original interest in central Asia had been to discover the origins of his native Magyar language, echoing nineteenth-century scholarly concerns with the origins of languages and cultures.

Needless to say, Csoma de Koras's work begins to feed into what Mathiassen (1996) describes as "Mythos Tibet." The first Portuguese visitor, Andrade, described the Tibetan people with great sympathy as the "unknown known" and Tibet as a promised land. The image further changed in the eighteenth century. Kant described Tibet as a dark and cruel theocracy, and Rousseau found the Tibetan government oppressive and bizarre. But by the nineteenth century, when scholarly interest in Tibet intensified, Mathiassen continues, "evolutionism, imperialism, romanticism and rationalism became part of the interpretation of Tibet." Even the rosy picture of Tibetan Buddhism as painted by Andrade was superseded by a view that saw Tibetan religion corrupted with folk religion and nonpure Buddhist beliefs. By the twentieth century, travelers, missionaries, English officials, fiction writers, and others famously completed the mystification of this land.

It stands to reason that the first Portuguese traders arriving in the Bay of Bengal area soon after the conquest of Goa were the first lexicographers, but the systematic study of languages of the Burmese kingdoms awaited the missionaries. One early attempt to compile a Burmese dictionary was by Sigismondo Calchi (1685–1728), appearing in 1725 (England 2001). Calchi was a Barnadite missionary dispatched to the courts of Ava and Pegu by Pope Innocent XII (1691–1700). Better documented is *Alphabetum Bermanum* (Alphabet of the Burmese Language), published in

Rome in 1776 and authored by the Jesuit Melchior Carpanio. This was the first work to offer a rendition of Pali script.[11]

There is no doubt that visiting Jesuits also made the first word lists of Thai, Lao, and Khmer languages. Two Europeans, Gerritt van Wuysthoff of the Dutch East India Company, followed by the Italian Jesuit Giovanni-Maria Leria, visited Laos in the 1640s. Leria, who remained for five years, learned the language but bequeathed no dictionary. It is also known that such missionaries as Guy Tachard, who accompanied the Siamese embassy in their audience with Pope Innocent XI (1676–1689), could speak the language. The Society of Foreign Missions of Paris, which launched its mission in Siam in 1669, undoubtedly pioneered the European study of social institutions of the kingdom, including language, yet it was not until 1850 that the French missionary-bishop D. J. B. Pallegoix published in Bangkok his *Dictionarium Latinum Thai* (Thai-Latin Dictionary). We are reminded that when British civil servant James Low researched his 1824 map of Siam, Laos, and Cambodia, he complained to his superiors of the "total absence of any Elementary Works" in the Thai or Siamese language (Sternstein 1995, 113).[12] In any case, the typographic press made a relatively late entry to Siam. The first book printed by this process was the *Kham Son Christang* (1796) in the reign of Rama I (1782–1809), the king who first established his capital in Bangkok. Authored by the French missionary Mgr. Garnault, who was responsible for bringing the press to Siam, it was composed in Romanized language in default of an indigenous script typeface.

## ORIENTALISM REVISITED

It is paradoxical that, in the first wave of globalization, the Portuguese, who successfully imposed their language as a generational lingua franca across the Eurasian maritime zone, lagged in Oriental studies. The exception was the Jesuits, but their example was not emulated by the state, at least until the Pombaline reforms, beginning in 1770, provided the political and institutional setting for scientific advance, leading to, for example, the creation of a College of Natural Philosophy at Coimbra University in 1772 and the founding of the Lisbon Academy of Sciences in 1799.

Meanwhile, the Dutch, French, English, and subsequently the Germans and Russians raised Indology and Sinology to a new level. The Napoleonic invasion of Egypt in 1798 was one harbinger of the future European appropriation of the Oriental "Other" and, in Said's (1978, 42) description, marked the advent of "modern European Orientalism." The arrival of the English East India Company in Bengal in 1757, coincident with the decline of Mughal power and the gradual consolidation of British imperial rule over the subcontinent, was another historical moment in the Orientalist framing of the expanding British possessions east of India.

One such marker of the European advance into Asian mental space, widely noted in this discourse, was Macaulay's "Minute on Indian Education" of February 2, 1835. Railing against the printing of Arabic and Sanskrit books in British India, Macaulay elaborated, "In India, English is the language spoken by the ruling classes. It is spoken by the higher class of natives at the seats of Government. It is likely to become the language of commerce throughout the seats of Government. It is the language of the two great European communities which are rising, the one in the south of Africa, the other in Australasia, communities which are every year becoming more important, and more closely connected with our Indian empire."

It is unlikely that late Tokugawa officials in Japan actually read this report, but, as observed, by the mid-nineteenth century, Japanese scholars were deserting *Rangaku* studies for English. Macaulay's notice not only foreshadowed the rise of the New Anglican school of Orientalism but also firmly established English as the hegemonic language for the next hundred years and beyond. To be sure, while English became the primary written language of educated Indians, we also acknowledge that, along with many other Asian civilizations, Chinese and Japanese have not lost their written or spoken languages. The postcolonial retention of English as an official language or as a language of commerce does not negate the role this code played in empire formation. The legacy of England's late colonial hegemony is in the way that English, in its many varieties, is the fastest-growing language of the current era, setting aside the spread of Mandarin Chinese and Spanish otherwise linked with demographics and history. But in the current globalization, English also expands as a second or third language.

## CONCLUSION

The development of European philological studies of Asian languages is often viewed as part of the process of empowerment and displacement associated with the rise of Orientalism. Such a view would appear to be confirmed by our discussion on the Arabic world, Indology, Malay world studies, the extinction of Tagalog script in the Philippines, and the Romanization of Vietnamese, illustrating to varying degrees the actions of rising European imperialism in foisting their languages and/or scripts on native peoples or otherwise displacing or marginalizing local tongues. Thus, in short time, Castilian/Spanish became the language of power in the Philippines, just as at a later date English became the language of administration in India and Malaya and Dutch in the East Indies. Even so,

Jesuit endeavor to produce lexicons of myriad minor languages along with such dominant codes as written Chinese and Japanese challenged but never threatened the political hegemony of China and Japan. Arabic remains to believers the language in which the Koran was revealed.

As we confirmed, Japan offers a countermodel to the Orientalist thesis insofar as it was Japanese officials who led the way in the early modern period in compiling lexicons and dictionaries of European languages as aids to actively stimulate *Rangaku* and European learning. China, Persia, and large swaths of the Arabic-speaking world, along with the peripheries of central Asia and the archipelago, remained and still remain either outside of or impervious to the trend signaled by Macaulay of the early nineteenth-century British Empire. Through the time frame of our first globalization, indeed to this day, print communities within countries and civilizations maintaining script-based alphabets (such as Arabic, Jawi Malay, Hindi, Urdu, Thai/Lao, and so on), along with those sharing ideograph-based systems (such as Chinese) or languages employing a combination of both (such as Japanese and Korean), appear to have culturally insulated themselves from many of the hybrid effects of cultural "contamination." Of course, it may be more than coincidence that many of these countries remained semicolonies or protectorates through the age of high imperialism rather than submitting to conquest along the pattern of the Americas and sub-Saharan Africa.

While Arab-Iberian crossovers reach back to the twelfth century, continuing through the Crusades, the rise of the Ottoman Turks prodded European courts into taking their enemies seriously. This we have seen in the role of Leiden and Paris together forming the incubator of serious Oriental studies. But biblical studies such as pioneered in Leiden soon proved an entrée into the study of languages of practical commerce and diplomacy, such as Persian and Arabic. The Dutch, French, and English, in particular among European nations, vied for dominance in the rapidly expanding academic field of Oriental studies, by the eighteenth century also defined as embracing Sanskrit, Chinese, and Malay, among other languages and dialects, unlocking the knowledge and empowerments necessary for establishing commercial bridgeheads and future colonial empires.

## NOTES

1. Setting aside partial Spanish translations and translations into Latin, the first translation of the Koran into a modern European language was an Italian version by Andrea Arribene (1547), forming the basis of the first German translation by Solomon Schweigger (Nuremberg, 1616), in turn forming the basis of the first translation into Dutch (Hamburg, 1641).

2. For example, for a study, inter alia, linking Jones with a Hindu revival in British India, see Kopf (1965).

3. See Andaya (2001), who allows the origins of Melayu ethnicity developing along the Straits of Malacca as early as the seventeenth century. The Melayu political center, variously Sumatra and the peninsula, was resolved only in the nineteenth century by British political and ideological intervention that contrived to position the Malacca sultanate as "the cradle of Malay civilization."

4. We allow that a "Chinese Vocabulary of Malacca Malay Words and Phrases" was compiled for the use of Chinese traders at the port city between 1403 and 1511.

5. The dictionary is the subject of a major inquiry by Lombard (1970).

6. For an overview of historic descriptions of Timor and cognate languages, see Hull (1998).

7. For a translation and interpretation, see Coblin and Levi (2000).

8. Sinkang was the place opposite Tayouan, where the Dutch originally settled in 1624, today known as Sin-chhi in Tainan County. Several texts in Romanized Sinkang dialect were published, including Daniel Gravius's *Het heylige evangelium Mathheu* (The Gospel of St. Matthew), published in 1661. Gravius was a member of the Dutch Reformed Church. See Chiung (2002).

9. In 1862, the press, styled Imprimerie Neerlandaise, printed (in French with two pages in Japanese) a catalog of Siebold's library, interestingly a total of 700 books, ranging from voyages of discovery to works on China and Japan to language and natural and physical sciences.

10. Long denounced by Vietnamese anticolonialists, a street once dedicated to Rhodes in Saigon has been restored. Likewise, his commemorative stone in Hanoi has been rediscovered and his contributions to the development of Vietnamese language and culture praised by leading officials (Marr 2000).

11. The first full-scale account of Burma (Ava) in English was Michel Symes (1800).

12. Lexicology of Lao and Khmer languages developed in tandem only with the great French missions of exploration of the upper Mekong in the late nineteenth century, namely, those of Jean Moura (1878) and M. Massie (1894).

# 10

# A Theory of Global Culturalization

The Southeast Asian archipelago throughout our 1500–1800 time frame was the locus of intense European cultural and racial creolization. As I develop below, creolization was not restricted to linguistic form but embraced a range of cultural crossovers that came to be embedded in specific local cultures and even mainstreamed into dominant cultures. Such borrowings and adaptations run the gamut from cuisine, music, and games to artistic form. Importantly, the concept of crossovers challenges the binarism inherent in the Orientalist critique. I further argue that modern-day Indonesia, especially the Flores-Timor zone, along with the Moluccas, the Philippines, and East Timor, owe their present-day character to this history of European-Asian contact. To be sure, not all cultural contact was Asian-European but equally involved the process, still ongoing, of Arabization, Indianization, and Sinicization. The Malayanized Chinese communities of Penang and Malacca are cases in point. In any case, certain of these creolized communities came to constitute "nations," such as the Philippines and East Timor; others part communities, such as the "Portuguese" of Malacca and the Macanese of Macau; others vestigial minorities within new nation-states; and others simply disappearing through intermarriage and assimilation. This chapter seeks to identify, albeit selectively, the processes of creolization, "crossover," and the broader questions of what might be called historical ethnicity and identity arising out of the first globalization.

## CREOLE CULTURES,
## CREOLES, AND CREOLIZATION

Compared to the mixing and meeting of various Asian peoples arising from migrations, trade contacts, and conquest, creole cultures, by definition, emerged out of the Columbian exchange, products of the miscegenation of conquistadores and their native subjects. But with the major demographic shifts stemming from the Atlantic slave trade, the Caribbean–Latin American zone was transformed forever, giving rise to a range of creoles and creole cultures from Louisiana to Cuba to Martinique and Guyana, and to the Afro-creole of the River Plate, sometimes termed "plantation creoles." While the Brazils of the world actually celebrate their creoleness and while the creole culture of, for example, New Orleans has come to be celebrated by writers from William Faulkner to Lafcadio Hearn, other settler zones had cause to actively suppress racial mixing, and many creoles, such as the "colored" peoples of South Africa, were actively discriminated against. Where Protestant England and Holland developed forms of racial separateness in their respective colonies, Portugal deliberately fostered new cultures, especially out of, and out of the need for, miscegenation. This in fact was the famous injunction of Alfonso de Albuquerque on his conquest of Goa, mindful that demography handicapped Portugal's overseas expansion. The case of the equatorial Atlantic island of São Tome off the west coast of Africa, virtually untouched by humans before 1485, is illustrative. Peopled successively by African slaves from Benin, intermarried with Portuguese descendants of Angolan slaves, freed slaves, and other immigrants from Cape Verde and Mozambique, a new Portugalized creole society developed in what Hagemeijer (1999, 74–88) describes as the "Babel islands" of the Gulf of Guinea.

What then are creole languages? Isabel Tomás (1990, 56) has provided an appropriate definition: "Creoles are mother tongues of comparatively recent origin arising from linguistic encounters in specific historical, social, political and linguistic situations." Despite their "youth," and notwithstanding their oral emphasis, creoles attain the same degree of complexity and subtlety of expressive power as all other languages. Even so, many creoles are discriminated or ranked lower than dominant codes. As discussed later in this chapter, this was the case of the Portugalized creole of Malacca alongside Malay. While the Portugalized creole of Macau suffered no discrimination, its longevity became threatened by the existence of a prestige language in the form of standard Portuguese. But creole can in certain circumstances gain prestige, such as in independent Cape Verde and Guinea-Bissau, where liberation movements pragmatically adopted creole as national language. In other situations, such as Haiti, a diglossia comes into being where two often mutually incomprehensible variants coexist in the same community as in (High) French and (Low) French-based African creole. To degrees, such can be discerned in newly independent East Timor as Portuguese regains status, but the number of speakers remains relatively low alongside creolized Tetum, the lingua franca and "language of East Timorese nationalism" (Tanter, Selden, and Shalom 2000, 254).

What, then, were the specific historical, social, and political situations giving way to new linguistic encounters? We observe that, in the first globalization, Europeans came to constitute enclaves, whether as seasonal traders, such as on the coast of China and in Hirado and Nagasaki in Japan; as residents of fortresses, such as at Mombassa, Mozambique Island, Colombo, Galle, Malacca, and Solor and in the Moluccas; or as privileged inhabitants of *intramuros* (well-guarded fortress cities), as in Macau, Manila, Goa, and Batavia. Even so, by overcoming barriers thrown up through class and religion, some Europeans, invariably male, lived outside these social constraints. With time, creolized communities of Portuguese and their *mestiço* (mixed-race descendants) developed across Asia besides, as alluded, the Americas and the African littoral.[1]

In the early 1600s, the fortified city of Manila hosted a multiracial group of Indians, Javanese, Portuguese, French, Dutch, Flemings, Italians, Greeks, and African slaves along with the Spanish ruling class. Chinese traders from Fujian and Japanese Christian exiles formed separate communities outside the city walls. The major social test imposed on these communities under the Iberian flag was the imperative to convert to the Catholic religion. Victims of Spanish pogroms, the Chinese soon fell in line. Not only did Chinese mestizo classes develop from liaisons with Spanish, but a profound mixing of Chinese and "Indios" or native Filipinos led to the development of a new cultural layer in colonial society.

Historic Malacca offers a prime example of Asian-Asian "creolization" alongside Eurasian creolization. The major locus of trade connecting India, Java, China, and the Ryukyus, the Malacca sultanate, prior to its conquest by the Portuguese in 1511, like other maritime marts in the archipelago, was a highly cosmopolitan city. Even today, Muslim coreligionists in modern Malaysia may be Arab-Malay, Indian-Malay, Javanese-Malay, or even Sino-Malay with many subethnic affiliations. Needless to say, the arrival of Portuguese missionaries imposed Catholicism as a new social marker. Writing of the "Luso-Malays" of seventeenth-century Malacca, Thomaz observes that, above all, it was from female slaves that *mestiços* were born with the children set free on the payment of a small sum. But also in Malacca, a new Christian group emerged from *klings* (or people of Indian descent) and their slaves. It was from this group that new Christians were drawn. Only with the arrival of the Jesuits was a more active proselytization policy entered against the local Muslim population. At the beginning of the seventeenth century, there were 7,400 Christians (*orang*

**Figure 10.1. Malacca viewed from shipboard, from Argensola's *Histoire de la Conquete des isles Moluques par les Espagnols, par les Portugais & par les Hollandais* (1707). A slightly fanciful view of a naval clash offshore the strategic Portuguese-held trading emporium and port of Malacca astride the strategic straits of the same name. (Author's collection)**

*Serani*) living in Malacca dispersed around the town as opposed to residing in any specific quarter (Thomaz 1998).

Writing in 1583 of late sixteenth-century Goa, Linschoten was well placed to observe of Goa society that numerous Portuguese in India were married with "the natural-born women of the Country, and the children proceeding of them are called Mestiços that is half countrymen" (Linschoten, in Purchas 1905–1907, 229).

As Dampier wrote of early eighteenth-century Lifau, a key port on Timor servicing the sandalwood trade, while formal authority lay with a Portuguese sent from Goa, at the time of his visit the place was under the command of one Alexis Mendosa, a *mestiço* (the scion of "a Mungrel-Breed of Indians and Portugueze"). As Dampier elaborated, though they pretended to be under the king of Portugal, "they are a sort of lawless People, and are under no Government" (Dampier 1745, 177–78). The *topasse*, or Laratuqueiros, named after their stronghold at Larantuca on Flores, sometimes known as "Black Portuguese," survive today as a mixed-race Catholicized element on both Timor and Flores islands.

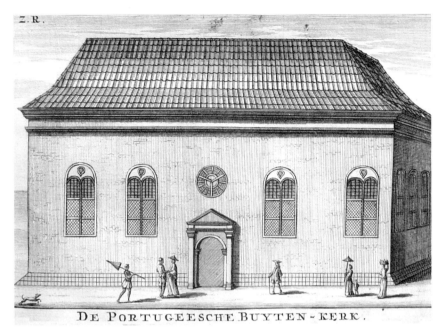

DE PORTUGEESCHE BUYTEN-KERK.

**Figure 10.2. Portuguese church in old Jakarta, from Valentijn's** *Oud en Nieuw Oost-Indien* **(1724). Sited in the Tugu district of Batavia/Jakarta, the Portuguese church long served the creolized community of the port city, even surviving until recent decades. (Reproduced with permission of Nagasaki University Library)**

The etymology of *topasse* is obscure. A generic term applied to the products of Portuguese-Asian liaisons, *topasse* enjoyed wide currency in a Portuguese Indian context from the sixteenth century on, reflecting its likely derivation from the Malayalam word for "two languages" or "interpreter" or, in Hindi, *dobashi* (cf. Yule and Burnell 1903). An early reference to the term occurs in correspondence written in October 1545 from the kingdom of Kandy to the king of Portugal referring to the "Topaz who had come as the topaz of the factory." In 1604, the Dominican friar Gabriel Quiroga de San Antonio encountered (or wrote of) *topasse* on the Coromandel coast of India (Cabaton 1914, 184). From a letter written by the viceroy of India to the Portuguese court in 1619, we learn that, in the absence of Portuguese guards in the Malacca fort, "topazes" were preferred to the exclusion of "troublesome" Japanese, Javanese, or Malays. The Dutch official Kaempfer observed in Ayutthaya a "village inhabited by a Portuguese race begot by black women." In another observation on the proliferation of Portugalized communities in Southeast Asia, English sea captain Alexander Hamilton (1727) mentions some 200 *topasse* or Indian Portuguese settled and married in Cambodia (cf. Gunn 1999b, 92–94).

Tokugawa Japan appears to be singular in its solution to the emergence of Portuguese and Dutch creole societies on the island of Kyushu at Nagasaki and the small offshore island of Hirado, where Portuguese, Dutch, and English traded in the seventeenth century. Under the infamous exclusion laws directed at Christians, in 1636 all children of mostly Portuguese liaisons, some 287, were expelled to Batavia. Three years later, children of Japanese-Dutch liaisons were likewise destined for a lifetime exile in the colonial port city, many joining the residents of the *Nihonmachi* (Japan town) in Batavia's Christian quarter. Among the exiles was the celebrated Eurasian daughter of a Japanese notable, Cornelia van Nijenrode, who married the head Dutch East India Company merchant at Hirado, François Caron. A woman of undoubted accomplishment, Cornelia quickly rose through the echelons of Dutch colonial society. But on being widowed and remarried to a powerful company lawyer, as Blussé (1986) has related, Cornelia fell foul to fierce Dutch Christian patriarchy, having been stripped of her inheritance. Her striking portrait hangs today in the Rijksmuseum in Amsterdam, to where she traveled. Another example of mestizo communities from the Dutch East Indies is that of the island of Kisar near Timor, where exiled Dutch soldiers spawned a race of *mestizen*.

But the relationship between metropolitans and creoles, whether Eurasian, Euroafrican, or Euroamerican, has often historically been contestatory. We have offered the single example of the black Portuguese of the archipelago. Anderson goes further in developing a thesis of "creole functionaries and creole printmen" as playing decisive historical roles, a reference to the transmission of European nationalism to eighteenth-century Latin America. The Philippines also enters this discourse in the person of José Rizal (1861–1896), Eurasian author of a celebrated novel, *Noli me tangere* (Don't Touch Me; 1886) and nationalist hero in the struggle against corrupt Spanish rule. Citing Charles Boxer (1969b, 266), Anderson describes the rise by the seventeenth and eighteenth centuries of racial bars and exclusions in European overseas empires, in any case fitting the ideology of the Atlantic slave trade. But ironically, he continues, Enlightenment thinkers such as Rousseau, who embedded creoles in savage hemispheres, also influenced the crystallization of distinctions between metropolitans and creoles (Anderson 1983, 60–61).[2]

## PORTUGUESE AS FIRST WORLD LANGUAGE

The importance of Portuguese language as a language of trade and commerce was well recorded in European writings of the eighteenth century;

however, it is only in the modern period that Portugalized creole languages of Asia have been comprehensively studied. One attempt was made in 1883 by German linguist Hugo Schichardt (1842–1927) in his "Bibliographic Créole." Indeed, there is reason to acknowledge the role of Portuguese as a world language long before French (and English) (Valkhoff 1975). The research of David Lopes (1867–1942) first demonstrated the importance of Portuguese language as a lingua franca over a wide swath of maritime Asia across three centuries as well as the development of creole languages in Asia and the degree that Portuguese language influenced local vernaculars (Lopes 1969). Another to research this subject was the Goa-born Sanskritist and linguist Mons Rodolfo Sebastiao Dalgado (1855–1922), author of *Portuguese Vocables in Asiatic Languages* (1936). We merely note Portuguese usage in Brazil and the Portuguese creoles of Africa, including São Tome and Guinea Bissau.

Sometimes the distinction is made between "trade languages," pidgin languages, and lingua franca. One example of pidgin is China Coast pidgin, combining English, Chinese, and some Portuguese terms, with its origins in the British trading post established in Guangzhou in 1640. In fact, creole language, like creole culture, should be seen as rooted in two cultures, one descended from a European descendant, such as the French creole of Louisiana or the Portuguese creole languages of West Africa. We do not deny the possibility of Asian creole languages, such as those stemming from the Chinese diaspora. Hokkien-inflected Baba Malay, with its origins dating from the first Chinese contacts with Malacca, is the most representative, surviving among "Malayanized" Chinese communities in modern-day Penang, Malacca, and Singapore.[3] Chinese-native interactions in such places as Java, the Philippines, and Thailand also led to rich linguistic borrowings from Chinese dialects, such as in Jakarta or Betawi Malay. Equally, we do not deny other European language–based creoles, such as "Singlish," the indigenized variety of English spoken in Singapore with its rich borrowings from Chinese dialects, Malay and Tamil. But strict to our definition, we are here concerned with Portuguese creoles.

In his bibliographical survey of Portuguese creole languages that evolved in Asia, Tomás (1992) explains how the evolution of creole languages reflects a historical process, stemming from the first Portuguese maritime expansion, a catchword embracing discovery, commerce, Christianization, conquest, slavery, emigration, miscegenation, and colonialism. Needless to say, by their diversity and vast geographical spread, the study of Portugalized creole languages requires insights into the cultural specificities of the host nations and peoples, whether African, American, or Asian. Not surprisingly, Tomás's work ranges over the India coast, Diu, Damão, Bombaim (Bombay), Korlai, Goa, Cochin, and Malabar, among other sites. Ceylon is a special case, as is Malacca (and Singapore), along with the eastern archipelago, Macau (and Hong Kong). This work offers an exhaustive list of travel reports where it was observed that Portuguese was spoken across wide space. Often the Portuguese usage is described as archaic or degraded, and the reporter expresses surprise at its longevity or its survival in surprising places.

For example, Campos, writing in 1919 of the Portuguese in Bengal, observes that Portuguese language served as a lingua franca not only in the Portuguese settlements of Hoogley and Chittagong but also in such interior parts of India as the banks of the Ganges and the Bramaputra, wherever the Portuguese traded. But, he explains, the language survived the extinction of the Portuguese settlement and became a mandatory language for employers of the English East India Company, indeed spoken well by Robert Clive, from 1763 British governor of India. Campos grants that, at the time of his writing, Portuguese survived only in the form of loanwords incorporated into Bengali, Hindi, and other Asian languages (Campos 1919, 173, 209).

Campos is not alone in asserting that Portuguese language became a lingua franca in the East, notably in the coastal regions and among traders from India, the Malay Peninsula, Pegu, Siam, Tonkin, Cochin China, Basra, and Mecca. Writing in the early eighteenth century, Alexander Hamilton (1727, xii) observed that, "along the seacoast the Portuguese have left a vestige of their languages tho' much corrupted, yet it is the language that most Europeans learn first to qualify them for a general converse with one another, as well as with the different inhabitants of India."

According to Subrahmanyam (1999, 226), the modern historian of the far-flung Portuguese *Estado da India* trading network, we should pay heed to the special role played by creolized "political adventurers." Numbering over 1,000, these Luso-Asians entered the employ of numerous Asian kingdoms and sultanates, such as at Kandy and the Toungoo dynasty in Burma, but were also scattered around the Bay of Bengal on the Coromandel coast and at myriad points in mainland and island Southeast Asia, including Laos and Siam. Outside the official *Estado* system yet indispensable all the same, they represented, in Subrahmanyam's words, "forms of trans-cultural synthesis which Portuguese officialdom and religious authority could scarcely approve of." This is a reference not only to the conversion of some to Islam but also to their abandonment of the Iberian tradition in favor of local dress, usages, and cuisine.

A small literature has captured the dogged survival of the creole of the Christianized dwellers of the Batavia/Jakarta suburb of Tugu. The case of the Malayo-Portuguese creole of Malacca (Malaquero), also known as Papia Kristang, has also merited attention (Baxter 1988). The English naturalist Alfred Wallace (1869, 21), who visited in the 1860s, described the language of the descendants of the Portuguese of Malacca "with the admixture of a few Malay words" a "useful philological phenomenon," albeit "ruefully mutilated in grammar." To wit, "the verbs have mostly lost their inflections, and one form does for all moods, tenses, numbers and persons." While the survival of Kristang cultural elements today might also be attributed to modern attempts to preserve this group's identity and to win national recognition, there is a sense that such support has come at the loss of certain "traditional" forms (O'Neill 2002). But just as elements of this language group still survive in Kuala Lumpur and Singapore, a variety once found on Pulau Tikus in Penang is believed extinct. Elsewhere in the archipelago, varieties of Portuguese creole known as Ternateno are spoken in the Catholicized communities of Banda and Ambon. We also observe the ceremonialized use of Portuguese in such church ceremonies as the *confreria* of Larantuca on Flores. Larantuca was a major center of Portuguese activity prior to settlement of Timor.

While to be sure linguistic borrowings are not the central defining feature of creole languages, they do stand as a signifier of a deeper historical creolization of cultures. In this vein, echoing Campos (1919), we should also not ignore the continuing influence of Portuguese vocabulary on such Southeast Asian languages as Indonesian/Malay, languages of the Indian continent, and those of Japan (Tomás 1992). Lexical and other studies of Sinhala, Khmer, Malay, Japanese, and Moluccan languages, along with Tetum, as discussed later in this chapter, have revealed the extent of Portuguese borrowings. Teixeira offers a list of 272 Portuguese words current in Malay, from *ajidan* (*ajudante* [adjutant]) to *zaitum* (*azeitone* [olive tree]). Contrariwise, he offers twenty-five Malay words current in Portuguese, from *amouco* (*amok*) to *veniage* (*berniaga* [trade]) (Teixeira 1963, 474–84).

Additionally, Braga observes, the Portuguese often adopted older Asian cognomens for their trade items but gave them a new Portuguese form and spelling that later became generalized across many other Asian societies by entering their languages and dialects. Moreover, many were adopted by later generations of newcomers. Offering the examples of currency, Braga contends that the Portuguese coined such non-Chinese terms as "picul," "catty," "tael," "mace," and "candareen," all of which entered English language. In the world of Hong Kong, such Portuguese terms as "praia" and "compradore" entered ordinary discourse. We have mentioned the special terms used to describe Chinese punishments, namely, "cangue" and "bastinado." Other terms of Indian origin were imported east by the Portuguese, such as "shroff" and "factor," along with "amah," "coolie," "lascar," and even "catamaran." Furthermore, such Chinese words as "chop," "chit," and "mandarin" were first popularized in Portuguese, as were "junk," "pirate," and "typhoon." Trade vocabulary also figured, such as "porcelain," "parasol," "palanquin," "kimono," "calico," and "tafeta," among others. The list of words either from Portuguese or popularized by Portuguese extends to fruits ("banana," "mango," "papaya," and "coconut") and even includes animals ("buffalo" and "alligator") along with insects ("mosquito") (Braga 1942b).

Such borrowings range from the thousand or so words of Portuguese that entered Nagasaki dialect from the time of its origins as the terminal trading port for Portuguese merchants arriving from Macau (1571), including hundreds of Christian terms in use during the first century of contact to the score or more Portuguese derivatives that palpably remain in modern Japanese. These famously include *pan* (bread), *botan* (button), *bidoru* (glass), *kappa* (raincoat), *konpeito* (comfits), and *karuta* (cards). It is notable, however, that Portuguese continued to be used as a language of communication with other European traders in Japan until the early part of the eighteenth century despite the final expulsion of the Portuguese in 1639. This was because the Spanish (1592–1624), the English (1613–1623), and the Dutch (1609–1854) were obliged to use a language familiar to the Japanese interpreters. According to Tai Whan Kim (1976, 9), this may account for the predominance of Portuguese loanwords in modern Japanese dating from the sixteenth and seventeenth centuries.

Equally, modern scholarship has thrown into relief the longevity of Indo-Portuguese creoles in the most isolated and abandoned communities, such as among the 700 remaining members of the Korlai (Chaul) community of Bombay, not to mention Daman, Diu, and Goa. Such modern lexicographers as Dalgado (1893) have recognized the influence of Portuguese on Konkani, just as the first missionaries recognized the importance to learn and catechize in the major spoken code in Goa. Sar Desai (1997, 145–57) observes that the impact of Portuguese on Konkani was far more considerable than that of English on Marathi or other Indian languages. Post-1961, with the resumption of Indian sovereignty in Goa, use of Devangiri script has made a comeback, just as deliberate attempts have been made to purge Konkani of Portuguese vocables. Korlai creole is also threatened not only through the introduction of loanwords from Marathi but also because of the reorganization of syntactic order away from creole toward a convergence with Marathi (Tomás 1990). On Ceylon, vestiges of creole are found in Colombo, Kandy, Trincamelee, Galle, and Batticaloa. The language of the Ceylon Malays (Hussainmiya 1990, 19–20), the Kaffirs, and the Burgher community is of special interest. The Burghers (people of Portuguese and Dutch descent), with their cultural homeland in Batticaloa, and the Kaffirs (people of African descent), who have their cultural homeland near Puttalam in Northwest Province, are both mother-tongue speakers of Portuguese creole, although some lost it to Dutch, and today some Burghers have opted for English (Silva de Jayasuriya 2000, 19).[4]

We should not ignore, as mentioned, the oral features of creole languages. Almost invariably, creoles are spoken languages, learned out of formal settings and transmitted orally. Indeed, it would be hard to imagine if more than a small percentage of speakers of the sixteenth- and seventeenth-century Portuguese world language were literate. In any case, global literacy in this era, whether in Europe or in Asia, was a restricted literacy outside religious communities, courts, aristocracies, trade journals, and military dispatches. As residents of zones of contact, we can also assume that the creole communities were bilingual or multilingual and that a great deal of code switching took place as one of the defining features of what Cheng (1999, 4) calls the Portuguese "ideology of ecumenicalism."

Finally, this discussion on Portugalized creoles should not ignore the special role of *jurubassa* (*juru bahasa*), a Malay term that entered Portuguese language in the sixteenth- and seventeenth-century trading circuits from Timor to Macau to Nagasaki, where it came to designate the role of the interpreter without whom the all-important official and trade contacts could not have been maintained. Even the arrival of English and Dutch speakers in Japan from the 1600s on did not displace the role of the *jurubassa*. In any case, it would take generations before Japanese interpreters mastered Dutch, much less English. In China, the European traders were no less dependent on their interpreter, also known as *linguas*. The Dutch mission to Beijing in 1794, for example, were in thrall to their *lingua* engaged in either Macau or Guangzhou. Under other guises, the interpreters continued their intermediary role until the late twentieth century in colonial Macau and Hong Kong, with the Macanese central in this niche.[5]

## THE LITTLE WORLD
## OF THE MACANESE AND TIMORESE

Macaense or Macanese society, albeit in great decline, is better studied than other Portugalized creole societies if only because of its longevity and protection by Portugal as the colony of Macau until 1999. Loosely defined as *filhos* (and) *filhas da terra*, or "local-born sons or daughters of two cultures," one lusophone and one Asian, the Macanese literally straddled two worlds. Originally, other parents could be Goan, Malaccan, or, even more remotely distant, Timorese, African, or Japanese, suggesting a mingling of mostly Asian races. Also known as Nhonha, after the Malay-Hokkien ethnonym Nyonia of the Baba Chinese community of Malacca, the "Malay" element was undoubtedly important in the foundation of this community. It was only in a later period that Portuguese began to legitimize their marriages with Chinese,[6] and that Portuguese patrilinearity came to be emphasized.

In fact, all these elements combine when one comes to analyze various cultural traits assimilated into Macanese culture. These include distinct

Macanese cooking, Talu, Portuguese billiards introduced into Macau by the Jesuits in 1712, and African-style board games known in Macau as *chonca* (Amaro 1994). From fieldwork conducted in East Timor in March 2000, I was able to confirm the popularity of the Timor version of the latter game, styled *songhe* in Tetum, also observing that, unlike in Malacca and Macau, the Timor version is simply hewn from the earth. Without exception, my informants could not hazard the origins of the game, believing it to be indigenous.

But Macanese dialect, Makista (Maquista), or *lingua Macaista*, affords a prime example of cultural creolization. With a vocabulary of some 700 borrowings from Malay, Japanese, and Indian languages, Batalha (1958) found the dialect in a state of transition leading to decadence. While some of her elderly informants could speak a code not intelligible to metropolitan Portuguese, adolescents in the official school system were caught between two influences, vacillating between old linguistic habits and the standard form. While over a long time creole had achieved stability, by the mid-twentieth century the dialect had entered a decadent stage and, at the time of Batalha's research, had reached the level of extreme instability, leading to convergence with standard Portuguese. From a scrutiny of written form, letters, and so on, Batalha has constructed word lists of imported Indian, Malay, and other languages assimilated into Macaense along with Chinese (Batalha 1958; Lessa 1995). Doubtless as well, a diglossia existed well before a process of "decreolization" set in (Tomás 1990). In any case, the sense of extinction of this patois has been foreseen for some time, as Macanese families either migrated, failed to keep up the tradition, or graduated from Portuguese or English schools as fluent speakers of neither or both those languages. In the words of Tomás (1990), Makista stands as an example of linguistic suicide, especially in the face of "corrective pressures" to conform to standard Portuguese.

The longevity of Portuguese language on Timor, ruled by Lisbon until 1975, should not surprise, but the retention of Portuguese as lingua franca by the surviving band of guerrillas who fought a twenty-four-year war against Indonesian occupiers surprised many otherwise ready to accept the linguistic and cultural incorporation of the half-island into the Republic of Indonesia (Gunn 2000, 215–26). Timor offers a counterpoint to Macau and even Malacca, especially insofar as the Lusitanian heritage has survived the Indonesian occupation in interesting ways. As Portuguese governor of Timor, Affonso de Castro observed of mid-nineteenth-century Dili, a majority of indigenous chiefs along with inhabitants spoke *crioulo* (Castro 1867, 328). Nevertheless, the ancient creole of the Bidau *bairro* (quarter) of Dili faded after World War II, especially as subsequent generations entered the official Portuguese school system for the first time (Baxter 1990).

A historical *bairro* originally peopled by mixed Florenese and African elements, Bidau keeps its traditions alive in a *confreira* held for a long time annually on October 13. According to my informant, Francisco Amaro, proclaimed *chef de suco* (village chief) of Bidau-Lecidere, the *confreira* takes the form of a procession bearing a statue of Bunda Maria, also known as Nossa Senhora do Rosario. Traditionally, the Bunda Maria resided in a designated residence (the last owner was the *reina* [queen] of Bidau from July 31 to August 1, 1988), although today it resides in a rebuilt *capella* (chapel) on the original nineteenth-century Bidau church site. Although many *confreira* can be seen in Dili today, the Bidau *confreira* is unique in the sense of lending out the Maria to a family custodian, although certain parallels exist in the Philippines. Zialcita (1998, 285–89) observes that, contrary to European and Latin American forms where *cofraida* are owned by the church, in the Philippines the practice of parading the *patung* (mummified bones) is entrusted to the richest and most respected family. Similarly, it would be easy to read into the Bidau *confreira* an example of the longevity of pre-Christian beliefs, also raising the question as to why the practice was stopped in 1988.

As described by Affonso de Castro (1867), Raphael das Dores (1907), and other lexicographers, by the mid-nineteenth century many hundreds of Portuguese words had entered Tetum-Praça, the major code spoken in Dili, the capital of Portuguese (East) Timor. Specifically, Castro (1867, 325) explained that Portuguese words were used in default as terms for objects not encountered before the *conquista*. "Portuguese" terms entering Tetum also included other Asian borrowings, such as *katana* (machete), the preferred instrument of violence, as it were, a Japanese import, just as exports of *katana* as a trade item from Japan in the seventeenth century reached Macau and, at a later date, possibly Timor. This situation compares with Mozambique, where no creole emerged. Nevertheless, the Indonesianization of East Timor during the period of Indonesian subjugation (1975–1999) also gave way to a new lexicon of "Malayo"-Tetum. But with the end of the illegal and brutal Indonesian occupation of East Timor in 1999 and the decision by East Timorese leaders to adopt Portuguese and Tetum as official languages, an expanded lexicon of Portugalized terms in Tetum and other dialects is assured. In fact, this process is already under way as children entered Portuguese-medium primary schools from the first weeks of the new millennium. This is not to say that Portuguese will supplant Tetum or other dialects as the primary speech communities outside elite circles but only that its domain will expand under official patronage. But whether Tetum or Tetum lexified with Portuguese will achieve a status in East Timor analogous with the creoles of São Tome, Cape Verde, and Guinea-Bissau also remains to be seen. Language issues are bound to be contested in independent East Timor, especially as Indonesian remains the preferred print language and especially given the high priority placed on English by the interim United Nations administration (1999–2002).


## MEXICO-SPANISH-PHILIPPINES
## CULTURAL TRANSACTIONS

Not surprisingly, an intense cultural traffic attended the famous Acapulco–Manila galleon trade. The impact on Mexican and Peruvian material and cultural life created by the import of Chinese ceramics, silks, Japanese lacquerware, Macau-made religious objects, and such indigenous Philippine goods as mother-of-pearl-inlaid furniture and craft goods was no doubt significant, especially, it should also be pointed out, the traffic in Asian goods that went beyond trade in luxuries to include basic cotton and consumer goods and such cultural imports as rockets and fireworks to Lima by 1656 (Obregón 1964; Nuñez 1980, cited in Garcia de los Arcos 1998, 12). The reverse flow of imports from Mexico into the Philippines was also significant but is less researched. Taking architecture as a standard, Mexican historian Jorges Loyzaga has researched how European forms were modified in New Spain and then retransmitted, possibly by Mexico-born craftsmen or Spanish residents, to influence the architecture of the Philippines in the seventeenth and eighteenth centuries (cited in Garcia de los Arcos 1998, 11). The UNESCO World Heritage Site of Vigan or Ciudad Fernandino in IIolos del Norte Province of the Philippines is cited as the "best-preserved example of a planned Spanish colonial town in Asia."

We might add that the Portuguese stucco plaster technique introduced into southern China was later reexported to such "overseas" Chinese enclaves as Penang and Phuket in distinct Sino-Portuguese architectural style. In Nagasaki dialect, the term for applying cement plaster to walls is termed "Amacao," suggesting its Portuguese Macau origins. While the role of traveling Mexican merchants and the Mexican garrison in the Philippines has also only recently been researched, their agency as cultural brokers can also be taken for granted, as indeed was the better-documented case of Spanish missionaries arriving from Mexico.

Still, it has puzzled some that Castilian or Spanish did not strike deeper roots in the Philippines as in Latin America. Popular explanations hold that this owed to the relatively small number of Spanish, never over 5,000 for most of the colonial period, even allowing that toward the end the number expanded to defend against growing nationalism. Unlike Latin America, where a *criollo* class of local-born Spanish created a Hispanic society, the extreme isolation of the Philippines discouraged immigration, much less a female presence. Nevertheless, Spanish was the language of administration, and, as observed, religious texts in Spanish were printed.

Even so, the missions worked the people in their indigenous languages, and Spanish texts were orally transmitted and memorized, a labor assisted by bilingual Filipino catechist translators called *ladinos*. While certain *ladinos*, such as Gaspar Aquino de Belen, author of a Tagalog passion play *Mahal Na Passion ni Jesu Christong* . . . (Beloved Passion; 1704), had their works published, their audiences were restricted and controlled. Nevertheless, *ladino*-style poetry appeared sporadically throughout the seventeenth and early eighteenth centuries (Lumbera 1968). The prototypical octosyllabic verse form pioneered by Aquino de Belen also found its resonance in subsequent centuries in the form of traveling plays or theater celebrating the life and sufferings of Jesus Christ.

It is not surprising that Hispanicized family names also emerged as part of Catholic Filipino identity. The assigning of names of saints to Christian converts dated back to the first missions, but with the publication in 1849 of *Catalogo Alfabetica de Appelidos* (Catalogue of Names by Alphabet) under the governor-generalship of Narasco Claveira, the assignation of approved Hispanicized names became more systematic. Doubtless, status considerations eased acceptance. In any case, names came to be modified to fit local linguistic conventions. But names may belie identity. Such is the case of Wallace Nolasco, the protagonist in Timothy Mo's novel *Monkey King* (1978). As Christina Cheng (1999, 148–49) analyzes, the Macanese, Wallace, is so genetically and linguistically assimilated into Macau Chinese culture that little remains of his hybrid background or "his shadowy buccaneer-ancestors" but his name. No doubt, we could find examples in Manila society where ancestry is either suppressed or celebrated according to situation.

The domain of spoken Spanish in the Philippines during colonial times was restricted by the standards of Mexico and other former colonies and, in any case, lost rank dramatically in the first decades of the American occupation, even though Spanish loanwords remaining in Filipino speech are numerous. Nevertheless, outside elite circles where Spanish was the language of the *illustrados*, a Spanish creole developed among the uneducated in places where Spanish-indigenous contact was most intense. This was at Cavite, the Spanish naval shipyards where the Manila galleons were constructed, and at Zamboanga, from 1635 a fortified garrison for Spanish and Mexican soldiers on the frontier of the Muslim Sulu zone. The linguistic legacy is the creole known as Chabacano, a Spanish word meaning "clumsy" or "awkward." In Cavite, Chabacano comprises a mixture of Spanish, Tagalog, and other dialects. The Chabacano of Zamboanga, by contrast, comprising a mixture of Spanish, Cebuano, and local dialects, began to acquire its own distinctive linguistic form. In a description of Chabacano and an attempt to transcribe this oral language, Camins (1989) observes four speech characteristics, namely, archaic Spanish borrowings; words of Latin American, particularly Mexican, origin;

vulgar Spanish; and adopted Spanish words. Singularly, Chabacano de Zamboanga continues to survive as a true creole, even as the language of local radio stations, despite the impact of mass media in Tagalog and recent demographic changes arising from local conflicts. Also stemming from the galleon trade, a limited vocabulary originating from indigenous American languages (especially Nahuatl) is believed to have entered certain Philippine languages, although this remains in the realm of linguistic anthropological research (Garcia de los Arcos 1998, 14).

## CULTURAL CROSSOVERS

By definition, "cultural creolization" implies a range of cultural crossovers, not only associated with the emergence of creole languages and communities, but also with specific local and dominant cultures as they too became subject to new influences. Such borrowings and adaptations ran the gamut from cuisine, music, and games to artistic form. I also suggested that the concept of crossover challenges the binarism in the Orientalist critique. Perhaps one of the best examples of ambivalences in the Eurasian encounter, as illustrated here, comes from seventeenth-century Japan, where political seclusion (*sakoku*) did not preclude an active and ultimately subversive cultural exchange with Europe. But China, India, and the archipelago also fit the pattern.

One of the most celebrated and oft-quoted texts on cultural crossovers is Yule and Burnell's *Hobson-Jobson* (1903). Originally published in 1886, *Hobson-Jobson* has become synonymous with the concept of assimilation of foreign words to the sound pattern of the adopting language. Researched from a major search of the extant historical travel literature, *Hobson-Jobson* is a glossary of some thousands of words of "Indian" origin that have entered English language since Elizabethan times. Such were "calico," "chintz" and "gingham," but the number of such "outlandish guests" swelled as the English East India Company deepened its presence in the East. As with the previously cited examples, words such as "shawl," "bamboo," "pagoda," "typhoon," "monsoon," "mandarin," and "palanquin" were modifications of an "Indian" proper name. Even so, as we have already discussed, certain of these terms entered English through Portuguese. With the gradual assumption of British administration in India, a very large number of terms of Persian and Arabic derivation were assimilated into English, especially related to revenue. Hindustani, Urdu, and Chinese likewise left their mark. Words of Malay derivation entering English include "paddy," "godown," "compound," "rattan," "amok," "prow," and "junk," but again via Portuguese. In turn, lexical borrowings from Asian languages in Portuguese language would require a separate inquiry, even setting aside the major influence of Arabic dating from the Moorish occupation of the Iberian Peninsula.

Taking ceramics as a measure, following on from the Portuguese trade, the Dutch East India Company began to play a primary role in introducing Chinese and Japanese porcelain to Europe. In Europe, the demand for the characteristic blue and white *kraak*-ware (a term derived from the Portuguese *carrack*) surged, as tableware became an important indicator of status in bourgeois society and then, importantly, extended beyond the bourgeois and aristocratic classes. Typically produced in the kilns of Jingdezhen in China's Jiangxi Province, the center of world porcelain production between 1350 and 1750, the manufacturers extended the range of products from traditional Chinese plates to European-style lidded jars, candlesticks, beer mugs, and so on to meet a seemingly insatiable European and later American market. Lisbon had earlier taken over from Venice as emporium for Chinese products entering Europe that the Dutch in turn distributed throughout Europe. The earliest specially commissioned porcelain from China were glazed pieces decorated in cobalt blue featuring an armillary sphere, the emblem of King Manuel I, the Portuguese coat of arms, and the coats of arms of the Jesuits along with prominent Portuguese families, all combined with Chinese decorative touches. These date from the Shengde reign (1506–1521) and are to be found in the porcelain room of the Marques de Abrantes Palace. Just as the export of porcelain to Europe surged during the Wanli reign (1573–1620), so the number of traders in porcelain in Lisbon rose to seventeen in the early seventeenth century. From an early period, Portuguese potters began to reproduce Chinese porcelain (Monteiro 1994).

But with the turmoil associated with the transition from the Ming to Qing, the Dutch, from their base in Nagasaki in Japan, turned to the Arita kilns of Hizen (today's Saga Prefecture), which subsequently became the major supplier of *kraak* porcelain. Known locally as *Imari-yaki*, this was a distinctive polychrome decoration on a blue underglaze. After much experimentation, the potters at Delft in the Netherlands also began imitating *Imari*-ware with a result that blue and white delftware came to superficially resemble the Asian models.[7]

By the seventeenth century, however, a range of Asian products were entering Europe via global trading circuits. Just as the names of Indian fabrics entered European languages, so Indian plastic arts found their place in aristocratic society. For example, in Portugal, the marquis of Fronteira, João de Mascarenhas, furnished his late seventeenth-century palace with Indo-Portuguese furniture. From an early date, Chinese-style decorative panels were built into the sixteenth-century library of Coimbra University. Louis XIV, who had lent his support to the Jesuit project to help build the *Yuanming yuan* (summer palace) in Beijing (replete with European clocks, plumbing, and flora), also commissioned the Trianon de Porcelaines and other Chinese architectural touches in Versailles. In Europe, "Jappanware" was a synonym for a range of Japanese lacquered products exported by the

Dutch from Nagasaki to the Indian coast and beyond. Another variation on the hybrid porcelain theme is that of Jesuit ware, or Chinese porcelain decorated with European subject matter derived from engravings brought to China by the Jesuits. Produced during the reign of Qianlong (1736–1796) for the export market, many pieces included Christian subjects.

If the first-arriving Portuguese and their African slaves were a major spectacle in Tokugawa Japan, the first "New World" visitors in Europe were no less the objects of wonderment. We have passed allusion to the Japanese ambassadors to late Renaissance Europe and the first official visitors from the Siamese court to Versailles, but one of the first Chinese visitors to be received in this circle was the Christian convert Michael Alphonsus Shen Fu-tsung, accompanied from Macau by Jesuit missionary Philip Couplet. In 1684, Shen was summoned by the Sun King to demonstrate chopstick techniques. In 1687, he helped catalog Chinese manuscripts in the Bodleian Library at Oxford, attracting the attention of James II. Today, Shen is remembered in the form of an oil painting in the Royal Collection at Windsor, executed by John Riley at royal command. Shen died near Mozambique in 1691 on the return journey. A visiting "Prince of Timor" also graced the court of Louis XV (Gunn 1999b, 94). A no less exotic— albeit homesick—visitor to Europe was the Tahitian Aotourou. As Diderot remarks of the young celebrity in *Supplément au Voyage de Bougainville*, discussed in chapter 2, "He grew bored with us," just as Aotourou urged Bougainville to return him to his island paradise.

We have already observed the early globalization of New World species and food crops, but cuisines were also the product of an intense cultural hybridization. For example, the modern Japanese word for bread (*pan*) is derived from the Portuguese *pão*. Nagasaki's famed *kasutera* (castella) pound cake of reputed Portuguese origin has achieved the status of a national cultural icon in Japan. As Gaspar da Cruz (1905, 328) related of late sixteenth-century Guangzhou, a city then frequented by Portuguese merchants, "They make very good bread which they learnt to make of the Portuguese." Also acknowledging a Chinese tradition of making cakes from wheat flour, the Dominican's observation of the distinctive Portuguese bread, as still made in Macau, is credible. Other cuisines of creole origin, such as the Baba-style cooking in Malacca, Penang, and even Singapore, along with Macanese cooking in Macau, have even achieved a revival with tourist interest, just as "fusion food" has entered the twenty-first-century vocabulary as a product of the current globalization. It is interesting in this respect to consider that, to this day, rice forms a more important part of diet among Portuguese than in other European nations, suggesting a reverse legacy of Portugal's early globalizing reach.

Another example of early globalization of cultural form and taste comes from Nagasaki. In 1706, the Dutch in Nagasaki were surprised to be offered coffee with a Japanese meal served by the *bugyo* (local magistrate). But this authority had already acquired a taste for Spanish wine, which had long entered the list of mandatory gifts and bribes offered by the Portuguese and Dutch to their Japanese interlocutors.

One striking cultural survival from the Portuguese–Japanese exchange of the early seventeenth century is the European playing card. Images of the game being played by *nanban-jin* (foreigners) in Japan can be found on surviving *byobu-e* (screen art). Styled in modern Japanese *karuta* after the Portuguese *carta*, they were originally known as Tensho *karuta* after the Tensho period (1573–1592) and produced in sets of forty-eight. Popularized among the samurai classes during the Edo period (1600–1868), the game was proscribed along with other forms of gambling, only to evolve into other *karuta* games, such as *hanafuda* (flower cards), *uta karuta* (poem cards), and *iroha karuta* (ABC cards), revived in the modern period as a New Year "tradition." The poem cards were in fact an outgrowth from an original Japanese game using sea shells on which text was painted, while the ABC cards, which evolved in the late eighteenth century, added pictures. In some variants, players were supposed to match scenes from the Japanese literary classic *Genji Monogatari* or to match scenes with lines of poetry. To be sure, there is little resemblance between the alchemic Arabesque-patterned design of the original Tensho *karuta* and the modern mass-produced survival except for rectangular shape and inscribed numbers or pictures.[8]

Allowing that the European playing card has Oriental and plausibly Indian origins, at least introduced into Spain by the Moors, Amaro (1995a, 98) has researched the introduction and survival of European card games in Macau. Still known in Macanese circles as *cartas manilha* as opposed to *cartas Chinas*, she found that Chinese and Occidental card games are played side by side, "often with hybrid rules." While *cartas manilha* suggests a Spanish connection, in fact this ancient Portuguese card game also survives in Malacca.

Musical adaptation in Latin America and the Caribbean and the subsequent globalization of African and Latin musical forms is part of our contemporary world culture. Brito (1996) writes that the first Portuguese navigators used music and dance as a way of making initial contact with people of other cultures. The expedition of Peter Cabral that left Lisbon for India in March 1500 was accompanied by trumpets, kettledrums, *sistra* (rattles), flutes, and bagpipes, just as all major fleets heralded their arrivals, triumphs, and feast days with musical performances.

But the acceptance of Latin musical form along with instrumentation has been far more restrictive in Asia. In Nagasaki, where European music was taught in Jesuit missionary colleges at least until the final exclusion acts of the early seventeenth century and where the Dutch on

Deshima island regularly hosted miniconcerts, there do not appear to be any local or national musical borrowings or even survivals from this period. Indeed, one enduring image of the Portuguese age in Japan is the depiction of a lute player and singer on a *nanban* screen depicting social customs of foreigners. European forms of musical notation were adopted in Japan only during the Meiji period. Macau is obviously a special case where European musical notation has deep roots. But the Kangxi emperor also encouraged Western music and the teaching of Western musical theory at the court and set up Jesuit Tomes Pereira as head musician of a small band. At a more popular level, Western music reached church audiences in China from the early sixteenth century, although this had faded by the end of the eighteenth (Huang Qichen 1998, 120–21).

Yet the impact of Latin musical form on the archipelago is significant, even setting aside the Philippines. Kartomi (1996) writes that the Portuguese-Malay musical style developed as a result of Portuguese and *mestiço* contacts with Malay coastal areas of the archipelago, especially during the Malaccan period. By contrast, Islamic and pre-Islamic musical forms proved to be more resilient in the upland zones of Java and Sumatra. Especially, the Portuguese elements include harmonic relationships between violin and vocals, influencing melodic innovation. The synthesis gave way to such Malay/Indonesian forms as *kapri, dondang, sayang, bangsawan,* and *keroncong.* While localized as *kerocong tugu,* the genre of music is linked to the old Tugu or Betawi quarter of Jakarta around the site of a Portuguese church established in 1661. As the music of an underclass, *keroncong* shares some features with *fado,* the musical form that emerged from the Afro/Indian/Portuguese underclass of Lisbon. According to Kartomi (1996), *keroncong* is both a repertoire and a musical style distinguished by its crooning singing style and its unique instrumentation using European harmonics created through the use of plucked or bowed strings. *Keroncong* can also be described as an orchestra based on violin, flute, guitar, ukulele, banjo, cello, and bass. With the advent of radio, the form has been widely disseminated and popularized throughout the archipelago.

We can also adduce specific local varieties of Portugalized melodies in Timor, Flores (especially in Sica and Larantuca), Menado, and the Moluccas. Violin (*biola*) is also an instrument of choice in the Flores and Timor islands along with the *gambus,* although this instrument could also be of Middle Eastern origin. Such instruments may be played at *pesta* (from the Portuguese *festa* [festival]), including, for example, on the occasion of funerals or marriages (cf. Kartomi 1996). In Goa, musical form introduced by the Portuguese, notably folk songs sung in two-voice harmony, even casts its influence in modern Hindi film music (Issar 1997, 175).

## PORTUGALIZED/HISPANICIZED TOPONYMS

Not surprisingly, as the first world language of trade, Portuguese also bequeathed a plethora of invented toponyms, many of which have endured, others Anglicized, others "indigenized," and still others universalized.

The invention and Portugalization of the now universalized names of China, Cochin China, Korea, and Japan are special cases in point. The transition from "Grand Cathay" to "China" cannot pass without mention. As the Spanish missionary Navarette wrote, "It is well known that the name China (which the French and Italians pronounce Cina) is not the proper appellative of the empire, but a name given it by estrangers trading thither. The Portuguese first took it from them; and afterwards the Spanish in the Philippine islands." Navarette agrees with the Jesuit missionaries and authors Trigault and Kircher that China was but a Portuguese corruption of "Sina" or "serica," a term for "silk." Other theories exist, but early European missionaries in China were struck that China had no proper name of its own, "Middle Kingdom" aside, but adopted reign names. Navarette continues that the Portuguese corruption of "Je Pun" led to "Japan" and the corruption of "Kao Li" to "Coria" or "Korea" (Navarette 1732, 1–2). "Cochinchina," as southern Vietnam was known under French rule, was another Portuguese invention. According to Borri (1732), "Cochin" was a Portuguese corruption of "Kio Chi" or "Cochi," a Japanese term for "Annam," but to distinguish the place from Cochin in India, they termed it "Cochin-China."

The invented Portuguese toponym for "Formosa" coexists with "Taiwan," the form the Dutch universalized. The Pescadores islands in the "Taiwan" straits also endure on modern maps along with its local toponym. "Flores," dubbed "Cabo da Frolles" by Rodrigues, remains the name of the island in the eastern archipelago. The mid–Indian Ocean island group of Diego Garcia, today a U.S. base, is still on the map. Pedra Branca/Batu Putih is a rock prominence today disputed by Singapore and Malaysia. "Bombay" and "Ceylon," corruptions of "Bombai" and "Ceilão," respectively, have both been indigenized in postcolonial times. Certain toponyms, of which the "Cape of Good Hope" is well known, have been Anglicized from the original Portuguese. Hundreds of other toponyms denoting reefs, shoals, atolls, and other maritime features dot the modern maritime map, legacy of trailblazing seafarers and traders. Not surprisingly, Portuguese toponyms remain residual in Malacca, such as in "Cape (Cabo) Rachado," a Famosa fort, and in the Malayanized *terankerah*, a corruption of *tranquiera*, meaning "palisade." The exceptions are invented toponyms imposed in the "Portuguese Settlement" after its creation in 1930, such as streets named after de Albuquerque, Sequira, Teixeira, Araujo, and Eridia, figures related to Malacca's conquest and history. Only a handful of recently invented Portuguese toponyms survive in

Nagasaki today, including site indicators of some of the dozen or so former churches and, along with it, the Misericordia (Gunn 1997).

On the other hand, it is also not surprising that in Portugal's last remaining Asian colonies, Macau and Timor, Portuguese toponyms were imposed even at the level of street names. In the case of Macau (Teixeira 1979a), where hand-painted *azulejos*-style ceramic name plates are struck in Portuguese and Chinese, more than a few of the toponyms have seventeenth-century origins, even though the Portugalized forms never supplanted familiar Chinese usage. It would thus be more accurate to pronounce on Macau's double toponymy, especially as many Portuguese street names have little relevance or resonance with local Cantonese speakers.[9] Thus, Avenida Almeida Ribeiro, Macau's main commercial street, named after a former minister of colonies, is universally known locally as Sam Ma Lou, or "new street of horses." Rua Nova a Guia, leading to a lighthouse, is known locally as Street of the White Turbans, after the Sikhs who once frequented this area.

While Portuguese and other European place names in Asia never displaced indigenous toponyms, such as largely occurred in the Western Hemisphere, it is also the case that, sailing west, the Spanish added their own repertoire of place names. The Ladrones (robber islands), named by the Magellan voyage, was one that persisted. The strait named after Spanish sailor Torres is another, as is Solomon (Salaman), the islands also discovered by the Spanish in the late sixteenth century. Of the myriad Hispanicized place names on New Guinea and the Solomons mapped and mentioned in Antonio de Herrera's *Historia General del Mundo* (General History of the World; 1601), an extract entering Purchas XIV as "Description of the West Indies," and of the dozen or so recorded on Hondius's *Insulae Indie Orientalis* (1635), only "Nova Guinea" and "Solomons" has stuck. Drawing on a map by the Jesuit Alfonso Lopez, Bellin (ca. 1750) offered "Marianes" as an alternative to "St. Lazarus." "Marianas" is the form that has endured. The major exception is the Philippines, where Hispanicized toponyms coexist with native ones and those introduced by the American colonizer. A glance at a map reveals that only the Muslim-predominant areas of the south successfully resisted what might be called the "Magellan revolution" and its missionary push.

Nevertheless, we observe a kind of seventeenth-century map war, as a rising hegemon took over from a waning one. And so the island dubbed "Mauritius" by the first visiting Dutchman in 1598 and, in turn, "Ile de France" by the French replaced "Ilha do Cerne," the name given by Portuguese Domingos Fernandez in 1505. "Madagascar" was also a contested toponym in the seventeenth century, coexisting with "St. Laurence" until the former won out. Some new toponyms simply never stuck, such as "Cape San Diego," the name applied by the Spanish to the northern tip of Formosa during their brief tenure on the island.

Early Portuguese maps of the southern regions of Japan reflected the discoverer's penchant for naming, but, as Michel has observed, only the designation "Santa Clara" for the Uji island group (Ujiginto) near Kyushu survived into the nineteenth century. Even so, he observes, the names in European maps of Japan are largely Japanese. An exception was the Dutch explorations of the northern region of Japan in 1643, "the de Vries expedition," bequeathing to Dutch cartography (the world map of John Blaue of 1647) such ephemeral toponyms as "Bay de Goede Hope," "Strait de Vries," and "De Compapanjis Landt," none of which persisted. An exception is La Perouse Strait, separating Sakhalin and Hokkaido, missed in the fog by de Vries but "discovered" in 1787 by the French explorer (Michel 1993, 38, 50). Only in the eighteenth century was the coastline of Korea mapped by Europeans, leaving it studded with toponyms derived from French, English, and Russian, including memorials left behind by La Perouse in 1787 (Tennant 1996, 198). Nor was there a total fixity in the way that indigenous place names came to be transcribed in various European languages. Standardization awaited a modern era.

While European toponyms never totally supplanted indigenous forms outside of zones of settler colonialism, we recall as well that Arab and other Asian seafarers developed their own repertoires of Asian toponyms to aid their navigations. As modern students of Chinese chronicles are well aware, from at least the time of the great Ming sea voyages, China also developed its own oceanic cartography, with matching toponyms to boot. But we here recall the European and creole renderings of what might be called civilizational space, albeit a contested space when it came into conflict with other great crusading Asian civilizations. A modern example is the Chinese insistence in dubbing the Spratly islands of the South China Sea "Nan Xa," alternatively "Truong Sa" in Vietnamese (Gunn 1991).[10]

## CONCLUSION

Typically, European colonialism in Asia encouraged intra-Asian migration from countries of high population density, such as India, China, and Vietnam, to the frontier zones of the countries we call today Indonesia, Malaysia, Cambodia, Burma, and Laos. But we should not confuse the little Indias, Chinatowns and Arab streets, and other ethnic quarters of Asian cities with the distinctive creolized communities that emerged as a result of the first European contact. If we are to define creolization as a strictly ethnic mixing by marriage, we are to miss the point that creole communities, where one side was European, usually Portuguese or Spanish, led to the development of a new cultural synthesis around religion, morality, language, fashion, and food besides other cultural borrowings and ecumenical forms.

We may ponder whether the first creole communities in Asia carried the seeds of what today we gloss as westernization/globalization. Many of these communities lived a privileged life, being the first to embrace the religion of the Europeans and to effect their fashions and privileged in some ways by access to the European power centers, whether by blood, as concubines, as compradores, or as interpreters. Yet others were outcast, rejected by native communities as much as by the Europeans. Modern Malaysia/Singapore/Indonesia/India/Sri Lanka have obviously inherited highly creolized communities, not only stemming from the first globalization, such as in historical Goa and Malacca, but also as a result of demographic changes wrought by later-arriving colonialisms. Their survival, much less celebration, in the age of postcolonial nationalism has been variant across these nations, especially where, almost everywhere, they have become victims of communalism and state-directed political correctness. While the liberation of East Timor, following a quarter century of aggressive Indonesian acculturation, offers new life to the largest creole community of early twenty-first-century Southeast Asia, it remains to be seen how East Timor identity will be forged or at least actively created.[11]

In the current globalization, English alone has emerged as world language. Dutch especially, and even the language of diplomacy, French, lost rank in the mid- to late twentieth century as their respective empires dissolved. But in the first globalization, we have demonstrated that Portuguese—even more than Arabic, Persian, or Turkish and with greater currency than even Spanish—became the first world language in the sense of its usefulness and currency in commercial transactions across oceans and continents. Even as a language of eastern trade, English superseded Portuguese only in the eighteenth and nineteenth centuries.

## NOTES

1. The etymology suggests as much. Whereas the Spanish *criollo* carries the sense of a person native to a locality, the Portuguese *crioulo* is a diminution of *cria*, or "person raised in a house," especially "servant," from *cria*, "to bring up," in turn derived from the Latin "to beget." Baba Malay is the distinctive patois spoken by especially Malacca-born Chinese.

2. We are not referring to the Creole Spanish aristocracy of Spanish America, a reference to local-born Spanish as opposed to metropolitans. Spanish Creole were subject to various discriminations and sometimes allied themselves with mestizos, Indians, and black slaves but were generally seen by the latter as part of the repressive colonial order. Neither are we referring to localized Dutch creoles (Blussé 1986).

3. Ansaldo and Mathews (2002) describe Baba Malay as a case of creolization without European input and important to Chinese linguistics "as the clearest case of creolization involving a Sinitic language."

4. Books in Indo-Portuguese were printed in Colombo in the 1820s by the Wesleyan Mission Society. Manuscript versions of "Portuguese Song Batticaloa" and "Songs of the Kaffrinha—Portuguese Negro Songs," recorded in British colonial times, and roots of modern Kaffir songs have been translated into standard Portuguese and English by Silva de Jayasuriya (2000).

5. The term *jurubassa,* historically correct in historical Nagasaki, was confirmed to me in 1999 in Nagasaki by a Tetum-speaking Timorese as a received term in that language.

6. As related by Spence (1998, 31), Fernão Mendes Pinto, author of *Perigrinação de Fernam Mendez Pinto* (1614), mythologized a faux creole household in China long before such liaisons actually occurred. Head of the fictionalized Sino-Portuguese household is the real personage of Vasco Calvo, a Portuguese merchant imprisoned during the disastrous Tomé Pires embassy of 1517.

7. These insights are derived from the symposium and exhibition held in Nagasaki in 1999, "Ceramics Crossed Overseas: Jingdezhen, Imari and Delft from the Collection of the Groninger Museum."

8. Just as Spanish- and Portuguese-suited cards number forty-eight, so the *hanafuda* deck comprises forty-eight cards. A modern reproduction of Tensho *karuta* currently stored at the Tekisui museum in Hyogo reveals striking visual similarities with Portuguese cards, notably knobby intersecting swords and cudgel designs. Just as depictions of dragons on Portuguese cards are singular in Europe, so they appear on the Tensho *karuta.*

9. The choice of Portuguese as official language in East Timor made by the Timorese leaders in late 1999 has revived traditions suppressed during the twenty-five years of Indonesian conquest. In short time, Indonesian names were removed from public buildings and so on, while a select number of Portugalized toponyms have been coined to reflect recent history, such as "Avenida Liberadade de Imprensa" and "Rua dos Martires de Patria" replacing "Jalan Tien Soeharto," named after the wife of the Indonesian dictator. In any case, few Portugalized toponyms outside of street names ever gained currency in the former colony, the efforts of the Salazar regime notwithstanding. See Gunn (2000, 227–51).

10. Another contested toponym with civilizational overtones is the sea between Korea and Japan. On April 1, 1999, the permanent mission of the Democratic People's Republic of Korea to the United Nations released a background paper titled "It Is 'East Sea'—Not 'Sea of Japan,'" citing the works of seventeenth-century European geographers referring to the "Sea of Korea," "Oriental Sea," or "East Sea," including charts by Guillaume de Lisle (1705) and Jacques Nicolas Bellin (1752) along with "Map of Asia" drawn by Katsuragawa Hosho in 1784. Delegations from North Korea and South Korea had previously lobbied on this question at the Sixth UN Conference on the Standardization of Geographical Names, held in New York from August 25 to September 3, 1992.

11. For a rare discussion in print on Timorese identity arising out of a public seminar convened in Dili in March 2002, see Gunn (2001) and Mattoso (2001).

# Conclusion

While we recognize the flow of peoples, trade, and ideas across the Eurasian landmass back to antiquity, the Eurasian exchange (1500–1800), as we have described it with reference to the complex crossover of ideas, languages, and philosophies, was revolutionary in terms of its first globalization effect. Just as we found a close correlation between specific exchanges and time frame, whether late Renaissance or early Enlightenment (late Ming or early Qing from a Chinese perspective), so the Asia we have described was multipolar with respect to polity and civilization. Finding broad parity between Europe and the core Asian civilizations through most of our period, we have also raised questions as to the various receptions and impacts of European religion and science on a range of Asian civilizations and societies and, indeed, the impact of Asian civilizations on European philosophy and intellectual fashion insofar as that can be measured. This conclusion offers a summary of these exchanges, impacts, and effects.

## THE EURASIA EXCHANGE

Tracking the maritime silk roads in the age of European expansion, our narrative follows close on the great Ming voyages of the late fifteenth century, cutting a swath through the coastal zones and ports in a vast crescent from the Indian to the Pacific Oceans. As we have seen, and as summarized here, it was in certain of these Asian ports and strong points that the Europeans developed beachheads that became sites of intense cultural exchange. By contrast, we have demonstrated the awe-inspiring strengths of Asia's core areas: the great Islamic empires, including the Mughal Empire with its capitals in northern India; the Chinese Empire, including its tributary satellites; and Japan under the Pax Tokugawa. Not only was each the fount of powerful bureaucratic polities, but each supported social structures and technological achievements comparable with and often superior to that of Renaissance Europe. Given the strength and scale of the Asian core areas, it was not surprising that European interlopers first infiltrated peripheral zones, either by strength (European seaborne power held the edge with its mobile firing platforms) or through alliance. Where European missionary advance was restricted in continental situations, the Iberian formula of missionary-colonizers as applied in the Americas prevailed in more insular situations (Goa, the Philippines, the Moluccas, Timor-Flores, and even Vietnam).

Perhaps only in the Chinese mandarinate did the Europeans meet their peers, or superiors, in the production of knowledge for knowledge's sake outside strictly religious doctrine. China's civilizational legacy—including its complex bureaucracy, its social order and philosophical underpinnings, its thriving economy, its urban development, its imposing range of practical technologies, and its sheer vastness and population density— also greatly impressed the first European visitors since the age of Marco Polo. In an age before opium wars and blustering imperialists, the reception of China in Europe in the hands of Jesuit interpreters and Enlightenment thinkers was unrivaled, especially if contrasted to the ideology of the American *conquista* on the one hand and parodies of Islam on the other. From the other side (while it lasted), the reception by the Ming and Qing courts to Jesuit cosmography and Renaissance accomplishments could hardly have been bettered (setting aside delusions of mass Christian conversions). All things considered, the first major European encounter with China since the Mongol era was a relatively felicitous affair.

We do not deny the empire-building and imperialistic interventions of Euro-America over Asia that climaxed in the nineteenth and twentieth centuries, one that built on the earlier European expansion. Surveying the impact of Europe on the Americas along with much of Africa, we can say that European weaponry and organization prevailed against less well-defended tributary and lineage systems. The lack of resilience of Amerindians to diseases borne by the conquistadores is frequently mentioned in the literature, and, indeed, the peoples of other peripheries such as Australia and the Pacific Ocean islands shared their fate. No major ideological contest confronted the Iberians and subsequently the Dutch, the British, the French, the Germans, and eventually the Americans in their conquest of the peoples of the Americas and the coasts of Africa.

In contradistinction to the conquest of the Americas, China, Japan, Korea, Vietnam, and Mughal India, along with the Buddhist kingdoms of

Ayutthaya and Pegu, adroitly managed to set the terms of the Eurasian encounter over much of the period of our inquiry: the sixteenth through the eighteenth century. The Portuguese in Macau paid rent to China and in Nagasaki offered elaborate bribes to shogunal authorities, whereas on the Malabar and Coromandel coasts of India, along with the East Indies, the European presence was more in the form of enclaves and outposts as opposed to colonies and dominions. Japan, we have viewed, was singular in managing the Eurasian exchange to its advantage, not only by keeping the Europeans at a distance but also by selectively borrowing and adapting "Western learning" to its advantage.

In Asia, the Europeans were brought to their senses by empirical observation. Cosmographic verities reaching back to the Middle Ages no longer held up in the light of new discoveries and the new geographies. The discoveries hastened the Enlightenment and buried the alchemical and obscurantist pseudosciences of medieval Europe. While the Ptolemaic and Poloean images of Eurasia died hard, the Iberian *portalan* maps and Jesuit descriptions provided irrefutable new geographical and other evidence. Even the violence of the New World *conquista* and the obscurantism surrounding the Holy Inquisition tended to set the Iberian nations further apart from Protestant Europe, as signaled by the rising political and commercial fortunes of the United Provinces free from Spanish rule. Leiden and, in turn, Paris (and London), we viewed, also emerged in this period as major centers and founts of new knowledge on the Orient.

Still, there were skeptics on both sides. The fetish for the bizarre in Europe actually drove a marketplace in imaginary utopian literature that played on prejudice associated with Christian doctrine, narrow biblical interpretation, or other pre-Copernican interpretations. The rising print technology, married to the production of images, changed the way people viewed the world. Unimaginable in this day of instant global imaging, the production of New World images in Europe between 1500 and 1800 was mediated by a relatively closed circle of engravers in the employ of bourgeois and state patrons and printers. The subject requires further research, but, excepting images of the natural world, the number of two-dimensional representations of the New World, Asia included, could be counted in the thousands only, with some countries and cultures hardly represented at all. A relatively small number of engravers and families of publishers recycled and retooled the most wooden images of Asia, oblivious to the wealth of discoveries by voyagers and travelers. Some, we have revealed, were faked or confabulated, just as literatures of the fantastic fed a titillated, rising mass public audience.

While animist Philippine society, along with the Marianas and the Moluccas, definitely fell into the Holy Iberian confrontationist mold, just as much of maritime Southeast Asia underwent a profound Islamicization in an age of civilizational contest, East Asia avoided the most debilitating elements of the "Eurasian exchange" during the first wave of globalization, in turn allowing a different set of outcomes during the high tide of European imperialism. As we have seen, Japan, Korea, and Vietnam, precisely those civilizations most closely drawn into the tributary-trade orbit of China, were resilient or selective in the way they adapted or adopted the religious or secular knowledge of Renaissance Europe. Almost without peer in the European New World, China under the early Qing was able to turn the tables on the Jesuit interlopers, assimilating their knowledge where it corrected or added to cartography or astronomical knowledge, rejecting their religion, and even offering up to Europe a powerful, awe-inspiring model of governance in the Confucian bureaucratic system.

Whereas the Spanish *conquista* of the Americas massively disrupted the pre-Columbian economies and societies, Europe's trade in Asia fired up commerce and created new demands and stimuli not only in the larger polities but also in the most unlikely peripheral formations. But where the New World went into dramatic demographic decline, Asia experienced demographic consolidation and, as alluded in chapter 8, levels of urbanization unknown in the world. Just as the Columbian exchange kicked off with the first disembarkation, so globalization's first wave brought to Asia vital new food sources, new products, and new technologies. It may be coincidental—it may be contingent on a host of ecological and cultural factors—but it happens that the zones of Asia that historically were long able to take effective measures to restrict the European military, political, and cultural advance and particularly avoided direct colonization (namely Japan, Korea, and China) have today levered themselves into regional if not global economic primacy.

## ROOTS OF DIVERGENCE?

Our time frame, spanning the incorporation of the New World (1500) to the advent of the industrial revolution (1800) and the decline of the Chinese Empire, coincides with what Frank (1998, 344) singles out as the two major "inflections" of world history. Intellectual change in Europe, we have explained, was long incubating, although I am loathe to accept Eurocentric interpretations that push European exceptionalism back to earlier epochs. The roots of the divergence on the road to modernity between Europe and China, although this has not been our main theme, strike back to the early discoveries, the Columbian exchange, the rise of print media, the Copernican revolution, and the Enlightenment in general. Contra the genre of economic history reaching back to Adam Smith's *Wealth of Nations* (1776), this book has viewed Eurasia as the premium global arena of major intellectual exchange, the crucible where Arab and Asian knowledge came to be critically digested. Gunpowder, the art of printing, the floating compass, and the lateen sail are oft-cited examples of an early exchange to Europe's profit. All this suggests that, beginning with Renaissance Europe, the exchange with Asia was much less one-sided and far more multifaceted than is often acknowledged. This we have illustrated with reference to the Jesuit mission, not only of far-reaching importance for its intellectual contributions to early Qing China science but also in the way that newly gained knowledge of the East profoundly influenced the Enlightenment philosophes.

The rising tide of commerce in Europe consequent on the first globalization sometimes obscures the fact that change was always a condition in Asia. Stagnation was never an apt characterization for India under the Mughals, Japan under the Tokugawa, and China under the Ming and Qing, to mention only the biggest players. While entertaining the European traders, the courts of these great civilizations at first welcomed philosophical debate as much as they sought new knowledge of navigation and geographical awareness as well as access to new weapons and silver brought by the European seafarers. Closure—and apparent stagnation to the extent that this occurred in China and Japan—was more out of fear of losing control of the conditions of engagement, with the Philippines under Spanish rule as an obvious negative example frequently raised by the Tokugawa to justify the expulsion of Christian missionaries. This book adds extra weight and new dimensions to the view that cultural and philosophical interchange was incubating in the courts and ports of Asia ahead of the great epoch of imperial domination and in ways that were far healthier.

Still, intellectual involution appeared to be entrenched across the Confucian world. No spirit of skepticism entered mainstream Chinese thought by the time of the Qing. Ottoman achievements in empire building and administration were not matched by technological advance. Only late Tokugawa Japan came to emulate the spirit of European Enlightenment inquiry. By contrast, drawing on the Columbian exchange and the Eurasian exchange together, Europe emerged "enlightened" from the late Renaissance out of decadent medievalism. Ours is not an argument in defense of European exceptionalism, as we have gone to pains to emphasize the degree of mutual intellectual curiosity and crossover between East and West. Nevertheless, the Central Kingdom's rejection of the tenets of the Copernican revolution, as much as its prickly defense of Confucian and neo-Confucian orthodoxies in the face of counterevidence supplied by the new physical sciences, ultimately stymied intellectual development in the world's largest and most populous economy.

Europe, especially the northern tier, first experienced an industrial revolution. Enlightenment advances in sciences and technology, advancing on Renaissance knowledge, simply gave Europe the technological edge over the rest of the world. The question as to why Asia lagged in technological accomplishment should not detain us here. Francesca Bray (1997) elaborates that historians of technology have imposed a master narrative that opposes "modern to traditional, active to passive, progress to stagnation, science to ignorance, West to rest, and male to female." While Bray's concerns are to explain how technologies defined women's place in Chinese society as integral to the historical process, she also offers a powerful critique of the teleological method and assumptions of Joseph Needham's multivolume *Science and Civilization in China*. As Needham demonstrated, the Central Kingdom was ahead of Europe until about 1450. For 1,000 years prior, Chinese science was simply inaccessible to Europe. Herself a Needham collaborator, Bray allows the influence of the "master" in demonstrating that the history of modern science was in fact a world history but that the failure of medieval Islam, the Incas, and even China in this interpretation confirms the master narrative that only the West was truly dynamic. Consistent with Bray's culturally textured reading of technology as a form of cultural expression, actually derived from her study of everyday life, women, and cultural history of imperial China, I have also been concerned with the manner of technological civilization confronted by the first European visitors in their encounter with Asia. While I have not explored here differential levels of technology across civilizations and we doubt the possibility of generalizing across many cultures, states, and civilizations, we are also cognizant of Bray's understanding of technology as a form of cultural expression.

To offer our own examples of technology as cultural expression, Gaspar da Cruz was full of wonderment at naval development and cannonry that he witnessed in early sixteenth-century China. Early sixteenth-century visitors to the archipelago, such as Antonio Pigafetta, were struck more by the energy of their would-be antagonists than their overall naval-military supremacy, but all European seaborne visitors to the archipelago were taken by the sheer variety of sailing craft revealing various influences, whether indigenous or hybrid Chinese, Indian, or Arabic. Augustin Beaulieu was upbeat about the naval prowess, metalwork, and craft of early seventeenth-century Aceh but entered his reservations as well. Such visitors to mid-sixteenth-century Japan as Luís Fróis were equally overwhelmed by the standard of craft and its artistic quality. Jesuit visitors were also well positioned to comment on metallurgy in Japan, wanting techniques soon borrowed from both Korea via China and the Iberians. But Japan was also one of the first points of technological transfer between East and West, from Portuguese firearms to medicine to European learning, as well as being a major source and conduit for European curiosity on East Asia.

Because the Japanese were demonstrably fast learners in military skills and other sciences, it is tempting to speak of a Japanese "exceptionalism" with its roots in the sixteenth and seventeenth centuries. But the complexity of the question of technological levels, technological diffusion, and cultural context is also addressed from another angle by Fróis (1994, 114), who remarked, "Chez nous, il ya des moulins mus par le vent, l'eau ou des bêtes, au Japon, tous ce qui moulu se fait avec les roues manuelles poussée à la force des bras" (In our land, there are windmills moved by the wind, water, or beasts, in Japan, all that is ground by wheels is done by manual force).

Japan's experience also affords lessons for the divergence thesis. While recent historiography eschews a view of social stasis under the three-century Tokugawa "seclusion," supported by our evidence of lively cultural interchange, it is also likely that Japan's withdrawal from active participation in the Asian maritime trade during the epoch of first globalization left a commercial void that the Portuguese, Dutch, and British were bound to fill. Japan's rise to industrial behemoth from the mid-nineteenth century is often touted as a model of late industrialism. Of course, Japan's new convergence with the West also coincided with its grasp of Western learning even prior to the arrival in the mid-nineteenth century of American Commodore Perry's famous black ships. Ironically, Japan had to be persuaded to reenter the industrial world economy/world system to help itself.

## THE CREOLIZATION EFFECT

The first globalization also ushered in a creolization of cultures on a global scale, especially outside the cores of the great Eurasian civilizations. While it might be argued that ancient empires across the Afroeurasian landmass had always imposed their cultures or enslaved their enemies, European seaborne expansion of the 1500s to the 1800s was sui generis. The sheer volume of exchanges in men, ideas, languages, and technologies was of a different order, just as the translations and missionizing of the conquistadores proved revolutionary. The creolization of cultures emerging out of these encounters was dramatically experienced in the zones of intense contact where European traders and missionaries congregated. Out of these multivalent exchanges (the Eurasian exchange) emerged a new hybridity of cultures around religion, language, cuisine, artistic form, costume, and racial mixing in the zones of intense European-Asian contact. Here, creole languages emerged as lingua franca alongside Portuguese as a trade language or what we allow as the first world language of consequence. As I have been at pains to emphasize, whether we live in New York, Paris, Beijing, or Tokyo, many of the cultural crossovers we take for granted today have their origins in the first globalization.

Today we observe creolizing trends throughout the world, including the United States, shaped by immigration and demographic expansion especially but not exclusively of Hispanic speakers alongside Anglo-American culture. But the present-day fusion of cultures stemming from economic globalization should not be confused with the emergence of creole nations out of creole communities that gelled during the first two centuries of European expansion. Brazil and the Caribbean republics offer the best examples, but Asia, Goa, Macau, the Philippines, and East Timor also fit the pattern. Typically, the Asian examples have emerged from Portuguese or Spanish conquest of peripheral zones remote from the civilizational heartlands. The typical marker of conquest was conversion to Catholicism and the use of Portuguese or Spanish as the language of power along with the emergence of mixed-race communities. Such mixed-race communities could also include Chinese-native liaisons, especially in the Philippines, or, in the case of East Timor, could also include Goan-Timorese or Afro-Timorese alongside Portuguese parentage. Of our Asian examples, only the Philippines and East Timor levered themselves to independent statehood. The first prime minister of independent East Timor, Mr. Mari Alkatiri, is of Yemeni Arab-Timorese background, while the president, José "Xanana" Gusmão, is of mixed Portuguese-Timorese ancestry. More than one president of the Republic of the Philippines has acknowledged Chinese ancestry.

## ENVOI ON ORIENTALISM

This study has traced the origins of Orientalism and Oriental studies to the sixteenth century. In that age, indeed to this age, Christocentrism faced down Islamocentrism, with possibly Sinocentrism forming the largest world historical tribute-collecting empire of all. While the Iberian conquests irredeemably drew the world into a common system of exchange, linked especially by long-distance sea trade, we must await a mature European Enlightenment before the connection between Orientalism and imperialism became organic.

But who was learning from whom during the first two centuries of the new global order? Had Orientalism as a totalizing ideology of domination been called into being? To be sure, from the Caribbean to the Philippines, the conquistadores imposed their languages of power, reworked native grammars, and changed native mentalities and societies forever. Such was the great transformation that only anthropology and archaeology could recover these lost worlds of preconquest America even within our time frame. In the context of the Americas, only *criollos* (Anglo-Franco-Hispanic), true creoles or *ladinos*, and liberated slaves would recover their "nationalisms," albeit within the framework of European nation-state. From Asia, we have mentioned the cases of the Philippines and, with independence in May 2002, East Timor. (In 1999, Macau acquired a fifty-year dispensation from China, ostensibly respecting Portuguese language and culture.) Few native claimants to independence, to my knowledge, repudiated their acquired language or "faith," at least at the level of nation-state, notwithstanding a plethora of nativistic challenges from Australian aborigines to the Chiapos of Mexico.

But continental Asia was a different story, as we have discussed with reference to China, India, and Japan. Here, the Jesuits and other Europeans passed through a long phase of ideological contestation, adaptation to native belief, wonderment, mystification, confabulation, and disbelief, even though the fruits of mass conversion were always elusive. Precocious cultural relativism on the part of early Enlightenment Europe helped Europe rid itself of many medieval, if not yet all, religious (and racial) prejudices. Civilization remained contested terrain to European missionaries and colonizers alike. But fantasy and allegory also helped cushion the unknown, to reinforce the old verities against an avalanche of counterevidence afforded by both the Copernican revolution and the eyewitness traveler accounts.

As I have sketched of the early expansion literature, the new cartographies, and encyclopedic church studies, an active cultural exchange was engendered from the early sixteenth century between West and East, between centers and peripheries that went beyond strict dualities. Just as Iberian agents in Asia encountered teeming metropolitan centers on a scale unimaginable in Europe, not to mention complex bureaucratic states and deeply entrenched economic networks, so these ancient civilizations were correspondingly eager to entertain the knowledge revealed by the agents of distant Europe. But in Asia, reception to heterodox ideas and philosophies depended on a host of contingent local factors. Contrary to the Orientalist orthodoxy, Japan demonstrated that the new science in the hands of a reformist literati could become the cutting edge of radical change, even if this revolution against the neo-Confucian orthodoxy was long in the making.

## LESSONS OF GLOBAL HISTORY

The salutary lessons of a globalizing history is to seek unities, crossovers, and exchanges between and among competing civilizations. To be sure, at the onset of the first globalization there was much more to astonish and wonder. The world, at least the known world, revealed itself to late Renaissance Europe as a kaleidoscope of little cultures, a babel of languages, a smorgasbord of cuisines, a circus of styles and fashions, and a riot of colors and smells. It also provoked a fear of the unknown. The unknown also depended on where one stood, at least with reference to theological debates in Christian Europe. Civilizational diversity was also the norm in our time frame. Even the number of princelings and states far exceeded the roll call of the UN General Assembly. Global standards, world time, digital communications, air travel, cosmopolitanism, cultural relativism, the modern Olympics, planet earth, and McWorld awaited the new globalism, its prophets, and its doomsayers.

We have not here sought to analyze the making of a global economy. While I have independently supplied an analysis of Japan's location within a global division of labor (1500–1800) (Gunn 1999a), the present work is simply not an economic reading of the making of the world system. Rather, we have offered Eurasia as the key world historical arena of civilizational contest and borrowings. In so doing, we are in line with Goody's (1996) sense of a holistic Eurasia, although we are not prepared to endorse the sense of Europe's accidental priority within this huge landmass of myriad states and many civilizations.

But in offering an ostensibly culturalist reading of the first globalization, have we also ignored the question of global accumulation and economic empowerment? Not at all. Rather than presenting a culturally overdetermined argument, we have presented the other side of the coin of economism reaching back to Adam Smith. Consistent with an integrated world history approach, we have argued that without the ideological superstructures of schools, churches, presses, and missionary activities, the circuits of commerce and trade reaching from Europe to Asia could not have flourished. Our thesis of Eurasian cultural metamorphoses restores Asia to its rightful civilizational equivalence or even preeminence in an era before the rise of industrialism and imperialism.

To summarize, in this book I have been concerned primarily with the making of the European or, rather, Eurasian world system as an ideological and cultural as opposed to an economistic system. By privileging the superstructure of ideas and mediating institutions in my analysis of the Eurasian world system, I have departed from both conventional Wallersteinean European world system analyses and the divergence school. Moreover, by underscoring the radical break in world history in 1500 ushered in by the European expansion, we allow the dawn of the capitalist epoch with its roots in Europe itself. But equally, drawing a line at the year 1800, we prefigure the rise of full-blown European industrial society and the age of Eurocentric imperialism. Between 1500 and 1800, I have captured a long period of metamorphosis reflecting the ebb and flow of ideas and their uneven receptions and adaptations across the vast Eurasian space. The binary East–West "Asian values" argument has always been flawed. No part of the world besides the most remote and isolated anthropological zones was outside some form of globalization and creolization of culture by the long sixteenth and seventeenth centuries. The tension between cultural relativism and universalism is very much a modern-day phenomenon, but, as this book has been at pains to state, the roots go back to the era of the first globalization stemming from the Eurasian encounter.

# References

These references include all books or authors mentioned in the text (many exceedingly rare and not directly consulted). Increasingly, however, images of incunabula and other classics are made available for perusal via Internet sites hosted by major libraries and archives. While certain books listed are reprints, in all cases I seek to offer the earliest publication date and, where possible, data on the first and/or most accessible English language imprint.

Abreu Mousino, Manuel de. 1617. *Breve discurso en se cuenta la conquista del Reyno de Pegu, et la India de Oriente. Hecho por los portugueses desde el ano de mil y seyscientos hasta el de 603.* Lisbon: Pedro Craesbeek.

Abu-Lughod, Janet. 1989. *Before European hegemony: The world system AD 1250–1350.* New York: Oxford University Press.

Acosta, Cristobal de. 1578. *Tractado de las drogas y medicinas de la india orientales.* Burgos, Spain: N.p.

Acosta, Nicolas de. 1638. *Breve relacion del martyrio del padre Francisco Marcelo Mastrillo de la Compañia de Jesus: martyrizado en Nangasaqui . . . en 17 de octubre de 1637.* Madrid: N.p.

Adams, Percy G. 1962. *Travelers and travel liars 1660–1800.* Berkeley: University of California Press.

Adams, Will. 1625–1626. "Letters," in Samuel Purchas (ed.), *Hakluytas posthumus or, Purchas his pilgrimes: Contayning a history of the world in sea voyages and lande travells by Englishmen and others . . . .* Glasgow: Glasgow University Press, 1905–1907.

Aduarte, Diego. 1640. *Historia de la provincia del Sancto Rosario de la Orden de Predicadores en Philippinas, Japon y China.* Manila: Colegio de Santo Thomaz.

Albuquerque, Afonso de. 1557. *Commentarios do grande Afonso Dalbuquerque, capitam geral governador da India.* Lisbon: João de Barreyra.

———. 1874–1884. *The commentaries of the great Affonso de Albuquerque (1500–1580): The second viceroy of India* (trans. from Portuguese ed. of 1774). London: N.p.

Aleri, Guilo. N.d. *Tchifang wai ki.* N.p.

Alexander, William. 1802. *The costume of Turkey.* London: N.p.

———. 1805. *The costume of China, illustrated in forty-eight coloured engravings.* London: W. Miller.

Almeida, António de. 1976. "Presenças etnobotânicas brasileiras no Timor português." *Memórias de academia das ciências de Lisboa: Classe de ciencias* 19: 157–83.

Almeida, Manoel de, Emanuel Diaz, and Julien Baldinotti. 1629. *Historire de ce qui'est passe es royaumes d'Ethiopie en l'année 1626 jusqu au mois de mars 1627. Et de la Chine; en l'année 1625 jusques en feburier de 1626. Avec une briefue narration du voyage qui s'est fait au Royume de Tunquim nouvellement descouvert: tirées des lettres adressées au R. Pere Générale de la Compaigne de Jesus.* Paris: Sebastien Cramoisy.

Alpinius, Prosper. 1745. *Medicine Aegyptiorum.* N.p.

Amaro, Ana Maria. 1994. *Três jogos populares de Macau.* Macau: Instituto de Macau.

———. 1995a. "Iberian tradition card games in Macao." *Review of Culture,* no. 23 (2nd ser.): 87–89.

———. 1995b. "The 'illusive' Macanese women." *Review of Culture,* no. 24 (2nd ser.): 7–14.

Andaya, Leonard Y. 2001. "The search for the 'origins' of Melayu." *Journal of Southeast Asian Studies* 3, no. 32: 315–30.

Anderson, Aeneas. 1796. *A narrative of the British Embassy to China in the years 1792, 1793, and 1794 containing the various circumstances of the Embassy with customs, and manners of the Chinese and a description of the country towns, cities, etc. . .* London: J. Debrett.

Anderson, Benedict. 1983. *Imagined communities: Reflections on the origins and spread of nationalism.* London: Verso.

———. 1998. *The spectre of comparisons: Nationalism, Southeast Asia and the world.* London: Verso.

Andrade, António de. 1625. *Novo descobmimento do gram Cathayo, ou reinos de Tibet, pello padre Andrade da Companhia de Ieusu portuguez, no anno de 1624.* Lisbon: Matteus Pinheiro.

Anonymous. N.d. *Compositio et operatio astrolabio.* N.p.

———. N.d. *Macau: Cartography of the west-east encounter.* Macau: N.p.

———. 1570. *Cartas de Japão.* Coimbra: N.p.

———. 1576. *Historia da provincia de St. Cruz.* N.p.

———. 1590a. *De missione legatorium Iaponensium.* Macau: N.p.

———. 1590b. *Relação des grandes alterações & mundanças que ouve em as Reynos de Japão nos annos de 87 & 88.* Coimbra: N.p.

———. 1593a. *Doctrina christiana en lengua española y tagala.* Manila: N.p. (National Historical Commission, Manila, 1973).

———. 1593b. *Doctrina christiana en letra y lengua China.* Manila: N.p.

———. 1593c. *Pien cheng-chiao chen-ch'uan shih-lu.* Manila: N.p.

———. 1593d. *Shih-lu: Tradado de la doctrine de la Santa IIglesia y de ciencias naturales.* Manila: N.p.

———. 1621. *Dotrina Christiana.* Manila: St. Pauls (in Ilocano).

——. 1665. *An exact relation of the embassy sent by the East India Company of the United Provinces to the Great Tartar Cham, or emperour of China . . .* N.p.

——. 1689. *Vrende geschiedenissen in Cambodia en louwen-lant, in Oost-Indien.* Harlaam, Netherlands: Pieter Castleyn.

——. 1714. *The travels of several learned missionaries of the learned society of Jesus into divers parts of the archipelago, India, China and America containing a general description of the most remarkable towns; with a particular Account of the customs, manners and religions of these several nations.* Trans. from the French original. London: N.p.

——. 1771. *Alphabetum Brammanicum seu Indostanum universitatis Kasi.* Rome: Typis Sac. Congregation de Propag Fide.

——. 1776. *Alphabetum Bermanum seu bomanum regni avaefinitmarum-que regionum.* Rome: N.p.

——. 1779–1784. *Transactions of the Batavian society of arts and sciences.* Batavia: N.p.

——. 1790. *Histoire générale des voyages ou nouvelle collection de toutes les relations de voyages.* 24 vols. Paris: Didot.

——. 1807. *The costumes of Indostan.* London: Edward Orme.

——. 1830. "A short account of the island of Bali: Particularly of Bali Baliling." *Singapore Chronicle* (June).

——. 1903–1905. *An excellent treatise of the Kingdome of China, and of the estate and government thereof: Printed in Latine at Macao a citie of the Portugals in China, AN DOM. 1590 and written dialogue-eise. The speakers are Linus, Leo and Michael.* Comp. by Richard Hakluyt. Glasgow: The Principal Navigations.

——. 1935. *Livros antigos Portuguezas/Early Portuguese books, 1489–1600 in the library of His Majesty, the King of Portugal described by H.M. King Manuel in three volumes, 1570–1600 and supplement 1500–1597.* London: Cambridge University Press/Maggs Bros.

——. 1977. "Hanoi: From the origins in the nineteenth century." I. *Vietnamese Studies,* no. 48: 1–777.

——. 1991. *Livro das plantas, das fortalezas, cidades e povoações do Estado da India Oriental com as descrições do maritimo dos reinos e provincias onde estão situadas e outros portos principais daquelas partes,* (Luis Silveira, ed.), Contribuição para a história das fortalezas dos Portugueses no ultramar. Lisbon: Ministério do Planemento Territorial Commission to the Commemoration of the Portuguese Discoveries.

——. 1993. *Ancient town of Hoi An.* National Committee for the International Symposium on the Ancient Town of Hoi An. Hanoi: Gioi Publishers.

Anquetil-Duperron, Abraham-Hyacinthe. 1778. *Législation orientale, ouvrage dans lequel, en montrant quels sont en Turquie, en Perse et dans l'Indoustan, les principes fondamentaux du governement . . .* Amsterdam: Chez Marc-Michel Rey.

Ansaldo, Umberto, and Stephen Mathews. 2002. "The Minnan substrate and creolization in Baba Malay." www.hku.hk/linguist/staff/mathews/baba.html.

Anson, George Lord. 1748. *A voyage round the world in the years MDCCXL.* Vols. I–IV. N.p.

Anville, Jean Baptiste Bourguignon de. 1737. *Nouvel atlas de la Chine.* The Hague: N.p.

Arago, Jacques Etienne Victor. 1823. *Narrative of a voyage round the world in the Uranie and Physicienne corvettes commanded by Captain Freycinet during the years*

*1817, 1818, 1819, and 1820 on a scientific expedition undertaken by order of the French government in a series of letters to a friend.* London: Treutel and Wurtz, Treutel, Jun and Richter.

Aresta, Antonio. 1997. "Portuguese Sinology: A brief outline." *Review of Culture*, no. 31 (2nd ser.): 3–16.

Argensola, Bartolomeu, Leonardo de. 1609. *Conquista de las islas Malucas al Rey Pilipe III.* Madrid: A. Martin.

———. 1707. *Histoire de la conquete des isles Moluqes par les Espagnols, par les Portugais & par les Hollandais.* Amsterdam: Jacques Desbordes.

———. 1708. *The discovery and conquest of the Moluccas and the Philippine Islands.* London: N.p.

Arrillaga, Paulino. 2001. "'Latinos' take pride in their Indian roots." *South China Morning Post*, January 2.

Arvieux, Laurent d'. 1728. *Voyage fait par ordre du Roy Louis XIV dans La Palestine, vers le Grand Emir, chef des princes Arabes du desert, connus sur le nom de Bedouins, ou d'Arabes Scenites, qui se disent la vraie posterité d'Ismael fils Abraham. Ou il est traité des moeurs & des coutumes de cette naiton. Avec la description générale de l' Arabie, faite par le Sultan Ismael Abdulfeda, traduite en François sur les meilleurs, manuscrits, avec des notes.* Amsterdam: Steenhouwer.

Auber, Peter. 1834. *China, an outline of its government, laws, and policy and of the foreign embassies to and intercourse with that empire.* London: Parbury, Allen, and Co.

Ayusawa, Shintaro. 1953. "The types of world map made in Japan's age of national isolation." *Imago Mundi* 10: 123–28.

———. 1964. "Geography and Japanese knowledge of world geography." *Monumenta Nipponica* 19: 41–61.

Bacon, Francis. 1627. *New Atlantis.* London: N.p. www.levity.com/alchemy/atlantis.html.

Bailey, Gauvin Alexander. 2000. *Art on the Jesuit missions in Asia and Latin America, 1542–1773.* Toronto: University of Toronto Press.

[Balbi, Gaspero.] 1625–1626. In Samuel Purchas (ed.), *Hakluytas posthumus or, Purchas his pilgrimes: Contayning a history of the world in sea voyages and lande travells by Englishmen and others . . . .* Glasgow: Glasgow University Press, 1905–1907.

[Baldaeus, Philip.] 1704. *A true and exact description of the most celebrated East-India coasts of Malabar and Coromandel, As also of the ile of Ceylon by Philip Baldaeus, minister of the word of God in Ceylon.* Amsterdam, 1672. In A. Churchill and J. Churchill (eds.), *A Collection of voyages and travels,* vol. 3 (pp. 501–822). London: At the Black Swan in Paternaster Row.

Baldeus, Philip. 1672. *Naaukeurige beschryvinge van Malabar en Choromandel der zelver aangrezende ryken, en het machtige eyland Ceylon.* N.p.

Baldinotti, Guilano. 1626. *La relation sur le Tonkin: Relation du voyage fait au Royaume de Tunquin novellement decouvert.* Macau: N.p.

Ball, V. (ed.). 1889. *Travels in India by Jean Baptiste Tavernier,* vols. 1 and 2 (trans. from French ed. of 1676). London: Macmillan.

Bankoff, Greg. 1999. "Devils, familiars and Spaniards: Spheres of power and the supernatural in the world of Seberina Candelaria and her village in early 19th century Philippines." *Journal of Social History* 33, no. 1: 37–55.

[Barbosa, Duarte.] 1918, 1919. *The Book of Duarte Barbosa: An account of the countries bordering on the Indian Ocean and their inhabitants*. M. L. Dames (trans. and ed.), 2nd ser., 1, no. 44, 2, no. 49. London: Hakluyt Society.

Barreto, Luís Filipe. 1997. "Secular and clerical cultures: Macau's cultural dynamics, ca 1560–ca 1660." Part II, *Macau Magazine* (Macau).

Barros, João de. 1539. *Grammatica da lingua portuguesa*. Lisbon: Casa de Luis Rodrigues.

———. 1552a. *Asia: dos factos que os Portugueses fizeram no descobrimento e conquista dos mares e terras do Oriente*. Lisbon: G. Galharde.

———. 1552b. *Decadas da India*. Lisbon: N.p.

———. 1628–1645. *Decadas da Asia*. 10 vols. Lisbon: N.p.

Bartoli, Daniello. 1660. *Dell' historia della Compagnia di Giesu il Giappone*. Rome: N.p.

Bary de, William Theodore, et al. 1960. *Sources of Chinese tradition*, vol. 1. New York: Columbia University Press.

Batalha, Graciete Nogueira. 1958. "Estado actual do dialecto Macaense." *Revista Portuguesa de filologia*, 177–213.

Baudier, Michel. 1669. *Histoire de la cour du roy de la Chine*. Paris: Estienne Limosin.

Bauhinus, Caspar. 1623. *Pinex theatri botanici Caspari Bauhini*. Basileae Helvet: N.p.

Baxter, Alan N. 1988. *A grammar of Kristang (Malacca creole Portuguese)*. Canberra: Australian National University.

———. 1990. "Notes on the creole Portuguese of Bidau." *Journal of Pidgin and Creole Languages* 5, no. 1: 1–38.

Bayer, Gottlieb Siegfried. 1730. *Museum sinicum, in quo sinicae linguae et literaturae ratio explicatur*. Petroli: Typographia Academiae Imperatoriae.

Bayton-Williams, Ashley. 1999. "Beginner's guide: woodcuts." www.mapforum.com/8wood.htm.

[Beaulieu.] 1745. "Memoirs of Admiral Beaulieu's voyage to the East-Indies." In John Harris (comp.), *Navigantium atque itinererium bibliotheca . . .*, vol. 1 (pp. 717–44). London: Thomas Bennet.

Beaumont. 1672. *The emblem of ingratitude: A true relation of the unjust, cruel, and barbarous proceedings against the English at Amboyna in the East Indies, by the Netherlands governor and council there . . . with remarks upon the whole matter faithfully recorded from anciet and modern records*. London: Printed for William Hope.

Beawes, William. 1752. *Lex mercatoria or the merchant' directory being a compleat guide to all men in business*. London: Printed for the author by John Moore.

Beekman, Daniel. 1718. *A voyage to and from the island of Borneo, in the East Indies*. London: Printed for T. Warner at the Black Boy and J. Bailey at the Dove.

Beekman, D. 1718. *A voyage to and from the island of Borneo, in the East Indies*. Folkestone and London: Dawson of Pall Mall.

Beekman, E. M. (trans., ed., and annot.). 1995. *The Ambonese curiosity cabinet*. New Haven, Conn.: Yale University Press.

Belen, Gaspar Aquino de. 1704. *Mahal na passion ni Jesu Christong panginoon natin na tola*. Manila: N.p.

Bellegarde, M. l'Abbé de (Jean Baptiste Morvan). 1708. *A general history of all voyages and travels throughout the old world and new world, from the first ages to the present time*. Amsterdam: Edmund Corll.

Bellin, J. N. 1748. *La Chine avec la Corée et les Parties de la Tartarie les Plus Voisines Tirée des Cartes que les Jesuites Missionaires ont Levees les Années 1708 jusqu'en 1717.* Paris: N.p.

———. 1764. *Le petit atlas maritime.* 5 vols. Paris: N.p.

Belon, P. 1553. *Les observations de plusieurs singularitez et choses memorables, trouvées en Grece, Asiae, Judée, Egypte, Arabie, & autres pays estranges.* Paris: N.p.

Bencardino, Filippo. 1998. "China in European cartography between the fifteenth and seventeenth centuries." *Review of Culture,* no. 34/35 (2nd ser.): 11–34.

Beranger, Jean Pierre. 1788. *Collection de tous les voyages autour du monde.* 9 vols. Paris: N.p.

Bergeron, Pierre, et al. 1735. *Voyages faits principalement en Asie dans les XII, XIII, XIV, et XV siecles.* La Haye: N.p.

Bernier, François. 1671–1672. *Histoire de la derniere revolution des états du grand Mogul (1670–1671).* N.p.

Bhabha, Homi K. 1994. *The location of culture.* New York: Routledge.

Blair, E. H., and J. A. Robertson, eds. 1903–1909. *The Philippine islands, 1493–1898.* 55 vols. Cleveland: Arthur H. Clark Co.

Blanc, Marcel de. 1604. *Histoire de la revolution de Royaume de Siam arrivé en l'année 1688.* Lyon: N.p.

Blancas de San José, P. Francisco. 1604. *Libro de los cuatro postrimerios del hombre.* Bimendo: Juan de Vera.

———. 1610. *Arte y reglas de la lengua tagala.* Bataan: por Tomas Pinpin.

Blanco, Padre Manuel. 1837. *Flora de Filipinas.* C. Lopez, N.p. (Manila: Estab. tip de Plana y ca. 1877–80).

———. 1993. Text by Pedro G. Galende. *Flora de Filipinas.* Manila: San Augustin Convent.

Blaue, Jean. 1642, 1667. *Le grand atlas.* Amsterdam: J. Blaue.

Blaut, J. M. 1993a. *1492: The debate on colonialism, Eurocentrism, and history.* Trenton, N.J.: Africa World Press.

———. 1993b. *The colonizer's model of the world: Geographical diffusionism and Eurocentric history.* New York: Guilford.

———. 2000. "Environmentalism and Eurocentrism." *Geographical Review* 89, no. 3: 391–408.

Blussé, Leonard. 1986. *Strange company: Mestizo women, and the Dutch in VOC Batavia.* Providence, R.I.: Foris Publications.

Bondt, Jacob de (Jacobus Bertius). 1642. *De Medicina Indorum.* N.p.

———. 1658. *Historiae naturalis et medicae Indiae orientalis liber quintis de quadrupedibus, avibus & picibus.* In Willem Piso (ed.), *De Indiae utrius re naturali et medica.* Amsterdam: N.p.

Bonifacio, Giovani. 1588. *Christian pueri institutio adolescentio.* Macau: N.p.

Bordone, Benedetto 1528. *Libro di Benedetto Bordone . . . or isolario.* Venice: N.p.

Borri, Christoforo. 1631. *Relation de nouvelle mission de les péres de la compagnie de Jesus au Royaume de la Cochinchine.* Rome: N.p. (Lille: Pierre da Rache, 1631).

———. 1704, 1732. "An account of Cochin-China, in two parts." In A. Churchill and J. Churchill (eds.), *A Collection of voyages and travels,* vol. 2 (pp. 737–838). London: At the Black Swan in Paternaster Row.

Bouchon, Geneviève. 1979. "Les premiers voyages portugais à Paris et à Pegu (1512–1520)." *Archipel* 18: 127–58.

Bougainville, Louis Antoine de. 1771–1772. *Description d'un voyage autour du monde par la fregate du Roi et la flute l'Etoile en 1766, 1767, 1768 & 1769.* 2 vols. Paris: Chez Saillant & Nyon.

Bougas, Wayne A. 1990. "Patani in the beginning of the XVIIth century." *Archipel* 39: 113–38.

Boulainvilliers, Comte Henri d'. 1731. *Histoire des Arabes, avec la vie de Mahomed par M. Le Compte de Boulainvilliers.* Amsterdam: Pierre Humbert.

Bourges. 1666. *Relation du voyage de Monseigneur l'Evéque de Beryte vicaire apostolique du Royaume de la Cochinchine . . . par la Turquie, la Perse, les Indes et jusqu'au Royaume de Siam.* Paris: Denys Bechet.

Bowring, Sir John. 1857. *The King and people of Siam with a narrative of the mission to that country in 1855,* vol. 1. London: John W. Parker.

Boxer, Charles, R. 1948. *Three historians of Portuguese Asia.* Macau: Imprensa Nacional.

———. 1951. *The Christian century in Japan 1549–1650.* Berkeley: University of California Press (Carcenet Press, 1993).

———. 1953. *South China in the sixteenth century: Being the narratives of Galeota Pereira, Fr. Gaspar da Cruz, O.P., Fr. Martin da Rade O.E.S.A.* London: Hakluyt.

———. 1969a. "A note on the Portuguese reaction to the revival of the Red Sea spice trade and the rise of Atjeh, 1540–1600." *Journal of Southeast Asian History* 10, no. 3: 415–28.

———. 1969b. *The Portuguese seaborne empire, 1415–1825.* New York: Knopf.

——— (ed. and trans.). 1984. *Seventeenth century Macau.* Hong Kong: Heinemann.

———. 1985. *Portuguese conquest and commerce in South Asia, 1500–1750.* London: Varium Reprints.

———. 1993. *Macau na epoca da Restauração.* Lisbon: Fundação Oriente.

Boym, Michael. 1656. *Flora Sinensis.* Venice: N.p.

Boym, Michael. *Specimen medicinae Sinicae* (Zhongguo yifa juli). N.p.

Braccioini, Gian Francesco Poggio. 1431–1448. *Historia de varietate fortunae.* N.p.

Braga, Jack. 1942a. "Early European printing in China" (April 7, reprint from *Renascimento,* Macau).

———. 1942b. "Notes on the lingua franca of the East" (October 2, reprint from *Renascimento,* Macau).

Braudel, Fernand. 1976. *The Mediterranean and the Mediterranean world in the age of Philip II.* 2 vols. New York: HarperColophon.

Bray, Francesca. 1997. *Technology and gender: Fabrics of power in late imperial China.* Berkeley: University of California Press.

Breyne, Jacob, and William Ten Rhijne. 1674–1678. *Exoticarum aliarumque minus cognitarum plantarum centuria prima.* Dansk: N.p.

Brewer, Carolyn. 2001. *Holy confrontation: Religion, gender and sexuality in the Philippines, 1521–1685.* Manila: Manila Institute of Women's Studies, St. Scholastical's College.

———. 2002. "Baylan, asog, transvestism, and sodomy: Gender, sexuality and the sacred in early colonial Philippines." www.murdoch.edu.au/intersections.html.

Brito, Manuel Carlos de. 1996. "Sounds from the discoveries: Musical aspects of the Portuguese expansion." *Review of Culture,* no. 26 (2nd ser.): 3–22.

Bruton, William. 1638. *Newes from the East Indies; or a voyage to Bengalla.* N.p.

Buglio, Luigi. N.d. *Yu lan sifang yeo ki.* N.p.

Bulag, Uradyn, F. 1998. *Nationalism and hybridity in Mongolia.* Oxford, U.K.: Clarendon Press.

Burbidge, F. W. 1989. *The garden of the Sun.* Singapore: Oxford University Press.

Burmann, J. 1737, 1777–1778. *Thesaurus Zeylanicus, exhibens plantas in insula Zeylana nascentes.* Amsterdam: N.p.

Busbecq, Ogier Ghiselin. 1582. *Itinera Constantinopolitanum et amasianun.* N.p.

Cabaton, Antoine. 1914. *Bréve et veridique relations des evénements du Cambodge par Gabriel Quiroga de San Antonio.* Paris: Ernest Leroux.

Caetano, Maria Paula (intro.). 1990. *Breve discurso, em que se conta a conquista do reino do Pegu na India Oriental: Manuel Abreu Mousinho.* Lisbon: Publicações Europa-America.

Camins, Bernadino S. 1989. *Chabacano de Zamboanga handbook and Chabacano English-Spanish dictionary.* Zamboanga City, Philippines: First United Broadcasting Corp.

Camões, Luiz Vaz de. 1572. *Lusiadas.* Lisbon: N.p.

Campanella, Tommaso. 1602. *Civitas solis* (The city of the sun). N.p. www.levity.com/alchemy/citysun.html.

———. 1981. *La citta del sole: Dialogo poetica/The city of the sun: A political dialogue.* Daniel J. Donno (trans). Berkeley: University of California Press.

Campbell, Judy. 2002. *Invisible invaders: Smallpox and other diseases in aboriginal Australia 1780–1880.* Melbourne: Melbourne University Press.

Campbell, W. M. 1903. *Formosa under the Dutch.* London: Kegan Hall, Trench, Trubner.

Campos, J. J. A. 1919. *History of the Portuguese in Bengal.* Calcutta: Butterworth and Co.

Candidius, Georgius. 1627. *A short account of the island of Formosa.* N.p.

Cardim, António. 1646. *Fasciclus a Japonicus floribus.* Rome: N.p.

Careri, John Francis Gemeli. 1704, 1732, 1744–1747. "A voyage round the world." In A. Churchill and J. Churchill (eds.), *A Collection of voyages and travels,* vol. 4 (pp. 1–572). London: At the Black Swan in Paternaster Row.

Carey, William 1818. *Dialogues intended to facilitate the acquiring of the Bengalee language.* Serampore: Mission Press.

Carletti, Francesco. 1964. *My voyage around the world: The chronicles of a sixteenth century Florentine merchant (1701).* New York: Pantheon.

Caron, François and Joost Schouten. 1671. *A true description of the mighty kingdoms of Japan and Siam. Written originally in Dutch by Francis Caron and Joost Schotten and translated into English by Captain Roger Manley.* London: R. Boulter (repr. from the English ed. of 1663, ed. with intro. by C. R. Boxer [London: Argonaut Press, 1935]).

Carpanio, Melchior. 1776. *Alphabetum Bermanum.* Rome: N.p.

Carrascalão, Natalia. 1998. *Vamos jantar a Timor.* Macau: Carrascālao.

Carvalo, Alexandro, and Manuel João Ramos. 1999. "O Nile Azul: De paraiso terrestre á Etiopie/The Blue Nile: From the earthly paradise to Ethiopia." In *O destino etiope do Preste Joao/The Ethiopian destiny of Prester John* (pp. 17–27). Lisbon: Museu Nacional de Arte Antigo.

Castanheda, Fernão Lopes de. 1552. *Historia do livro segundo do descobrimentos & conquista da India pelos Portuguesas.* Coimbra: N.p.

Castelo, Claudia Orvalho. 1993. "The history as told by João Rodrigues." *Review of Culture*, no. 17 (2nd ser.): 103–74.

Castillon, J. 1774. *Anecdotes Chinoise, Japonais, Siamois, Tonquinoises, etc.* Paris: N.p.

Castro, Affonso de. 1867. *As possessões portugeusas na oceania.* Lisbon: Imprensa Nacional.

*Catholic Encylopedia.* 1914. New York: The Encyclopedia Press Inc. www.newadvent.org/cathen.

Catz, Rebecca, D. (ed. and trans.). 1989. *The travels of Mendes Pinto.* Chicago: University of Chicago Press.

[Cavendish, Sir Thomas.] 1745. "Voyage around the world." In John Harris (comp.), *Navigantium atque itinererium bibliotheca . . .*, vol. 1 (pp. 14–28). London: Thomas Bennet.

Chakraborti, Phanindra Nath. 1994. *Rise and growth of English East India Company: A study of British mercantile activities in Mughal India.* Calcutta: Punthi Pustak.

Chandler, David P. 1976. "Maps for the ancestors: Specialized topography and echoes of Angkor in two Cambodian texts." *Journal of the Siam Society* 64 (pt. 2, July): 176–87.

———, et al. (eds.). 1987. *In search of Southeast Asia: A modern history.* Sydney: Allen & Unwin.

———. 1993. *A history of Cambodia* (2nd ed.). Boulder, Colo.: Westview Press.

Chang, Kuei-sheng. 1970. "Africa and the Indian Ocean in Chinese maps of the fourteenth and fifteenth centuries." *Imago Mundi* 24: 21–30.

Chardin, John. 1686, 1720. *Travels in Persia 1653–1677.* 2 vols. London: N.p.

Charlevoix, Pierre François-Xavier de. 1715, 1736, 1756. *Histoire de l'établissement des progres et de la decadence du Christianisme dans l'empire du Japon.* Paris: N.p.

Chase-Dunn, Christopher, and Thomas D. Hall. 1997. *Rise and demise: Comparing world-systems.* Boulder, Colo.: Westview Press.

Chater, James. 1815. *A grammar of the Cingalese language.* Colombo: Printed at the Government Press by Nicholas Bergman.

Chatterton, E. Keble. 1927. *Old ship prints.* London: John Laie, The Bodley Head Ltd.

Chaucer, Geoffrey. 1391. "Treatise on the astrolabe." N.p.

Chaudhuri, Kirti N. 1985. *Trade and civilization in the Indian ocean.* Cambridge, U.K.: Cambridge University Press.

Chen, Arthur. 1997. "Connecting east and west through Jesuit perspective." *Review of Culture*, no. 27/28 (2nd ser.): 155–68.

Ch'en Ching-Ho. 1968. *The Chinese community in the sixteenth century Philippines.* East Asian Cultural Studies series, no. 12. Tokyo: Center for East Asian Cultural Studies.

Chen Shouyi. 1998. In Adrian Hsia (ed.), *The vision of China in the English literature of the seventeenth and eighteenth centuries* (pp. 87–114, 215–48, 283–300). Hong Kong: Chinese University Press.

Cheng, Christina Mui Ning. 1999. *Macau: A cultural Janus.* Hong Kong: Hong Kong University Press.

Chirino, Pedro. 1604. *Relación de las islas Filipinas.* Rome: N.p.

Chiung, Wi-vun Taiffalo. 2002. "Romanization and language planning in Taiwan." http://home.kimo.com.tw/de-han/pehoeji/lomaji/3.htm.

Choisy, Francois Timoleon. 1687. *Journal du voyage de Siam fait en MDC.LXXXV. et MDC.LXXXVI.* Paris: Sebastien Mabre-Cramoisy: N.p.

———. 1710. *Le Prince Kouchimen, histoire tartare, et Dom Alvar de Sol, Histoire Napolitaine.* Paris: N.p.

Churchill, Awnsham, and John Churchill (eds.). 1704, 1732, 1744–1747. *A collection of voyages and travels. Some now first printed for original manuscripts, Others translated out of foreign languages, and now first published in English. To which are added some few that have formerly appear'd in English, but do now for their exellency and scarceness deserve to be re-printed.* 4 vols. London: At the Black Swan in Paternaster Row.

Cinatti, Ruy Vaz Monteiro Gomes. 1959. *Explorações botânicas em Timor,* vol. 4. Lisbon: Ministerio da Colonias.

Claver, Martin. 1638. *El admirable y excelente martiro en el Reyno de Japan de los benditos Padres fra Bartolome Gutierrez, fray Francisco de Graçia, y fray Thomas de S. Augustin, religiosos de la orden de San Augustin . . . y de otros compañeros suios hasta el año de 1637.* Manila: Printed by Colegio de Santo Thomas Luís Beltran.

Claveria y Zaldua, Narciso. 1844, 1973. *Catalogo alfabetico de apellidos.* Manila: N.p.

Clerc, M. 1769. *Yu le Grand et Confucius, historire Chinoise.* Paris: N.p.

Coblin, W. South, and Joseph Abraham Levi (eds.). 2000. *Francisco Varo's grammar of the Mandarin language (1703): An English translation of Arte de la langue Mandarina.* Intro. by Sandra Breitebach. Amsterdam: John Benjamin.

Cobo, Juan. 1593. *Bien zhengjiao zhenchuan shilu.* Manila: University of São Tomé.

———. 1595. *Myong sim bo-gam/Espejo rico del claro coraz.* Madrid: N.p.

Columbus, Christopher. 1493. *Epistola de insulis nuper inventis.* Basel: N.p.

Commelin, Izaak (ed.). 1646. *Begin ende voortgang vande vereenigde Neederlandtsche geoctroyeerde Ooste Indische Compagnie.* 2 vols. Amsterdam: N.p.

Cooke, Edward. 1712. *A voyage to the south sea, and round the world . . . in the years 1708, 1709, 1710, and 1711 . . . Wherein an account is given of Mr. Alexander Selhkirk . . . upon the unihabited island of Juan Fernandes.* London: N.p.

Cooper, Michael S. J. 1994. *Rodrigues the interpreter: An early Jesuit in Japan and China.* Tokyo: Weatherhill.

Copernicus, Nicolas. 1543. *De revolutionibus orbium coslestium.* N.p.

Cordier, Henri. 1883a. *Essai d'une bibliographie des ouvrages publiés en Chine par les européens au XVII et au XVII siècle.* Paris: Ernest Leroux.

———. 1883b. *Bibliotheca Sinica: Dictionnaire bibliographique des ouvrages relaties à l'empire Chinoise.* Paris: N.p.

———, and J. M. Lenhart. 1912. "Tibet," *Catholic encyclopedia,* vol. 14. New York: Robert Appleton.

Corrêa, Gaspar. 1858–1866. *Lendas da India.* Lisbon: Academia Real das Sciencias.

Cortesão, Armando. 1935. *Cartographia e cartógrafos portugueses dos seculos XV e XVI.* 2 vols. Lisbon: Edicão da Seara Nova.

Cortesão Armando, and Henry Thomas. 1938. *Carta das nvas que vieram a el Rei Nossa Senhor de descobrimento do Preste João (Lisboa 1521). Texto original e estudo critico.* Lisbon: N.p.

Costa, Ignacio da. 1662. *Sapienta Sinica.* Jiangzi: N.p.

———. 1659. *Sinarum scientia politico-moralis.* Canton: N.p.

Costa, João de. 1588. *De natura novi orbis.* N.p.

Couplet, Philippe, et al. 1686–1687. *Confucius Sinarum philosophus, sive scienta Sinensus latine exposita . . . adjecta est tabula chronologica Sinicae monarchiae.* Paris: Danielem Horthemels.

Courtois, Ponce (ed.). 1769. *Yu le Grand et Confuncios histoire Chenois.* Paris: N.p.

Couto, Diogo do. 1597 (1602). *Decada IV.* Lisbon: N.p.

Coyer, François Gabriel. 1752. *A supplement to Lord Anson's voyage round the world: Containing a discovery and description of the island of Frivola . . . to which is prefixed an introductory preface by the translator.* London: N.p.

Crawfurd, John. 1820. *History of the Indian archipelago. Containing an account of the manners, arts, languages, religions, institutions and commerce of the inhabitants.* 3 vols. Edinburgh: Constable and Co.

Cro, Stelio (ed.). 1975. *Description de la Sinapia, peninsula en la Tierra Austral: A classical utopia of Spain.* Hamilton, Ontario: McMaster University Press.

Crosby, Alfred W. 1973. *The Columbian exchange: Biological and cultural consequences of 1492.* Westport, Conn.: Greenwood Press.

Cruz, Gaspar da. 1569. *Tradado onde se contam muito por extenso as cousas da China / Iractado em que se c'am muito por esteso as cousas da China.* Evora: Andre de Burgos.

———. 1905. "Friar Gaspar da Cruz: A treatise of China and the adjoining regions." In Samuel Purchas (ed.), *Hakluytas posthumus or, Purchas his pilgrimes: Contayning a history of the world in sea voyages and lande travells by Englishmen and others . . .,* vol. 11 (pp. 474–565). Glasgow: Glasgow University Press, 1905–1907.

Cruz, Martin de la, and Juan Badiano (trans.). 1552, 1939. *Libellus de medicinalibus idorum herbis.* Baltimore: N.p.

Cubero, Sebastian Pedro. 1688. *Peregrinacion que ha hencho de la mayor parte del mundo . . . con las cosas mas singulares que le han sucedido, y visto, entre tan barbaras nacionese, su religion, ritos, ceremonias, y otras cosas memorables, y curiosas, que ha podido inquirir. Con el viage por tierra, desde España, hasta las Indias Orientales.* Zaragoza: por Pasqual Bueno.

Cuvier, George. 1828. *Histoire naturelle des poissons.* Paris: Chez F.G. Levrault.

Cyrano de Bergerac, Savinien. 1657. *Histoire comique des états et empires du soleil.* Paris: N.p.

———. 1687. *The comick history of the states and empires of the worlds of the moon and sun.* London: N.p.

———. 1976. *Other worlds; the comical history of the states and empires of the moon and sun.* Trans. by Geoffrey Strachan. London: New England Library Science Fiction Series.

Dalgado, S. R. 1893. *Diccionario Konkani-Portuguez.* Bombay: N.p.

———. 1936. *Portuguese vocables in Asiatic languages.* Baroda, India: Oriental Institute.

Dalrymple, Alexander. 1770–1771. *An historical collection of the several voyages and discoveries in the south Pacific ocean.* London: N.p.

Dampier, William. 1699. *Voyages and descriptions in three parts, viz. 1. A Supplement of the voyage round the world . . . 2. Two voyages to Campeachy . . . 3. A discourse of trade winds . . .* London: Printed for James Knapton.

———. 1708–1711. *A voyage to New-Holland, etc. in the year 1699.* 2 vols. London: N.p.

———. 1745. "First voyage around the world." In John Harris (comp.), *Navigantium atque itinererium bibliotheca . . .,* vol. 1 (pp. 865–908). London: Thomas Bennet.

Daus, Ronald. 1989. *Portuguese Eurasian communities in Southeast Asia, local history and memoirs.* Singapore: Institute of Southeast Asian Studies.

Davidson, J. A. 1977. "Brunei coinage." *Brunei Museum Journal* 4, no. 1: 43–81.

Davis, Henry. 2001. "Cartographic images." www.henry.davis.com/MAPS.

Davis, John Francis. 1815. *San-yu-low, or the three dedicated rooms. A Tale. Translated from the Chinese.* Macau: East India Company Press.

De Bry, Johan Theodor. 1612–1614. *Florilegium novum.* Frankfurt: N.p.

——, and Johann Israel de Bry. 1606, 1613. *Indiae Orientalis septima.* Frankfurt: N.p.

De Bry, Johann Theodore. 1590–1620. *Grand Voyages.* Frankfurt: N.p.

De Bry, Johann Theodore. 1598–1634. *Petit Voyages.* Frankfurt: N.p.

Defoe, Daniel. 1719. *The life and strange surprising adventures of Robinson Crusoe, etc.* London: W. Taylor.

Dellon, Gabriel. 1688. *Relation de l'Inquisition de Goa.* Paris: D. Horthemels.

Deus, Jacinto de. 1690. *Vergel de plantes, e flores de provincia da madre de deus dos Capuchas Reformados.* Lisbon: Miguel Deslandes.

Dhiravat na Pomberja. 1993. "Ayutthaya at the end of the seventeenth century: Was there a shift to isolation?" In A. Reid (ed.), *Southeast Asia in the early modern period: Trade, power and belief* (pp. 250–72). Ithaca, N.Y.: Cornell University Press.

Diamond, Jared. 1997. *Guns, germs, and steel: The fates of human societies.* New York: W. W. Norton.

Diaz, Emmanuel. 1615. *Thien wên lüeh* [Explicatio sphaerae coelestis]. China: N.p.

Diderot, Denis. 1772. *Supplément au voyage de Bougainville.* Paris: N.p.

Dieu, Lodewik (Louis) de. 1639. *Rudimentae linguae Persicae.* Leiden: N.p.

Dores, Raphael das. 1907. *Diccionario Teto-Portugues.* Lisbon: Imprensa Nacional.

[Drake, Francis.] 1745. "The voyage of Sir Francis Drake round the globe." In John Harris (comp.), *Navigantium atque itinererium bibliotheca . . .,* vol. 1 (pp. 19–24). London: Thomas Bennet.

Drakenstein, Hendrik Reede tot. 1683–1703. *Hortus Indicus malabaricus.* 12 vols. Amsterdam: N.p.

Dryden, John. 1673. *Amboyna, or the cruelties of the Dutch to the English merchants.* London: N.p.

Dudley, Robert. 1646. *Del arcano del mare.* Florence: N.p.

Dufour, P. S. 1685. *Tractatus novi de potv caphe, de chinensium thé et de chocolata.* Paris: P. Muguet.

Durante, Castor. 1567 (1585). *Herbario nuovo.* Venice: G. Hertz.

Dye, Morris 1999. "The empire winds down." http://salon.com/travel/feature/1999/12/18/macao.

Ecluse, C. de L'. 1592. *Aliquot notae in garciae aromatum historium.* Antwerp: N.p.

Eden, Richard. 1555. *The decades of the newe worllde or West Indies.* London: G. Powell.

——. 1677. [finished by Richard Wills]. *The history of travayle in the west and east Indies, and other countreys lying eyther way, towardes the fruitfull and ryches Moluccas.* London: R. Jugge.

Edney, Mathew H. 1993. "Cartography without progress: Reinterpreting the nature and historical development of mapmaking." *Cartographica* 30, no. 2–3: 54–68.

———. 1997. *Mapping an empire: The geographical construction of British India, 1765–1843.* Chicago: University of Chicago Press.

Elliott, Mark C. 2000. "The limits of Tartary: Manchuria in imperial and national geographies." *Journal of Asian Studies* 59, no. 3: 603–47.

Emmerson, Donald, K. 1994. "'Southeast Asia': What's in a name?" *Journal of Southeast Asian Studies* 15, no. 1: 1–21.

Encarnação, Antonio da. 1665. *Breve relaçam das cousas, que nestes annos proximos, fizerão os religios da Ordem dos Pregadores, e dos prodigios, que succedeaõ nas Christandades do sul, que correm por sua conta na India Oriental.* N.p.

England, John C. 1997. "Early Asian Christian writings, 5th–12th centuries: An appreciation." *Asia Journal of Theology* 11, no. 1: 154–71.

———. 2001. "Asian Christian writings in the sixteenth to eighteenth centuries." www.missionstudies.org/asia.

Eredia, Manuel Godhino de. 1851–1852. *Malaca, l'Inde méridionale et le Cathay: Facimilé du manuscrit autographe de la Bibliothèque Royale de Belgique.* Brussels: L. Jansen.

Erpenius (Thomas van Erpen). 1631. *Grammatica Araba quinque libris methodice explicita.* Leiden: N.p.

Escalente, Bernadino de. 1577. *Discurso de la navigation que les portugueses hazena los reinos y provincias del Oriente y de la noticia q se tiene de las grandezas del Reino de la China.* Seville: N.p.

Esteves, Thomas. 1640. *Arte da lingua canarim.* Goa: N.p.

Fausset, David. 1993. *Writing the new world: Imaginary voyages and utopias of the great southern land.* Syracuse, N.Y.: Syracuse University Press.

Favre, Pierre-François. 1740. *Lettres edifiantes et curieuses sur la visite apostolique de M. de La-Baume que d'Halicarnasse, la Cochinchine en l'annee 1740 . . .* Neuchtael, Switzerland: N.p.

Fell, R. T. 1988. *Early maps of South-East Asia.* Singapore: Oxford University Press.

Fellows, Thomas Bernard. 1895. *Faba Arabica, vulgo caffatum carmen.* Lyons: N.p.

Ferguson. 1773. *Dictionary of the Hindustan language.* London: N.p.

Fernandes, Miguel Senna, and Alan Norman Baxter. 2000. *Maquista Chapado: Vocabulario e expressoes do crioule português de Macau.* Macau: Instituto Internacional de Macau.

Ferreira, Fernanda Durão. 2000. *The Portuguese origins of Robinson Crusoe.* London: Minerva Press.

Feynes, Henri de. 1615. *An exact and curious survey of all the East Indies even to Canton, the chieffe cittie of China.* London: Thomas Dawson for William Arondell.

Fitch, Ralph. 1921. In William Forster (ed.), *Early travels in India: 1583–1619.* London: Oxford University Press.

Floor, Willem. 2001. "Dutch-Persia relations." www.iranica.com.

Flynn, Dennis O. 1996. *World silver and monetary history in the 16th and 17th centuries.* Aldershot, U.K.: Variorum.

Foigny, Gabriel de. 1676. *La terre Australe connue.* Geneva: N.p.

———. 1692. *Les avantures de Jacques Sadeur dans la decouverte et le voiage de la Terre Australe. Contenant les coutumes & les moeurs des Australiens.* Paris: N.p.

———. 1993. *The southern land, known.* Syracuse, N.Y.: Syracuse University Press.

Fortune, Robert. 1847. *Three years wandering in the northern provinces of China . . . with an account of the agriculture and horticulture of the Chinese, new plants, etc.* London: N.p.

Foss, Theodore. 1994. "Jesuit cartography: A Western interpretation of China." *Review of Culture*, no. 21 (2nd ser.): 133–56.

Fourmont, Etiènne. 1737. *Meditationes Sinicae.* Paris: N.p.

———. 1742. *Linguae Sinarum Mandarinicae grammatica duplex.* Paris: Chez Hippolyte-Louis Guerin.

Foust, Clifford M. 1992. *Rhubarb, the wondrous drug.* Princeton, N.J.: Princeton University Press.

Frank, Andre Gunder. 1998. *ReOrient: Global economy in the Asian age.* Berkeley: University of California Press.

———, and Barry K. Gills. 1993. *The world system: Five hundred years or five thousand?* London: Routledge.

Freeman, J. 1835. *Dictionary of the Malagasy language in two parts.* An-Tannanarive, Madagascar: N.p.

Frei, Henry. 1984. "Japan discovers Australia: The emergence of Australia in the Japanese world-view, 1540s–1900." *Monumenta Nipponica*, no. 39: 55–81.

French, Roger. 1991. "Medicine in western Europe during the fifteenth century." In Mário Gomes Marques and John Cule (eds.), *The great maritime discoveries and world health* (pp. 39–53). Proceedings of the First International Congress on the Great Maritime Discoveries and World Health, September 10–13, 1990, Lisbon.

[Fróis, Luís.] 1589. *Carta do Padre Luis Fróes da Companhia de Jesus.* Lisbon: N.p.

———. 1976–1984. *Historia de Japam.* 5 vols. Lisbon: Edition de Jose Wicki, Biblioteca National.

———. 1994. *Traité de Luis Fróis, S.J. (1585) sur les contradictions de moeurs entre Européens & Japonais* (trans. by Xavier de Castro and Robert Schrimpf, intro. by José Manuel Garcia; 2d ed.). Paris: Editions Chandeigne.

———. 2001. *Tratado das contradições e diferenças de costumes entre a Europa e Japão* (ed. by Rui Manuel Loureiro). Macau: Instituto Português de Oriente.

[Fryke, Christopher, and Christopher Schweitzer.] 1997. *Voyages to the East Indies (1700).* Intro. by C. Ernest Fayle. New Delhi: Asia Educational Services.

[Funnell, William.] 1745. "The voyage of William Funnell round the world, as mate to Captain William Dampier." In John Harris (comp.), *Navigantium atque itinererium bibliotheca . . .*, vol. 1 (pp. 131–50). London: Thomas Bennet.

Gabriel de S. Antonio. 1604. *Relation breve et veridique des evénéments du Royaume du Cambodge.* Trans. by A. S. Pablo de Valladolid and Antoine Cabaton. Paris: Ernest Leroux, 1914.

Gallilei, Galileo. 1635. *Systema cosmicum.* Amsterdam: Elzevioun.

Galvão, António. 1601. *The discovery of the world from their first original unto the yeere of the Lord 1555.* London: G. Bishop.

———. 1625, 1905. "Book of the discovery of the world." In Samuel Purchas (ed.), *Hakluytas posthumus or, Purchas his pilgrimes: Contayning a history of the world in sea voyages and lande travells by Englishmen and others . . . .* Glasgow: Glasgow University Press, 1905–1907.

———. 1971, ca. 1544. *A treatise on the Moluccas.* Ed. and trans. by Hubertus. Rome: F. Jacobs.

Gama, José Basilio da. 1769. *O Uraguai*. Uruguay: N.p.

Garcia, José Manuel. 1994. "Preface." In *Traité de Luis Frois. S.J. (1585) sur les contradictions de moeurs entre Européens & Japonais* (pp. 1–23). Paris: Editions Chandeigne.

Garcia de los Arcos, Maria Fernanda. 1998. "Philippine historical studies in Mexico." *Asia Research Trends*, no. 1: 1–23.

Garnault. 1796. *Kham son Christang*. Bangkok: N.p.

Gaubil, Antoine. 1758. "Memoire sur les iles que les Chinois appellent iles de Lieou-kieou par le Pére Gaubil, missionnaire de la Compagnie de Jesus á Peking." N.p.

Geertz, Clifford. 1981. *Negara: The theater state in 19th century Bali*. Princeton, N.J.: Princeton University Press.

Gerarde, Jean. 1597. *The herball or general historie of plantes*. London: John Norton.

Gervaise, Nicolas. 1688. *Description historique du Royaume de Macaçar*. Paris: Hilaire Foucault.

———. 1688. *Histoire naturelle et politique du Royaume de Siam*. Paris: Claude Barbin.

———. 1989. *The natural and political history of the Kingdom of Siam*. Trans. by John Villiers. Bangkok: White Lotus Press.

Giddens, Anthony. 1991. *The consequences of modernity*. Stanford, Calif.: Stanford University Press.

Giorgi, Antonio Agostino. 1762. *Alphabetum Tibetanum missionum apostolicum commodo editum*. Rome: N.p.

Gobien, Charles Le. 1700. *Histoire des Isles Mariannes nouvellement converties à la religion chrétienne*. Paris: N.p.

[Goes, Benedict.] 1811. *The travels of Benedict Goes, a Portuguese Jesuit from Lahore in the Mongol's empire: Early seventeenth century essays on China, Tibet and Central Asia*. London: Longmans.

Goes, Damião de. 1549. *De bello cambaire ultimo commontan tres*. Louvain: N.p.

Goldsmith, Oliver. 1760–1761. *Citizen of the world; or, letters of a Chinese philosopher, living in London, to his friends in the East*. London: N.p.

Goldstone, Jack A. 1987. "Cultural orthodoxy, risk, and innovation: The divergence of east and west in the early modern world." *Sociological Theory* 5: 119–35.

———. 1991. *Revolution and rebellion in the early modern world*. Berkeley: University of California Press.

———. 2002. "The rise of the West—or not? A revision to socio-economic history." http://sociology.uc.davis.edu/personal/faculty/stgold2.htm.

Golius, Jacob. 1635. *Lexicon Arabico-Latinum*. Leiden: N.p.

Gonçalves, Joachim Alfonso. 1829. *Arte China constante de alphabeto e grammatica comprehendo modelos das differentes composicoens*. Macao: Real Collégio de São José.

———. 1841. *Lexicon magnum Latino Sinicum*. Macao: Real Collégio de São José.

Gonçalves, José Julio. 1968. "A informação nas provincias do Oriente" (Elementos para o seu estudo). *Colóquios sobre as Províncias do Oriente* 2, no. 81: 227–363. Estudos de Ciencias Politicas e Sociaias. Lisbon: Junta de Investigaçoes do Ultramar Centro de Estudos Politicos e Sociais.

Goodman, Grant. 1986. *Japan: The Dutch experience*. London: Athens Press.

Goody, Jack. 1996. *The East in the West*. Cambridge, U.K.: Cambridge University Press.

Gothard, Artus. 1614. *Dialogues in the English and Malaiane languages.* Trans. by Augustine Spalding. London: N.p.

Gouveia, António de. 1611. *Relacam que se tratam as gueras e grandes victorias que alcançar o grande rei de Persia.* Lisbon: Pedro Crasbeek.

———. 1671. *Innocentia victrix sive sententia comitiorum imperij sinici pro innocentia Christiane religionis. Lata juridice per Annum 1669.* Quam cheu, China: N.p.

Gove, Philip Babcock. 1941. *The imaginary voyage in prose fiction: A history of its criticism and a guide for its study, with an annotated check list of 215 imaginary voyages from 1700 to 1800.* New York: Columbia University Press.

Gravius, Daniel. 1661. *Het heylige evangelium Mathheu.* N.p.

Green, John. 1745. *New general collection of voyages and travels.* London: Thomas Astley.

Grelot, Guillaume. 1680. *Relation nouvelle d'un voyage de Constantinople.* Paris: N.p.

Groeneveldt, W. P. 1880. *Historical notes on Indonesia and Malaya, compiled from Chinese sources.* VBG (Jakarta: Bhratara, 1960).

Grotius, Hugo. 1626, 1646. *De jure belli ac pacis libri tres.* Amsterdam: Johan Blaeu.

Grove, Richard. 1996. "Indigenous knowledge and the significance of south-west India for the Portuguese and Dutch constructions of tropical nature." *Modern Asian Studies* 30, no. 1: 121–43.

Gu Wei-ming. 2002. "Cooperation and contradiction: Portugal and the Holy See in the ecclesiastical affairs of China in the 17–18th centuries." *Review of Culture,* no. 2 (International ed.): 90–95.

Guedes, Maria Ana Marques. 1998. "The Portuguese in Burmese Literature." *Review of Culture,* no. 35 (2nd ser.): 215–16.

Guignes, Joseph de. 1759. *Memoires dans lequel on prouve, que les Chinois sont une colonie Egyptienne. Lu dans l'assemblée publique de l'Académie Royale des inscriptions & belles-lettres, le 14 Novembre 1758. Avec un précis de memoirs de M. l'Abbé Berhelmy sur le lettres, Phénisiennes.* Paris: N.p.

———. 1770. *Le Chou King: Un des livres sacres des Chinois.* Paris: M. N. Tilliard.

Guillot, Claude, et al. 1990. *The Sultanate of Banten.* Jakarta: Gramedia.

Gumilev, L. N. 1987. *Searches for an imaginary kingdom: The legend of Prester John.* Cambridge, U.K.: Cambridge University Press.

Gunn, Geoffrey C. 1991. "Anglo-French rivalry over the Spratlys (1930–1937): An aspect of world historical incorporation." In R. D. Hill, N. G. Owen, and E. V. Roberts (eds.), *Fishing in troubled waters* (pp. 262–83). Hong Kong: Hong Kong University, Centre of Asian Studies.

———. 1996a. *Encountering Macau: The rise of a Chinese city-state on the periphery of China, 1557–1999.* Boulder, Colo.: Westview Press.

———. 1996b. "Imagining Nagasaki." *Tonan Ajia Kenkyu-jo* 38: 37–52.

———. 1997. *Language, power, and ideology in Brunei Darussalam.* Southeast Asia series, no. 99. Athens: Ohio University Center for International Studies.

———. 1999a. *Nagasaki in the Asian bullion trade networks.* Monograph 31. Nagasaki: Nagasaki University, Southeast Asian Research Center.

———. 1999b. *Timor Loro Sae: 500 years.* Macau: Livros do Oriente.

———. 2000. *New world hegemony in the Malay world.* Trenton, N.J.: Africa World Press.

———. 2001. "Língua e cultura na construção da identidade de Timor-Leste." *Camões: Revista de letras e culturas lusófonas,* no. 14 (July–September): 14–25.

Gupta, Kanchan. 1999. "Recall the Goa Inquisition to stop the Church from crying foul." www.rediff.com/news/1999/mar16gupta.htm.

Gutiérrez, Fernando G. 1993. "A survey of Nanban art." *Review of Culture*, no. 17 (2nd ser., October–December): 70–102.

Haex, David. 1631. *Dictionarium Malaico-Latinum et Latino-Malaicum.* N.p.

Hagemeijer, Tjerk. 1999. "The Babel islands: Creolization in the Gulf of Guinea." *Camões: Revista e letras de culturas Lusofonas*, no. 6: 74–88.

Hagenaar, Heinrik. 1672. *Anmerkungen Heinrech Hagenars au Franz Carons beschreibung des reichs Japan.* Nuremburg: N.p.

———. 1725. "Voyage de Henry Hagenaar aux Indes Orientales." In R.A. Constantin de Renneville (ed.), *Recueil des voyages qui ont servi al'establissement et au progrez de la Compagnie des Indes Orientales*, vol. 9. Rouen: Pierre Cailloue.

Hager, J. 1801. *Elementary characters of the Chinese.* London: N.p.

Hakluyt, Richard. 1582. *Voyages touching the discovery of America.* London: N.p.

——— (comp.). 1589, 1598, 1599, 1600. *The principall navigations, voyages and discoveries of the English nation . . . within the compasse of these 1500 Yeeres . . .* London: Bishop and Newberie.

———. 1928. *The voyages traffiques & discoveries of foreign voyagers.* Intro. by John Masefield. London: Dent and Sons.

Halbfass, William. 1998. *India and Europe: An essay in understanding.* Albany: State University of New York Press.

Halde, Jean-Baptiste du. 1735. *Description geographique, historique, choronologique, politique . . . de l'empire de la Chine.* 4 vols. Paris: P. G. Le Mercier.

———. 1735, 1734–1743, 1748. *The general history of China containing a geographical, historical, chronological and physical description of the Empire of China, the Chinese Tartary, Corea and Tibet indicating an exact and particular account oftheir customs, manners, relgions, art and sciences. The whole adorn'd with curious maps, and variety of copper plates.* 4 vols. London: John Watts.

———. 1741. *A description of the empire of China.* London: N.p.

Hall, Basil. 1818. *Account of a voyage of discovery to the west coast of Corea and the great Loo-Choo island.* London: John Murray.

Hall, Joseph. 1605. *Mundus alter et idem sive Terra Australis ante hac semper ingocnita longis itinerbus peregrini academici nuperrime lustrata.* Frankfurt: N.p.

Hamashita, Takeshi. 1994. "The tribute trade system and modern Asia." In A. J. H. Latham and Heita Kawakatsu (eds.), *Japanese industrialization and the Asian economy* (pp. 91–107). London: Routledge.

———. 1995. "The future of northeast Asia-Southeast Asia." In Stephen Kotkin and David Wolf (eds.), *Rediscovering Russia in Asia, Siberia and the Russian Far East* (pp. 312–29). New York: M. E. Sharpe.

Hamel, Henrik. 1608. *Journal van de ongeluckige voyage van't jacht de sperwas.* Rotterdam: N.p.

———. 1668; 1670. *Relation du naufrage da vaisseau hollandais, sur la coste d'isles de Quelparte.* Paris: N.p.

———. 1745. "An account of the shipwreck of a Dutch vessel on the coast of the isle of Quelpaert, together with a description of the Kingdom of Corea" (trans. from French). In A. Churchill and J. Churchill (eds.), *A collection of voyages*, vol. 4 (pp. 607–32). London: At the Black Swan in Paternaster Row.

Hamilton, Alexander. 1727. *A new account of the East Indies.* London: John Mosman.

Hanna, Willard, A. 1991. *Indonesian Banda: Colonialism and its aftermath in the nutmeg islands.* Banda Neira, Indonesia: Yayasan Warisan dan Budaya Banda Neira.

———, and Des Alwi. 1990. *Turbulent times past in Ternate and Tidor.* Moluccas, Indonesia: Rumah Budaya Banda Neira.

Harris, John (comp.). 1745 (orig. 1705). *Navigantium atque itinerantium bibliotheca or a complete collection of voyages and travels consisting of above six hunded of the most authentic writers.* 2 vols. London: Thomas Bennet.

Hartshorne, Richard. 1939. *The nature of geography.* Lancaster, Pa.: Association of American Geographers.

Harvey, Paul A. S. 1993. "After Columbus: Englishmen and the non-Europeans, c. 1600." In *Portuguese voyages to Asia and Japan in the Renaissance period* (pp. 57–92). Proceedings of the International Conference, Sophia University, September 24–26, Tokyo.

[Hasan ibn Yaz, Ab Zaid, al-Srfi.] 1718, 1733, 1744. *Ancient accounts of India and China by two Mohamadean travellers, who went to those parts in the 9th century.* London: Harding.

Hennequin, Victoire Antoine. 1849. *Un Chinez em Paris buscando a communuismo.* Coimbra: N.p.

Hermann, Paul. 1717. *Musaeum Zeylanicum.* Leiden: N.p.

Hernandez, Eloisa May P. 2000. "The Spanish colonial tradition in Philippine visual arts." www.ncca.gov.ph/CONTEMPORARY/VISUAL%20ARTS/visual_spanishprint.htm.

Hernandez, Francisco. 1570. *Historia natural de la Nueva Espana.* N.p.

Hernandez, Vicente, S. 1999. "Trends in Philippine library history." Proceedings of 65th IPLA Council and General Conference, August 20–28, Bangkok.

Herrera, Antonio de. 1601–1615. *Historia general del mundo.* Madrid: N.p.

———. 1601. *Descripcian de las Indias Occidentales.* Madrid: N.p.

Heylyn, Peter. 1621. *Mikro'Kosmos: A little description of the great world.* Oxford, U.K.: William Turner.

———. 1652. *Cosmographie in four books: Containing the chorographie and historie of the whole world and all the principal kingdoms, provinces, seas and isles thereof.* London: Henry Seile.

Hezel, Francis X. 1982. "From conversion to conquest: The early Spanish mission in the Marianas." *Journal of Pacific History* 17, no. 3–4: 115–37.

Hill, John. 1759. *Exotic botany illustrated in thirty-five figures.* London: N.p.

Hisakawa, Sukehiro. 1989. "Japan's turn to the west." In *The Cambridge history of Japan*, vol. 5 (pp. 432–87). Cambridge, U.K.: Cambridge University Press.

Ho, Ping-ti. 1955. "The introduction of American food plants into China." *American Anthropologist* 57: 191–201.

Hori, Tatsunosuke. 1862. Eiwa-taiyaku-shuchin-jisho (A pocket dictionary of the English and Japanese language), Edo (Tokyo): Yosho-Shirabedo-koro.

[Houtman, Cornelis.] 1598. *The descrption of a voyage made by certain ships of Holland into the East Indies.* London: John Wolf.

Houtman, Frederik van Goud. 1604. *Spraeeck ende woord-bieck in de Maleyasche ende Madagascarsche talen.* Amsterdam: N.p.

Hsia, Adrian (ed.). 1998. *The vision of China in the English literature of the seventeenth and eighteenth centuries.* Hong Kong: Chinese University Press.

Huang Qichen. 1998. "Macao: A bridge for cultural exchange between China and the West in the sixteenth and seventeenth centuries." *Review of Culture,* no. 21 (2nd ser.): 157–84.

Hull, Geoffrey. 1998. "The languages of Timor 1772–1997: A literature review." In *Studies in languages and cultures of East Timor,* vol. 1 (pp. 1–24). Macarthur, Australia: University of Western Sydney.

Humboldt, Alexander von. 1845–1862. *Kosmos.* 5 vols. Stuttgart: N.p.

Humboldt, Friedrich Wilhelm. 1836–1839. *Uber die Kawi-sprache auf der insel Java.* Berlin: N.p.

Hung, Ho-fung. 2000. "Imperial China and capitalist Europe in the eighteenth-century global economy." *Review,* no. 4: 473–513.

Hussainmiya, B. A. 1990. *Orang rejimen: The Malays of the Ceylon rifle regiment.* Bangi: Penerbit Universiti Kebangsaan Malaysia.

Hymowitz, Theodore. 1990. "Soybeans: The success story." In Jules Janick and James Simon (eds.), *Soybeans: The success story, Advances in new crops* (pp. 139–63). Portland, Ore.: Timber Press.

Ikeda, Satoshi. 1996. "The history of the capitalist world-system vs. the history of East-Southeast Asia," *Review (Fernand Braudel Center)* 19, no. 1 (winter): 49–77.

Inamura Sampaku. 1769. *Haruma wage.* Edo (Tokyo).

Incarville, Pierre Nicholas le Chéron d'. 1772. "Memoire sur le vernis de la Chine." In Jean-Felix Watin, *L'Art de peintre, doreur, vernisseur.* Paris: N.p.

Ishii, Yoneo (ed.). 1998. *The junk trade from Southeast Asia: Translations from the Tôsen Fusetsu-gaki, 1674–1723.* Data Paper series, Sources for the Economic History of Southeast Asia, no. 6. Singapore: Institute of Southeast Asian Studies.

Issar, T. P. 1997. *Goa dourada: The Indo-Portuguese Bouquet.* Bangalore: N.p.

Jacobs, Hubert (ed. and annot.). 1980. *Documenta Malucensia (1542–1577).* Rome: Jesuit Historical Institute.

———. 1988. *The Jesuit Makasar Documents 1615–1682.* Rome: Jesuit Historical Institute.

Jansen, Marius. 1989. "Japan in the early nineteenth century." In *The Cambridge history of Japan,* vol. 5 (pp. 50–111). Cambridge, U.K.: Cambridge University Press.

[Jartoux, Pierre.] 1711. *A letter from Father Jartoux, missioner of the Society of Jesus to F. Procurator General of the Missions of India and China.* Peking: N.p.

Johnson, John [Johannes Jonstonus.] 1650. *Theatrum universale omnimium animalium, placium, avium, qudrupedium . . .* Frankfurt: N.p.

———. 1633, 1652. *Atlas novus.* Amsterdam: N.p.

Johnson, Maurice, Kitagawa Muncharu, and Philip Williams. 1977. *Gulliver's travels and Japan.* Moonlight series, no. 4. Doshisha, Japan: Doshisha University, Amherst House.

Johnson, Samuel. 1739. *The history of Rasseles, Prince of Abyssinia.* N.p.

[Jones, William.] 1799–1807, 1867. *The works of Sir William Jones. With a life of the author, by Lord Teignmouth.* 13 vols. London: Printed for John Stockdale and John Walker.

Kaempfer, Engelbert. 1712. *Amoenitatum exoticarum.* Lemgo, Germany: Meyen.

———. 1727. *The history of Japan.* London: Printed for the translator.

———. 1729. *Histoire naturelle, civile, et ecclésiastique de l'Empire du Japon.* La Haye: Chez P. Grosse & J. Neaulme.

———. 1987. *A description of the Kingdom of Siam.* Trans. by John Scheuchzer, intro. by H. K. Kuly. Bangkok: White Orchid Press.

Kane, Daniel. 2000. "Mapping 'all under heaven': Jesuit cartography in China." www.mercatormap.com/404_jesuit.html.

Kant, Immanuel. 1795. *Perpetual peace: A philosophical sketch.* N.p.

———. 1802, 1882. *Physical geography.* Edition by Rink. N.p.

Kapista, Peter. 1990. *Japan in Europe: Texte und billdokumente zur europaishen Japankenntsis von Marco Polo bis Wilhelm von Humboldr.* Munich: Indicium.

Kartomi, Margaret. 1996. "Portuguese musical imprint of the Malay-Indonesian World." *Review of Culture,* no. 26 (2nd ser.): 25–35.

Kathirithamby-Wells, J., and John Villiers (eds.). 1990. *The Southeast Asian port and polity: Rise and demise.* Singapore: Singapore University Press.

[Khoo, Dionysius.] 1744. "Dionysius Khoo, a native of China . . ." In John Harris (comp.), *Navigantium atque itinererium bibliotheca . . . ,* vol. 2 (pp. 960–70). London: Thomas Bennet.

King, David A. 1999. *World-maps for finding the direction and distance to Mecca.* Leiden: E. J. Brill.

Kircher, A. 1670. *Le Chine illustrée monuments tants sacrées qua profanes.* Amsterdam: N.p.

Kitson, Peter J. 1998. "Romanticism and colonialism: races, places, peoples, 1785–1800." In Tim Fulford and Peter J. Kitson (eds.), *Romantic circles: Romanticism and colonialism.* Cambridge, U.K.: Cambridge University Press.

Knox, Robert. 1681, 1682, 1692. *An historical relation of the island of Ceylon in the East Indies.* London: Robert Chiswell.

Kobata, Atsushi, and Mitsuga Matsuda. 1969. *Ryukuan relations with Korea and South Sea countries: An annotated translation of documents in the Rekidai Hoan.* Kyoto, Japan: Kobata.

Kochhar, R. K. 1991. "Science in British India 1. Colonial tool." *Current Science* 63, no. 11 (December): 689–94.

Koda, Shigetomu. 1939. "Notes sur la presse Jésuite au Japon et plus spécialement sur les livres imprimés an caractères Japonaise." *Monumenta Nipponica* 2: 374–85.

Kopf, David. 1965. *British orientalism and the Bengal renaissance.* Berkeley: University of California Press.

Kraam, Alfons, van der. 2000. "The Dutch in Siam: Jeremias van Vliet and the 1636 incident at Ayutthaya." University of New England Asia Centre Asia Papers, no. 3: 1–14.

Krishna, Bal. 1924. *Commercial relations between India and England (1601 to 1757).* London: George Routledge & Sons.

Kulmus, J. A. 1722, 1759. *Anatomische tabellen.* Leipzig: N.p.

Laborinho, Ana Paula. 1993. "Accounts of travellers to the Far East." *Macau* (Special issue): 141–46.

———. 1994. "The role of language in evangelization strategy." *Macau* (Special issue): 108–14.

Lach, Donald F. 1965. *Asia in the making of Europe, vol. I: The century of discovery.* Books 1 and 2. Chicago: University of Chicago Press.

———. 1969. *Asia in the making of Europe.* Chicago: University of Chicago Press.

———. 1991. *Asia in the eyes of Europe: Sixteenth through eighteenth centuries.* Catalog. Chicago: University of Chicago Library. www.lib.uchicago.edu/e/su/southasia/lach.html.

Laet, Joannes de. 1631. *De imperio Magni Mogolis, sive, India vera comentarius e variis auctoribus congestus.* Amsterdam: Elzervitiana.

Landes, D. S. 1998. *The wealth and poverty of nations: Why some are so rich and some so poor.* New York: W. W. Norton.

Langhenez, Bernardt. 1598. "The description of a voyage made by certain ships of Holland into the East Indies with their adventures and successes: etc." London: Imprinted by John Wolf.

Laufer, Berthold. 1924. *Tobacco and its use in Asia.* Chicago: Field Museum of Natural History.

Laval, François Pyard de. 1615–1616. *Discours du voyage des Français aux Indes Orientales.* Paris: N.p.

Lecomte, Louis. 1696. *Nouveaux memoires sur l'etat present de la Chine.* Paris: N.p.

Legge, John. 1965. *Indonesia.* Englewood Cliffs, N.J.: Prentice Hall.

———. 2000. "The writing of Southeast Asian history." In N. Tarling (ed.), *The Cambridge history of Southeast Asia: From early times c.1500* (pp. 1–52). Cambridge, U.K.: Cambridge University Press.

Legrand, Joachim. 1728. *Voyage historique d'Abissine du R.P. Herome Lobo de la Compagnie de Jesus.* N.p.

Leibniz, Gottfried von. 1697. *Novissima Sinica.* N.p.

Leitão, Humberto. 1948. *Os Portugueses em Solor e Timor de 1515 a 1702.* Lisbon: Livraria Sé de Costa.

Lemos, Jorge de. 1585, 1991. *Historia dos cercos que Achens, & Iaos Puserão a Malaca.* Intro. and notes by João C. Reis. Lisbon: N.p.

Leshock, David, B. 2000. "To conquer our right heritage: The medieval map and travel narratives as constructions of European identity." www.hfni.gsend .gwu.edu/~humsci/inter/leshock.html.

Lessa, Almerindo. 1995. "The population of Macao: Genesis of a mestizo society." *Review of Culture*, no. 23 (2nd ser.): 56–86.

Lethinois, André. 1769. *Avvenimenti memorabili del Principe Baldassare figlio primogenito del Re di Timor e Solor nell isole Molucche esposta a sua naesta Christianissima.* Paris: Knapen.

Levi, Abraham (ed.), and Sandra Breitebach (intro.). 2000. *Francesco Vero's grammar of the Mandarin language.* Amsterdam: John Benjamins Publishing Co.

Li Tana. 1998. *Nguyen Cochinchina: Southern Vietnam in the seventeenth and eighteenth centuries.* Ithaca, N.Y.: Cornell University, Southeast Asia Program Publications.

Lieberman, Victor. 1990. "Wallerstein's system and the international context of early modern Southeast Asian history." *Journal of Asian Studies* 24, no. 1: 70–90.

———. 1993. "Was the seventeenth century a watershed in Burmese history?" In A. Reid (ed.), *Southeast Asia in the early modern period: Trade, power and belief* (pp. 214–49). Ithaca, N.Y.: Cornell University Press.

———. 1995. "An age of commerce in Southeast Asia? Problems of regional coherence—A review article." *Journal of Asian Studies* 54, no. 3 (August): 796–807.

Linnaeus, Carl. 1735. *Fundamenta botanica.* Uppsala: N.p.

———. 1738. *Classes plantarum.* Uppsala: N.p.

———. 1753. *Species plantarum.* Uppsala: N.p.

Linschoten, Jan Huygen van. 1596. *Itinerario, voyage ofte schipvaert naer oost ofte Portugaels Indien inhoudende een corte beschryvinghe der selver landen ende zee-custen.* Amsterdam: Cornelis Claesz.

———. 1558. *John Huighen van Linschoten: His discovers of voyages into ye Easte and West Indies.* Trans. by John Wolfe. London: N.p.

———. 1583, 1905. "John Huighen van Linschoten, his voyage to Goa and observation of the East Indies (abbreviated)." In Samuel Purchas (ed.), *Hakluytas posthumus or, Purchas his pilgrimes: Contayning a history of the world in sea voyages and lande travells by Englishmen and others . . .,* vol. 10 (pp. 303–18). Glasgow: Glasgow University Press, 1905–1907.

Liu Dun. 1998. "Western knowledge of geography reflected in Juan Cobo's *Shilu,* 1593." Paper presented at the Conference on History of Mathematics: Portugal and the East II, October 10–12, Macau. www.ihns.ac.cn/members/liu/doc/cobo.htm.

Lizares, Adrian V. 2000. "Garden rises from history's ruins." *Philippine Daily Enquirer,* March 10.

Lobato, Manuel. 1999. *Politica e comércio dos Portugueses na insulindia: Malaca e as Molucas de 1575 a 1605.* Macau: Instituto Português do Oriente.

Locke, John. 1690. *Essay concerning human understanding.* London: N.p.

Lodewycksz, Willem. 1558. "D'eerste Boeck: Histoire van Indien vaer inne verhaelt is de avontueren die de Hollandtsche schepen bejeghent zijn." In G. P. Rouffaer and J. W. Ijzerman (eds.), *De eerste schipvaart der Nederlanders naar Oost-Indië onder Cornelis de Houtman 1595–1597.* 3 vols. (The Hague: Martinus Nijhoff 1915–1929).

Lombard, Denys. 1967. *Le Sultanat d'Atjeh au temps d'Iskandar Muda, 1607–1636.* Paris: EFEO.

———. 1970. *"Le Spraek ende woord-boek" de Frederick de Houtman.* Paris: EFEO.

———. 1990. *Le carrefour javanais.* 3 vols. Paris: Editions de l'EHESS.

———. 1996. *Augustin de Beaulieu . . . Memoires d'un voyage aux Indes Orientales, 1619–1622: Un marchand Normand à Sumatra.* Paris: EFFEO.

———. 1997. "Comment on Sakurai's paper." In *Proceedings of the International Symposium Southeast Asia: Global Area Studies for the 21st Century* (pp. 125–27). Kyoto: Kyoto University, Center for Southeast Asian Studies.

———, and Jean Aubin (eds.). 2000. *Asian merchants and businessmen in the Indian Ocean and the China seas.* Chenai: Oxford University Press.

London, Jack. 1915. *The jacket (star rover).* New York: Grosset & Dunlap.

Lopes, David. 1969. *Expansão da lingua Portuguesa no Oriente nos séculos XVI, XVII e XVIII.* 2 vols. Porto: Portucalense Editora.

Lord, Henry. 1704. "A display of two foreign sects in the East Indies, 1630." In A. Churchill and J. Churchill (eds.), *A Collection of voyages and travels,* vol. 6, pt. 8 (pp. 328–42). London: At the Black Swan in Paternaster Row.

Loubère, Simon de la. 1691, 1986. *Du Royaume de Siam.* 2 vols. Paris: Coignard.

Loureiro, Juan de. 1790. *Flora Cochinchinesis sistems plantas in regno Cochinchina nascentes, quibis accedunt aliae oservatae in Sinensi imperio, Africa orientali, Indiaeque, locus variius. Omnes disposiate secudrum Systema Sexulae Linnaeanum.* Lisbon: N.p.

Loureiro, Rui Manuel. 1996. *O manuscrito de Lisboa da "Suma Oriental" de Tomé Pires.* Macau: Instituto Português do Oriente.

———. 1997. "European books and libraries in sixteenth century Portuguese India." *Review of Culture*, no. 31 (2nd ser.): 17–30.

Lourido, Rui d'Avila. 1994. "A Portuguese seventeenth century map of the south China coast." *Santa Barbara Portuguese Studies* 1: 240–71.

Love, Ronald S. 1996. "Rituals of majesty: France, Siam, and court spectacle in royal image-building at Versailles in 1685 and 1686." *Canadian Journal of History/Annales Canadiennes d'Histoire* 31 (August): 171–98.

Lucas, Henry. 1934, 1960. *The Renaissance and the Reformation*. New York: Harper & Row.

Lumbera, Bienvenido. 1968. "Tagalog poetry during the seventeenth century." *Philippine Studies*, no. 16: 99–130.

Lundolph, Job. 1698. *Grammatica lingua Amharicae*. Frankfurt: N.p.

Lutz, Walter (ed.). 1994. *Japan, a cartographic vision: European printed maps from the early 16th–19th century*. Munich: Prestel.

Lynch, Jack. 1999. "Orientalism as performance art: The strange case of George Psalamanazar." Paper presented at the SUNY Seminar on Eighteenth-Century Literature, January 29. http://andromeda.rutgers.edu~jlynch/Papers/psalm.html.

[Ma Huan.] 1433, 1997. *Ying-yai sheng-lan/The overall survey of the ocean's shores.* Notes by J. V. J. Mills. Bangkok: White Lotus Press.

Mackerras, Colin. 1975. *The Chinese theatre in modern times: From 1840 to the present day.* London: Thames & Hudson.

———. 1989. *Western images of China*. Hong Kong: Oxford University Press.

Magahaes (Magalhaes), J. Gabriel de. 1688, 1997. *A nova relação da China*. Macau: Fundacão Macau.

———. 1688. *A new history of China*. Trans. by John Ogilby. London: N.p.

Mailla, Joseph Anne Marie Moyriac de. 1777. *Histoire general de la Chine, ou Annales de cet empire . . .* Paris: N.p.

Mandeville, John. 1480, 1481. *Itineranium*. Milan: Pietro de Cornero.

———. 1499. *The voyage and travaile of Syr Iohn Maundevile knight*. London: Wynkyn de Worde.

Manguin, Pierre-Yves. 1972. *Les Portugais sur les côtes du Vietnam et du Champa.* Paris: Adrien Maisonneuve, Publications de l'Ecole Française de Extrême-Orient.

[Marco Polo.] 1922. *O livro de Marco Polo, O livro de Nicolao Veneto por Pegio Florentim e carta de Jeronimo de Santo Estevam, conforme a impressão de Valentim Fernandes, feita em Lisboa em 1502*. Fasc. Lisbon.

Marini, Gio Filippo de. 1665. *Historia et relatione del Tunchino e del Gaippone con la vera relatione ancora d'Altri Regni, e provincie di quelle regioni, e del loro governo politico*. Rome: N.p.

———. 1996. *A new and interesting description of the Lao Kingdom (1642–1648)*. Bangkok: White Lotus Press.

Marks, Robert B. 1998. *Tigers, rice, silk and silt: Environment and economy in late imperial south China*. Cambridge, U.K.: Cambridge University Press.

———. 2002. *The origins of the modern world: A global and ecological narrative*. Lanham, Md.: Rowman & Littlefield.

Marques, Mário Gomes, and John Cule (eds.). 1991. *The great maritime discoveries and world health*. Proceedings of the First International Congress on the Great Maritime Discoveries and World Health, September 10–13, 1990, Lisbon.

Marr, David. 1971. *Vietnamese anticolonialism 1885–1925.* Berkeley: University of California Press.

——. 2000. "From history and memory in Vietnam today: The journal Xua & Nay." *Journal of Southeast Asian Studies* 31, no. 1 (March): 1–25.

Marsden, William. 1783. *The history of Sumatra.* London: N.p.

——. 1812. *A grammar of the Malayan language with an introduction and praxis.* London: Printed for the author by Cox and Baylis.

Martini, Martinus. 1654. *De bello tartarico historia.* Rome: N.p.

——. 1655. *Novus atlas sinensis.* Amsterdam: N.p.

——, and Alvaro Semedo. 1667. *Historie universelle de la Chine.* Lyon: N.p.

Martyr, Peter. 1504. *Mondo nuovo.* Venice: N.p.

Mason, George Henry. 1800. *The costume of China.* London: N.p.

——. 1604. *The punishments of China illustrated with twenty-two drawings.* London: Printed for William Miller by William Bulmer and Co.

Massie, M. 1894. *Dictionnaire Latien.* Paris: N.p.

Matelief, Cornellis. 1608. *Historical (An) and true discourse of a voyage made by Admiral Cornellis Matelief the younger into the East Indies, who departed out of Holland in May 1665. With the besieging of Malacca and the battaile by him fought at sea against the Portugues in the Indies with other discoveries.* London: William Harrett.

Mathiassen, Charlotte. 1996. "Mythos Tibet." *Nordic Newsletter of Asian Studies* 2 http://130.225.203.37/articles/issues/1996/2/mythos.

Matos, Manuel Cadafaz (intro.). 1988 (orig. 1588). *Ioanne Bonafacius, Christiani pueri instituti.* Macau: Instituto Cultural de Macau.

Mattoso, José. 2001. "Sobre a identidade de Timor Lorosa'e." *Camões: Revista de letras e culturas lusófonas,* no. 14 (July–September): 6-15.

Maverick, Lewis A. 1941. "Pierre Poivre: Eighteenth century explorer of Southeast Asia." *Pacific Historical Review* 10, no. 2 (June): 165–77.

Mayanagi, Makoto. 2002. "The import and reprinting of Chinese medical books during the Edo period." www.hum.ibaraki.ac.jp./hum/chumbun/mayanagi/paper02netherlandsEng.htm.

Maxmillian of Transylvania. 1523. *De Moluccis insulis.* Cologne: Cervicornus.

McCune, George M. 1946. "The exchange of envoys between Korea and Japan during the Tokugawa period." *Far Eastern Quarterly* 5, no. 3 (May): 308–25.

McIntyre, Kenneth Gordon. 1987, 1989. *The secret discovery of Australia.* Sydney: Pan.

Medhurst, Henry. 1830. *English and Japanese and Japanese and English vocabulary.* Batavia: N.p.

Meilink-Roelofz, M. A. P. 1962. *Asian trade and European influence in the Indonesian archipelago between 1500 and about 1630.* The Hague: Nijhoff.

Meletius, Joseph. 1562. *Geographia.* Venice: Willibald Pirckheimer.

Mendoza, Juan Gonzalez de. 1585. *Historia de la cosas mas notable, ritos y costumres del gran reyno de la China.* Rome: Vincencio Accotti.

——. 1586. *Dell' historia dell China.* Trans. by F. Auanzo. N.p.

——. 1853–1854. *The historie of the great and mightie kingdom of China and the situation there of: Together with the great riches, huge cities, politike government and rare inventions of the same.* 1st ser., pt. 1. London: Hakluyt Society. (Republication of first English translation by R. Park, 1588. N.p.)

Meuden, W. J., van de. 1974. "Suvaranadvipa and the Chryse Chersonesos." *Indonesia*, no. 18, (1974): 1–40.

———. 1975. "Ptolemy's geography on mainland South-East Asia and Borneo." *Indonesia*, no. 19 (April): 1–32.

Meurs, Jacob de. 1680. *Ambassades memorables de la Compagnie des Indes Orientales des Provinces Unies*. Amsterdam: N.p.

Michel, Wolfgang. 1993. "Japanese place-names on old Western maps." In Walter Lunz (ed.), *Japan: A cartographic vision*. Munich: Prestel-Verlag.

———. 2000a. "His story of Japan—Engelbert Kaempfer's manuscript in a new translation: Review article." *Monumena Nipponica* 55, no. 1 (spring): 109–20.

———. 2000b. "Inner landscapes—Japan's reception of Western conceptions of the body." www.jsps-club.de/pages/Treffen1999.html.

———. 2000c. "Travels of the Dutch East India Company in the Japanese archipelago." www.rc.kyushu-u.ac.jp/~michel/publ/books/04/04aenglish.html.

Miles, John. 1684. *A true relation of ther great victory, obtained by the King of the Abissines called Prester John, against the Turks: Taking the flourishing city of Habalee, and destroying 10,000 Ottomans*. London: Printed by C. Groom.

Milton, Giles. 1999. *Nathaniel's nutmeg: How one man's courage changed the course of history*. London: Hodder & Straughton.

Mimoso, João Sardinha. 1620. *Relacion de la real tragicomedia con que los Padres de la Compania de Jesus en su Colegio de S. Anton. de Lisboa recibieron a la Magestad Catolica de Felipe II de Portugal . . .* Lisbon: Jorge Rodriguez.

Miranda, Rocky V. 1985. "Diogo Ribeiro's 'Vocabulario de Lingoa Canarim' and its historical significance." In R. Teotonio de Souza (ed.), *Indo-Portuguese history. Old issues, new questions* (pp. 196–202). New Delhi: Concept.

Mo, Timothy. 1978. *Monkey king*. New York: William Morrow and Co.

[Mocquet, Jean.] 1996. *Voyage à Mozambique & Goa: La relation de Jean Mocquet (1607–1610)*. Preface by Dejanirah Couto, annot. by Xavier de Castro. Paris: Editions Chandeigne.

Molina, Alonso de. 1571. *Vocabulario en lengua castellana y mexicana*. Mexico: Antonio de Spinola.

Moll, Herman. 1715–1754. *The World described*. London: Bowler.

———. 1717. *Atlas geographicus*. London: N.p.

Monardes, Nicholas. 1565. *Dos libros el uno trata de todas las cosas q trae de nras Indias Occidentales*. N.p.

Montague, Mary Wortley. 1763. *Letters of the Right Honourable Lady Mary Wortley Montague*. London: N.p.

Montanus, Arnoldus. 1680. *Atlas Japannesis being remarkable addresses by way of Embassy for the East India Company of the United Provinces to the Emperor of Japan containing a description of their several territories, cities, temples and fortresses, their religious laws, and customs, their prodigous wealth and gorgeous habits, the nature of the soil, plants, beasts, hills, rivers and fountains with the character of ancient and modern Japan*. Trans. by John Ogilby. London: N.p.

———. 1671. *Atlas Chinesis*. London: T. Johnson.

Monteiro, João Pedro. 1994. *A influéncia Oriental na ceramica Portuguesa do seculo XVII/Oriental influence on 17th century Portuguese ceramics*. Lisbon: Museu Nacional do Azulejo.

Montesquieu, Charles de Secondat. 1721. *Les lettres d'un Persan.* Paris: N.p.
———. 1748. *De l'esprit des loix.* Paris: N.p.
More, Thomas. 1516. *Utopia.* N.p.
Morejon, Pedro. 1619. *A briefe relation of the persecution lately made against the catholike Christians in the Kingdom of Japonia.* Saint-Omer: English Jesuit College.
———. 1621. *Historia y relacion de los svedido en los Reinos De Japon y China . . .* Lisbon: Juan Rodriques.
Morga, Antonio de. 1609a. *History of the Philippine islands: From their discovery by Magellan in 1521 to the beginning of the XVII century.* Mexico: N.p. (Separate publication from E. H. Blair and J. A. Robertson, *The Philippine islands, 1493–1898* [Cleveland, Oh.: Arthur H. Clark Co., 1907])
———. 1609b. *Sucecas de las islas Filipinas dirigida a don Christoval Govez de Sandoval.* Mexico: N.p.
Morris, Peter. 2002. "Introduction to human geography: The ecological perspective: Understanding human-environment relations." http://homepage.smc.edu/morris_pete/human/hg02c.html.
Morrison, Robert. 1815–1823. *Dictionary of the Chinese language.* Macao: East India Company Press by P. P. Thoms.
———. 1823a. *A grammar of the English language: For the use of the Anglo-Chinese College.* Macao: East India Company Press.
———. 1823b. *The Holy Bible.* 23 vols. Malacca: Anglo-Chinese College.
———. 1828. *Vocabulary of the Canton dialect.* Macao: East India Company Press by G. J. Steyn.
Moseley, C. W. D. (trans. and intro.). 1993. *The travels of Sir John Mandeville.* London: Penguin.
Mosely, Benjamin. 1800. *A treatise on sugar with miscellaneous medical observations.* 2nd ed. London: John Nicholls.
Moura, Jean. 1878. *Vocabulaire français-cambodgien et cambodgien-français.* Paris: N.p.
Mousinho, Manuel de Abreu. 1990. *Breve discurso em que se conta a conquista do Reino do Pegu na Índia Oriental . . . no ano 1600.* Intro. by Maria Paula Caetano. Portugal: Publicações Europa-America.
Mueller, Max. 1862. *Lectures on the science of language.* New York: N.p.
Mundy, Peter. 1919. *The travels of Peter Mundy, in Europe and Asia, 1608–1667 (Part I) Travels in England, Western India, Achin, Macao, and the Canton River, 1634–1637.* Hakluyt XLV, 2nd ser. London: Hakluyt Society.
———. 1942. *Macau na epoca da restauração (Macao three hundred years ago).* Macau: Imprensa Nacional.
Mungello, D. E. 1999. *The great encounter of China and the West, 1500–1800.* Lanham, Md.: Rowman & Littlefield.
Munster, Sebastian. 1544. *Cosmographia.* Basel: N.p.
Nakamura, H. 1939. "Les cartes du Japon qui servaient de modèle aux cartographes européens au debut des relations de l'Occident avec le Japon." *Monumenta Nipponica* 2: 100–23.
Navarette, Dominic Fernandez. 1732. "An account of the empire of China, historical, political, moral and religious, written in Spanish by the R.F.F. Dominic Fernandez Navarette." In A. Churchill and J. Churchill (eds.), *A Collection of voyages and travels,* vol. 1 (pp. 1–380). London: At the Black Swan in Paternaster Row.
Nebrija, António de. 1492. *Grammatica Castillana.* Madrid: N.p.

Needham, Joseph. 1954. *Science and civilization in China: Vol. I. Introductory orientations.* Cambridge, U.K.: Cambridge University Press.

———, with Wang Ling. 1959, 1972. *Science and civilization in China. Vol. 3: Mathematics and the sciences of the heaven and earth.* Cambridge, U.K.: Cambridge University Press.

Neek, Jacob Cornelis van. 1663. *Journael van de tweede reys gedaen by den heer admirael Jacob van Neck, naer Oost-Indien, met ses scheepen in den jare 1600* . . . Amsterdam: G. J. Saeghman.

Neves, Jaime Ramolhete. 1994. "The Portuguese in the Im-Jim War?" *Review of Culture,* no. 18 (2nd ed., January/March): 20–27.

Ngai, Gary M. C. 2000. "Macau: An ideal base to develop Sino-Latin ties." Paper presented at the World Conference on Globalization and Latin Humanism, May 1–3, New York.

Nguyen Van Hoan. 1993. "Hoi An—Vietnam's centre for cultural contacts with the world in the 17th century." In *Ancient town of Hoi An* (pp. 176–83). Hanoi: Gio Publishers.

Nicholl, Robert (ed.). 1975. *European sources for the history of the sultanate of Brunei in the sixteenth century.* Bandar Seri Begawan, Brunei: Muzium Brunei.

———. 1986. "A note on the Velarde map." *Brunei Museum Journal* 6, no. 2: 72–82.

Nieuhoff, Johannes. 1665. *L'ambassade de la Compagnie Orientale vers l'empereur de la Chine.* Leiden: J. de Meurs.

———. 1669. *An embassy from the East India Company of the United Provinces, to the Great Tartar Cham, Emperor of China.* London: John Macock.

———. 1745. "Voyages and travels into Brasil and the East Indies." In A. Churchill and J. Churchill (eds.), *A Collection of voyages and travels,* vol. 2 (pp. 1–329). London: At the Black Swan in Paternaster Row.

———, and Arnold Nieuhoff. 1669–1671. *An embassy from the East India Company of the United Provinces to the great Tartar Cham, Emperor of China.* London: John Macock.

Nolte, Henry N. 1999. *Indian botanic drawings, 1793–1868.* Edinburgh: Royal Botanical Garden.

[Noort, Oliver van.] 1745. "The voyage of Oliver van Noort." In John Harris (comp.), *Navigantium atque itinerantium bibliotheca,* vol. 1 (pp. 29–32). London: Thomas Bennet.

Nuñez, Estuardo. 1980. "Heullas e influencias de Oriente en la cultura peruana de los Siglos XVI y XVII." In Ernesto de la Torre Villar (ed.), *La expansion hispanoamericana en Asia: Siglos XVI y XVII* (pp. 149–302). Mexico: FCE.

Obregón, Gonzalo. 1964. "Influencia y contrainfluencia del arte oriental en la Neuva España." *Historia Mexicana* 14: 191–302.

Ocampo, Ambeth R. 1999. "Jesuit charted 1st accurate RP map." *Philippine Daily Enquirer,* November 2.

Odoroco, de Pordenone. 1771. *Elogio storico alle gerta del beato Odorico con la storia da lui dettata de suoi viagggi Asiatica.* Venice: Antonio Zatta.

Oliveira, Fernão de. 1536. *Grammatica da lingogem Portuguesa.* Lisbon: Germão Galharde.

Oliveira, Isócrates. 1975. *Itinerário de Camões no Extremo Oriente.* Lisbon: *Boletim da Sociedade de Geografia,* 71–89.

O'Neill, Brian Juan. 2002. "Multiple identities among the Malacca Portuguese." *Review of Culture,* no. 4 (International ed., October): 81–105.

Orazio de la Pena, Francesco. 1742. *Relacion del Reyno del Gran Tibet.* Rome: Mesnier.

Orta, Garcia da. 1563, 1903. *Colóquios dos simples, e drogas he cousas mediçinais da India e assi dalgûas frutas achadas nella, onde se tratam algûas cousas tocantes amediçina pratica e otras cousas boas, pera saber.* Goa: Quinquêncio e Endem.

Ortelius, Abraham. 1570. *Theatrum orbis terrarum.* N.p.

Osorio, Geronimo. 1581. *Histoire de Portugal.* Paris: N.p.

Palafox y Mendoza, Juan de. 1670. *Histoire de la conqueste de la Chine par les Tartars/Historia de la conquista de la China por el tartaro.* Paris: Antonio Bertier.

———. 1723. *Histoire de la conqueste de la Chine.* Amsterdam: N.p.

Pairenin, Dominique. N.d. *Ki ho youen pe.* N.p.

Pallegoix, D. J. B. 1850. *Dictionarium Latinum Thai.* Bangkok: Typographic Press, College Assumption.

———. 1854. *Dictionarium linguage Thai sive Siamensis interpretatione Latina, Gallica et Anglica.* Paris: N.p.

Panduro, Lorenzo Hervás y. 1800–1818. *Catalogo de las lenguas de las naciones conocidas, y numeracion, division, y clases d estas segun la diversidad de sus idiomas y dialectos . . .* Madrid: N.p.

Papillon, Thomas. 1680. *A treatise concerning the East India trade: Being a most profitable trade to the Kingdom and best secured and improved by a company and a jointstock.* London: N.p.

Paz, Ramiro V. 1999. *Dominio Amazónico.* Bolivia: Plural Editores.

Penzer, N. M (ed.). 1926. *George Psalamaazaar, an historical and geographical description of Formosa,* vol. 2. London: The Library of Impostors.

Piccolomini, Aeneas Aykviis. 1509. *Cosmographia pii Papae in Asiae et Europae eleganti descriptione.* Paris: N.p.

Pietsch, Theodore W. (ed.). 1995. *Fishes, crayfishes and crabs: Louis Renard's natural history of the rarest curiosities of the Indies.* Baltimore: The John Hopkins University Press.

———. 2000. "Commentary, *Poissons, ecrevisses et crabes.*" www.octavo.com/aboutthebooks/rndpss/index.html

[Pigafetta, Antonio.] 1969a. *Magellan's voyage: A narrative account of the first circumnavigation.* New Haven, Conn.: Yale University Press.

———. 1969b. *The voyage of Magellan, The journal of Antonio Pigafetta.* Engelwood Cliffs, N.J.: Prentice Hall. (Fasc. *Le voyage et navigation faict par les espignolz es isles Mollucques* [Paris: N.p., 1525].)

———. 1975. In Robert Nicholl (ed.), *European sources for the history of the Sultanate of Brunei in the sixteenth century.* Bandar Seri Begawan, Brunei: Muzium Brunei.

Pinpin, Thomas. 1610. *Librong pagaaralan nang manga Tagalog nang Uicang Castila.* Bataan, Philippines: N.p.

Pinto, Fernão Mendes. 1614. *Peregrinação de Fernam Mendez Pinto.* Lisbon: Pedro Crasbeck.

———. 1692. *The voyages and adventures of Ferdinand Mendez Pinto: A Portugal: During his travels for the space of one and twenty years in the Kingdoms of Ethiopia, China, Tartaria, Cauchinchina, Calammham, Siam, Pegu, Japan, and a great part of the East-Indies.* London: H. C. Gent.

———. 1989. *The travels of Mendes Pinto.* Ed. and trans. by Rebecca D. Catz. Chicago: University of Chicago Press.

Pires, Benjamin Videre. 1998. "Mutual influences between Portugal and China." *Review of Culture*, no. 6 (July–September): 76–83.

[Pires, Tomé.] 1944. *The suma oriental of Tomé Pires: An account of the East from the Red Sea to Japan, written in Malacxca and India in 1512–1515.* 2 vols. Ed. and trans. by Armando Cortesão. London: N.p.

Piso, Willem. 1658. *De Indiae utrius re naturali et medica.* Amsterdam: N.p.

Plutschow, Herbert E. 1991. *Historical Nagasaki.* Tokyo: Japan Times.

Poivre, Pierre. 1797. *Oeuvre complêtes.* Paris: N.p.

Polo, Marco. 1447, 1483. *Divisament du monde.* Gouda: N.p.

———. 1579. *The most nobel and famous travels of Marcus Paulus, one of the nobilitie of the state of Venice into the east partes of the world.* London: Ralph Nevvbery.

Pomeranz, Kenneth. 2000. *The great divergence: China, Europe, and the making of the modern world economy.* Princeton, N.J.: Princeton University Press.

Prevost, A. F. 1746–1770. *Histoire générale des voyages.* Paris: N.p.

Priolkar, A. K. 1961. *The terrible tribunal for the East: The Goa Inquisition.* New Delhi: Voice of India.

Prolova, L. 2000. "Siberia mapping: Exhibition." National Library of Russia. www.nfr.8101/eng/exib/siberia/sib009.htm.

Psalmanazar, George. 1704. *An historical and geographical description of Formosa, an island subject to the emperor of Japan.* London: N.p.

———. 1764. *Memoirs of commonly known by the name of George Psalmanzar, a reputed native of Formosa, written by himself, in order to be published after his death.* London: N.p.

Ptolemy. 1477, 1478, 1490, 1548, 1562. *Geographia.* Rome: Arnold Buckinck.

[Ptolemy] Claudii Ptholomei Alexandrini. 1478. *Cosmographia.* Rome: Arnold Buckinck.

Purchas, Samuel (ed.). 1905–1907. *Hakluytas posthumus or, Purchas his pilgrimes: Contayning a history of the world in sea voyages and lande travells by Englishmen and others . . .* Five books, 1625–1626; 20 vols. Glasgow: Glasgow University Press.

[Pyrard de Laval, Francois.] 1887–1890. *The voyage of Francois Pyrard of Laval to the East Indies. The Maldives, the Molucas and Brazil.* London: N.p.

Quan Zhongshu. 1998. "China in the English literature of the eighteenth century." In Adrian Hsia (ed.), *The vision of China in the English literature of the seventeenth and eighteenth centuries.* Hong Kong: Chinese University of Hong Kong Press.

Quesnay, François. 1767. *Le despotisme de la Chine.* Paris: N.p.

Quincey, Thomas de. 1822. *Confessions of an English opium-eater.* London: Printed for Taylor & Hessey.

[Quiroga de San Antonio, Gabriel.] 1914 (orig. 1604). Antoine Cabaton, *Brève et véridique relation des evénéments du Cambodge.* Paris: Ernest Leroux.

Rafael, Vincente L. 1993. *Contracting colonialism: Translation and Christian conversion in Tagalog society under early Spanish rule.* Durham, N.C.: Duke University Press.

Ramada Curto, Diogo. 1997. "Representations of Goa: Descriptions and travel accounts." In *Stories of Goa* (pp. 45–85). Lisbon: National Museum of Ethnology.

Ramusio, Giovanni Battista. 1550–1559. *Delle navegationi et viaggi.* 3 vols. Venice: N.p.

Rangel, Miguel. 1635. *Relaçam das Chrisrandades e ilhas de Solor, etc.* Lisbon: Lourenço Cresbeck.

Raynal (Raignal), Guillaume Thomas. 1770, 1780. *Histoire philosophique et politique des establissemens et du commerce des Européens dans les deux Indes.* Paris: N.p.

———. 1776. *Philosophical and political history of the settlements and trade of the Europeans in the East and West Indies*, vol. 1. Trans. by J. Justamond. Dublin: N.p.

Rebello, Gabriel. 1561. *Historias das Molucas*. N.p.

Reid, Anthony. 1988. *Southeast Asia in the age of commerce 1450–1680*. New Haven, Conn.: Yale University Press.

———. 1993. (ed.) *Southeast Asia in the early modern era, trade, power, and belief*. Ithaca, N.Y.: Cornell University Press.

———. 2000. *Charting the shape of early Modern Southeast Asia*. Singapore: Institute of Southeast Asian Studies.

———, and Lance Castles. 1975. *Pre-colonial state systems in Southeast Asia*. Monograph 6. Kuala Lumpur: Malaysian Branch of the Royal Asiatic Society.

———, and Takeshi Ito. 1999. "A precious Dutch map of Aceh, c. 1645." *Archipel* 57: 191–208.

Reinhartz, Dennis. 1997. *The cartographer and the literati: Herman Moll and his intellectual circle*. Lewiston, Me.: Edwin Mellen Press.

———. 2000. "Geography, literature, and empire: Herman Moll, his maps, and his friends." www.mercatormap.com/402_cart.html.

Reitinger, Franz. 2000. "Discovering the moral world: Early forms of map allegory." www.mercatormap.com/404_moral.html.

Rémusat, Jean-Pierre Abel. 1816. *Elements de la grammaire Chinois*. Paris: N.p.

Renard, Louis. 1719. *Poissons, ecrevisses et crabes, et diverses couleurs et figures extraordinaires, que l'on trouve autour des Isles Moluques, et sur les côtes des terres Australes*. Amsterdam: N.p.

———. 1995. *Fishes, crayfishes, and crabs: Louis Renard's natural history of the rarest curiosities of the seas of the Indies*. Intro. by Theodore W. Pietsch. Baltimore: The Johns Hopkins University Press.

Renneville, R. A. de Constantin. 1702–1706, 1725. *Recueil des voyages qui ont servi à l'etablissment et aux progres de la Compagnie des Indes Orientales*. 5 vols. Amsterdam: N.p.

Reynolds, Frank E. 1978. "Buddhism as universal religion and as civic religion: Some observations on a recent tour of Buddhist centers in central Thailand." In Bardwell L. Smith (ed.), *Religion and legitimation of power in Thailand, Laos, and Burma* (pp. 194–203). Chambersburg, Pa.: Anima Books.

Rhodes, Alexandre de. 1631. *Dictionarium Annamiticum Lusitanum et Latinum*. Rome: N.p.

———. 1650. *Relazione de' felici successi della Sante Fede nel Regno di Tunchino*. N.p.

———. 1651 (orig. 1630). *Histoire du royaume de Tunquin er des grands progrez que la prediction*. Lyons: Devenet.

———. 1652. *Relation des progres de la Foy au Royaume de la Cochinchine*. N.p.

———. 1854. *Voyages et missions du Pere Alexandre de Rhodes de la Compagnie de Jesus en la Chine et autres royaumes de l'orient*. Paris: Julien.

Ribeiro, Diogo. 1973. *Vocabulario da lingoa Canarina com versam Portugueza*. Lisbon: N.p.

[Ribeiro, João.] 1836. *Fatalidade histórica da ilha de Celão*. In Collecção Noticias para a Historia e Geographia das Nações Ultramarinos, Academia Real das Sciencias de Lisboa. Lisbon: N.p.

———. 1909. *The historic tragedy of the island of Ceilão*. Colombo: N.p.

Ricaut, Pierre. 1670. *Histoire de l'état present de l'empire Ottoman.* Paris: N.p.

Ricci, Matteo. 1621. *Istoria de la Chine á cristiana empresa hecha en ella por la Compania de Jesus.* Seville: Veirarano.

Richard, J. 1778. *Histoire naturelle, civile et politique du Tunquin.* Paris: Chez Moutard.

Richardson, John. 1806–1810, 1877–1880. *A dictionary, Persian, Arabic and English . . . A new edition . . .* 2 vols. London: Charles Wilkins, William Bulmer & Co.

Riddell, Peter. 2001. *Islam and the Malay-Indonesian world: Transmission and response.* Singapore: Horizon Books.

Ritter, Carl. 1817. *Die erdkunde.* N.p.

Rizal, José. 1886. *Noli me tangere.* Berlin: N.p.

Rodrigues, Francisco. ca. 1513. *Livro da geographia oriental.* Manuscript.

Rodrigues, João. 1604. *Arte da lingoa de Japão composto pello Padre João Rodriguez Portugues de Companhia de Jesu.* Japan: N.p.

———. ca. 1605. *Vocabulario de Japon declarado.* Manila: Tomas Pinpin.

———. 1615, 1624. *Arte breve da lingoa Japoa de arte grande da mesma lingua.* Macau: N.p.

———. 1620. *Historia da igreja do Japão.* N.p. (Macau, 1954–55).

Rodrigues, Luis. 1540. *Verdadeira informacão das terras do Preste João.* Lisbon: N.p.

Roger, Abraham. 1651. *De open deure tot het verborgen Heydendom.* Leiden: N.p.

[Rogers, Woodes, and Stephen Courtney.] 1745. "The voyage of Captain Woodes Rogers in the *Duke* and Captain Stephen Courtney in the *Duchess*, round the world." In John Harris (comp.), *Navigantium atque itinerantium bibliotheca,* vol. 1 (sec. 16). London: Thomas Bennet.

[Roggewain.] 1745. "An account of Commodore Roggewain's expedition, with three ships for the discovery of southern lands, under the direction of the Dutch West India Company from an original manuscript." In John Harris (comp.), *Navigantium atque itinerantium bibliotheca,* vol. 1 (pp. 281–305). London: Thomas Bennet.

Romain, Pierre Martiny. 1666. *Relation nouvelle et curieuse des royaumes de Tunquin et de Lao.* Paris: N.p.

Roque, Jean de la. 1715. *Voyage de l'Arabie par l'ocean oriental et le detroit de la mer rouge . . . 1708, 1709 et 1710 . . . Un memoire concernant l'arbre et le fruit de cafe.* Paris: N.p.

Ross, Alexander. 1649. *The Alcoran of Mahomet translated out of Arabique into French by the Sieur du Ryer . . . And newly Englished for the satisfaction of all that desire to look into the Turkish vanities.* London: N.p.

Roth, A. W. 1821. *Novae plantarum species praesertim Indae Orientalis.* N.p.

Rouffaer, G. P., and J. W. Ijzerman. 1925. *De eerste schpvaart der Nederlanders naar Oost-Indie onder Cornelis de Houtman 1595–1597,* vol. 2. The Hague: Martinus Nijhoff.

Rousseau, Jean-Jacques. 1755. *Discours sur l'origine et les fondements de l'inégalité parmi les hommes.* Amsterdam: M. M. Rey.

Royle, J. F. 1833–1839. *Illustrations of the botany and other branches of the natural history of the Himalayan mountains and the flora of Cashmere.* London: N.p.

Rudgely, Richard. 1998. "Tobacco." *The Encyclopedia of psychoactive substances.* Boston: Little, Brown and Company.

Ruggiero, Michele. 1584. *Tian-zhu shilu.* Macau: N.p.

Rumphius, Georgius Everhardus. 1705, 1766. *Amboinische raritaten . . .* Amsterdam: N.p.

———. 1750–1755. *Herbarium Amboinense.* N.p.

———. 1999. *The Ambonese curiosity cabinet.* Trans., ed., and annot. by E. M. Beekman. New Haven, Conn.: Yale University Press.

Ryer, André du. 1630. *Rudimenta grammatices linguae Turcicae.* Paris: N.p.

Ryer, André du. 1647. *L'Alcoran de Mahomet, translaté d'arabe en français.* Leiden: N.p.

Sá, Artur Basilio de. 1955. *Documentação para a historia da Missões da Padroado Português do Oriente: Insulindia,* vol. 3. Lisbon: N.p.

Saccano, Metello. 1635. *Relation de progrez de la foy au Royaume de la Cochinchine.* Paris: N.p.

Sahagun, Bernandino de. 1583. *Psalmodia Christiana.* Mexico: N.p.

Said, Edward. 1978. *Orientalism.* London: Routledge & Kegan Paul.

———. 1983. *The world, the text, and the critic.* Cambridge, Mass.: Havard University Press.

Saliba, George. 2001. "Seeking science from the land of Islam." www.columbia.edu/~gas/1/project/visions/visions.html.

Salverda, Reinier. 1990. "Linguistics and the Dutch." Inaugural lecture delivered at University College London, November 26. www.ucl.ac.uk/dutch/rsearlym.htm.

Sande, Duarte de, and Alessandro Valignano. 1590. *De missione legatorium Japonen.* Macau: N.p.

Sansom, G. B. 1977 (orig. 1950). *The Western world and Japan: A study in the interaction of European and Asiatic cultures.* Tokyo: Tuttle.

Santarem, Manuel Francisco de Barros y Sousa. 1848. *Atlas composé de mappemondes, de portulans, et de cartes hydrographiques et historiques.* Paris: N.p.

Santos, Hector. 1996. "Literacy in pre-Hispanic Philippines." www.bibingka.com/dahon/literacy.htm.

———. 2001a. "Extinction of a Philippine script." www.bibingka.com/dahon/extinct/extinct.htm.

———. 2001b. "The Tagalog script." www.bibingka.com/dahon/extinct/extinct.htm.

Santos, João Camilo dos. 1999. "From myth to reality: The Portuguese literature of the discoveries." *Portuguese Studies Review* 7, no. 2 (spring–summer): 129–42.

São Tomas, Frei Alberto de. 1969 (orig. 1788). *Virtudes de algumas platas da ilha de Timor.* Preface by Francisco Leite de Faria, intro. by José d'Orey. Lisbon: Ministerio do Ultramar.

Sar Desai, Mandai Rai. 1997. "Portuguese influence on the Konkani language." In *Stories of Goa* (pp. 45–85). Lisbon: National Museum of Ethnology.

Sardo, Susana. 1996. "The reception of European music in Asia: The case of Mando in Goa." *Review of Culture,* no. 26 (2nd ser.): 48–54.

Saris, John. 1941. *The first voyage of the English to Japan.* Transcribed and collated by Takanobu Otsuka. Tokyo: Toyo Bunka.

Saunders, Graham. 1994. *A history of Brunei.* Kuala Lumpur: Oxford University Press.

Savage, Victor R. 1984. *Western impressions of nature and landscape in Southeast Asia.* Singapore: Singapore University Press.

Savenije, Henny. 2002. "Hendrik Hamel." www.cartography.henny-savenije.pe.kr/hamel.htm.

Scalliet, Marie-Odette. 1997. "Une curiosité oublié: Le livre de dessins faits dans un voyage aux Indes par un voyageur hollandais' du Marquis de Pauling." *Archipel*, no. 54: 57–62.

Schouten, Jost. 1645, 1646. *Beschrijving van hetmachtig coninckrijck Japan*. Amsterdam: N.p.

Schouten, Wouter. 1676, 1707. *Oost-Indische voyage*. 2 vols. Amsterdam: N.p.

Schuchardt, Hugo. 1883. "Bibliographic créole." *Revue Critique* 15: 314–18.

Scudery, Madelaine de. 1654. *Carte de tendre*. Paris: N.p.

Semedo, Alvaro. 1642. *Imperio de la China*. Madrid: N.p.

———. 1642, 1994. *A relação da grande monarquia da China*. Macau: Fundacão Macau.

Semmelink, I. 1885. *Histoire de cholera aux Indes Orientales avant 1817*. Utrecht: N.p.

Short, Kevin. 2001. "When's a potato not a potato?" *Daily Yomiuri*, November 6.

Siebold (Sieboldt), Philip Franz von. 1832. *Nippon*. Leiden: N.p.

———. 1859. *Geographical and ethnological elucidations to the discoveries of Gerrits Vries, commander of the flute Castricum AD 1643 in the east and north of Japan to serve as a manager's guide in the navigation of the east coast of Japan, and to Jezo, Krafte and the Kuriles*. Amsterdam: Frederik Muller.

———. 1862. *Catalogue de la bibliotheque apporté du Japon par Mr. Ph. F. de Siebold*. Dezima: Imprimerie Neerlandaise.

Silva de, Daya. 1987. *The Portuguese in Asia: An annotated bibliography of studies on Portuguese colonial history in Asia, 1498–c.1800*. Bibliotheca Asiatica 22. Zug: IDC.

Silva de Jayasuriya, Shihan. 2000. "Sri Lanka Portuguese creole verses." *International Institute for Asian Studies Newsletter*, February 21.

Silva, Sebastião Maria Apparicio da. 1889. *Diccionario de Portuguêz-Tétum*. Macau: Typographia do Seminario.

Sivin, Nathan. 1995. *Science in ancient China: Researches and reflections*. Ashgate: Varium.

Smith, George Vinal. 1977. *The Dutch in seventeenth-century Thailand*. DeKalb: Northern Illinois University Press.

Smith, Richard J. 1996. *Chinese maps*. Hong Kong: Oxford University Press.

Smithies, Michael. 1990. *The Siamese embassy to the Sun King*. Bangkok: Editions Duang Kamol.

Solvyns, François Balthazar. 1807. *The costume of Indostan*. London: Edward Orme.

Sonnerat, Pierre. 1782. *Voyage aux Indes Orientales et a la Chine*. Paris: N.p.

———. 1806. *Collection de planches pour servir au voyage aux Indes Oriental et a la Chine*. Paris: Dentu.

Sorel, Charles. 1671. *De la conaissance des bons livres, ou examen de plusieurs auteurs. Supplement du traitez de la conaissance des bons livres*. Paris: N.p.

Sousa, Acacio Fernando de. 1997. "The Orient and other reports: From Zacuto to the failure of the qualitative leap of new publishing in Portugal." *Review of Culture*, no. 30 (2nd ser.): 167–72.

Sousa, Luis de. 1767. *Histoire de S. Domingos particular de reino, e conquistas de Portugal*. Lisbon: N.p.

Sousa, Manuel de Faria e. 1666. *Da Asia Portuguesa*. 3 vols. Lisbon: H. Valente de Oliveira.

———. 1695. *Portuguese Asia or the history of the discovery and conquest of India by the Portuguese, containing all their discoveries from the coast of Africa to the farthest parts of China and Japan, all their battles at sea and land, sieges and other memorable actions; a description of these countries, and many particulars of the religion, government and customs of the nations, etc.* Trans. by John Stevens. London: C. Brume.

Souza, Teotório da, and Charles J. Borges (eds.). 1992. *Jesuits in India in historical perspective.* Macau: Instituto Cultural de Macau, Xavier Center of Historical Research.

Speed, John, 1627. *Prospect of the most famous parts of the world.* N.p.

Spence, Jonathan D. 1996. *God's Chinese son: The Taiping heavenly rebellion of Hong Xiuquan.* New York: W. W. Norton.

———. 1998. *The Chan's great continent: China in Western minds.* London: Penguin.

———. 1999. *The search for modern China.* 2nd ed. New York: W. W. Norton.

Spongberg, Stephen A. 1993. "Exploration and introduction of ornamental and landscape plants from eastern Asia." In J. Janick and J. E. Simon (eds.), *New crops* (pp. 140–47). New York: Wiley.

Springer, Balthazar. 1505–1506; 1515. *Of the newe lâdes of ye people founde by the messengers of the Kynge of Portygale named Emanuel. Being the description of the voyage of D. Francisco de Almeida from Lisbon to India in 1505 . . .* Antwerp: John of Doesborowe.

Sramek, Joseph. 2001. "Sir William Jones (1748–1794): The 'good' Orientalist?" Parts 1–3. www.suite101.com/article.cfm/british_history/18551></18554></15899>.

Sternstein, Larry. 1995. "'Low' maps of Siam." *Journal of the Siam Society* 73 (pt. 1–2, January–July): 132–56.

Stevenson, Edward Luther. 1921. *Terrestial and celestial globes.* 2 vols. New Haven, Conn.: Hispanic Society of America by Yale University Press.

Struys, John. 1684. *The voyages and travels of John Struys.* London: Abell Swalle.

Stuart-Fox, Martin. 1977. *A history of Laos.* Cambridge, U.K.: Cambridge University Press.

Suárez, Thomas. 1999. *Early mapping of Southeast Asia.* Singapore: Periplus.

Subrahmanyam, Sanjay. 1988. "Commerce and conflict: Two views of Portuguese Melaka in the 1620s." *Journal of Southeast Asian Studies* 19, no. 1: 62–79.

———. 1997. "The romantic, the Oriental and the exotic: Notes on the Portuguese in Goa." In *Stories of Goa* (pp. 27–29). Lisbon: National Museum of Ethnology.

———. 1999. "Manila, Melaka, Mylapore . . .: A Dominican voyage through the Indies, ca. 1600." *Archipel* 57: 223–42.

Swiderski, Richard. M. 1991. *The fake Formosan: George Psalmanazer and the eighteenth century experiment of identity.* San Francisco: Mellon Research University Press.

Swift, Jonathan. 1726. *Gulliver's travels or travels into several remote nations of the world Including the Voyages to Lilliput, Brobdingnag, Laputa, Balnibarbi, Luggnagg, Glubbdubdrib, and Japan.* London: Printed for Benj Motte.

———. 1729. *A modest proposal for preventing the children of poor people in Ireland from being a burthen to their parents or country . . .* N.p.

Symes, Michael. 1800. *An account of an embassy to the Kingdom of Ava, etc.* London: J. Debray.

Taberd, Jean-Louis. 1838. *Dictionarium Anamitico-latinum er Latino-Anamiticum.* Serampore, India: N.p.

Tachard, Guy. 1688. *A relation of the voyage to Siam performed by six Jesuits sent by the French king to the Indies and China in the year 1685.* London: N.p.

Tai Whan Kim. 1976. *The Portuguese element in Japanese: A critical survey with glossary.* Supplement 5. Coimbra: Revista Portuguesa de Filologia.

Tanter, Richard, Mark Selden, and Stephen R. Shalom (eds.). 2000. *Bitter flowers, sweet flowers: East Timor, Indonesia, and the world community.* Lanham, Md.: Rowman & Littlefield.

Tarling, Nicholas (ed.). 2000. *The Cambridge history of Southeast Asia.* 4 vols. Cambridge, U.K.: Cambridge University Press.

Tavernier, Jean-Baptiste. 1675. *Nouvelle relation du serrrail du grande signier.* Paris: N.p.

———. 1676–1677. *Les six voyages.* Paris: N.p.

———. 1889. *Travels in India by Jean Baptiste Tavernier,* vols. 1 and 2 (trans. from French ed. of 1676). Ed. by V. Ball. London: Macmillan.

Teiva, de Diego. 1548. *Commontarios de rebus in India apud dium gestarannosalatus nostrae.* Coimbra: N.p.

Teixeira, Manuel. 1961–1963. *The Portuguese missions in Malacca and Singapore (1511–1958).* Vol II: Malacca; Vol. III: Singapore. Lisbon: Agência-Geral do Ultramar.

———. 1979a. *Toponimia de Macau.* Vol. I Macau: Imprensa Nasional Macau.

———. 1979b. "The church of St. Paul in Macau." *STVDIA* (Revista Semestral), no. 41–42 (January–December): 51–111.

———. 1988. "The IVth centenary of printing in Macau." *Review of Culture,* no. 6 (July–August): 3–10.

Tennant, Roger. 1996. *A history of Korea.* London: Kegan Paul International.

Thevenot, Melchisedech. 1663–1673. *Relations de diverse voyages curieux.* 4 vols. Paris: N.p.

Thomaz, Luís Filipe, F. R. 1995. "The image of the Archipelago in Portuguese cartography of the 16th and early 17th centuries." *Archipel* 49: 79–124.

———. ca. 1998. *Early Portuguese Malacca.* Macau: CTMCDP.

———. 2001. "Reconhecimento preliminar do patrimônio histórico-cultural subsistente em Timor-Leste." Manuscript.

———. 2002. *Babel Loro Sa'e: O problema linguístico de Timor-Leste.* Lisbon: Cadernos/Instituto Camões.

Thomaz, Luis Filipe, F.R., and Denys Lombard. 1981. "Remarques preliminaires sur un lexique Portugais-Malais inédit de la Bibliotheque Nationale de Lisbonne." In Nigel Philips and Khaidir Anwar (eds.), *Papers on Indonesian languages and literatures.* London: Indonesian Etymological Project, School of Asian and Oriental Studies; Paris: Association Archipel.

Thongchai Winichakul. 1994. *Siam mapped: A history of the geo-body of a nation.* Honolulu: University of Hawaii Press.

[Thunberg, C. P.] 1784. *Flora Japonica . . . sistens plantas insularaum Japonicarum . . . Lipsiae.* Mileriano: N.p.

———. 1796. *Voyages de C.P. Thunberg, au Japon, par le cap de Bonne Espérance, les Isle de la Sonde, etc.* 2 vols. Paris: N.p.

———. 1809. "Voyage to the Indian seas and Japan between the years 1770 and 1779." In *A collection of voyages and travels for the discovery of America to the commencement of the nineteenth century. In twenty-eight volumes,* vol. 6 (pp. 292–95). London: Richard Philips.

———. 1825a. *Florula Ceilanica.* Uppsala: N.p.

———. 1825b. *Florula Javanica.* Uppsala: N.p.

Tibbetts, G. R. 1979. *A study of Arabic texts containing material on Southeast Asia.* Leiden: E. J. Brill.

[Tomas, Alberto de São.] 1969. *Virtudes de algumas plantas folhas, cascas e raizes de differente avores da ilha de Timor.* Lisbon: Ministério de Ultramar.

Tomás, Isabel. 1990. "The life and death of a creole." *Review of Culture,* no. 9 (February–April): 55–65.

———. 1992. *Os crioulos Portugueses do Oriente: Uma bibliografia.* Macau: Instituto Cultural de Macau.

*Transactions of the Society instituted in Bengal for enquiring into the history and antiquities.* Calcutta: East India Company Press.

Trento, Giovanni Battista. 1566. *Mappe-monde nouvelle papistique.* N.p.

Trexler, Richard. 1995. *Sex and conquest: Gendered violence: Political order and the European conquest of the Americas.* Ithaca, N.Y.: Cornell University Press.

Trigault, Nicholas. 1615. *De Christiana expeditona apud sinas.* Augsburg: N.p.

———. 1625. *The collection of sounds and writings of the Western scholars* [in Chinese]. N.p.

———. 1673. *Descriptio regni Japoniae et Siam.* N.p.

Turpin, François-Henri. 1771. *Histoire civile et naturelle du Royaume de Siam, et des révolutions qui sont bouleversé cet empire jusqu'en 1770.* 2 vols. Paris: Costard.

Vairrase [Veiras], Denis. 1675, 1677–1679. *The history of the Severites or Severambi, a nation inhabiting part of the third continent commonly called Terra Australes Incognitae.* London: N.p.

Valdes, Tamon. 1995. *Fernando, report in which by order of his Catholic Majesty (may God protect him), the stronghold, castles, forts and garrisons of the Provinces under his royal dominion in the Philippine islands are listed.* Madrid: Santande Investment S.A.

Valentijn, François. 1724–1725. *Oud en nieuw Oost-Indien.* Amsterdam: J. van Braam.

Valkhoff, Marus-François. 1975. *Miscelâna Luso-Africana* Lisbon: Junta de Investigações Cientificado Ultramar.

Vallejo, Ross M. 2000. "Books and bookmaking in the Philippines." www.noca.gov.ph/ORGANIZATION/SCH/LIBRARIES/libraries_books.htm.

Van Braam, André Everard. 1798. *An authentic account of the embassy of the Dutch East India Company to the court of the emperor of China in the years 1794 and 1795 . . .* 2 vols. London: Phillips.

Van Hagendorp 1779–1781? (p. 234)

Varenius, Bernard. 1649. *Descriptio regni Japoniae et Siam.* Amsterdam: Elsevinium.

———. 1650. *Geographia generalis.* Amsterdam: Elsevinium.

———. 1733. *A compleat system of general geography.* N.p.

Varo, Francisco. 1703. *Arte de la engua Mandarina.* Canton, China: N.p.

[Varthema, Ludovico di.] 1928 (orig. 1510). *The itinerary of Ludovico di Varthema of Bologna from 1502 to 1508.* Trans. by John Winter Jones. Southampton, U.K.: The Arganaut Press.

Vaughn, W. 1804. *Narrative of Captain Woodward and four seamen . . . surrendered themselves up to the Malays, in the island of Celebes.* London: N.p.

Vega, Lope de. 1618. *Triunfo de la fee en los reynos del Japon, por los años de 1614 y 1615.* Madrid: N.p.

Velarde, Pedro Murillo. 1749a. *Geographia historia.* Madrid: N.p.

———. 1749b. *Historia de la provincia de Filipinas de la Compañia de Jesús.* Manila: N.p.

Velde, Paul van der, and Rudolph Bachofner. 1992. *The Deshima diaries Marginalia 1700–1740.* Tokyo: Japan-Netherlands Institute.

Verbeist, Ferdinand. 1673. *Ling tai yi xiang zhi.* Peking: N.p.

———. 1674, 1687. *Astronomia European sub Imperatore Tartare Sinico Cam Hy.* N.p.

———. 1726. *Gu jin tu su ji jeng* [Imperial encyclopedia]. Ed. by Cheng Meng Le. Peking: N.p.

Vermeulen, A. C. J. 1986. *The Deshima dagregisters: Their original table of contents,* vol. I, 1680–90. Leiden: Intercontinenta.

Vespucci, Amerigo. 1504. *Mundus nouus.* Augsburg: Johannes Otmar.

———. 1515. *Sensuyt le nouveau monde & navigations faictes par emeric vespuce Florentin. Des pays & isles nouvellement trouvez auparavant a nous inconneuz tant en l'Ethiope que Arrabie, Calichut et autres plusiers regions éstranges.* N.p.

———. 1604. *Lettera al soderni.* Lisbon: N.p.

Vickers, Adrian. 1989. *Bali: A paradise created.* Berkeley, Calif.: Periplus.

Vlekke, Bernard H.M. 1965. *Nusantara: A history of Indonesia.* The Hague: W. van Hoeve Ltd.

Voltaire, François. 1733. *Orphelin de la Chine.* Paris: N.p.

———. 1757. *Candide ou l'optimisme.* Paris: N.p.

———. 1763. *Traité sur la tolérance.* Paris: N.p.

———. 1773. *Fragments sur l'Inde et sur le general Lalli.* Paris: N.p.

———. 1924. *The philosophical dictionary.* Trans. by H. I. Woolf. New York: Knopf. ("Voltaire's philosophical dictionary," http://history.hanover.edu/texts/voltaire/volindex.htm, 2002)

———. 1961. *Mélanges.* Paris: Galimand.

Vos, Fritz. 1975. "Master Eibokken on Korea and the Korean language . . ." *Transactions of the Royal Asiatic Society, Korea Branch* 50: 7–42. www.henny-savenije.demon.nl/FritsVos/index.htm.

Wade, Geoffrey P. 1986. "Po Luo and Borneo—A re-examination." *Brunei Museum Journal* 6, no. 2: 13–35.

Waley-Cohen, Joanne. 1999. *The sextants of Beijing: Global currents in Chinese history.* New York: W. W. Norton.

Wallace, Alfred Russel. 1869. *The Malay archipelago: The land of the orang-utan, and bird of paradise, a narrative of travel with studies of man and nature.* London: N.p.

Wallerstein, Immanuel. 1974. *The capitalist world-system, Vol. I, Capitalist agriculture and the origins of the European world-economy in the sixteenth century.* New York: Academic Press.

———. 1996. "Eurocentrism and its avatars: The dilemmas of social science." Keynote address at ISA East Asian Regional Colloquium, "The Future of Sociology in East Asia," November 22–23, Seoul, South Korea (cosponsored by Korean Sociological Association and International Sociological Association).

Wands, John Millar (ed.). 1981. *Another world and yet the same: Bishop Joseph Hall's mundus altar et idem.* New Haven, Conn.: Yale University Press.

Wang Gungwu. 1964. "The opening of relations between China and Malacca 1403–05." In J. Bastin and R. Roolvink (eds.), *Malayan and Indonesian studies— Essays presented to Sir Richard Windstedt on his eighty-fifth birthday* (pp. 87–104). London: Oxford University Press.

Wann, Louis. 1915. "The Oriental in Elizabethan drama." *Modern Philology* 12: 123–47.

Waterhouse, David. 1996. "The earliest Japanese contacts with Western music." *Review of Culture,* no. 26 (2nd ser.): 36–47.

Watin, Jean-Felix. 1772. *L'art de peintre, doreur, vernisseur.* Paris: N.p.

Watson Andaya, Barbara. 1997. "Review article: The unity of Southeast Asia: Historical approaches and questions." *Journal of Southeast Asian Studies* 28, no. 1: 161–71.

Webb, John. 1669. *An HISTORICAL ESSAY endeavouring a probability that the language of the Empire of China is the primitive LANGUAGE.* London: N.p.

Wesdin, Phillip. 1977 (orig. 1790). *Sidharubam seu grammatica Samsordamica cui accedit dissertatio historico-critica in linguam Samsordamicam vukgo Samscet dictam.* Rome: N.p.

Wheatley, Paul. 1961. *The golden Cheronese.* Kuala Lumpur: University of Malaya Press.

Whelan, Christal. 1994. "Japan's vanishing minority: The kakure Kirishitan of the Goto islands." *Japan Quarterly* 41, no. 4: 434–49.

Wiles, John. 1684. *A true relation of their great victory, obtained by the King of the Abissines called Prester John, against the Turks: Taking the flourishing city of Habalee, and destroying 10,000 Ottomans . . .* London: N.p.

Wilkins, Charles. 1785. *The Bhagavad-geeta, or, dialogues of Kreeshna and Arjoon in eighteen lectures and notes.* London: N.p.

Wilkins, John. 1638, 1640. *The first book: Discovery of a new world or a discourse tending to prove, that it is probable there may be another habitable world in the Moone. With a discourse concerning the possibility of a passage thither.* London: John Norton.

Wills, John E., Jr. 2001. *1688: A global history.* New York: W. W. Norton.

Wills, Richard. 1557. *History of travayle in the West and East Indies.* London: N.p.

Wiltens, Caspar. 1623, 1706. *Vocabularium, afte woorteboeck.* The Hague: N.p.

Witsen, Nicolas. 1692, 1695, 1705, 1785. *Noord en oost Tartaryen.* Amsterdam: N.p.

Wong, R. Bin. 1997. *China transformed: Historical change and the limits of European experience.* Ithaca, N.Y.: Cornell University Press.

———. 2001. "Entre monde et nation: Les régions Braudeliennes en Asie," *Anales HSS,* no. 1 (January–February): 5–41.

Wood, Frances. 1995. *Did Marco Polo go to China?* London: Seeker & Warburg.

———. 2000. "Marco Polo's readers: The problem of manuscript complexity." *Asia Research Trends,* no. 10 (pp. 67–75). Tokyo: Center for East Asia Cultural Studies for UNESCO, Toyo Bunko.

Woodside, Alexander B. 1971, 1988. *Vietnam and the Chinese model.* Cambridge, Mass.: Havard University Press.

———. 1976. *Community and revolution in modern Vietnam.* Boston: Houghton Mifflin.

———. 1998. "Reconciling the Chinese and Western theory worlds in an era of Western development fatigue (A comment)." *Modern China* 34, no. 2: 121–34.

Wuystoff, Gerrit van. 1699. *Vrende geshiedenissen In de koninckrijeken van Cambodia en Louwen Land in Oost Indien, zederi den Iare 1635, tol den Iare 1644.* Haarlem: N.p.

———. 1993. *Journal de voyage de Gerrit VAN WUYSHOFF er de ses assistants au Laos (1641–1642).* Ed. by Jean Claude Lejosne. Metz, France: Centre de Documentation et d'Information sur le Laos.

Wyche, Peter. 1689. *A short relation of the river Nile: Of its sources and currents, of its overflowing the campagnia of Agypt, till it runs into the Mediterranean, and of other curiosities/ written by an eye-witness, who lived many years in the chief kingdoms of the Abyssine empire.* London: Printed for John Martin.

Wyld, Johnny. February 2000. "Prester John in central Asia." *Asian Affairs* 31 (old ser., 87, pt. 1): 3–13.

Xavier, Francis. 1556. *Conclusiunes philosophicus.* Goa: Colégio de São Paulo.

———. ca. 1557. *Catecismo da doutrina Crista.* Goa: Colégio de São Paulo.

Xavier, Jerome. 1602. *Mirat al quds.* N.p.

Yonemoto, Marcia. 2000. "The 'spatial vernacular' in Tokugawa maps." *Journal of Asian Studies* 59, no. 3: 647–66.

Yule, Henry. 1866. *Cathay and the way thither: Being a collection of medieval notices on China, I, Preliminary Essay on the Intercourse Between China and the Western nations previous to the discovery of the Cape route.* London: Hakluyt Society.

———, and A. C. Burnell. 1903. *Hobson-Jobson: The Anglo-Indian dictionary.* London: Murray.

Zacuto, Abraão. 1496. *Almanach perpetuum.* Leira: Abraão d'Orta.

Zaide, Gregorio F. 1980. *Takayama Ukon, Japanese Christian daimyo; Japanese town in Manila during Spanish times; and Japanese population in the Philippines during Spanish times.* Kanazawa, Japan: Seiken Bunko.

Zannetti, Bartholomeo. 1610. *Annua della Cina del 1606.* Rome: N.p.

Zialcita, Fernando N. 1998. "Survivances prechretiennes dans le culte de la 'Sainte Sepulture' aux Philippines/Peninggalan pra-kristen dalam pelaksanaan ibadat 'pemakaman suci' di Filipina." In *Dialog Prancis-Nusantara* (pp. 285–89). Jakarta: KCNRS-Lasema/Yayasan Ober Indonesia.

# Index

Note: Page numbers in *italics* refer to illustrations.

# About the Author

**Geoffrey C. Gunn** teaches international relations in the Faculty of Economics of Nagasaki University. He is a graduate of Melbourne, Queensland, and Monash universities in the broad fields of Asian history and government. He is the author of a number of books, monographs, and papers on Indochina, the Malay world, Macau, Nagasaki, and East Timor. He is an editor of *Journal of Contemporary Asia* (Manila).

**DATE DUE**